Antonia Ford House

Oliver House/Bailiwick Inn

Fairfax Court House

Confederate Memorial

Fairfax Jail

Moore-McCandlish House

Five Chimneys/Farr House

© CHAD WAGNER-96

Fairfax, Virginia:
A City Traveling Through Time

By
Nan Netherton
Ruth Preston Rose
David L. Meyer
Peggy Talbot Wagner
Mary Elizabeth Cawley DiVincenzo

History of the City of Fairfax Round Table
Fairfax, Virginia
1997

City of Fairfax

Mayor: John Mason

Council Members

J. Anthony Coughlan   Samuel P. Mershon
Jeffrey C. Greenfield   Gary J. Rasmussen
Julia P. Lyman   R. Scott Silverthorne

History of the City of Fairfax Round Table Members

Delegate John H. Rust, Jr., Chairman

Diane C. Cabe	Suzanne S. Levy	Gary J. Rasmussen
Thomas P. Dugan	Claudia J. Lewis	Constance K. Ring
John H. Gano	Randolph H. Lytton, Ph.D.	Robert C. Russell
Wallace S. Hutcheon, Jr. Ph.D.	Patricia M. Pflugshaupt	Carole T. Scanlon
Traci L. Kendall	Edgar A. Prichard	Senator Jane H. Woods

Claire A. Luke, Executive Assistant

Library of Congress Cataloguing in Publication Data: LC# 97-077248

ISBN: 0-914927-26-4

The American Legion

History of Post No. 177

On October 23rd, 1945, the late Comrade Amos Chilcott donated about 9 acres of apple orchard and open field on Oak Street to erect a Post Veteran's Memorial Home and Community Center. His motivation for this selfless act is lost to history, but one can surmise that it was love for his country and belief in the purpose for which American fighting men and women struggled for four long years. The history of Post No. 177 and the building it occupies are intertwined.

The date was November 13th, 1944 and far from the raging conflict that continued to ravage Europe and Asia, a group of veterans met in Fairfax, Virginia to establish an American Legion Post. The purpose was to provide a local organization for the returning World War II veterans where they could not only seek assistance in returning to civilian life, but also provide a common meeting place where veterans could discuss their experiences and enjoy the company of comrades-in-arms.

The first meeting was held at the Fairfax County Trial Justice Court, leading to the incorporation and charter of Post No. 177 in January, 1945. For several years, meetings were held in the Town Hall, Elementary School, members' homes and local establishments. After years of planning and difficulties with material shortages and restrictive regulations, the first shovel of dirt for the Veteran's Memorial Home and Community Center was turned in February, 1951. Construction was slow over the next 5 years, with donated labor and materials, and borrowed money.

The minutes of meetings in the early 50's shows the finances of the Post as "less than a shoestring". With little more than three hundred dollars in the general fund, a $2.00 expenditure for the use of a projector required board approval! With determination however, the members forged ahead.

In 1952, a cornerstone was obtained from the remnants of the White House renovation. It was inscribed with the Legion motto "For God and Country" and contained a chamber for the names of W.W.I, W.W.II and Korean Conflict dead from Fairfax County. The stone itself enjoys a remarkable history in that it was quarried on Squires Creek in Fairfax County in 1794 and still bore the smoke stains of the British fire of 1812.

In the early part of 1955, meetings were held in the Post home for the first time. Permanent lighting, restrooms and temporary heating were in-

The Post Home ca. 1958.

The late Amos Chilcott, Benefactor of the Post.

stalled for the 10th anniversary dinner in May of that year. 1955 also saw the beginning of Little League baseball with a diamond built in the rear of the building.

A loan of $25,000 enabled the remaining brickwork and the roof to be completed. By 1956, the ground floor was completed, a kitchen was installed and the "rumpus room" enlarged. A lease was made with the Little League for the present ballfield bordering Cedar Street which was billed as "the finest Little League stadium in Northern Virginia."

With culmination of the Post home in sight, a loan of $110,000 was obtained to finish the building, with the exception of the two side porches. (The original plans called for a covered balcony and a screened porch on either side of the building at the second story level.)

The long anticipated completion of the Post home was attained in 1957. Radio station WCFR (now WEEL) occupied a portion of the ground floor, providing much needed revenue. Chilcott Hall was used for the first time in May when the Evangelical Lutheran Congregation held Lenten services. The Hall was open to the public on May

18th and 19th, followed by a Back-To-God program on the 20th. With a beautiful facility in hand, the Post began a season of events — the 10th District Convention, July 4th fireworks, weddings, parties and fund raisers.

A new wave of pride of accomplishment spurred the members and officers to plan the ultimate completion of the side porches and an ambitious undertaking to build an Olympic size swimming pool on the adjoining grounds. Consideration was given to the amount of debt being carried by the Post and the plans were shelved. As time passed and the 50's became the 60's, the Post home buzzed with a flurry of activities. The Sons and Daughters of the American Legion performed civic duties. The Ladies Auxiliary sent young ladies to Girls State. (The Legion sent boys to Boys State). The Post had a majorette program with uniforms and a Junior American Legion baseball team.

Disaster struck early in the morning of September 14th, 1964. A fire believed to have started in the kitchen quickly spread and grew to an inferno. By sunrise, all that remained of a once elegant structure was a burned out shell. Gone was the radio station, the club room, Chilcott Hall and all of the amenities.

Undaunted, the Post held a meeting on September 21st to discuss the fate of the Home. Initially, the reality of the fire struck home with the revelation that the building's insurance did not cover the mortgage.

An engineering firm was hired to evaluate the remaining structure, with results that the brick portion, though fire scarred was sound and could support a new building. A new plan was made to rebuild the main building in much the same form as before, but with a completely finished basement, allowing the entire first floor to be devoted to a ballroom and adjacent meeting or small party room.

Many months of planning and considerable financial difficulties dragged construction and completion of the Post Home for the next two years. On April 26, 1967, the Post received a Certificate of Occupancy from the City of Fairfax. The price tag for this precious document was $2.50. After two and one-half years and tens of thousands of dollars in construction costs, including thousands of hours of donated labor, Post No. 177 was home again.

Over the next 30 years, as the Post's fortunes waxed and waned and then grew solvent, a few modifications were made to the Home. Additional parking, an enlarged clubroom, nee "rumpus room", a bar and kitchen on the upper level as well as food service facilities for the club level.

Changing times saw the Majorettes leaving for the High School. The youth baseball team was absorbed by the Little League. As the membership grew older, golf replaced more strenuous activities. But the Post's many civic and charity programs began to flourish with active support of Veteran's Hospitals where residents and patients receive much needed comfort items. Girls and Boys State programs are well funded as are the Thanksgiving and Christmas food baskets which are donated to the needy.

With the trials and tribulations of 50 plus years fading into the past, the future of Post No.177 and the building it occupies looks confident. With nearly a thousand members, there is an active Auxiliary and Sons of the American Legion, both dedicated to civic and charitable purposes. The

First meeting in the unfinished rumpus room in 1955

Home is receiving a face lift with landscaping, awnings and interior improvements which will enhance its ambiance well into the next century.

The history of Post No. 177 continues to be written and will continue as long as the Post endures. The founders have all departed, and as the builders and rebuilders are entering their golden years, they too will leave the heritage of the Veterans Memorial Home and Community Center to a new generation.

Standing in the great hall named for its benefactor one can almost hear the echoes of his footsteps, as he makes his rounds to admire his accomplishment. But as Amos Chilcott reposes within sight of a great memorial, his grave unadorned save for his name, let us remember him and his legacy with the words of William Shakespeare:

And thou in this shalt find thy monument,
When tyrants' crests and tombs of brass are spent.

For God and Country
R. E. Mercier
Historian
Post No. 177, The American Legion

Post home nearing completion in 1957

The Americanette Majorettes posing on the portico in front of the Post Home. The portico was lost in the fire of 1963.

Contents

The Patrons of History

Presented below are the people who made publication of this book possible. The assistance of these patrons of history is gratefully acknowledged.

Our City Publishers
(Contribution of $5,000 or more)

- City of Fairfax, Virginia
- American Legion Post 177
- Country Club of Fairfax
- Fairfax Nursing Center

Our Town Editors
(Contribution of $2,500 or more)

- The George Mason Bank
- Media General Cable of Fairfax
- Van Metre Companies
- Virginia Power
- Washington Gas

Our Chapter Reporters
(Contribution of $500 or more)

- Tom Davis for Congress
- Fairfax City Observer
- Patriot National Bank
- Price Cosco Wholesale
- The Rotary Club of Fairfax, Virginia
- In Memory of Mr. and Mrs. J. Frank Swart, James E. Swart & Robert A. Swart

Our Page Bylines
(Contribution of $250 or more)

The Margaret Kilpatrick Adams Family
An Anonymous Donor
Burdette, Halstead & Smith, P.C.
Andy and Holly Bud, in Memory of Kitty Britt
Chocolate Lover's Festival
Jean and Barrie Cook
The Charles Darcey Family
Fairfax City Republican Committee
Law Firm of Evan H. Farr, P.C.
Friends of the Fairfax City Regional Library
The Ted Grefe Family
Stephanie F. Gruendl
In Memory of Harry J. Hall
In Memory of A. William Henn
Barnard and Nancy Lee Jennings
Juanita C. Kipp
In Memory of Robert F. Lederer, Sr.
Randolph and Ellen Lytton

Mayor John Mason
Peter and Susanne Max
McCandlish & Lillard, P.C.
Janice and Jon Miller & Family
Mosby Woods Community Association
In Memory of LTC Herbert W. Mylks
John and Mary Petersen
In Memory and Honor of the Pobst Family
Gary and Mary Jo Rasmussen
Reniere & Associates - Hal Reniere
In Memory of Virginia Richardson Ritchie
In Memory of Jeanne J. Rust
Dr. Barry Soffran
Carole T. Scanlon
Robert E. Stafford and Family
Steve & Carol Wolfsberger & Jerry Minter
Jane and Jim Woods
In Loving Memory of Howard Franklin Young, Sr.

Acknowledgments

The writing of a book which seeks to cover over 200 years of the history of a special place requires assistance and cooperation from numerous resource people. The chair of the History of the City of Fairfax Round Table, John H. Rust, Jr., and his committee members provided strong support throughout the duration of the project. Professor Randolph Lytton was especially attentive as chair of the Reading Subcommittee, as was Diane Cabe, chair of the Graphics Subcommittee.

The staff of the Virginia Room history collection at the Fairfax City Regional Library was always resourceful as each author combed through references searching for appropriate materials. Suzanne Levy, Anita Ramos, Brian Conley, Karen Ann Moore and Marjorie Schoenberg were all patient and helpful. Malcolm Richardson's newspaper indexes were invaluable. Ben Levy assisted with a large assembly of images from the Virginia Room's photographic archive as a school community project.

Assistance was appreciated from the staffs of the Arlington County Public Library Virginia Room; and the Manuscript Collections of the Library of Virginia, the Virginia Historical Society and the Library of Congress.

The five authors are particularly indebted to architect Charles R. Wagner for his skillful pen-and-ink sketches of local buildings and monuments for this pictorial history book. It was great to have the enthusiastic cooperation of four more resource people: Tony Chaves and Randolph Lytton, who loaned historical postcards from their collections; Lee Hubbard, who loaned images from his historical prints collection; and Scott Boatright, who in addition to providing some additional images, took photos and copied numerous pictures. Bill Harrah and Traci Kendall developed the concept of the dust jacket illustration.

Special thanks are due to former Mayors Edgar A. Prichard and John H. Rust, Sr. for their careful review of the text. They provided unique perspectives of the City and its history. Their personal recollections led to lively discussions about our heritage and history.

Working in the Town and City Council minute books, 1927 to 1996, required time, attention and desk space, and City Manager Robert Sisson, City Clerk Jackie Henderson and their office staff as well as staffs of the various City government departments and the City school staffs were helpful. Claire Luke and her staff from the Central Fairfax Chamber of Commerce provided both communications and office skills.

With the mechanical necessities of preparing the history book for actual printing, we had the assistance of Frederick Hafner of Higher Education Publications and his staff, particularly designer Mary Pat Rodenhouse. Word processing skills were provided by Carol and David Dunlap.

Many and varied were the contributions by others whose names follow: Amanda Ahlerich, Louise Armitage, Barry Baker, Vivian Baltz, Loraine Bauer, Patricia Beck, Earl

Berner, Paul D. Briggs, Diane Cabe, Mike Cadwallader, Chris Cawley, Elizabeth M. Cawley, Edward J. Cawley, Jr., Jackie L. Cawley, Kevin Cawley, Tom Cawley, Fran Chester, Gerry Collings, Candy Contristan, Sue Cotellessa, Amy Craig, Bankhead T. Davies, Margaret Dewar, Mary Kate DiVincenzo, Tim DiVincenzo, Tommy DiVincenzo, Kevin Dunn, Fay Fahs, Chris Fow, Blaine Friedlander, Richard R. Fruehauf, Judith M. E. Fugate, Joan Gano, John Gano, Laurel Gauthier, John Gecan, Norma Gecan, Shelby Goletz, Jimmy Harris, Jackie Henderson, Ruth Hill, Thomas Hill, Todd Hoffman, Susan Hogge, Lee Hubbard, David Hudson, Wilma Huff, Daryl Humrichouser, Jim and Gay Nell Jacks, William Page Johnson, Joseph Jones, Roseanne Kelly, Frederic and Alice Kielsgard, Pat King, Robert Lisbeth, Jeanne Maruszewski, Dawn Maskell, Gary F. "Buddy" Matthews, Ann Mattingly, Ted McCord, Gary A. Mesaris, Cindy Meyer, Janice Miller, Stephen L. Moloney, Jane Montante, Chris Mullen, Lisa Mussenden, Ross Netherton, Alta Newman, Ed San Nicholas, Sue Otto, Patrick Rodio, Joan Rogers, Carl Rose, Robert C. Russell, Adrian Schagrin, Shirley Shaffer, James R. Shull, John J. Skinner, Edith Sprouse, George Stepp, Karen S. Struble, Howard Stull, Mitch Sutterfield, John Veneziano, Barbara Welch, Gayle Werling, Susan Wiczalkowski, Ellen Wigren, Vicki Wildermuth Hope Yarbrough and Lehman Young.

The Authors:
Nan Netherton
Mary Beth DiVincenzo
David Meyer
Ruth Rose
Peggy Wagner

Foreword

Some of us were born here, others discovered that they had married Fairfax as well as their spouse, and still others stopped here in search of employment and found a home. Each of us in our own way has come to love this small city in the center of northern Virginia - this oasis of charm in the suburban desert. That is why all of the members of the History of the City of Fairfax Round Table welcomed the opportunity to publish a book about the City of Fairfax, Virginia, its origins and our roots.

In September 1995, the Central Fairfax Chamber of Commerce and Historic Fairfax, Inc. joined forces to create the History of the City of Fairfax Round Table, whose charter charged it with the responsibility to research, write, publish, produce, finance, and distribute a useful, attractive and enduring history of the City of Fairfax, Virginia. Those of us who have served on the Round Table believe we have met that charge, bringing you a book which is well-researched and carefully written, filled with facts, photographs and stories from our past. We hope that you find the book as much fun to read as we had in publishing *Fairfax, Virginia: A City Traveling Through Time*.

The book is not simply a chronology of events in the City. Rather, as former Mayor Ed Prichard proposed, the book has been built around those events which we believe define the City of Fairfax. The book also is the first publication to provide some insight into the turbulent events after World War II, which transformed the City from a sleepy country town into a suburban city. The book provides good insight into the independent thinking and often visionary foresight that define this small city. In these pages, you will learn what makes the City a beacon of character in the faceless sea that is northern Virginia.

We are fortunate that local historian Nan Netherton led her talented team of writers, Mary Elizabeth DiVincenzo, David Meyer, Ruth Preston Rose and Peggy Wagner, in putting together a first class history book. You may well be familiar with the quality of Nan's research and writing from her earlier books. But you probably do not know the leadership and concern which she brings to the publication of a history book. There are many discussions, many decisions, and many concerns when you publish history. We will be forever grateful to Nan for her able scholarship, vast experience and calm in the face of every storm. Without her guidance and good sense, this book would never have been published.

Those of us in the Round Table are a group of eager amateurs. We are grateful for the professional help which we received from our publisher, Frederick "Fritz" Hafner of Higher Education Publications. Fritz gave far more to us that this book will ever earn for his company. He contributed his time, his patience and his goodwill. His joy and excitement about the history book kept all of us enthused. For Fritz, as for all of us, this book was a labor of love.

We are also grateful to the citizens and businesses in northern Virginia who gave special contributions which made the publication of this book possible. Please take a look at our donor page -- these are the people and organizations who truly have made history, they deserve our recognition and our thanks.

In addition, a heartfelt thanks to Claire Luke and the able staff of the Central Fairfax Chamber of Commerce. They contributed the know-how, the support and the common sense that kept our volunteer Round Table moving forward during the past two years. Be it big jobs or small details, no task was too much, no demand too great. Thanks to the Chamber for all they did.

Most of all, we are grateful to you for joining us in our pursuit of the history and heritage of the City of Fairfax, Virginia. Your purchase of this book contributes directly to Fairfax. All net proceeds from the sale of the book will be divided between the Chamber's Margaret Kilpatrick Adams Memorial Scholarship Fund and the Fairfax Museum and Visitors Center. Each year the Chamber grants scholarships based upon academic achievement and citizenship to seniors at our local high schools who will study humanities, architecture, art design or business. The Fairfax Museum and Visitors Center is a small gem in the center City, providing interpretation about our City and preserving our past. It is one of the centerpieces in defining the community that is the City of Fairfax. The success of this book will materially contribute to the success of young people in our community and to the preservation of our heritage. Thank you for your contribution to the City and its citizens.

When you read this history and learn about the people who have come before you, remember that each of them was just like you -- a citizen who cared about his or her community, and who tried to make a difference. You can make a difference too.

History is happening all around you right now. You can play a part in shaping the defining events in your community for future generations to share.

Make some history yourself as you travel through time!

Historically yours,

John H. Rust, Jr., Chairman
History of the City of Fairfax Round Table

October 6, 1997

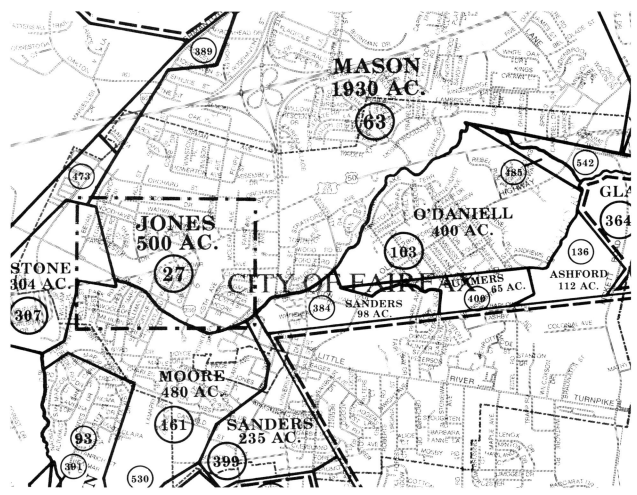

The above excerpt showing the City of Fairfax and its environs comes from a published cadastral map prepared by Beth Mitchell showing early English property owners' boundaries superimposed on a modern street map. It accompanies her book, Beginning at a White Oak . . . Patents and Northern Neck Grants of Fairfax County, Virginia, *published in 1977. Courtesy of the Fairfax County Office of Comprehensive Planning*

1.

Indians, Rangers and English Settlers
Prehistory to 1800
by Ruth Preston Rose

When early explorers first came to the region around the Chesapeake Bay, they found the area west of the bay to be made up of peninsulas, the northernmost of which lay between the Potomac and the Rappahannock rivers. Captain John Smith's 1608 map was surprisingly accurate and has provided settlers and historians detailed information about the land and its inhabitants at the time of initial European contact. The Indians of the Northern Neck were Algonquian-speaking, semi-sedentary peoples who lived at least part of the year in villages near the rivers and the tributary streams. Typically, the women of these communities gardened, built homes, and cared for children while the men hunted, fished, and made war. The earliest known European foothold was established close to the confluence of the Potomac and Rappahannock rivers, the region inhabited by the Chicacoan Indians, a branch of the Powhatan chiefdom. The area would later become Northumberland County in the 1640s.[1] As the settlers moved westward, new counties were formed to take care of the growing population of Europeans, and consequently the Indians were pushed ever farther from their ancestral homes ultimately abandoning the area to join the Piscataway Indians on the Maryland banks of the Potomac and also pushing westward beyond the Blue Ridge.

While no archaeologists have identified significant Indian sites in the City of Fairfax, the numerous prehistoric objects found in the region testify to the long occupation in the area by native peoples.[2] A stone axehead was found on a farm a few miles from

As many as 18 different native American societies are thought by archaeologists to have been present in Fairfax County during the past 12,000 years. Stone projectile points for spears and arrows, as well as stone tools like this stone axe made by early groups, are frequently found in the Fairfax area. Photo by Scott Boatright. Courtesy of the Fairfax Museum and Visitors Center

the City of Fairfax, and it is believed that potential sites of the earliest inhabitants may be found within the City along Accotink Creek and Daniels Run. Beneath the historic downtown area there may yet remain significant deposits of archaeological material that could provide useful information to the student of history. Rust Hill, behind Truro Church, is one of the areas of the city where prehistoric artifacts have been found.[3]

In 1649, the exiled Prince Charles, who would later become Charles II of England, granted all of the land

The County, Town and City were named for the family of the Right Honorable Thomas, Sixth Lord Fairfax, Baron of Cameron, and Proprietor of the Northern Neck in Virginia (1693-1781).

The above portrait attributed to the painter, Sir Joshua Reynolds, is owned by the Alexandria-Washington Lodge No. 22, A.F.&A.M., Alexandria, Virginia. Used with permission. Photo by Marler Studios. Courtesy of the Fairfax County Public Library Photographic Archive

The Fairfax Coat of Arms used by Thomas, Sixth Lord Fairfax was quartered to represent the families of both his mother and father. The Culpepers are represented by the diagonal stripe and the Fairfaxes by the parallel horizontal bars with a rampant Scottish lion. The family's title is Scottish. Arms painted by the College of Heralds, London, England

lying between the Potomac and the Rappahannock rivers to seven of his loyal followers, among whom were two members of the Culpeper family. Known as the Northern Neck Proprietary, the entire peninsula eventually became the property of Thomas, Lord Culpeper, at whose death the land passed to his daughter, Catherine. The marriage of Catherine to Thomas, Fifth Lord Fairfax, eventually brought the property into the Fairfax family. The Northern Neck Proprietary, whose boundaries were determined in 1746 to extend westward to "the first heads or springs" of the Potomac and Rappahannock rivers, ultimately included over five million acres.

That some settlers were in the region of the City of Fairfax before the end of the seventeenth century is indicated by reports of Indian depredations against the English around 1691, after which Lord Culpeper suggested that small bands of light horsemen range

through the wooded areas. Afterwards, ten men under Captain Thomas Owsley ranged from "above the Occoquan to the head of the [Potomac] river." According to the journal of David Strahane, a group of rangers operated from the Occoquan to Sugarland Run from June through September of 1692.[4]

Beth Mitchell's map, "Patents and Northern Neck Grants of Fairfax County, Virginia," accompanied by the book *Beginning at a White Oak*, records the early land ownership. Of the first 605 land grants, 29 were given in the 17th century. William Fitzhugh's 21,996-acre grant of 1685, later called "Ravensworth," was the largest and one of the earliest grants made in the County. The northwestern corner of the property reached into present-day City of Fairfax.[5] Under the proprietorship, quit-rents were collected from the grantees. Agents of the proprietors made grants and collected rents until 1747 when Thomas, Sixth Lord

Fairfax, Baron of Cameron, son of Thomas, Fifth Lord Fairfax, came to Virginia to take personal control of his vast estate. His cousin, William Fairfax, acted as proprietary agent while living at Belvoir, the home that he built in 1741. Lord Fairfax lived for a while at his cousin's home, then established his own seat at Greenway Court, in Frederick County in the Shenandoah Valley, where he welcomed the men who came from far and wide to pay their respects and to conduct business.[6] When Fairfax County was formed from old Prince William County in 1742, it was named for the proprietor.

In colonial Virginia, as in the mother country, the Anglican Church was the state church, and therefore played an important role in the governance of the citizens. Political leaders were usually also church officials—vestrymen and wardens. The vestrymen made levies and assessments on the parishioners, kept records of attendance at church services in order to discipline delinquents, and selected ministers. They also were responsible for the care of the poor and the apprenticeship of orphans. Some of their responsibilities extended beyond the church building and the congregation into such activities as the storage of tobacco collected for the church and the upkeep of roads in the parish. The City of Fairfax is located in the original Truro Parish, established in 1732, ten years before there was a County named Fairfax.[7]

When Fairfax County was formed in 1742, justices for the new court were often vestrymen of Truro Parish. Landowners who were both vestrymen and justices from the area where the City of Fairfax now exists included William Ellzey, William Fairfax, William Payne, Henry Gunnell, John Colvill and George William Fairfax.[8] The first known Courthouse was built on the estate, Springfield, on land belonging to William Fairfax, and located on Accotink, Wolf Trap, Pimmit, and Scott's runs, near present-day Tysons Corner.[9] George Washington and George Mason, whose estates were in the eastern part of the County, on the Potomac River, had great influence on both local and national government. Both men were justices of Fairfax County and vestrymen of Truro Parish[10]. Ten years after the County's first known Courthouse was built at Springfield, merchants of Alexandria petitioned for approval of a new Courthouse in the port town, established in 1749. This request was approved and the County's second Courthouse functioned in Alexandria between 1752 and 1800.[11]

In 1774, a new era began in the government of Fairfax County. The American colonies had rebelled against the British Stamp Act of 1765 and the subsequent Intolerable Acts of 1774. Mason's Declaration of Rights influenced the 1789 French Declaration of the Rights of Man, and served as a model for the Bill of Rights to the U. S. Constitution.[12]

Washington was chairman of the Fairfax Committee of Safety and was a delegate to the Continental Congress, which in 1775 created an army to oppose the British. In the following year, he was made commander-in-chief of the Continental Army. Virginia Governor Patrick Henry in 1777 ordered that the militia of Fairfax County be put on Continental pay. Initially, 200 men from Fairfax County were called to serve in Washington's army.[13]

The Church of England remained the established church in Virginia until 1786 when the General Assembly adopted Thomas Jefferson's Statute for Religious Freedom, separating church and state.[14] Meanwhile, the population of Fairfax County continued to grow, and a new parish was formed in the eastern part of the county in 1765, called Fairfax Parish. To make religious services more accessible to western parishioners of Truro Parish, it was decided at a meeting of the vestry in February 1766 to build a new church "on the middle ridge, near Ox Road . . . on Land supposed to be belonging to Mr. Thomzon Ellzey."[15] A church warden, Edward Payne, of Hope Park, obtained the construction contract for the new place of worship and it became known as "Payne's Church."

Though Payne's Church has long since disappeared from the landscape, its memory is preserved in the design of the Truro Church chapel in Fairfax. The 18th century building was designed by the Virginia architect John Ariss (Ayres), who is believed to have been trained in England and to have had a hand in the design of some of Virginia's most refined houses.[16] The church was to be fifty-three and a half feet long and thirty feet wide. The exterior was to be made of bricks nine inches long and four and a half inches wide, with corners, windows and doors of "rubbed brick." The windows were to have sixteen lights "of the best crown glass," and the floors were to be of pine plank one and a half inches thick, the "Iles to be laid with Brick Tyle," the pews of pine, and an altar piece in the Ionic order. All details of the structure were carefully laid out by Ariss (Ayres), including the size of the cypress shingles for the roof. Edward Payne

Payne's Church was built on the Ox Road in 1768, near what is now Fairfax Station, to serve Colonial Anglican church members in western Fairfax. A replica of this church was built as a chapel for Truro Episcopal Church in the town of Fairfax in 1933. This photo of Payne's Church, taken about 1863, appeared in Philip Slaughter's History of Truro Parish. *Courtesy of the Virginia Room, Fairfax City Regional Library*

was to be paid £570 Virginia currency, and the designer of the church was to be paid forty shillings.[17] Located on Ox Road near Fairfax Station, the church has been replaced by Jerusalem Baptist Church, which was built on part of the old Payne's Church foundations.

Payne's Church was finished in 1768 and was in regular use until the American Revolution, when the increase in the size of nonconformist congregations resulted in the decline of attendance at the church. By the mid-1770s, the Baptist preacher Jeremiah Moore was finding followers in Fairfax, though his anti-establishment doctrine brought him into conflict with the authorities. Appearing before the court in 1773 on a charge of preaching without a license, he was fined £10, to be voided if he "be of good Behavior for a year and a day," and that he not preach until he obtained a license. He was not licensed to perform marriages until 1785. When the new Courthouse was completed in 1800, religious dissenters were dominant in Virginia, and Moore was permitted to preach in the new public building.[18]

The county court of Fairfax followed the original prototype established by Governor Sir George Yeardley in 1618, which called for monthly meetings where gentlemen justices heard both civil and criminal cases. The duties of the justices included maintaining order; levying taxes; settling claims; licensing taverns, warehouses and mills; and supervising elections. They also directed the administration of estates, supervised the care of indigents and orphans, and acted as judges in all but capital cases. The most frequent cases before the court were selling liquor without a license, drunkenness, assault, battery, trespassing, adultery, fornication, and swearing. Punishments in the 18th century included fines, whipping, ducking, and jailing. The term of service of indentured servants was sometimes extended as punishment.[19]

The fast-growing port town of Alexandria had been the county seat since 1752, but in 1789, the General Assembly of Virginia ordered that the Courthouse be moved to the center of the County after it was decided to cede Alexandria to the federal government as part of the District of Columbia. The new Courthouse was to be constructed on "the lands of William Fitzhugh, gentleman, or on the lands of any other person within one mile of the crossroads at Price's Ordinary."[20] That location would have been on the Ravensworth estate in the vicinity of present-day Annandale, near the intersection of Braddock and Backlick roads.

In 1798, when no successful plans for a new Courthouse had been made, the General Assembly instructed the justices of the Fairfax County Court to choose a suitable site and proceed to erect public buildings. Until a new Courthouse was built, the justices should "appoint any place for holding court as they should think proper."[21] Chosen from among the County's justices to act as commissioners for the new Courthouse were George Minor, Charles Little, James Wren, William Payne, and Dr. David Stuart.

George Minor was from a family that had long held land in the County and had been active in parish affairs. In 1789, he was an overseer of the poor after that function was handed over to the County following the dissolution of the established church. He was also a colonel of the County militia. Charles Little was a landowner in the County. He was of sufficient acquaintance with George Washington to be one of the men who verified the first President's will when it was recorded in court in January of 1800. Commissioner James Wren, a carpenter and joiner, was the designer of the new Courthouse. He also was the designer of Christ Church in Alexandria.[22] William Payne had been a vestryman and a church warden for Truro Parish and was a surveyor for Fairfax County. His father, William, had the distinction of almost fighting a duel over an election dispute with George Washington in 1755.[23]

David Stuart, who purchased Hope Park from Edward Payne in 1785, was a member of a prominent King George County family which was related to the royal family of Scotland. He was educated as a physician in Edinburgh, Scotland, and was married to Eleanor Calvert Custis, the widow of Martha Washington's son, John Parke Custis, thereby becoming linked with the leading family of the United States

Fresh tobacco leaves were packed tightly into barrels called casks or hogsheads, fitted with a frame and rolled by oxen, horses or men along crude early roads. These roads led from plantations and small farms to wharves at river landings such as Colchester and Alexandria. Here tobacco ships from London loaded them as cargo to be transported and sold at distant markets. Tobacco was the area's principal crop in the 1600s and 1700s and some of the local thoroughfares still retain the name of "rolling roads." Courtesy of the Smithsonian Institution

as well as of Fairfax County. As stepfather of George Washington Parke Custis, Stuart was responsible for the boy's property until he came of age, as well as for his own considerable land holdings. Stuart was a member of the General Assembly of Virginia and was one of the first commissioners of the District of Columbia.[24]

In 1791, Stuart was asked by President George Washington to make a report on the state of agriculture in northern Virginia. Washington wanted to know the rents on the land; what produce was grown; prices for articles sold on the farm and at market; prices of livestock; prices of butter, meat, and cheese; the price of wrought iron; and the taxes paid by residents.[25] The report that Stuart gave to Washington after several months of inquiry is valuable as a description of the conditions of agriculture in the late 18th century in Fairfax. Stuart reported that he found agriculture to be of a higher quality than he had expected, considering the fact that farms were operated by "black labourers and the more worthless wretches we employ to overlook them."[26] Wheat was replacing tobacco as the primary export crop and was being exported from Virginia in great quantity. Fairfax County provided pasture land of white clover for livestock, the prices of which were given in detail. The fee-simple rates for land ten miles from Alexandria and the river were 20 to 40 shillings per acre. State taxes on property were given in detail in pounds. At that time, the only federal government tax was six pence a gallon on stills, which had "excited some murmurs."[27]

Little is known about individual slaves who labored in Fairfax County. Their presence was little acknowledged except in tax lists, wills, and advertisements in *The Columbian Mirror and Alexandria Gazette*. On July 1, 1797, Nicholas Fitzhugh of Ravensworth sought a slave named Jacob who was described as "sprightly and engaging in his manner." Among Jacob's articles of clothing were a striped calico waistcoat and worn, turned-down boots. He was believed to be carrying a pig, a turkey and other stolen items. On August 9, 1798, Solomon Betton offered for sale 70 "likely Negroes" at Ravensworth, including men, women and children. Only Mount Vernon and Ravensworth had large numbers of slaves. According to the 1790 United States census, more than half of Fairfax County residents owned no slaves at all. Though treated as chattels, the slaves made important contributions to the achievements of their owners.

The decision was made to build the new Fairfax County Courthouse in 1798 at the crossing of Ox Road and the proposed turnpike extending west from Alexandria.[28] The five gentleman justices accepted an offer from Justice Richard Ratcliffe of four acres of land for which they paid one dollar. According to the court archivist, the late Constance Ring, "There are more than 500 references to Richard Ratcliffe in the Fairfax court records. He appears in 1771 being sworn a deputy sheriff. This was the first of an unbroken chain of public service positions which he held for fifty-four years. He served as sheriff, coroner, justice, patroller, Truro Parish overseer of the poor, Courthouse lot commissioner, jail inspector, superintendent of elections, poorhouse, road, and tax commissioner, master commissioner of the court, and designer and developer of the town which became the Fairfax County seat."[29]

In 1795, Richard Bland Lee was instrumental in getting the Virginia General Assembly to pass legislation authorizing the creation of the "Company of the Fairfax and Loudoun Turnpike Road," which later became known as the Little River Turnpike, or Route 236. Lee, who was one of the justices of Fairfax County when the first session of the new Courthouse was held in 1800, lived at Sully Plantation on a tract of land patented in the early 18th century by his grandfather, Henry Lee, a brother of Thomas Lee of Stratford Hall. Born at Leesylvania in 1761, Richard Bland Lee settled in Fairfax County near the end of the American Revolution. He became a member of the first Congress under the Federal Constitution, and played a pivotal role in the selection of a Potomac site for the new seat of government. In Philadelphia, Lee met his wife, Elizabeth Collins, daughter of a Quaker merchant.[30]

The northwest corner of William Fitzhugh's Ravensworth tract reached into the heart of what would become the City of Fairfax. Two years before the building of the new Courthouse, Richard Ratcliffe had purchased the thousand-acre corner portion of the tract from Augustine Jacqueline Smith and Henry Rose, who had purchased the property in 1797 from Battaile Fitzhugh, a descendant of William, the English immigrant.[31] In 1783, the upper half of Ravensworth was inherited by five of the sons of Major Henry Fitzhugh. They were Nicholas, Richard, Mordecai, Battaile and Giles Fitzhugh. Nicholas, a lawyer who was appointed by President Thomas

Jefferson to the U. S. Circuit Court for the District of Columbia in 1803,[32] may have been the first of his family to live on the tract. Among Jefferson's papers at the Library of Congress is a hand-drawn map sent by Nicholas Fitzhugh in 1804 to direct Jefferson through Ravensworth to avoid the use of public roads. The map shows Giles Fitzhugh's home and the "remains of an old House on a Hill that is to be avoided."[33] When Jefferson was President, he sometimes stayed with Richard Fitzhugh at his Ravensworth home en route between Washington and Monticello.[34]

The lower half of the Ravensworth tract was inherited by William Fitzhugh of Chatham, who began building a home there in 1795. *The Columbian Mirror and Alexandria Gazette* of May 31, 1798, carried an advertisement for the stud horse, Chatham, who would be "standing" at Ravensworth during the coming season. Named, no doubt, for Fitzhugh's home near Fredericksburg, the horse's pedigree was said to equal "any in America." Horse racing was an important sport in 18th century Virginia, and the breeding of fine horses was of interest to many local landowners.

With his purchase of the thousand-acre portion of the Ravensworth tract, Richard Ratcliffe was the owner of almost 3,000 acres of land. He had begun buying property there in 1786 before moving from Alexandria to the location of the future new Courthouse.[35] The mountain road ran past Ratcliffe's property, as did Ellzey's Church Road (now Old Lee Highway) and Ox Road. The proposed turnpike between Alexandria and Loudoun would run through Ratcliffe's land. He was in a perfect position to profit by the placement of the Courthouse at the crossroads of Ox Road and the Little River Turnpike.[36] On May 1, 1798, William Payne, who was County surveyor as well as a commissioner for the Courthouse, laid out four acres of Richard Ratcliffe's land "near Caleb Earpe's store." A corrected deed for the land was filed a year later on June 27, 1799.[37] Earp's store was one of only a few existing buildings in the vicinity of the new Courthouse site. Caleb Earp, a former deputy sheriff who operated the store, died in 1799, leaving Richard Ratcliffe, administrator of Earp's estate and owner of the land where the store stood, with the problem of collecting debts due the store. Ratcliffe replaced the store with a tavern and stables that were situated opposite the Courthouse.[38] In an advertisement in *The Columbian Mirror and Alexandria*

Gazette on February 1, 1800, Ratcliffe offered for rent his "Newly built two story" brick tavern with kitchen, "smoak house," stables, and other dependencies, stating that "it is conceived there are but few situations that offer greater advantages in that line than the above."

Before the establishment of Ratcliffe's tavern, travelers on the roads in the area may have found shelter at Price's Ordinary, several miles east on the road to Alexandria or a few miles west on the Mountain Road, now Braddock Road. On November 1, 1798, Anthony Thornton had an advertisement in the *Columbian Mirror and Alexandria Gazette* for his Eagle Tavern. It stated:

> The Subscriber takes this method of informing the Public that he continues to keep a House of Entertainment for Travellers at the Sign of the SPREAD EAGLE in the Town of Centerville, Virginia, where Travellers meet with Peace and Plenty, at his former prices. He at the same time returns his grateful acknowledgments to those travelling Gentlemen who have hitherto favoured him with their custom, and begs a continuance of their favors, which he hopes to merit, from his attention to business and desire to give satisfaction.

On April 16, 1798, the court ordered that the sheriff collect 35 cents for each tithable person in the County to pay for the new Courthouse.[39] On May 22, after the land had been laid out by William Payne, the court ordered the building of a Courthouse 40 by 30 feet, "with sixteen feet pitch with a twelve foot Portico, one Gaol forty feet by twenty . . ., One clerks office twenty four feet by eighteen . . . and one Gaolers House twenty four feet by eighteen . . ." The jail would have three rooms on the first floor and two on the second, with an addition on the back. The clerk's office should be "arched or covered with Slate or Tile," presumably for fire protection. There should also be stocks, a pillory and a whipping post. The commissioners were authorized to "let the building of the same to the lowest bidder" after advertising for three weeks in the Alexandria papers.[40]

John Bogue and Mungo Dykes were the contractors who were hired to do the work, and they completed the job early in 1800. Bogue was an Alexandria house and ship joiner, who arrived in Alexandria in 1795 on the ship *Two Sisters*[41]. The final payment for their work was made by the County in November of 1801.[42] In March of 1800, "the Justices of the County having been summoned for the purpose of receiving the Commissioners report for erecting a Courthouse Gaol and other Publick buildings for the use of the County Court, having taken the said report, into Consideration, do receive the said buildings as erected and ordered to be recorded . . ." The persons ordered to lay off ten acres of land for the court and adjoining the "Courthouse Gaol etc" also made a report.[43] Colonial Virginia statutes of 1748 stipulated that the jail be "well-secured with iron bars, bolts, and locks . . ." and that ten acres be laid off for the exercise of the prisoners.[44]

During the March court, William Deneale, "High Sheriff of Fairfax," requested that the court give him instructions "respecting the removal of the prisoners" from Alexandria to the new jail. The justices responded that they "would give no instructions to said Sheriff respecting said prisoners." After the justices handed down their ruling, Deneale "came into Court and protested against the sufficiency of the new Gaol erected for the County of Fairfax."[45] Without giving the sheriff's complaint further consideration, the court adjourned to the new Courthouse, to the "Court in Course," which would be in the following month.[46]

Following the adjournment of the March court, Sheriff Deneale placed a notice in the *Columbian Mirror and Alexandria Gazette* announcing that the County court had adjourned from Alexandria and would next be held at the new Courthouse "in the centre of the County, where all Suitors, & others having business, are hereby notified to attend, on the

The Fairfax County Courthouse, completed in 1800, was designed by architect James Wren, patterned after earlier market and town halls of Flanders, the Netherlands and England. The Courthouse was the nucleus of the Town of Providence when it was established in 1805. Drawing by Gloria Matthews, courtesy of the Fairfax County Office of Comprehensive Planning

George Washington's will, autographed on every page, is the best-known document recorded in the Fairfax County Courthouse. It is now secured in the nearby Judicial Center. Courtesy of the Clerk of the Circuit Court

third Monday of April next." The notice appeared regularly in the newspaper until time for the next court. Also in the notice was the announcement of an election to be held at the new Courthouse on the fourth Wednesday in April for a senator and "Representatives" for the next General Assembly of Virginia.

On April 21, 1800, the first court was held at the new Courthouse at the crossroads. The presiding justices were William Stanhope, Charles Little, David Stuart, William Payne and Richard Bland Lee. Three of them were commissioners of the new Courthouse. The clerk was George Deneale, who was also a captain of the Fairfax County militia. The first order of business was to record the will of Corbin Washington, a nephew of George Washington and brother of Judge Bushrod Washington, who was a Supreme Court Justice from 1798 to 1829. He had been married to Hannah Lee, a daughter of Richard Henry Lee.[47]

At the poll of voters at the Courthouse two days later, on April 23, Thomson Mason, a son of George Mason, won the senate seat, and Thomas Swann and Nicholas Fitzhugh were chosen as representatives. These state legislators represented both Fairfax and Prince William counties.[48]

With his design of the Fairfax County Courthouse, architect James Wren departed from the single-story plan usual in Virginia's colonial Courthouse, and produced a two-story building with a courtroom on the ground floor and jury rooms over the arched arcade.[49] A new design was appropriate for the heralding of a new century which would see even greater change in the County served by the Courthouse than had taken place in the previous one hundred years, when a wilderness peopled by Indians and the occasional European settler had become a thriving agrarian center.

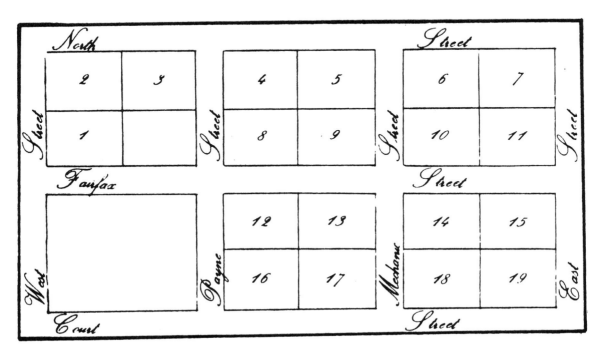

Town of Providence
1805

The above plat shows the Town of Providence established by the Virginia General Assembly in 1805 on 14 acres of land owned by Richard Ratcliffe "at the courthouse of Fairfax County. A postal village named Fairfax Court House." Courtesy of the Fairfax County Circuit Court Archives

2

The Town of Providence at the New Courthouse
1800 to 1860
by Nan Netherton

Through the colonial period in Virginia and up to 1870, judicial and administrative powers were vested in the county courts. The governor-appointed justices were responsible for the conduct of both public and private affairs. They set tax rates; approved licenses for the operation of mills, inns and peddlers; surveyed and maintained roads, bridges, and fords; and regulated welfare activities. The justices also influenced the selection of all other county officers. In the 1800s, much of the social and economic life of rural Virginia grew up around the monthly or quarterly "court days" at the county seat.[1]

Almost two years after the court held its first meeting in the new Courthouse, a new postal village was established on April 7, 1802. John Ratcliffe was the first postmaster, probably a son of entrepreneur and land speculator Richard Ratcliffe. The postal designation for the village by the post office department was "Fairfax Court House." A bronze plaque was placed in the 1800 Courthouse in 1995 by the Henry Clay Chapter, National Society, Daughters of the American Revolution (DAR), commemorating some of the contributions Richard Ratcliffe made to establish the Courthouse at what in 1805 became the Town of Providence; in 1874, the Town of Fairfax; and in 1961, the City of Fairfax.[2]

The Town of Providence was established on 14 acres of land owned by Richard Ratcliffe "at the court house of Fairfax County" in 1805, but the town was usually referred to by the earlier postal designation, "Fairfax Court House." The 12 trustees, all prominent men of the County, were Charles Little, William Payne, Richard Bland Lee, John Jackson, John C.

Hunter, Richard Coleman, Daniel McCarty Chichester, Henry Gunnell, Jr., Marmaduke B. Beckwith, Daniel Lewis, Francis Coffer, David Stuart, William Middleton and Richard Fitzhugh.[3]

Serviceable roads that enabled citizens to travel to the county seat, the markets, and other local places were slow to develop. Private companies throughout Virginia began building turnpikes and bridges in the late 1700s and early 1800s but found that they could not raise sufficient money to support expensive road-building projects and to maintain them. The state, through the General Assembly, became a financial partner in these enterprises. Toll gates were placed along the roads with scales to weigh wagons. Unfortunately, tolls collected did not cover the high maintenance costs.[4] The Virginia Board of Public Works was established in 1816 in order to cope with these and other problems.

If a County citizen wished to attend court when it was first opened at the crossroads in 1800, he could have obtained a refreshment for himself as well as hay and a place in the stable for his horse at Ratcliffe's Tavern. By 1805, a tavern, or ordinary, existed alongside "stables and other buildings" at the intersection of Main Street and Chain Bridge Road; where NationsBank now stands. Perhaps the building later known variously as the Willcoxen Tavern, the Union Hotel and the Fairfax Hotel had already been constructed by then, across from the Courthouse, where Earp's Store once stood. Eventually the hotel provided offices for local lawyers and judges as well as judges who needed accommodations when "riding the circuit."[5]

The Willcoxen Tavern was built early in the 1800s, on the site of an earlier, smaller inn built by Richard Ratcliffe, who probably enlarged Earp's Store or Ordinary. It was located on the corner where the NationsBank now stands, across the Little River Turnpike from the old brick courthouse. For more than 100 years, and under several names, it served the public until 1930 when it was razed and replaced in 1931 by the National Bank of Fairfax. Courtesy of Lee Hubbard

The few area roads that existed before 1800 had usually been built to accommodate the largest staple crop in Virginia from colonial times—tobacco. Almost every farmer grew the pungent plant and depended on being able to transport it to market for sale there. This necessitated what came to be known as "rolling roads" because tobacco hogsheads were rolled along them. These roads usually ran along ridges and connected tobacco lands with navigable waterways. They often followed old established Indian trails.[6]

The period between 1800 and 1861 was characterized by Virginia's increased state activity on roads encouraged by the demand of its residents. Fairfax Court House residents had friends and family who had "gone west" to the frontiers of Kentucky, Tennessee, Ohio and other newly-formed states, to find new and fertile land. The Commonwealth realized that good roads were important for better communication and closer commercial ties between east and west. People within the County saw the need for better roads,

particularly to encourage trade as the economic picture changed.[7] Like several areas in eastern Virginia, Fairfax lost population between 1810 and 1830 due to the extensive western movement. Emigrants were searching for new and more productive farm lands or for business opportunities.[8]

Seeing a need that was not being met, an ambitious young lawyer, William Smith, a native of Virginia, contracted in the early 1830s with the government of the United States to establish a line of United States mail and passenger post coaches from Washington City to Lynchburg. This line was routed through the towns of Fairfax Court House, Warrenton, Culpeper, Orange County Court House, and Amherst Court House, Virginia. Occasional advertisements in the *Alexandria Gazette* at the time assured prospective patrons that there would be "positively *no* racing" on their stage lines. A successful political candidate, Smith served in several elected positions before he was elected Governor of Virginia by the legislature in 1845 for a three-year term.[9]

Stage coach passengers moving through the Town of Providence might have seen some of the Town's buildings and residents as described under the designation of "Fairfax Court House P.O." in Joseph Martin's 1835 *Gazetteer*: "It contains besides the ordinary county buildings, 50 dwelling houses, for the most part frame buildings, 3 mercantile stores, 4 taverns and one common school. The mechanics are boot and shoe makers, saddlers, blacksmiths, tailors, &c. Population 200 persons; of whom 4 are attorneys and 2 physicians."[10]

Before Virginia's Underwood Constitution was adopted in 1870, education provided by the state was for paupers. Private academies for boys or girls had been established in the 1840s and earlier in Virginia. Dr. Frederick Baker, a surgeon born and educated in England, came to New York City in 1837, and soon met and married Hannah Marie Burgess. They had one child, Eugenia Davis Baker, nicknamed "Jane" or "Jennie." Land was cheaper in northern Virginia than in New York and the climate was more moderate, so the Bakers followed the lead of many other New Yorkers of the period.[11] They moved to Fairfax in 1843, and in 1844, Dr. Baker took the constitutional oath in the Fairfax County Court and became a citizen of the United States.[12]

In 1845, Dr. Baker bought a 15-acre tract on the north side of Little River Turnpike next to Zion Episcopal Church. There he erected a cluster of buildings for his residence and a private finishing school for girls, the first of the type in Fairfax County. Named "Coombe Cottage," the school attracted about

This brick Georgian-style structure has been somewhat altered since its construction in about 1810 by Dr. Samuel Draper, who lived there until 1842. A front porch has been removed and the first floor windows are actually French doors. Former outbuildings have been converted into small shops and a bookstore. Located at 10364 Main Street. Placed on the National Register in 1987. Photo by Carol L. Baird, courtesy of the City of Fairfax

The Ratcliffe-Allison house, erroneously known for decades as "Earp's Ordinary," is the City's oldest surviving residence and was the first city building to be placed on the National Register of Historic Places (1973). The oldest section of the house was built between 1805 and 1813 on land once owned by Richard Ratcliffe. In 1820, Gordon and Robert Allison acquired the house and used it as a post station and stagecoach stop. The brothers put an addition on the house, probably in 1830. It is located at 10386 Main Street, Courtesy of Lee Hubbard

Joshua Gunnell built this house on the corner of Sager Avenue and Chain Bridge Road early in the 1800s. It has been known as the "Oliver House" but is now called the Bailiwick Inn, a bed-and-breakfast establishment. The building design is a good example of townhouse-type Greek Revival architecture as represented by the entry portico and door surround. The interior workmanship shows excellent details. Located at 4011 Chain Bridge Road. This photo, taken about 1870, shows Mrs. Joshua Coffer Gunnell and her son, Henry Lewis Gunnell. Placed on the National Register in 1987. Courtesy of the Fairfax County Public Library Photographic Archive

Coombe Cottage was a private academy for young women in the Town of Providence during the decade prior to the Civil War. It was located on the property on the Little River Turnpike now owned by Truro Episcopal Church. The last building of several of the original school complex was demolished after this photo was taken in 1955. Courtesy of the Fairfax County Public Library Photographic Archive

80 students, some from local places and some from out of state. For a while, Antonia Ford of Fairfax was a student. (Please see Chapter III.) The tuition was $100 per year for the Academy, board and room. Subjects taught were English grammar, mathematics, history, geography, natural sciences, music, art, writing and the Bible. Most students attended for two years and their average ages were 13-16. A private diary, which survives to this day, was kept for the school year 1853-1854 by Frances Ellen Carper of Dranesville. During the Civil War, the school closed and never reopened.[13]

In the same decade, a new and exciting transportation scheme for Virginia was developed—a network of railroads. One of the local lines, the Orange and Alexandria Rail Road, was organized in 1848 to lay tracks southwest across Fairfax County from Alexandria to Gordonsville in Orange County.[14]

But why was the railroad not built through Fairfax Court House (Providence), the county seat? A Board of Public Works document which survives in the Virginia State Archives gives the probable answer. In the minutes of a stockholders' meeting of the Orange and Alexandria Railroad held in December 1849, the following resolution appears: "Resolved, that the President and Directors of this Company . . . shall

The Orange and Alexandria Rail Road Company, chartered in 1848, was laid across Fairfax and Prince William counties and eventually linked Alexandria with Gordonsville, Orange County, in central Virginia. Because a right-of-way was acquired in the southern part of the County, the tracks were not built through the county seat, called Fairfax Court House. The train stop closest was named Fairfax Station and for about 100 years it served Town of Fairfax shipments. Courtesy of artist Robert Clay, The Library of Virginia

Major passenger and mail service was provided from the 1830s through the 1850s by the Winchester and Alexandria Mail Stage. This passenger list illustrates what some of the conveyances looked like. It shows that Gordon Allison sold passenger Thompson his ticket. The roads used including the one through Fairfax Court House (Town of Providence) were often in deplorable condition. Railroads, first developed in the area during the 1850s, gradually replaced the stages. Courtesy of the City of Fairfax.

adopt the location on that route . . . which shall appear by the report of the Engineer to be the most direct, advantageous and cheap."[15]

Various landowners donated land so that the railroad could be built. The principal citizen among them was entrepreneur and Fairfax County Chief Court Justice Col. Silas Burke (after whom the village of Burke was named), who persuaded other landowners to follow his lead in giving land for the railroad right-of-way. Those who donated no doubt considered how their actions would benefit the community, but neither did they forget the benefits they themselves would enjoy.[16]

Still another local construction project featured a road made of wooden planks to facilitate easier travel than was possible on traditional packed earth or broken stone roads. The Providence Branch Plank Road Company was chartered in 1851 "for constructing a plank road from Fairfax Court House, running in a Southerly direction to some point on the Alexandria and Gordonsville Railroad at or near Paine's Church."

Route 123 from the City of Fairfax to Fairfax Station now follows this path, which was also a part of Ox Road.[17] This type of road was impractical because the planks soon warped and rotted in the moist climate.

When the railroad company survey of the right-of-way was completed to Gordonsville in 1853, a large number of Irish immigrants responded to advertisements for laborers to build the railroad. Many settled down later and built homes in the area. With the Hamill and Cunningham families, who had donated land in 1838 to the Diocese of Richmond for the purpose of constructing a church, the new Irish immigrants built St. Mary of Sorrows Catholic Church. The priest often celebrated Mass in boxcars standing at Fairfax Station, until the church building was completed in 1860. With a war between the North and South imminent, it was not long before the building was temporarily adapted for other than religious purposes.[18] The relatively tranquil pastoral life enjoyed by residents of Fairfax Court House and vicinity soon became disrupted by uniformed soldiers of both the North and South and their deadly weapons of war.

Wooden pavements called plank roads were widely used during the turnpike era in Virginia, using the abundant natural standing timber in the Commonwealth. Typically, a single track was about eight feet wide and on it were laid planks or logs placed crosswise. In time, severe warping and rotting occurred from frequent precipitation throughout each year, and the roads became useless. The Providence Branch Plank Road Company was chartered in 1851 "for constructing a plank road from Fairfax Court House, running in a Southernly direction to some point on the Alexandria and Gordonsville railroad at or near Paine's Church." Courtesy of The Library of Virginia

saint Mary's church

St. Mary of Sorrows Catholic Church was dedicated in September 1860 at Fairfax Station and has remained a local landmark ever since.
Courtesy of the artist, Charles R. Wagner

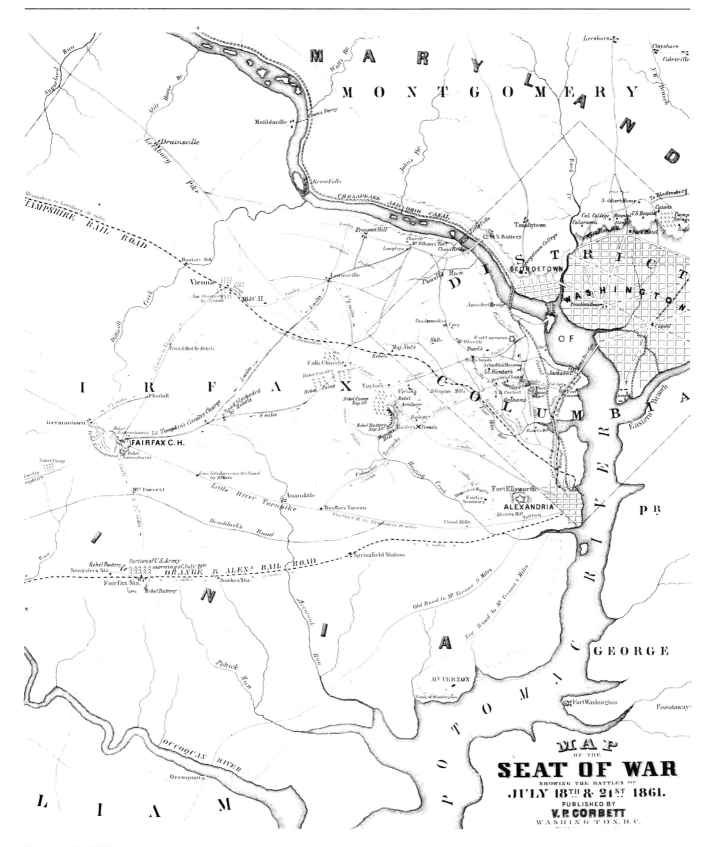

Cartographer V. P. Corbett produced a map in Washington, D. C. which he labeled "The Seat of War," in 1861. A portion of the map is shown here highlighting the area around Fairfax Court House. The American Civil War was reported more thoroughly than any war had been up to that time. Words, photographs, drawings and even paintings responded to the insatiable demand on the home front for details of events on the fighting fronts scattered over half a continent. Courtesy of the New York State Library

3.

Caught in the Crossfire: War and Its Aftermath, 1860-1870
by David L. Meyer

The decade of the 1860s for Fairfax Court House is a chronicle of a Civil War community that lived, suffered, and survived the conflict on the front line. While this front line was more geographic than strategic, the Fairfax Court House area experienced its share of economic and physical devastation wrought by the tens of thousands of troops that passed through the crossroads that circumscribed and defined the Courthouse and its adjacent community. The presence of the Courthouse brought great symbolic importance to the region for both the North and the South. As the legal center for Fairfax County, only 16 miles from the Federal City of Washington, the Courthouse was the repository of records for a region that had produced some of the early Republic's greatest leaders—George Washington, George Mason, and Richard Bland Lee, among others.

The Courthouse also represented legitimacy for the local government during the war. Its possession and occupation by both sides at different times during the war, while not a strategic imperative, did serve as some measure of control of the region. While securely in the hands of the North by 1863, the Courthouse and its community changed hands twice during the early part of the war. The community's populace was decisively Southern in its sympathies but had its share of Northern "loyalists." Consequently, Civil War life in the little town was spiced with raids, spies, kidnappings, and disputed and divided loyalties.

Northern Virginia's initial response to the growing secessionist movement was typically Virginian, loyal to its southern connections but cautiously respectful of 70 years experience with a Federal republic which many of its early residents helped design and create. Indeed at the outset of 1860, when many political leaders and legislatures in the lower South were espousing the right of secession, appropriating funds for military forces, and calling for a convention on Southern rights, Virginia took the lead in asserting that Southern grievances could be addressed and resolved within the framework of the Union.

Fairfax County in 1860 had 11,834 residents, including 672 free blacks (6%), 3,116 slaves (26%), and 8,046 whites (68%).[1] During the preceding decade, subtle but significant changes had contributed to Fairfax's slow response to secession. Emigration from Northern states created enclaves of loyalist support, such as the "New York Staters" who had settled in Oakton and Vienna, just to the north of Fairfax. Large plantation farming had been replaced by smaller operations, reducing the economic necessity and viability for slave labor.[2] New railroads opened Northern markets to Fairfax and further encouraged the influx of new residents. These residents brought with them different political affiliations (former Whigs, American party supporters, and Republicans) and religious denominations (for example, Quakers, northern Presbyterians, American Baptists, among others).

John Brown's raid on the Federal arsenal at nearby Harpers Ferry in October 1859 (in an attempt to instigate a slave uprising in Southern states) fueled the growing schism within the Democratic party, thus ensuring the election of Lincoln a year later on November 6, 1860. Over the next three months, 10 Southern states seceded. Only three states (Texas, Tennessee, and Virginia) decided to submit ordinances of secession to voters for ratification.

In Virginia, newly-elected Governor John Letcher reluctantly authorized the election of delegates to a convention to address Virginia's relation to the Federal government (the call for a convention having been forced upon him by the General Assembly). In Fairfax County, William H. Dulaney ran as the moderately Unionist candidate against Alfred Moss, a mild secessionist. A debate was held at the Fairfax Court-house on January 21. Dulaney's advocacy of continued negotiation with the North held sway with County voters. Dulaney defeated Moss 836 to 628.[3]

Despite Virginia's democratic deliberateness in electing delegates and convening them in Richmond in April, events elsewhere in the South moved quickly. The seizure of Federal arsenals and forts in the South was making the prospects for peace untenable. On April 12, Confederate forces fired on Fort Sumter, located on a small island in the harbor of Charleston, South Carolina. Two days later in Richmond, despite the "nay" votes of Fairfax delegate Dulaney and others, the Virginia convention approved secession 88 to 55.[4]

Technically, the Virginia convention approved a referendum on secession to be put before the voters, which was scheduled for May 23. However, in the intervening five weeks, Virginians were preparing for war. On April 25, 1861, Company D of the 17th Regiment of the Virginia Infantry, known as the "Fairfax Rifles," was mustered on the grounds of Fairfax Courthouse. In all, three volunteer companies (two cavalry and one infantry) were mustered into service for Virginia from Fairfax. Additionally, control of the two railroads that ran through Fairfax County were in the hands of Virginians.[5]

The movement toward "Virginia solidarity" made approval of the secession referendum a certainty. In mid-May, William Dulaney declared at a public forum in Fairfax, "the course of the [Lincoln] administration made it the imperative duty of every loyal son of Virginia to strike for her independence."[6]

The vote in Fairfax County was 1,231 for secession and 289 against.[7] The voting process at this time was oral. A voter declared his preference publicly (women were not enfranchised) and the clerk of the court recorded the results.[8]

Several incidents of intimidation of Unionist voters have been recorded. In one example, Robert Townsend Sisson, who resided on Ox Road in Fairfax and whose family had been in Fairfax County since the Revolution, headed to the Courthouse to vote in the referendum. Sisson was decidedly a Union supporter and proud of his father's service in the Revolutionary War. At the Courthouse he encountered State Senator Henry W. Thomas and told Thomas of his intention to vote "Union." Thomas replied that if Sisson wished to enjoy continued good health, he would do better not to vote at all. Sisson accepted Thomas' counsel and returned home.[9]

This engraving was published in a newspaper of the period. It depicts a "Brilliant charge of United States Cavalry through the village of Fairfax Court House" on June 1, 1861. Courtesy of The Library of Virginia

In another instance, a local farmer named William D. Smith traveled to Accotink to vote and found Confederate cavalry present. Despite verbal harrassment and threats to his safety and property, Smith voted to support the Union. Accotink, along with Lewinsville and Lydecker's, were the only three precincts where a majority voted to remain in the Union.[10]

Unionists did not fare well during the months leading up to secession. In the village of Flint Hill (now Oakton) just north of Fairfax Court House, "New York Staters" (as they were derisively referred to by Southern supporters) were harrassed for subscribing to the New York *Tribune*, whose editor was the abolitionist Horace Greeley. Tom Moore, a proslavery advocate and descendant of colonial Baptist preacher Jeremiah Moore, gave an ultimatum to these Northerners—"cancel [the] subscriptions or 'get out'!" The New Yorkers refused to do either; by the time of the secession referendum, the Post Office had ceased to deliver the newspaper.[11] More trouble for these loyalists was yet to come.

The day following the May 23 referendum, Union forces secured Washington, D.C., by posting guards at the Virginia entrances to bridges over the Potomac River and sent the New York Zouaves into the City of Alexandria. The Zouaves were under the command of Colonel Elmer Ellsworth who, upon entering the city and seeing a Confederate flag flying on a hotel known as the Marshall House, ran into the hotel, climbed to the rooftop, and tore the flag down. The proprietor of the hotel was a Fairfax native, James William Jackson, who had previously operated the Union House/Ratcliffe Tavern in Fairfax until February 1861, when he was offered the proprietorship of the Marshall House. Jackson had a flag patterned after the "stars and bars" and had placed it on the rooftop. When Jackson witnessed what Ellsworth had done, he shot and killed him. Corporal Francis Brownell who was accompanying Ellsworth then shot and killed Jackson. Jackson's wife and daughter escaped Alexandria with Jackson's business partner, Amos Fox. Ellsworth was a personal friend of President Lincoln, who arranged for his funeral to be held in the Pink Room of the White House. Jackson's remains were first interred at the Jackson house on Swinks Mill Road.[12] In 1896, he was reinterred in a family plot at the Fairfax Cemetery.[13]

While Union forces were being posted around Washington and Alexandria, Confederate volunteers took up sentry duty in areas just west and south,

including Fairfax. One such Confederate sentry was Peyton Anderson of Fairfax, who was stationed at what is now the intersection of Blake Lane and Lee Highway. On the afternoon of May 26, Anderson became quite hungry and upon seeing eight-year-old James Walker, asked him to bring him some breakfast the next morning. The next day, Jimmy Walker's mother prepared some food for Anderson at their farmhouse just north of his sentry post on the road that led to Falls Church. As Jimmy carried the food to Anderson, two horsemen confronted the boy and asked if there were any soldiers in the area, to which young Walker replied, "Oh yes, there's one just at the top of the hill." The riders thanked him and disappeared. As Walker was crossing the stream at the bottom of the hill, he heard shots. He arrived moments later and learned that Anderson had been wounded and taken prisoner. Anderson is recorded as Fairfax County's first wounded soldier and is sometimes claimed as the first casualty of the war. A monument to Anderson was placed at the intersection of Blake Lane and Lee Highway in 1927. It was later moved to Route 50/29/211 in Fairfax, where it now stands in the 9700 block of Lee Highway.[14]

Two days after the shooting of Anderson, on May 29, Charles Sutton and Squire Millard of Flint Hill, two unabashed New Yorkers, left their homes and families after being threatened by men at the Fairfax Courthouse, most likely in response to the wounding of Anderson. They later returned to help their families flee; their actions were wise, for later a number of their Northern neighbors were arrested and sent to the Libby Prison in Richmond.[15]

As the caldron of war neared its boiling point, greater violence was simply a matter of time. The defensive cordon established by Federal troops to defend Washington excluded Fairfax Court House and its environs, creating a zone of contention from Lewinsville through Vienna and Flint Hill to Fairfax Court House. These areas were constantly reconnoitered by Northern and Southern scouts, with pickets established by both sides in the same places at different times. The confusion and uncertainty of local residents was considerable, with property, livestock, crops, and personal safety always in jeopardy.

The turmoil of the region was exacerbated by the movement of civilians fleeing Federal troops that were entering Alexandria, Falls Church, Langley, and other nearby areas. Families often moved with little or no notice. The Rev. John P. Johns, Assistant Bishop of

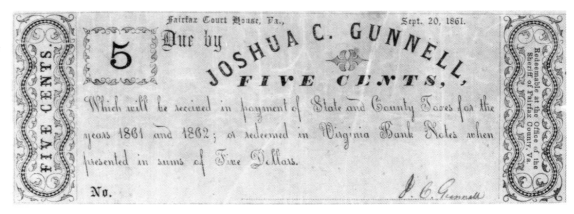

This is an example of paper money printed at Fairfax Court House, Virginia during the Civil War by Joshua C. Gunnell. Courtesy of Lewis Leigh, Jr.

the Episcopal Diocese who lived near the Virginia Theological Seminary in Alexandria, recorded his decision to leave, "On Friday morning, May 24, at an early hour the Federal forces took possession of Alexandria. It was now evident that I could no longer remain there unless I was prepared to be separated from the Diocese and restricted in official duties. . . . In two hours after the invasion I was on the road with those of my family who had not previously moved."[16]

At the same time, Judith B. McGuire, the wife of the Rev. John Payton McGuire, Principal of Episcopal High School in Alexandria, wrote in her diary: "Fairfax C.H., May 25, 1861. Alexandria and environs, including, I greatly fear, our home is in the hands of the enemy . . . About sunset (yesterday) we drove up to the door of this, the house of our relatives, the Rev. Mr. Brown."[17] The Rev. Richard Templeton Brown was serving The Falls Church in Fairfax Parish and Zion and St. John's in Truro Parish and was living at Fairfax Court House when hostilities commenced.

Eleanor M. B. Ewell (whose brother Albert would be killed at the Second Battle of Manassas) recalled the experiences of a relative who sought refuge in her home:

We had so far seen nothing of the real trouble already beginning in some places; but were to have a warning illustration. A connection of ours, Mr. William Slade, who had been for years a government clerk in Washington, with a home in that neighborhood, though on the Virginia side of the Potomac, arrived unexpectedly, bringing his two daughters. He stated that his home, near Langley, in Fairfax county, was no longer safe for his children—being constantly raided by the Union soldiery. We at once made them welcome. Edge Hill house, now vacant,

was placed at their service. They had brought with them a few household belongings and Mr. Slade soon returned to Langley with the hope of getting more. He came back empty-handed and in a fine towering rage. He had packed a wagon full of household goods and the horses were attached to it ready to start with a servant driving and Mr. Slade on horseback, when a band of the enemy surrounded and captured wagon, horses, and driver. The irate owner had only time to swear a good round oath, fire his pistol into their midst and make his escape. He settled down at Edge Hill, making the best of scanty means in hand, and continued with us for nearly a year. The family went to Richmond the next spring when our armies fell back in that direction.[18]

By the end of May, three units of Confederate soldiers (two cavalry and one infantry) were stationed at Fairfax Court House. These included the Warrenton Rifles (approximately 90 men) under the command of Captain John Quincy Marr, quartered in the Methodist Church located on the south side of the Courthouse; the Prince William Cavalry under the command of Captain Thornton (about 60 men) housed in the Episcopal church; and the Rappahannock Cavalry under Captain Green (about 60 men) who slept in the Courthouse itself. These troops were under the command of Lieutenant-Colonel Richard S. Ewell (who later became a general), freshly resigned as a Captain of a cavalry unit in the Federal army.[19]

On the night of May 31-June 1, a detachment of Company B, Second Cavalry under the command of Lieutenant Charles H. Thompkins with the Second Dragoons under Lieutenant David S. Gordon, numbering approximately 80, neared the town to scout enemy strength. After capturing a picket, these troops entered the town and were fired upon by Confederate troops from windows and rooftops. In the confusion and darkness, Captain Marr was killed by a stray bullet. Additionally, five Confederates were taken prisoner and removed to the Navy Yard in Washington. Three Union soldiers were killed or missing and four were wounded.[20]

John Quincy Marr, who died two days following his 36th birthday, was second in his class at the Virginia Military Institute when he graduated in 1846. He had served as a delegate from Fauquier County to the Virginia Convention that approved the secession resolution the preceding April. With his death, he became the first Confederate officer casualty of the war.[21] A monument to Marr was erected on the grounds of the Courthouse in 1904.[22]

The Courthouse first came under control of Union troops a month later as General Irvin McDowell, who had established his headquarters at "Arlington," and commandeered the home of Robert E. Lee, began moving his 37,000 man army west toward Manassas on July 18. He was to intercept Confederate General Joseph E. Johnston, who was leading his army of 9,000 north through the Shenandoah Valley. The ensuing battle on July 21, known as the First Battle of Manassas, was the first major conflict of the war.[23]

Confederate General Pierre G. T. Beauregard, who had advance warning of McDowell's movements, positioned his troops along Bull Run near Manassas Junction. By the early evening of July 21, Beauregard and Johnston, along with Generals Thomas J. Jackson (who earned the nickname "Stonewall" at Manassas) and Bernard Bee of South Carolina (who was killed in the afternoon fighting), held their Confederate forces firm against the well-equipped Union forces. When their lines broke, the overconfident and undisciplined Union army began a most disorderly retreat toward Washington, referred to by many participants as "the great skedaddle." The defeat would cost McDowell his command; Lincoln appointed General George B. McClellan to reorganize his army.[24]

The Confederate victory had come at a cost; the exhausted Southern forces were in no condition to pursue their enemy. The following day, Johnson deployed his troops in the Centreville area, building the largest military earthworks ever constructed up to that time.

In the aftermath of this Northern debacle, control of Fairfax Court House was securely in Southern hands for the next six months. Beauregard established his headquarters at Fairfax Court House and wanted desperately to mount a northern offensive into Maryland and Pennsylvania, possibly capturing Washington as well. Beauregard, a brilliant and somewhat self-promoting Creole from Louisiana, was a West Point graduate and probably the best artillery soldier of either army. Once established at Fairfax, he seized the opportunity to establish redoubts as close to Federal lines as possible, including some bluffs overlooking Washington City itself.[25]

Despite Beauregard's activist style, he was out-ranked by the more deliberative and cautious Johnston. Beauregard decided to present his case directly to the newly chosen President of the Confederacy, Jefferson Davis. On October 1, 1861, Davis met with Beauregard, Johnston, General Gustavus W. Smith, and their close advisors at the Willcoxen Tavern in Fairfax. The Confederate leadership gathered there decided that its army was in no position to mount an offensive against Washington City or begin a campaign into Northern territory. On October 3, Davis did take the opportunity to review Confederate forces on the grounds of the Courthouse, which was described as "a brilliant turnout."[26]

The winter of 1861-62 found the Federal troops in eastern Fairfax County and Confederate troops stationed at the heavily fortified camps at Centreville. With the exception of a few skirmishes, the positions of both armies remained relatively static during these months, with Fairfax Court House under Southern control.[27] With the onset of spring, however, both armies were on the move. The Confederate army withdrew from Centreville and Fairfax to take up new positions south of the Rappahannock to defend Richmond from what General Joseph Johnston knew would be an inevitable campaign by McClellan to capture the South's capital.

By this time, the Courthouse itself had ceased to function as a center for legal business and was simply used as a military outpost. Indeed, the Courthouse again became the site for an important deliberation on military strategy, this time with Union military leadership gathered in the building on March 13, 1862. McClellan and his commanders decided to move toward Richmond using a water route down the Potomac River, a strategy favored by McClellan over Lincoln's preference for a direct land assault. Thus McClellan's months of intransigence and unwillingness to move against Southern forces ended at the Courthouse conference.[28]

The withdrawal of thousands of Confederate troops that had been camped from west of Centreville to the east of Fairfax revealed the magnitude of the destruction over the winter. In less than one year, the devastation wreaked by soldiers living in primitive camps and relying mostly on their immediate surroundings for survival left the region a stark and hollow image of its former self. The destruction made a great impression on many Northern soldiers arriving to the region. William Maris Clark, a soldier from Chester, Pennsylvania, serving in the 28th Pennsylvania Infantry, had been bivouacked during the winter at Point of Rocks, Maryland. Clark described the area in a letter to his brother and sister dated April 27, 1862:

"... The trip was worth a great deal, as all the ground we traveled over, was fraught with scenes of interest; it is worth a travel from a great distance to see Manassas and the surrounding country. The Rebels have spent immense labor in fortifying that position it is surrounded on all sides by forts and Earth works of great size and strength, between the Junction and Bull Run nothing but one Fortification after another is to be seen. All their winter huts are still standing; At Bull Run we found that the bridge had been taken away by the late freshet, so we had to get out Cross over on the footpath, and get in a train from the other side. This caused quite a delay, so that night was coming on before we got started again. All the Country from Manassas to Fairfax, and further for what I know, is one vast barren waste: not a fence to be seen as far as the eye can reach, the land is horribly cut by thousands of wagon roads turning in different directions: the timber was all cut off last winter and used for fuel so I know that there is not enough timber left to fence the land."[29]

Jacob Heffelfinger, a Union officer, wrote in his diary of the countryside between Alexandria and Centreville in early 1862, "nothing along our whole route appears to have been held sacred from the devastation of the war. At one place I saw traces of a camp in a graveyard, some of the tents having been pitched immediately over the graves. The blackened ruins of dwellings line the road. At one place I saw a dead horse in one of the rooms of a deserted dwelling house."[30]

The withdrawal of Confederate troops from Fairfax Court House and the surrounding areas placed the region in Union hands for the remainder of the war. The Union forces immediately began the task of establishing a "loyal" civilian government and some semblance of economic and social order. When Virginia seceded from the Union, a "loyal" government was organized in Wheeling by Union supporters. These supporters had held a convention in May 1861 (in response to the secession convention held in Richmond in April of that year) and elected Francis Harrison Pierpont, a western Virginian with longstanding ties to the old Whig party, as governor. Thus with the arrival of Union forces to Fairfax Court House in early 1862, those men with Northern sympathies began to organize and press for local elections.[31] (Many were Northern immigrants who came to Fairfax County in the 1840s and 50s and were pacifist Quakers, and hence did not serve in the Union army.)[32]

On March 22, 1862, a meeting of the Unionists was held at the Courthouse. An appeal to Pierpont was drafted and within six weeks Pierpont issued a writ of election, which was held on May 22. A full complement of officers was elected. The same month postal service was resumed. Local residents had modest success in planting crops and minor commerce between localities resumed.[33]

Despite these efforts, this was still an occupied community in a country at war. Bitterness and enmity were crosscurrents among the populace; northern Unionists questioned the true commitment of native Unionists, both of whom were resented by Southern families whose sons, fathers, and brothers were on the battlefields for the Confederacy. Daily deprivations were exacerbated by the news of lost loved ones on battlefields south and west of Fairfax. Runaway slaves came to Fairfax seeking the protection of the Union army. Other slaves returned seeking the continuity of life on farms where they once served their owners. Some residents bartered with local soldiers and established friendships with many while other locals engaged in sabotage, theft, and spying for the Southern cause.

Efforts by the local Unionist government and army to bring some normalcy to Fairfax Court House was made all the more difficult by the presence of hundreds of troops concentrated in a village with a prewar population of only 300. Over the months of occupation, these troops came to struggle with the same deprivations experienced by the local population—lack of fuel, food, proper sanitation, and separation from family members. Military commanders had to

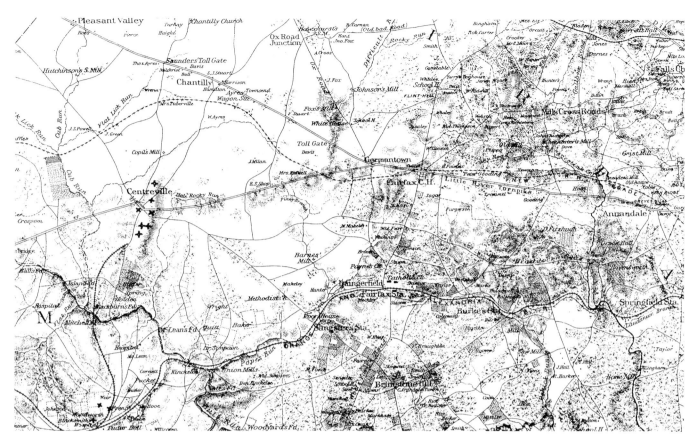

This is a portion of General Irvin McDowell's map of Northern Virginia showing Fairfax Court House. It was compiled in August 1862 by the United States Topographical Engineers Office. Courtesy of the Virginia Room, Fairfax City Regional Library

cope with the problems these conditions created among their soldiers, as well as the village population at large.

On the military front, McClellan's Peninsula campaign was unsuccessful in capturing Richmond. Incorrectly believing his forces were inferior in number and training, he moved hesitantly against the Confederate army. His extended battlelines along the Chickahominy River permitted Johnston to attack McClellan's 4th Corps on May 31-June 1. Despite Johnston's being severely wounded, the Confederate's performance strengthened their resolve and confidence. On June 1, Robert E. Lee was given command of the Army of Northern Virginia. At the same time, Stonewall Jackson began his brilliant campaign that moved his army north through the Shenandoah Valley. From March to June, Jackson's army of 18,000 pursued and attacked Union armies more than twice his number under the command of Generals Nathaniel Banks and John Fremont. In response, the Commander of the Union army, General Henry W. Halleck, consolidated the forces of McClellan and General John

Pope for a march toward Richmond via Manassas Junction. Lee's army moved quickly up the valley, setting in motion the rematch of Northern and Southern forces at Manassas on August 29-30, 1862.[34]

The Second Battle of Manassas saw thousands of Union troops passing west through the crossroads of Fairfax Court House in mid to late August. On August 29, Pope was attacked from the rear by Jackson, who destroyed his supplies lines; Pope's flank was subsequently attacked by Longstreet, who nearly destroyed his army. Pope never received the anticipated additional support from Generals Fitz-John Porter and McClellan, despite their close proximity, and retreated late August 30 toward Washington.[35]

The victorious but exhausted forces under Jackson and Lee pursued the retreating Union army toward Fairfax Court House, setting the stage for the most significant fighting of the war to occur in Fairfax County. The Battle of Chantilly (or Ox Hill, as referred to by Southern accounts) occurred east of Chantilly near what is now the intersection of U.S. Route 50 and State Route 608 (West Ox Road), just

Immediately following the Second Battle of Manassas (Bull Run), the only major battle to occur on Fairfax soil took place at Ox Hill (Chantilly). Although Union General John Pope managed to deflect Confederate General Lee's advance on Washington, Union control of Fairfax was disorganized for months after the fall 1862 campaign. Union Generals Isaac I. Stephens and Philip Kearny were killed during the battle. The engraving is entitled "The Death of General Stephens." Courtesy of the Virginia Historical Society

west of Fairfax. (A County park memorial to the battle now stands at West Ox Road and Memorial Drive.) By the afternoon of September 1, forces from both sides had manuevered to the point where heavy, direct firing and combat ensued. A low, violent thunderstorm began which hampered the ability of both armies to fire their weapons, and hand combat began with bayonets and musket handles. By the battle's end, two Union officers, Brigadier General Isaac Stevens and Major General Philip Kearny, had been killed. In a gesture of respect, General Lee had Kearny's body returned to Union forces under a truce flag on the morning of September 2.[36] Tactically, the Battle of Chantilly proved to have no victor. Southern forces were too exhausted and low on supplies and food to continue the assault on Union forces who, while outnumbering Southern forces, continued to suffer from a lack of a coordinated command. Their determination to ensure the security of Washington, D.C., hastened their retreat. The results of Second Manassas and Chantilly convinced Robert E. Lee to take his Army into Maryland in September, moving the central conflict away from the arena west of Fairfax Court House for the remainder of the war.[37]

The summer of 1862 also witnessed the entry of Clarissa (Clara) Harlowe Barton into the saga of the Civil War, and some of her earliest and most notable service occurred in the vicinity of Fairfax Court House. A native of Oxford, Massachusetts, Clara

Barton served as a school teacher for 18 years prior to her employment as a clerk in the U.S. Patent Office. In the spring of 1861, she organized a relief effort for wounded soldiers who had been brought to Washington. She wrote dispatches and appeals that were published in many Northern newspapers. She first appeared on the battlefield on August 9, 1862, when General Nathaniel Banks was defeated at Cedar Mountain. When she heard of the impending Second Battle of Manassas, she and four other women brought a train loaded with supplies to Fairfax Station. Under

Clarissa H. "Clara" Barton, eventually the founder of the American Red Cross, was a government clerk when, after the Second Battle of Manassas (Bull Run), she cared for wounded Union soldiers at Fairfax Station from the Battle of Ox Hill (Chantilly). Courtesy of The Library of Virginia

the supervision of Dr. James Dunn, she and her assistants provided care for 3,000 wounded soldiers. In what became a standard procedure on many battlefields of the Civil War, Barton laid straw on the ground and treated the wounded in open fields. Often staying up all night, Barton treated the wounded and dying by candlelight, risking fire from the straw to care for the soldiers.[38] At Fairfax Station, Barton oversaw the evacuation of the wounded on September 2, remaining until all soldiers were removed. Standing on the back of the last train, she observed Confederate forces moving into the area and burning the Station that had served as her headquarters.[39]

The autumn of 1862 witnessed Lee's first attempt to invade the North and isolate Washington from Northern cities. Following the Battle of Chantilly, Lee moved his army into Maryland.[40] McClellan's army met Lee's at Antietam on September 17, the bloodiest single day of the war (4,700 killed and 18,000 wounded). Lee immediately withdrew from the North to Winchester, and then to Fredericksburg in December, leaving the border areas of northern Virginia under tenuous Union control. As the winter began to arrive, the withdrawal of Southern forces a few miles west of Fairfax Court House revealed even more extensive destruction than was witnessed nine months earlier. On December 12, Company B of the 16th Regiment of the Vermont volunteers began a picket at the Courthouse. William Elbridge Knight, of Plymouth (Windsor County), Vermont, wrote to his wife about his arrival:

Fairfax Court House Dec 12th/62
Dear Jane

I will now try to give you a short history of our journey from our old camp We were called out a 2 o'clock this morning, struck tents at four & was on our way at five The ground was frose quite hard & we moved off briskly. we reached Cloud Mills a little after sun rise. here we rested about twenty minutes & looked around the battle grounds. the mills although nearly new & and of brick are almost shattered to pieces from here to fairfax Court I saw nothing worthy of note only the roads were lined with dead horses & mules & what we see everywhere here deserted plantations & mutilated buildings for when the union soldiers come to an old secesh rip goes his shanty. We have encamped for the night about a mile from the village. There is not much in this village worth notice only some of the houses look as though they had been shelled & some rebel earth works. I am so lame tonight I can hardly move. we have marched about 18 miles today & this afternoon the ground has thawed & the mud is ankle deep.[41]

Upon their initial arrival, these troops were moved around western Fairfax County in response to the uncertain movement of Southern troops. Two days after his arrival at Fairfax Court House, Knight's unit marched to Centreville. His description of the scene is graphic and haunting:

Union troops seized personal property frequently during the Civil War throughout northern Virginia, acting on orders from Union officers in many cases. Hay for horses and livestock for food were among many items taken for which, in some cases, compensation was given by the federal government after the war for losses suffered. Courtesy of The Library of Virginia

Centerville Dec 14th/62

Dear wife, We started from fairfax Court house yesterday at eight o clock and moved towards centervill. the road all along we found strewn with broken muskets knapsacks &c We crossed the battlefield of chantilla. the men on our side appared to be burried well but those that appeared to be on the rebel side were scersely covered up. I saw one that was thrown into a ditch head to the south, his head was above the surface of the earth. this looks rather hard to a green vermonter I tell you We marched 14 miles yesterday 6 miles farther than we need to get to the same place we are living on half rations for we have not got wagons enough to bring supplies to us. I tell you Jane when I think of those old farmers up there in vermont sitting in their easy chairs beside a comfortable fire & grumbling about the hard times I wish they could take our places through one march such as we have just had. a march of 26 miles in two days, half fed (for I had only one lb of bread & few apples that the Adutant gave me for two days rations) seventy lbs on their backs through mud & mire & then let them talk about hard times . . . . [42]

The Vermont soldiers learned quickly that despite the departure of Confederate forces, occupying the Fairfax Court House region was not without its dangers. On Christmas Eve, a soldier of the 14th Vermont regiment was murdered, shot in the head by a "secesh" farmer, who was immediately taken into custody. On Christmas Day, all duties for the Vermont soldiers were suspended and "Divine Services" were held for the soldiers.[43] The next day, a contingent of the Vermont soldiers marched northwest to the site of the September 1 fighting at the Battle of Chantilly with the grim task of burying many soldiers who had died and had been left in the fields.[44]

On December 28, however, conflict resumed. General J. E. B. Stuart led over 1,000 men on a raid of the Burke railroad station, part of the Orange & Alexandria line. Surprising the Federal troops who were grossly outnumbered, Stuart was able to remove the Union telegraph officer and substitute his own telegraph operator. Stuart began to intercept Union messages from Alexandria intended for the troops at Burke Station and Fairfax Court House and responded with bogus messages for nearly five hours. During this time his troops destroyed tracks and the rail line's

Confederate Major General James Ewell Brown "J.E.B." Stuart was just 29 years old when he made his famous raid in Fairfax County in December 1862. He captured Union supply wagons, cut telegraph lines, tore up railroad tracks and took prisoners. He benefitted from information provided by Antonia Ford of Fairfax Court House. *Courtesy of the Fairfax County Public Library Photographic Archive*

bridge over Accotink Creek.[45] After confiscating all the supplies he could, he sent a taunting yet jocular message to his Northern enemies:

Quartermaster-General Meigs,
United States Army:
Quality of the mules lately furnished me very poor.
Interferes seriously with movement of captured wagons.

J.E.B. Stuart.[46]

Stuart then headed north toward Fairfax Court House, where he had planned an attack on the garrison there. However, the Vermont soldiers, who were aware of the presence of Stuart's cavalry in the area, fired on the Confederates, who then circumvented the town, went north to Vienna and then west through Middleburg to the Confederate lines beyond Warrenton at Culpeper.[47]

By January 1863, the rhythm of life in and around Fairfax Court House began to find its daily pattern, shaped by its status as an occupied town in one of the northernmost points of the Confederacy. Routines applied to local citizens and Northern soldiers alike; while generally at odds with each other culturally and politically, they shared the common struggle for fuel, clothing, and food during the winter of 1863. Within one month of their arrival, there were serious illnesses among the soldiers, including an outbreak of measles that claimed numerous lives. William Elbridge Knight wrote his wife on January 9 from Fairfax Station:

> I am by the providence of God enjoying good health while so many of my fellow soldiers are called by the stern mandate of death to that other world away from the sound of the fife & drum the rattle of musketry. yes, they have gone & going where brighter scenes await them Where the wicked cease from troubling Where the weary are at rest There was 105 cases of measles in this regiment last month there will be more than that this month. they are coming down evry day with them.[48]

With nearly all trees and fence posts in and around Fairfax Court House used for fuel, hundreds of acres of land quickly became fields of frozen, muddy clay. William Knight wrote on January 22:

> we reached the [Fairfax] station about 10 o clock [in the morning] we rested until the Colonel picked out our camp ground. our tent did not get along till 9 o clock at night so late that we could not put it up that night. it began to rain about midnight & such a storm. The next morning we put up our tent & worked all day in the rain making things as comfortable as posible. got wet to my hide the first time I have got thoroughly wet since I have been out here but with the help of a little whiskey & some compasition I did not take cold. It is awful mudy here you never knew anything about mud in vermont It is just like mortar[49]

The presence of occupational forces did enable the North to begin the restoration of a loyalist government from among local Union supporters and the resumption of court proceedings. Governor Pierpont, who had administrative responsibility over those portions of northern Virginia controlled by Union forces, moved the County court to West End, near Alexandria.[50] By 1863, the Fairfax Courthouse building was only a structural shell, with its records pillaged and its interior seriously damaged.

The fate of George and Martha Washington's wills epitomizes the chaos and destruction wrought by the war. When Beauregard withdrew his troops from Fairfax in late 1861, the clerk of the court, Alfred Moss, removed George Washington's will and transported it to Richmond, where it was held for safekeeping until after the war, when it was returned to Fairfax. Martha Washington's will did not fare so well. In 1862, Northern soldiers were removing "trash" from the building when Col. David Thomson picked up some papers only to discover it was Martha Washington's will. Realizing its importance, the officer took it with him. The will surfaced 40 years later in England when Thomson's daughter sold it to J. P. Morgan. Only after Morgan's death and substantial legal pressure was brought to bear on Morgan's son, was the will returned to the County.[51]

Despite efforts to restore government and bring a semblance of normalcy to Fairfax, there was the ever-present danger of raids, sniper fire, and kidnappings from marauding bands of Confederate forces, especially those under the command of John S. Mosby. A lawyer by training, Mosby was originally from the Blue Ridge mountains of Virginia. After graduating from the University of Virginia, Mosby began a law practice in Southwest Virginia. Just prior to Fort Sumter, Mosby joined as a private under the command of J.E.B. Stuart. During Stuart's raids and scouting for Lee in the Peninsula Campaign and Stuart's ride around McClellan at Richmond in 1862, Mosby impressed Stuart with his judgement and restraint in tense encounters with Union patrols, his tactical assessments of enemy strengths and intentions, and most importantly to Stuart a tenacity to move quickly without rest or delay. Mosby had accompanied Stuart on his December 1862 raid at Burke Station and had received permission to remain in Fairfax County with nine men. This was the beginning of a campaign of harrassment and sabotage by Mosby that would continue in northern Virginia until the war's end.[52]

The most celebrated raid at Fairfax Court House during the war occurred during the early hours of Monday morning, March 9, 1863. The Union commander in Fairfax was a 25-year-old Brigadier General named Edwin H. Stoughton, who had established his headquarters (and living quarters) in the home of Dr. William Presley Gunnell, a local physician. This house (now the rectory of Truro Church) was one of the finest residences in Fairfax. Stoughton's penchant for drink and women quickly became a well-established fact among the locals and thus was used to strategic advantage by Mosby. As noted in Patricia Hickin's account, ". . .shortly after falling asleep, Stoughton suddenly awakened to a sharp slap on his

It was here in the home of Dr. William Gunnell on March 9, 1863, that Confederate Captain John Singleton Mosby and his men captured Union General Edwin H. Stoughton and, unnoticed, led the general, two captains, numerous soldiers and 58 horses out of the town in the middle of the night. The building became the Truro Church Rectory in 1873. Located on Little River Turnpike. Courtesy of Lee Hubbard

Antonia Ford was an enthusiastic supporter of the Confederate cause. After supplying General J.E.B. Stuart with information about Union movements around Fairfax Court House, he gave her a "commission" as major and named her his honorary aide-de-camp. She eventually married Joseph Willard, after she had been captured and held in a Union prison during the war. The couple had one son, also named Joseph. Courtesy of Lee Hubbard

bare rear. Stoughton. . .was none too alert. 'General,' asked the slim figure above him, 'did you ever hear of Mosby?' 'Yes, have you caught him?' 'No, but he has caught you.'"[53] Stoughton, along with two of his Captains, 30 soldiers in his immediate detail, and 58 horses, were led out of Fairfax under the cover of darkness.[54]

The reaction of Federal forces was predictable. Investigations ensued and the houses of many local residents were searched. At the residence of Edward R. Ford, Union soldiers discovered a document addressed to Mr. Ford's then 22-year-old daughter, Antonia, signed by J.E.B. Stuart. This document purported to be a "Commission" appointing Antonia an "honorary aide-de-camp" for her efforts during the preceding August in providing information to Stuart regarding Union plans prior to the Second Battle of Manassas. Lafayette Baker, U.S. Secret Service Chief, had received an unconfirmed report that Antonia Ford might have been involved in the Stoughton kidnapping. Baker sent a female agent to the Ford home in Fairfax to investigate, and the agent discovered the J.E.B. Stuart "Commission."[55] Antonia Ford's arrest on March 13 was followed a few days later by other Fairfax Court House residents, including Antonia's father, Edward Ford, and Joshua Gunnell, Amos Fox, and Thomas Love. All were imprisoned at the Old Capitol Prison in Washington. The occupation of Fairfax Court House by Union troops was becoming permanent as more Southern sympathizers were identified and removed from the immediate area.[56]

The story of Antonia Ford's arrest is not complete without reference to Joseph Willard, for his arrival in Fairfax and the events surrounding Antonia Ford's arrest would result in the Willards being connected to the life of Fairfax for three generations.

Upon his arrival at Fairfax Court House in 1862, Joseph Willard was 41 years old. Well-educated and well-traveled, he was also an experienced businessman. Willard was originally from Vermont. He left a job in New York to prospect for gold in California in 1849, while his brother, Henry, came to Washington and established a hotel in 1850. When gold prospecting proved unsuccessful, Henry invited his brother to come to the Federal City and join in the hotel enterprise. This venture was very successful and as the hotel business expanded in the 1850s, so did the Willards' influence and position in Washington. Despite his age and significant influence in Washington society, Joseph Willard's long-standing New England heritage and patriotism led him to join the Union army at the outbreak of the war.[57]

Willard was assigned to the staff of General Irvin McDowell, who occupied the Ford home and used it as his living quarters. The residence and the Courthouse building across the road also served as McDowell's headquarters; much military business was conducted in the home in close proximity to the Ford family. It was in this environment that Joseph Willard established a respectful, and increasingly cordial relationship with the Ford family.

These relations continued during the months leading to the Second Battle of Manassas. Willard remained in contact with the Ford family later when he was on the front lines with General McDowell. The exact nature of Joseph Willard's interest in Antonia Ford at this time is not ascertainable; however, upon learning of Antonia's arrest, Willard used his influence to arrange his transfer to General Samuel Heintzelman's command, which included overseeing prisoners in Washington, D.C. There he arranged for Antonia's eventual release. On September 18, 1863, she took an oath of allegiance to the United States and six months

Originally designed as a mid-19th century townhouse, this building was constructed about 1836, and has been refurbished and expanded in the early 20th century. It was the home of Antonia Ford, whose father, Edward R. Ford, was a Southern sympathizer who harbored Confederate soldiers. Located at 3977 Chain Bridge Road. Placed on the National Register in 1987. Courtesy of Lee Hubbard

After Confederate troops moved to the south, Union troops moved into the former Confederate outpost at Fairfax Courthouse. This was probably a T. H. O'Sullivan photo about June 1863, courtesy of the National Archives.

later Antonia Ford and Joseph Willard were married. Antonia's health had been severely compromised as a result of her imprisonment, an ordeal from which she never fully recovered. She died in 1871 at the age of 31, leaving one son, Joseph E. Willard.[58]

While the military drama of the war occurred in the theaters of Chancellorsville, Vicksburg, and Gettysburg in 1863, the occupation of Fairfax Court House became more secure during the months following Mosby's capture of Stoughton. Northern troops quickly organized themselves to receive mail and even family visitors on a limited basis. A camp newspaper was printed and circulated by one unit. However, efforts to establish a civilian government within those portions of northern Virginia under the control of Federal troops proved difficult. The results were a precursor to the Reconstruction period that would follow the war's end. The Pierpont government struggled from its beginning with the issue of legitimacy. Limited participation by voters (only men—and only white men at that—could vote and most "loyalist" men were elsewhere fighting in the Federal army) and the limited geographical area it actually represented made the Pierpont administration's claim as the "representative" government of Virginia the subject of jokes and derisive comments, even in the Northern press. The control it exercised over civilian life in Alexandria and Fairfax was limited and ephemeral at best, being dependent on the control exercised by Federal troops. Nonetheless, a convention was held in Alexandria on May 12, 1863, led by Job Hawxhurst of Fairfax, one of the leading native Unionists. The convention endorsed Pierpont and elections were held 16 days

later on May 28. The new government attempted to restore commerce (while restricting it to support the Federal cause), conduct court proceedings, and handle the massive influx of slaves, as well as Northern civilians arriving in the region to support the war effort or simply to be close to their husbands, sons, and brothers serving in the Army. These concurrent demands were overwhelming to the region. Despite the challenges, Pierpont's government passed legislation on December 19, 1863, calling for a constitutional convention to be held in early 1864.[59]

Although Francis Pierpont wanted a constitutional convention to strengthen the legitimacy of his government in Virginia generally, the convention's primary focus would turn on the issue of slavery. This was not necessarily viewed negatively by Pierpont, who continued to hold to a somewhat idealized view of a slavery-free, postwar Virginia. Personally, Pierpont was a committed abolitionist, having been raised in the Methodist Protestant Church, a denomination with a long-standing opposition to slavery. For those portions of northern Virginia under Pierpont's jurisdiction, Lincoln's Emancipation Proclamation, issued 12 months earlier on January 1, 1863, did little to clarify the issue for the citizens of Fairfax. Lincoln's Proclamation declared that all slaves in areas still in rebellion were "then, thenceforward, and forever free." This "limited" emancipation actually went no further than Congress had already gone legislatively on the issue. At the outset of the war, slaveowners in border areas demanded that their slaves be returned; Union generals had usually offered them protection and declared slaves as confiscated property that did not need to be returned. In 1862, at the urging of Radical Republicans, Congress prohibited the return of slaves to their owners. By the end of 1863, Pierpont was urging Virginia's Restored Government to emancipate all slaves within its jurisdiction.[60]

The attitudes of local citizens in Fairfax on the issue of freedom for their slaves appears to have changed considerably for many during the three years of war. The change in the size and operation of farms in northern Virginia beginning in the late 1840s and 1850s had already lessened landowners' reliance on slave labor and the tasks of those slaves that remained had become more varied. With the outbreak of the war and the departure of many able-bodied white men to fight in the Confederate army, much of the planting that was done in Fairfax was subsistance crops that no longer required slave labor. Many slaves long affiliated with their owners remained with these families, based on loyalty and/or practicality. The alternative of living in shanty towns, such as those which sprang up in Alexandria from slaves fleeing from southern parts of the Virginia (as well as some from the immediate region), offered only greater violence, hunger, disease, and exposure to the elements. White females, who frequently were the heads of local households, discovered that their slave families (particularly the children) were simply more mouths to feed in circumstances that were becoming more precarious as the war

became more protracted. Sarah Summers Clarke, who was raised at her grandparents' home at Fox Mill, three miles from Fairfax Court House, recalled 75 years later, "When the Emancipation Proclamation was issued...my mother called our Negroes together and told them that they were now free. She said they could do whatever they pleased and go wherever they wanted to go. They were at an utter loss what to do. They asked that they might stay with mother until the war was over. . . . 'Then we will see what we want to do,' they said."[61]

The Constitutional Convention met in Alexandria from February 13 through April 11, 1864, with the committed Unionist Job Hawxhurst representing Fairfax Court House. The convention results, while definitely Unionist in their effects, were tempered as a reflection of its Virginia locale. The new constitution outlawed slavery, required loyalty oaths for voters as well as candidates for public office, restricted former Confederate office holders from participating in the new Virginia government, and reduced residency requirements for voting (thus enfranchising those Northerners who had arrived in Virginia before and during the war, as well as those anticipated following the war). The new constitution also brought privacy to elections by providing for voting by secret ballot, thus ending the intimidating practice of oral votes.[62]

John Singleton Mosby and a few of his Rangers sat for this formal studio portrait about 1864. Front row, left to right: Walter W. Gosden, Harry T. Sinnott, O. L. Butler, I. A. Gentry. Middle row: Robert B. Parrott, Thomas Throop, John W. Munson, John Singleton Mosby, ? Newell, Charles H. Quarles. Top row: Lee Howison, W. Ben Palmer, John W. Puryear, Thomas Booker, A. G. Babcock, Norman V. Randolph and Frank H. Rahm. Used with permission of The Friends of Fairfax Station

The new constitution, as well as the subsequent Restored Assembly that convened in December 1864, did not provide for any practical benefits for former slaves beyond their freedom. They were not permitted to vote nor were they permitted to testify in court proceedings, thus severely limiting their avenues for legal redress of grievances. No provision was made for public education of blacks, despite personal appeals by Pierpont for these proposals. While Virginia's Unionist leaders were behind the war's effort to abolish slavery, they stopped short of actions that would have radically changed Virginia society in the postwar era.[63]

With the focus of Northern armies on Richmond and Petersburg, hostilities in the Fairfax Court House area diminished significantly in 1864, notwithstanding occasional raids by Mosby's men. It became increasingly clear that the Confederacy's defeat was simply a matter of time. Lincoln's reelection on November 8 and the adoption of the 13th Amendment by Virginia's Restored Assembly on February 9, 1865, prepared the citizens of Fairfax Court House for Lee's surrender at Appomattox Courthouse on April 9.

The war's end brought as much change to Fairfax Court House as the war itself. The summer months of 1865 saw the return of many sons, brothers, and fathers from battlefields across the South. For those local families who lost loved ones, the return of others was joy mixed with the anguished memories of their own tragedies. Families had to again adjust to the presence of those long absent. Many returning soldiers were shocked at the devastation of the area—countless homes, schools, barns, and churches had been completely destroyed for firewood, fields overgrazed by Union horses, wooded acreage cut, and roads badly degraded by sutler wagons, artillery, and thousands of troops. Some success in planting was achieved that year, despite nearly non-existent credit, farm implements, and livestock. The struggle to survive the war continued in the form of hard work to rebuild the community.

For freed slaves, the challenge was even more daunting. While many saw freedom as an opportunity for education and economic independence, others sought to maintain employment and living arrangements with former owners. Sarah Summers Clarke summed up her family's decisions regarding their slaves at the war's conclusion:

> "I would just love to take you all back with me,"Mother told our Negroes, "but I just can't do it. Times have changed, you are now free. I cannot feed you any longer. You must look out for

One of the town's houses occupied by Union troops during the Civil War was Blenheim, built in 1850 for Captain Rezin Willcoxen, owner of the tavern across Main Street from the Fairfax Courthouse. Attic walls in Blenheim still display legible graffiti left by Union soldiers, consisting of names, addresses and sketches. The Georgian-style building is located at 3610 Old Lee Highway. Photo by Edward Breitenbach, courtesy of the Fairfax County Public Library Photographic Archive

yourselves." Not one of our Negroes had left us during the war and all begged to go back with us. Many tears were shed.

> We never did believe in slavery. Lots of people in Virginia didn't believe in it either. Of course, farther south in the cotton fields and canebrakes people believed slaves were necessary. We had inherited our slaves and there was nothing to be done but to keep them. But we were glad the war ended as it did. Dozens and dozens of people said: "It ended just right." The people of Virginia after a year or two found that it was far better for them that the Negroes were free.[64]

Not all blacks chose or wished to remain with their former masters. Many saw their freedom as the opportunity to merge those semi-autonomous traditions nurtured in slavery, such as church and family, with the fledgling network created by free blacks prior to the war that included small businesses, mutual benefit efforts, and (when possible) the education of children.[65]

The future of the Fairfax Court House community, as well as northern Virginia as a whole, was influenced by several political developments. The assassination of Lincoln placed the Democrat Andrew Johnson against the increasingly radical Republican Party that controlled the U.S. Congress. The unwillingness of the assembly that had met under the Pierpont government to aggressively pursue equality for former slaves (by ensuring their enfranchisement, encouraging land ownership, extending credit, and providing for their public education) led the U.S. Congress in December 1865 not to recognize Virginia's first postwar representatives who included a number of former Confederates.[66]

The establishment of the Freedmen's Bureau in Virginia in June 1865 also ensured that there would be no return to antebellum life in Fairfax. Freed slaves throughout the South created an immediate and real challenge to the Union army. Thousands of former slaves walked off plantations and farms to cities and towns; this contingent of the population was homeless, jobless, and looked to the Union army and the Federal government to provide some answers to the question of their future. The response of the conservatives within the Pierpont government was to pass "Black Codes" that prohibited vagrancy and permitted coersive employment practices by whites. These laws, viewed by Unionists as "slavery in every respect except by name," fueled further distrust and anger by the Republican Congress toward the newly re-established State government.

The Freedmen's Bureau was tasked with providing immediate assistance to blacks in the form of food, clothing, and arranging contracts for renting of houses and land for farming. The Bureau also was relied on by blacks for protection from acts of violence and, for the first time, the public education of their children. Following blacks being granted suffrage by Congress in March 1867, the Bureau also sought to ensure black participation in local, state, and national politics.[67]

The freedmen in northern Virginia generally fared as well as could be expected in the first postwar years. Within seven months of the end of the war, bureau agents in Fairfax County reported that no blacks were relying on the Bureau for support. Fortunately, the demand for labor was strong, opportunities for sharecropping increased, and some blacks were able to purchase land by 1870.[68]

Notwithstanding some limited progress by freedmen in northern Virginia, the reemergence of control by former Confederates in the political life of most Southern states and the support their State legislatures received from President Andrew Johnson, enabled Radical Republicans in Congress to persuade their moderate allies to support legislation that turned Southern states into military districts. The purpose of the Reconstruction Act of 1867 was clear — military governors were to register black voters who, together with white Unionists, would elect legislatures that would, among other actions, approve the Fourteenth Amendment and draft new state constitutions guaranteeing black suffrage. Clearly, "[S]outhern intransigence played into the Radicals' hands."[69]

Rebuilding after the war's devastation meant different things to different people. To Richard Ratcliffe Farr on his return home after serving with Mosby's Rangers, it meant building a cottage for his mother Margaret on the Farr property. It was custom-built— no two doors or windows are the same size. The cottage was moved to its present location at 3901 Old Lee Highway in 1962. Placed on the National Register in 1987. Courtesy of the City of Fairfax

Voter registration under military control was completed in Virginia by the Fall of 1867 and elections were held on October 18-21. The Radical Republicans won a major victory, with Conservatives accusing the military of gerrymandering districts to ensure a victory by Unionists. Elected to represent Fairfax Court House was Orrin E. Hine of Vienna, and former Fairfax Court House resident John Hawxhurst was elected to represent Alexandria. Additionally, the Alexandria-Fairfax senatorial district was represented by Falls Church resident Linus M. Nickerson.[70]

The elected delegates convened in Richmond on December 11 to draft a new Constitution for the Commonwealth. Both Hine and Hawxhurst played leading roles at the convention, which was presided over by Judge John C. Underwood. Hine, Hawxhurst, and Underwood were all originally from New York State, having come to northern Virginia prior to the war. Their common heritage and war experiences significantly influenced the decisions that the Convention took with respect to the future of Virginia government in the postwar era.[71]

The convention drafted a new constitution that granted suffrage to blacks, established boards of supervisors elected by voters to govern counties, revamped taxation policies to rely more on revenue from property owners, and established a statewide system for public education.[72] The war that had destroyed so much of the cradle of the Republic was over and a time of rebirth had begun.

The oldest section of the brick Fairfax Elementary School was built in 1873, shown in this early photo. A front portion was added in 1912. After having been used for several different purposes, the building was restored and dedicated as the Fairfax Museum and Visitors Center on July 4, 1992. Located at 10231 Main Street. Placed on the National Register in 1992. From the postcard collection of Tony Chaves

4.

School Days, a War Memorial and a Masonic Hall, 1870-1900
by Nan Netherton

The story of the Town of Providence and the Town of Fairfax between 1870 and 1900 was one of a quiet agricultural area drifting through times of both moderate difficulties and moderate advances. The era's established rural and emerging village patterns of life reveal not only a charming serenity, but also suggest some subtle new directions the Town would take after the turn of the century. Leadership in County and Town was decidedly Southern. Former Confederates and Secessionists who were in positions of authority included Robert Wiley, Fairfax County treasurer; J. Owens Berry, Fairfax County surveyor and member of the Virginia House of Delegates; Henry W. Thomas and Daniel McCarty Chichester, Fairfax County circuit court judges; Mottrom D. Ball, Richard R. Farr and Thomas Love, attorneys; Dr. William D. McWhorton, first president of the Fairfax County Medical Society; and the Rev. Everard Meade, Episcopal minister.

A new type of county government was mandated by Virginia's 1869 Underwood Constitution, which was approved by the Federal government and ratified by the Virginia voters. Instead of being administered by appointed or elected court justices of the peace, counties were first divided into townships, and, later, magisterial districts, each represented by an elected supervisor. The resulting board of supervisors became the chief administrative body for the county and the towns within its borders, assuming many of the duties of the former county court justice system, including holding titles to the county's public properties.[1]

Another important mandate in the constitution was a more comprehensive publicly funded school system. Only four years after the change in state and local government, a two-story brick school was under construction in the Town on property sold for the purpose by the Sagar family of "Aspen Grove." The *Fairfax News* of September 5, 1873, was critical of the erection of a fine, expensive elementary school:

The brick school-house, 24 feet by 10 feet, 11 ft. ceiling, 2 stories high, now being built on the lot bought of Mr. Sagar, beyond the bridge at the eastern end of the village, is well under way, and will soon be completed, at a cost, perhaps, of $2,500 or $3,000. A less expensive building, for the present, would have done quite as well. We do not see the use of taking children, as must necessarily be the case, from humble homes—in fact, from cabins—and send them to a school in a fine building, so much better than what they live in and sleep in; and would it not be a wiser expenditure of money, for the children themselves, to let it go in the way of books and tuition, rather than a showy pile of bricks and mortar. This one is intended for white children. How long will it be before the negro people, on behalf of their children, will demand one for their use equally expensive, for that is our condition—we have to sustain two separate school establishments throughout the state, which now necessarily make it one of the most complicated and

Zion Episcopal Church was located on the north side of Route 236, on Main Street near the present Truro Episcopal Church. The first building was erected in 1843 with assistance from The Falls Church. Destroyed during the Civil War, this building shown replaced it after the war and served until it was replaced by the Truro Chapel in 1933. From the postcard collection of Tony Chaves

expensive systems of any people on earth. We should therefore proceed more cautiously, and work up slowly, according to our ability to do these things.[2]

It was almost four decades before a brick addition was put on the building.

Although residents of the Town were looking ahead to a better future, there were still upsetting reminders of the recent terrible war. One example was the report in 1873 of the following incident at Fairfax Station:

> Near the Depot, and just by the spot where Mr. Sisson's omnibus usually stands, at Fairfax Station, a box, containing human bones, became exposed, by the washing of the earth in a considerable drain of water, during the late rains, which, upon close examination, turned out to be, as is believed, the amputated legs and limbs of wounded soldiers, in the late war, they having the marks of the surgeon's saw upon them; and among these, was found a shoe. These relics were taken, by the order of Mr. J. E. Mitchell, the depot agent, to another spot and buried.[3]

The Orange, Alexandria & Midland Rail Road had just erected a new station house in 1873 serving Fairfax Court House "which has added much to the appearance of things thereabout and contributes to the comfort of the traveling community, and other persons doing business at that place."[4] Along with improved station facilities, an older transportation mode contin-

Duncan Chapel Methodist Church was built one block south of the Fairfax County Courthouse on Chain Bridge Road after the Civil War. It was replaced by the Fairfax United Methodist Church, built at the corner of University Drive and Stratford Avenue, in 1956. The old wooden church was used for county planning offices and the public library administrative offices in the 1960s. It was demolished in 1970. From the postcard collection of Tony Chaves

ued operation. A brief account which appeared in 1873 gave a personal view of the man who operated a regular seven-mile round-trip stage service from Fairfax Court House to Fairfax Station depot: "Mr. Robert Sisson, of Fairfax Court House, runs the most accommodating and pleasant stage route that connects with the W.C.V.M. and G.S.R.R., that from Fairfax Station to the Court House. In fact, Mr. Sisson's [stage] line is known as the *funniest* one south of Mason and Dixon's . . ."[5]

Although the Civil War had ended, small disturbances between residents of the Town were reported in the weekly newspaper. One incident involved an irate woman who approached the "worthy sheriff" with a pair of tongs and grasped either his nose or mouth with them. No apparent harm was done.[6] A barbecue attended by whites and blacks resulted in exchanges of blows and rocks during election week. One published comment was: "All this was the result of an attempt to harmonize the races."[7] On court day during Christmas week, 1874, there had been "only" two fights reported. One merchant had his stove upset. The fire inside was scattered about at the risk of burning up his goods and premises. The *Fairfax News* writer proposed: "that the State chemist be forthwith ordered here to analyze the whiskey at all the bars, as there must be something in it."[8]

In 1869, Culpeper County had decided to change the name of the county seat, "Fairfax," to "Culpeper." Fairfax County voters, finding that the name "Fairfax" was now available, had an Act of Assembly passed in Richmond changing the name of their county seat from "Providence" to "Fairfax" in 1874.[9]

Fewer than ten years after the war, a valuable description of the Town in 1873 was published in the *Fairfax News*. There was a great deal of optimism expressed: "Little by little, our village is being built up, and it is to be hoped ere long will be restored to its ante-bellum prosperity and size and even go far beyond what it then was."[10]

After commenting that R. R. Farr, county treasurer, was fitting up the old clerk's office for a treasury office, the *Fairfax News* editor enumerated the current businesses and buildings:

We now have four stores, two merchant tailors, one grocery, one bakery, one wheelwright and carriage shop, two hotels, one hostelry, a traveling butcher, two bar rooms, three schools, two doctors, six lawyers, three churches with a fourth expected, a brick kiln, a full share of 14th amendments [emancipated slaves] and lots of free dogs, besides being well supplied with wells, and any number of wheelbarrows. We have the prettiest location, the healthiest spot, and the scarcest money of any other outside, upside elevated space on top of the earth. But what especially gives interest and a name to the place is "the public square," full of trees, in the which is situated the clerk's office, the treasury building, the jail and the old Court House, with an unrivaled *well* outside, and Washington's *will* inside. Enough said . . .[11]

With the arrival of hot weather that same year, the editor of the *Fairfax News* wrote a little essay in a different vein describing the plight many a small town suffered across the country in the late 1800s when it was without a central sewage system:

TO WHOM IT MAY CONCERN.—There are certain little houses, not built for ornament, because they belong to none of the orders of architecture, nor are they of the Italian Villa

Joseph Cooper operated a thriving buggy manufactory and repair works on Main Street west of the County Courthouse for some years. This informative advertisement appeared in the Fairfax Herald *of July 13, 1888. Courtesy of the Virginia Room, Fairfax City Regional Library*

Old Fairfax Herald Print Shop, Friday, 13 July 1888.

Cooper's Carriage Shop shown here appeared on the 1878 Hopkins' map of Fairfax Court House. Courtesy of John H. Rust, Sr.

style, yet may be necessary buildings, that occupy conspicuous and prominent positions on the street near our office, and, as we think, very much out-of-place and have therefore been voted *nom con,* an insufferable nuisance as they stand. We only ask that they be, for decency and comfort sake, removed or deodorized.[12]

Many decades passed before permanent improvements in this situation were mandated by the Council of the Town of Fairfax.

Because Fairfax was the seat of a rural county, agricultural concerns were paramount among the Town's residents, some of whom farmed within the Town limits. The Central Farmers Club, formed in 1873, met at Fairfax Court House, and became an outspoken voice for more effective dog control laws and more and better railroad service to Washington markets.[13] In 1876, Richard Ratcliffe Farr was appointed Local Deputy of the State Grange (a national agricultural group also known as the Patrons of Husbandry) in Fairfax.[14] These active groups combined with other organizations and individuals to sponsor the "First Annual Farmers' Institute and Exhibition" which met at Fairfax Court House for three days in 1891. The meeting was held "for the interest of agriculture, to promote the welfare of our county and to aid in its development." The gathering was pronounced "very successful."[15]

The Farr Homeplace was built to replace the original family home, which was burned by Union soldiers during the Civil War. A large cross design was worked into each of the five brick chimneys. The building is an example of the Georgian style with a two-story colonnaded portico. The building's bricks were formed in the old clay pit nearby. Located at 10230 Main Street. Photo by Brian Conley, courtesy of the Fairfax County Public Library Photographic Archive

Distinguished town citizen R. Walton Moore's unpublished reminiscences dictated to his secretary in 1939 gave his distant memories of the Town of Fairfax in 1878:

The village, never very large, was then much smaller than it is now, and although now I think unusually attractive, was then most unattractive. The roads and streets were bad, with an absence of such trees as now line them; most of the homes, which had been largely deserted during the war, in poor repair. There was no water supply except what was furnished by individual wells; there was no method of lighting except by kerosene lamps; there was no public means of disposing of sewage, and of course there was no telephone service. Particularly in the winter time, the journey by highway to Washington was very difficult and tiresome, and the bridge facilities across the Potomac River were very poor.[16]

G. M. Hopkins published his important regional *Atlas of Fifteen Miles Around Washington* in 1879. Its detailed map of the Town of Fairfax contained a fascinating variety of information about the village at the time.[17] The document is a valuable record of old and new family names associated with the Town.

Six years after R. Walton Moore's description of the living conditions at Fairfax, *Chataigne's Virginia Gazetteer* (1884) listed businessmen and women, many with surnames which had been and would continue to be identified with Fairfax and its environs. Some of the names included magistrates J. R. Taylor,

The Donohoe House, built about 1880, was the 19th century home of Captain S. R. Donohoe, founder and publisher of the Fairfax Herald *weekly newspaper, beginning about 1882. Of Colonial Revival design, the house is one of the few examples in the City of late 19th century domestic architecture. Located at 3920 Chain Bridge Road, and placed on the National Register in 1987.*

Several other newspapers were published at Fairfax Court House in the early 1800s. They included the Fairfax Gazette *and the* Farmers' Intelligencer *in 1843, the* Providence Chronicle *in 1845, and the* Fairfax News *in 1846. The first three were short-lived, but the latter survived until 1872.*

Students and teachers posed for this picture at the Fairfax Elementary School in 1885. Courtesy of the Fairfax Museum and Visitors Center

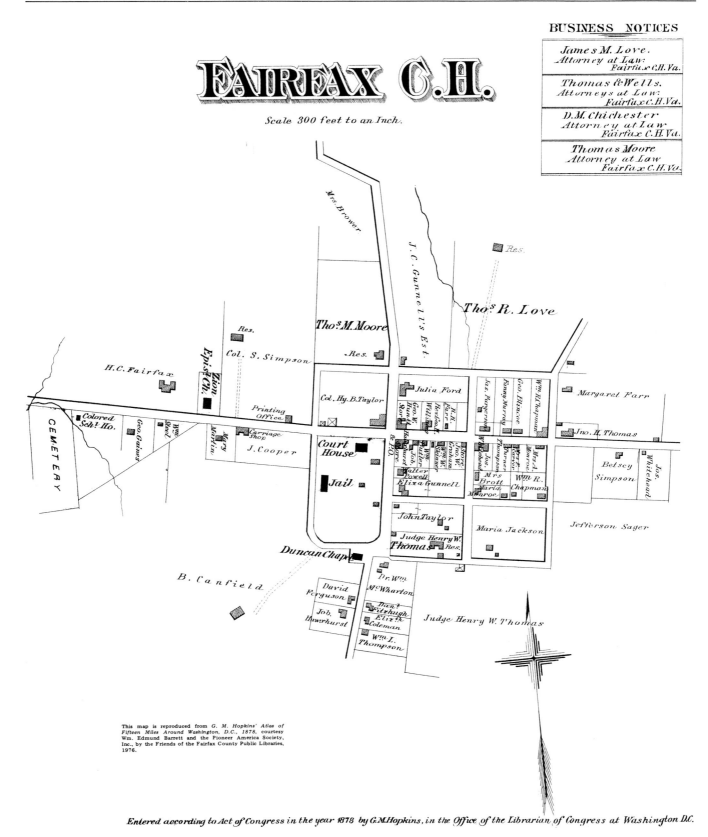

FAIRFAX C.H.

Scale 300 feet to an Inch.

This map is reproduced from G. M. Hopkins' Atlas of Fifteen Miles Around Washington, D.C., 1878, courtesy Wm. Edmund Barrett and the Pioneer America Society, Inc., by the Friends of the Fairfax County Public Libraries, 1976.

BUSINESS NOTICES

James M. Love.
Attorney at Law:
Fairfax C.H. Va.

Thomas & Wells.
Attorneys at Law:
Fairfax C.H. Va.

D.M. Chichester
Attorney at Law
Fairfax C.H. Va.

Thomas Moore
Attorney at Law
Fairfax C.H. Va.

Entered according to Act of Congress in the year 1878 by G.M.Hopkins, in the Office of the Librarian of Congress at Washington D.C.

This map of "Fairfax C. H." appeared in 1879 in G. M. Hopkins' Atlas of Fifteen Miles Around Washington, D. C. Besides showing the locations of Zion Episcopal Church and Duncan Chapel, it marks places of the Courthouse and jail, Cooper's Carriage Shop, and residences labeled Fairfax, Ford, Gunnell, Chapman, Fitzhugh, Hawxhurst, Thomas, Farr, Love and many other familiar family names. *Courtesy of the Friends of the Fairfax City Regional Library*

42

J. N. Ballard and R. Johnson; attorneys were F. P. Berkley, D. M. Chichester, M. D. Hall, Lucian Keith, James M. Love, T. R. Love, Moore & Son, and H. W. Thomas. S. R. Donohoe was editor and proprietor of the weekly newspaper, *The Fairfax Herald* (since 1881). The three physicians listed were C. M. Collins, W. D. McWhorton, and W. P. Moncure.[18]

Public education concerns occupied Fairfax townspeople on both state and local levels for several years in the early and mid-1880s. In early 1882, Fairfax's own Richard Ratcliffe Farr, former county treasurer, surveyor and three-term delegate to the State Assembly from Fairfax, was appointed Superintendent of Public Instruction of Virginia. He received criticism during his four-year administration in a poem published in the *Richmond State* newspaper:

> Haste thee, teacher, haste away
> Farr too long has been thy stay;
> Farr too bad thy words are spelt
> Much too strong thyself has smelt . . .[19]

Several men were appointed for brief terms by the State School Board to fill the position of Superintendent of Fairfax Schools in the late 1800s. However, when attorney Milton Dulany Hall accepted the appointment in 1886, he began a 42-year tenure during which great changes came to both the Town and the County of Fairfax.[20]

A prominent figure in post-war Fairfax was Captain John Newton Ballard. Born in Albemarle County, Virginia in 1839, he enlisted in the Confederate Army in South Carolina and served under both J.E.B. Stuart and John S. Mosby in Virginia. A wartime amputee, he continued in the service wearing a wooden leg. His active life had worn out three legs by 1884 when the State of Virginia furnished him a fourth. That same year, he married Mary Lillie Reid Thrift and they moved to her inherited property, "Fruit Vale Farm," on the Ox Hill Battlefield, where they lived for 48 years.[21]

During his long life following the war, Capt. Ballard served in positions in the Fairfax County government. His outstanding contribution to the community was as founder and first chairman of the Confederate Monument Association. After a vigorous fund-raising campaign in the Town and surrounding County, a large monument was erected with appropriate ceremony at the Fairfax Cemetery on October 1, 1890, dedicated to the Confederate soldiers of Fairfax who died or were killed during the Civil War, and was

John Newton Ballard was born on January 1, 1839, in Albemarle, Virginia. When the Civil War broke out, he enlisted in the Confederate Army. Eventually he joined with Mosby, and was badly wounded in one of his legs, which was amputated. After the war, in 1874 he married an heiress, Mary Thrift, who had inherited family property, Fruit Vale Farm, on the Ox Hill (Chantilly) Battlefield. Captain Ballard was able to raise funds to erect a monument in memory of the Confederate dead. It was placed on land earlier purchased by the Ladies Memorial Association, to whom the monument was presented when it was dedicated on October 1, 1890. Ballard died in 1922, having lived a long and useful life. Portrait from the Fairfax Herald, *courtesy of The Historical Society of Fairfax County, Virginia*

In 1866, land was purchased as a burial ground for Confederate soldiers who either lived or were killed in Fairfax County. After an active fund-raising campaign, a gray granite obelisk was dedicated to "the memory of the gallant sons of Fairfax." Many prominent guests attended the ceremony in 1890, including Virginia Governor William Fitzhugh Lee. Over 200 unknown Confederate soldiers are buried here, as well as 96 identified fatalities. Located at 10565 Main Street. Placed on the National Register in 1987. Courtesy of the artist, Charles R. Wagner

The Fairfax Confederate Monument Association assembled for a formal portrait about the time of the dedication of the monument in the Fairfax Cemetery. Prominent men and women of the community were led by the chairman, Captain John Newton Ballard, in their strong effort to memorialize the men who had given their lives in the Civil War conflict. Standing, left to right, are Miss Rose Thomas, Miss Lizzie Burke, Judge James Love, Mrs. Gurley, Mr. Gurley and George Pickett. Seated in the same order are George Harrison, Mrs. Thomas Moore, F. W. Richardson, Mr. Sager, R. Walton Moore, and George Gordon. Courtesy of Lee Hubbard

given to the Ladies Memorial Association of Fairfax, who had established the cemetery in 1866.[22]

One source of funds for the memorial was especially fitting. Two of John and Mary Ballard's sons hunted for relics on the Ox Hill Battlefield near their home and sold what they found to Civil War relic collectors. The boys then gave the proceeds to the Confederate Memorial Fund.[23]

The Jermantown Cemetery, on Main Street near Jermantown Road, had been established in 1868 for blacks who were prevented by segregation from being buried in the Fairfax Cemetery down the road. The Garden Club of Fairfax renovated the three-quarter-acre lot in 1990 with new trees and shrubs.

The 1888 *Virginia Gazetteer* published a healthy appraisal of Fairfax County, which included the Town of Fairfax, showing a gradual economic recovery from the devastation of the Civil War. It rated the transportation facilities as the best, there being hardly a place more than six or eight miles from at least one of the several railroads which traversed the County north, south, east and west. The farm land in general was considered good, producing corn, wheat, rye, oats, potatoes and other crops in abundance, while the raising of cattle, sheep and hogs was extensive. The fisheries on the Potomac still represented a thriving industry. The principal fish were shad, herring and sturgeon, and the work force included about 400 men, 150 vessels, representing $75,000 in capital, and an annual production of about 2,500,000 pounds valued at $42,000. Natural resources being extracted included red sandstone and gray granite, gold, iron, copper, asbestos and soapstone. Lumbering was an important industry, the timber being oak, pine, chestnut, locust and walnut.[24]

A tremendous leap forward was made in 1887 when Alexander Graham Bell's telephone, invented in 1876, arrived in the Town of Fairfax. The first phone was installed in the Willcoxen Tavern where the townspeople could go to make or receive calls. The charge was 10 or 15 cents per outgoing call.[25]

Fifty-three prominent businessmen of Fairfax Court House and vicinity were united in trying to solve a special problem in 1888. They petitioned Fairfax County Judge D. M. Chichester to deny a requested license for the sale of intoxicants within two miles of Fairfax Station. The petitioners stated that Fairfax Station on the Virginia Midland Railway (formerly the O&A) was not only their shipping point, but also the place they had to go to take passage on the trains, and therefore they had a real interest in sobriety and good order there. The two places where intoxicants were already sold had the effect of causing disorder and even danger to persons having business at Fairfax Station. They insisted drunkenness frequently met with there caused alarm and fear, especially to unaccompanied ladies. Drivers sent there for freight often got drunk, causing delay, loss of goods, and danger to teams and vehicles. The merchants lost their plea when William A. Davis of Fairfax Station was given a year's license "to sell ardent spirits" by Judge Chichester on May 21, 1888.[26]

Town of Fairfax telephone operator Miss Grace Dindlebeck was photographed at her central switchboard in 1928. Her subscribers made about 800 calls each 24 hours. Recollections vary as to whether telephone service began in the Town of Fairfax in the 1880s or 1890s. One of the first lines ran between Fairfax Courthouse and Fairfax Station on the Southern Railway. The Northern Virginia Telephone and Telegraph Company, organized in 1897, was purchased by M. E. Church and the Falls Church Telephone Company in 1901. He sold it to the Chesapeake and Potomac Telephone Company in 1916. Courtesy of the Fairfax County Public Library Photographic Archive

When the original County jail built about 1802 burned down in 1884, prisoners were temporarily housed in the Alexandria City jail until this building was completed in 1891. More space was necessary, and an addition was immediately ordered. A notable example of Italianate style, the structure's bricks were laid in common bond for the first section and in Flemish bond to match the adjoining Courthouse in the second addition. Iron cresting and finials decorate the hipped roof. When it was replaced by a new jail in 1952, this building was adapted for offices for other county government functions. Located at 10475 Main Street. Placed on the National Register in 1987. Courtesy of the artist, Charles R. Wagner

Fairfax Jail

There was no doubt about it. The railroads of Virginia needed extensive rehabilitation from war damage and post-war neglect. Between 1866 and 1894, entrepreneurs and politicians attempted to upgrade the systems. The Orange and Alexandria operated under more than eight names because of consolidations, receiverships, bankruptcies and reorganizations. Eventually, the Southern Railway consolidated a great many small railroads, including the former O&A, into the Southern System in 1894.[27]

From the 1890s to the early 1900s, the railroads encouraged the Good Roads Movement, which began in 1880, using box cars and flat cars on the railroads to publicize the need for improved roads and highways. These rail cars could accommodate the vehicles propelled by internal combustion engines—automo-biles, trucks and buses being shipped to dealers and drivers. Ironically, this generosity eventually led to a decline of freight and passenger service by rail in the first half of the 20th century, when highway vehicles with great speed and multiple routes became available.[28]

The peace and quiet of the Town of Fairfax was abruptly shaken by the unpleasant, distant sounds of war in 1898. Joseph E. Willard, son of Joseph C. and Antonia Ford Willard, was an attorney and owner of Washington's Willard Hotel who lived part of the year in Washington and part at "Layton Hall" in the Town of Fairfax. He raised Company I, Third Virginia Regiment to serve in the Spanish-American War. The Company served at Camp Alger and in Richmond. The *USS Maine* was sunk in Havana Harbor on February 15, 1898. U. S. troops were deployed to Cuba in June. The fighting lasted only a short time, and the war concluded with the signing of a peace treaty by the U. S. and Spain in Paris on December 10, 1898, less than ten months' time all together.[29]

Close to home, more than 23,000 soldiers came from 16 states to train in the U. S. Army's Second Corps temporary camp on a large farm between Falls Church and Fairfax near Merrifield. They marched, rode army horses and explored northern Virginia. The first soldiers arrived at the Falls Church train station on May 13, 1898. Camp Russell A. Alger closed, the last unit of troops leaving on September 9, 1898.[30]

Following the brief war, Joseph E. Willard built a neo-classical building now called "Old Town Hall." He had purchased a lot from Amanda Hailey on the corner of Little River Turnpike and the present University Drive. He and his wife, Belle L. Wyatt Willard, gave the hall and land on July 30, 1900, to the trustees of the Masonic Organization Henry Lodge No. 57.[31] The *Alexandria Gazette* of August 16, 1900, announced: "The new Masonic hall just built at Fairfax by Capt. J. E. Willard to replace the old lodge room which was burned some time since, was opened last night for the first time. . . ." Thus the Town of Fairfax greeted the new century with an impressive new facade and rising hopes. The imposing building, first called "Willard Hall," has now served as a community center for a great variety of activities for almost 100 years.

LOOK AHEAD-LOOK SOUTH

Small railroad companies such as the Orange and Alexandria had financial difficulties following the Civil War. Destruction of tracks and equipment was widespread during the war, and bankruptcies and reorganizations continued in the region for almost three decades after 1865. In 1894, the Southern Railway consolidated a large number of these short lines in its system and from that time on for almost 100 years provided passenger and shipping services to residents, farmers, and merchants in Fairfax via Fairfax Station. The Southern Railway merged into the Norfolk and Western Railroad and in 1982 became the Norfolk Southern. Courtesy of the Norfolk Southern

Two important buildings, both constructed in 1900, appear in this photo. The Fairfax Herald *newspaper office was in the structure so marked for more than six decades. When it ceased publication as a separate weekly, the printing equipment was moved to the graphic arts exhibit at the Smithsonian Institution. The building is located at 10400 Main Street.*

The Old Town Hall, shown behind the Herald *building, is a combination of architectural styles with its Tuscan Order columns and Federal-style details such as the fan-light window over the front door and the round-headed gabled dormers. The building was never used for the Town's government offices, but has been a social center for the community since it was constructed in 1900 by Joseph E. Willard, lieutenant governor of Virginia and ambassador to Spain. The Huddleson Library is housed in part of the building and meetings, dances, celebrations and ceremonies have been held in the structure for nearly 100 years. The building is located at 3999 University Drive. Photo by William Edmund Barrett, courtesy of the Fairfax County Public Library Photographic Archive*

The Old Town Hall has been a community center for almost 100 years. This depiction was drawn by artist Leonida Ivanetich of Annandale. Courtesy of the City of Fairfax

48

5.
Rails, Roads, Fairs and a Fire, 1900-1930
by Nan Netherton

There seemed to be a new wave of energy and enterprise as the 20th century began. This even extended to Fairfax townspeople and their problems of getting around their village on foot. *Fairfax Herald* editor Stephen Roszel Donohoe wrote in August, 1900 of the Town Council of Woodstock, Virginia voting to put in sidewalks as good as if not better than sidewalks in any other town in the Shenandoah Valley. The *Herald's* editor gave a gentle nudge to his own Town, writing: "When Fairfax exchanges her mud and gravel sidewalks for solid pavements, the people will feel just as the Woodstock people feel about the change."[1] It took some years for this welcome change to take place in Fairfax.

Several different advances in motorized transportation improved access to and from the Town of Fairfax. The Southern Railway was double-tracked between 1902 and 1904. The National Good Roads Movement was actively supported locally because its purpose in this rural area was to "Get Virginia's farmers out of the mud!" The local farmers, who had struggled with poor farm-to-market roads for decades, knew what that meant to the marketing of farm products.[2]

As roads improved, new, faster vehicles operated with internal combustion engines began with increasing frequency to force the slower farm animals to pull their carts and wagons off the main roads. Real estate development began to become an important business as people experienced greater ease in getting from place to place.[3]

A development plan for Fairfax Station conceived by an ambitious entrepreneur never became firmly established. E. R. Swetnam had the postal designation

changed to Swetnam in 1897. Shares were sold and a Town Hall was built there at the turn of the century. Swetnam was still promoting the idea of incorporation and development when he died in 1910. The plan seemed to die with him. The postal designation was changed back to Fairfax Station in 1921, and so it has remained to the present.[4]

An accomplished and distinguished citizen of the Town of Fairfax became interested in encouraging the extension of the electric trolley line from Falls Church to Fairfax and offered incentives to bring about the desired result. When his mother, Antonia Ford Willard, had died, Joseph E. Willard was a child of about seven years. His father, Maj. Joseph C. Willard, and his uncle, Henry Willard, were busy as the successful proprietors of the Willard Hotel in Washington, so the young boy was sent to the Town of Fairfax where he was raised by his Grandfather Ford. After his graduation from the University of Virginia Law School, he was elected to the Virginia House of Delegates in 1893 from Fairfax County. Elected Lieutenant Governor of Virginia in 1901,[5] Willard failed to win the Democratic primary for Governor in 1905, the same year he was appointed to the State Corporation Commission. The marriage of Willard's daughter, Belle, to Theodore Roosevelt's son, Kermit, was a "national event" in 1913 at "Layton Hall," the present site of the Safeway near Layton Hall Drive and Old Lee Highway. Even when he served as President Woodrow Wilson's minister and ambassador to Spain from 1913-1921, Willard sent $150 to the organizers of the Fairfax County Fair in 1916.[6]

The first clerk's office at the Fairfax County Courthouse in the Town of Providence was built in the early 1800s next to the Courthouse. A second clerk's office was built nearby after the Civil War and this earlier building continued to be used for a variety of community purposes. When prominent businessmen organized the National Bank of Fairfax in 1902, County officials agreed to let the bank officers conduct business in the old clerk's office because the new bank would be a financial asset to the Town of Fairfax and to the County. In 1905, a new bank building was constructed on the southeast corner of Sager Avenue and Payne Street (Chain Bridge Road). Courtesy of Lee Hubbard

Joseph E. Willard was the only son of Antonia Ford Willard and Joseph Willard. Born in 1863, he was a graduate of the University of Virginia Law School. He was elected lieutenant governor of Virginia in 1901. He later served as the United States ambassador to Spain. A member of the Willard Hotel family, his estate in the Town of Fairfax was called Layton Hall. In 1904, Joseph E. Willard, seeing the possibilities of delays in completion of the electric trolley line to the Town of Fairfax, offered $25,000 to the Washington, Alexandria & Falls Church Railway if it could complete the electric trolley to the Town of Fairfax within four months. The idea was a practical one and the county seat acquired a direct rail link to Washington before the original deadline. Courtesy of the Fairfax County Public Library Photographic Archive

This 1903 photo shows Fairfax as a true horse-and-buggy town—with a dirt road which was dusty in dry weather and muddy in wet. The view is eastward toward Annandale, with the Town Hall on the left at Mechanic Street, now University Drive. Courtesy of the Fairfax County Public Library Photographic Archive

When the electric trolley tracks ended at this station on Railroad Avenue in 1904, passengers complained about hiking up the steep hill to the Fairfax County Courthouse, the tavern, the main business district in Town, and to the residences within and close around the Town. Eventually, the tracks were extended up the hill to the Courthouse and the tavern was used as the trolley station. Courtesy of Lee Hubbard

This photo shows a trolley car parked across Main Street from the Willcoxen Tavern, about 1925. Courtesy of the Fairfax County Public Library Photographic Archive

The Layton Hall mansion shown here was part of the large Willard estate within the Town limits. The family was always generous with the use of the park-like property, inviting residents of the Town to use it for strolling, fishing, swimming, sledding and football. Photo taken about 1905. From the postcard collection of Tony Chaves

Always interested in his County's progress, he had made a financial gift to the Fairfax Central Road League in 1904 and at about the same time offered a reward of $25,000 to the Washington, Alexandria & Falls Church Railway if the company completed construction to Fairfax within four months. The new trolley line was completed ahead of schedule to the great joy of the townspeople who had long anticipated the new access the trolley would offer to Washington sites and markets.[7] The new Washington, Alexandria & Falls Church trolley line gradually replaced the passenger, farm-to-market, and mail services once provided by the steam-driven Southern Railway line through Fairfax Station.[8]

Symbolic of the new age the trolley would bring to the community was the passing in 1903 of Robert Lewis Sisson, who had carried mail and passengers between Fairfax Station and Fairfax Court House for 34 years, only failing to meet one train and that because the road to the station was blocked with snow. One Fairfax Herald reader figured that the 75-year-old stage driver had driven the equivalent of 10 times around the entire earth at three-and-one-half miles per trip. It was doubted that anyone had ever seen him in a bad humor or heard an angry expression from him. In eulogy, the Herald wrote:

The death of Robert L. Sisson closes a long and admirable life. . . . Old fashioned in appearance

and manners, he possessed the old fashioned virtues in the full degree. Honesty, conscientiousness, industry, affection for his family and friends, genuine courtesy, simple and earnest piety—these were the marks of a very fine and stainless character. . . .

He was survived by his daughters, Mrs. James W. Taylor and Mrs. George L. Perry.[9]

The turn of the century brought political change to the community. The Democratic party had been dominant since the end of Reconstruction and had gradually achieved a conservative consensus. There followed a strong movement to hold a constitutional convention in Richmond to consider a number of issues, the principal one being a disenfranchisement of negroes in state and local elections.[10]

Local resident R. Walton Moore served as Fairfax County's delegate to the Virginia Constitutional Convention in 1901, and he was named Chairman of the Legislative Committee. The Herald opined that the admitted object of the convention was to deprive the most ignorant and indolent members of the colored race of the right to vote. Not only did the convention restrict the black population's rights to vote, a denial of free textbooks to all students penalized the poorer blacks in particular. The Herald criticized the "ambition" to make classical scholars of the Negro race, questioning who would be left to do the "hewing of wood, the drawing of water and the hoeing of corn . . . since they have to be done by somebody?"[11]

Robert Walton Moore was born in 1859 and studied law at the University of Virginia. He was a Virginia state senator from 1887 to 1890 and a United States congressman from 1919 to 1931. President Franklin D. Roosevelt appointed him assistant secretary of state in 1933, and he worked in the State Department until his death in 1941. Courtesy of the Fairfax County Public Library Photographic Archive

On June 1, 1904, a gray granite monument was unveiled at the Town of Fairfax beside the Fairfax County Courthouse commemorating the location of the Civil War conflict on June 1, 1861, in which John Quincy Marr, Captain of the Warrenton Rifles, became the first Confederate officer killed in action. The day was wet and muddy, and many of the attendees came from long distances. The old Courthouse was filled to overflowing with veterans and other visitors to honor the occasion. Among them were Gov. Andrew Jackson Montague, Lt. Gov. Joseph Willard, Attorney General William Alexander Anderson, a number of court justices and other men of note including the Honorable R. E. Lee, Jr. As Susan Hunter Walker reported in the *Confederate Veteran* magazine: "A band stationed in the quaint balcony above the court chamber discoursed music between the speeches. The selections consisted chiefly of Southern airs, which augmented the enthusiasm inspired by the eloquence of the orators. It was a day of awakened memories and reminiscences, with reunions of old friends and comrades who had fought beneath the stars and bars—a day that will long be remembered in the hearts of all who were present."[12]

The dedication of the Captain John Quincy Marr Monument was held on June 1, 1904, on the Courthouse grounds. Despite the rainy weather, a large crowd attended the ceremony which included such notables as Governor Andrew Jackson Montague, Lieutenant Governor Joseph E. Willard and Attorney General Alexander Anderson. A band played on the courtroom balcony, the selections consisting chiefly of Southern airs. Courtesy of Lee Hubbard

Soon after the Marr Monument was dedicated in 1904, a large group of students and teachers from Fairfax Elementary School dressed up in their Sunday best to have a portrait made in front of the new memorial. Courtesy of Lee Hubbard

As the seat of County government, the Courthouse continued to be an active center of justice and commerce on court days. This photo of the interior taken in the early 1900s shows portraits of dignitaries of significance to the County's history. The place of honor, in the center, was given to Thomas, Sixth Lord Fairfax. *Courtesy of Lee Hubbard*

The first building erected specifically for the use of the National Bank of Fairfax was placed at the corner of Sager Avenue and Payne Street (Chain Bridge Road) in 1905. It is now The Community Bank. Courtesy of Lee Hubbard

If there had been any doubts about the Town of Fairfax entering a period of business growth, they must have been dispelled. The National Bank of Fairfax was organized in 1902 and first opened in the old clerk's office with R. Walton Moore, president. James W. Ballard, a son of Capt. John Newton Ballard, was a bank cashier. The first bank building was constructed in 1905.[13] A second strong indication of business growth was the awarding of a franchise for telephone and telegraph service. The Town of Fairfax Council passed an ordinance on July 5, 1904, authorizing placement of poles and electrical conductors on the public streets of the Town and to operate the telephone and telegraph lines for a period of 30 years.[14] The Town Council later accepted the bid of Southern Bell Telephone and Telegraph Company for the Town's franchise, worth $35.00.

A detailed description of the County seat in 1907 appeared in a booklet, *Industrial and Historical Sketch of Fairfax County, Virginia*, published by the board of supervisors. The text gave gentle nods to past history and a confident view of the future of the Town: ". . . advantageously situated on a high and commanding

Farr's steam mill, photographed about 1900, was built on the Farr property facing the Little River Turnpike near its intersection with Old Lee Highway. The building was the scene of many balls and germans (dances). Courtesy of Lee Hubbard

John and Albert Rust were photographed in front of Farr's Mill about 1905. Note the wooden boardwalk along Little River Turnpike. From the Rust Collection, Fairfax County Public Library Photographic Archive

point between the main line and Bluemont branch of the Southern Railway." After mentioning Gen. George Washington's will at the Courthouse, and the Gunnell House nearby where Ranger John S. Mosby had captured Union General Edward Stoughton, attention turned to changes which had taken place in the Town following the Civil War:

> While on the hills and in the valleys hereabouts can be found many evidences of the great conflict in the early "sixties," yet the hand of modern improvement has left no trace of these in the town. Coming out of the Civil War as a mere hamlet, with devastation on every hand, and the fortunes of its people much impaired, Fairfax has grown into a thriving town of several hundred inhabitants, with well-paved streets, a national bank, a hotel, excellent general stores, a well-equipped and up-to-date drug store, a prosperous newspaper (the *Fairfax Herald*, more than a quarter of a century old), a carriage and wagon factory, private and public schools, four churches, and a Masonic and other lodges. Here terminates the Washington, Arlington and Falls Church Railway, the completion of which, in the latter part of 1904, has not only infused new life into the town, but has assured its rapid and substantial growth.[15]

It is difficult for present residents of the City of Fairfax who were born after 1920 to imagine what daily life was like in the Town of Fairfax without the existence of radio, television or computers. But

John F. Jerman was an active and versatile businessman early in the 20th century as is proven by this advertisement he placed in the 1907 Industrial and Historic Sketch of Fairfax County. Not only was he a real estate agent, but he did bonding and loans and sold insurance. Jermantown Road between Oakton and Route 50 carries his name. Courtesy of the Fairfax County Public Library Photographic Archive

newspapers, books, magazines, public records, family records and reminiscences, and photographs provide revealing glimpses of some of the entertainment and recreation available in those times.

Music was almost a fundamental pursuit, starting with Sunday church services, church meetings during the week, and concerts on special occasions throughout the year. In 1905, the Fairfax Band was led by Prof. M. F. Shoddy.[16] Lt. G. W. Gaines was the leader in 1908 when the group was usually referred to as the Fairfax Brass Band and played a number of public concerts.[17] Community dances, called "germans"— dances consisting of intricate figures that are intermingled with waltzes—were given by the Fairfax Assembly for about 30 years.[18] The Fairfax Cotillion Club gave dances or "hops."[19] The Brass Band presented a number of selections at a meeting held at the Courthouse.[20] Another of the band's concerts was proudly reviewed by the *Herald*: "It is a pleasant fact to note that the Fairfax Brass Band has the encouragement of the best element of the town; their concert in the hall last week was very numerously attended and the ball that followed brought out the talent and beauty of the neighborhood."[21]

That same year (1906), the Fairfax Assembly gave "a very pretty german" in the Town Hall. Attendance was substantial despite the intense heat, and many came from some distance. It was led by Mr. J. J. Davies of Manassas and Miss Hattie Douglas of Alexandria.[22] A Christmas german was given by the Fairfax Assembly in the Town Hall—well-attended and greatly enjoyed by all

present.[23] Fairfax schools, both white and colored, gave plays from time to time as part of their activities,[24] and starting in the early 1920s, movies were presented at the Fairfax Town Hall each weekend.[25] Baseball games between local schools and against teams from nearby towns who rode the steam trains and trolleys to meet their schedules were popular diversions.[26] The Fairfax Country Club gave dances and eventually completed a golf course in 1927.[27]

Mary Donohoe McCandlish rode her pony sidesaddle when she went to the Fairfax Town Post Office on Main Street about 1905. The dormer windows of the Ford House can be seen in the distance, and the brick sidewalk in front of what is now the Hav-a-Bite restaurant. The post office was housed in a number of different places before occupying its present building. Courtesy of Nancy and Edgar Prichard

It was in front of the L. H. Young Livery Stables that this nostalgic photo of a two-horse open sleigh was taken about 1910. The establishment was located near the Groff funeral home, now Everly's. Courtesy of Lehman Young

Occasionally, valuable documents lost during the Civil War were returned. Unlike General George Washington's will, the will of his widow, Martha Dandridge Custis Washington, remained in the Fairfax Courthouse during the early part of the Civil War. Late in 1862, Union troops from New England occupied the building and were in the process of shoveling out debris when the files spilled on the floor. A lieutenant colonel named David Thomson picked up papers, recognized them as Mrs. Washington's multi-page will and took it home with him. After his death, his daughter, Mary Espy, sold the will which was later sold again to American financier J. P. Morgan. Word came to Fairfax officials that the precious document was part of Morgan's collection of rare memorabilia. Between 1908 and 1913, County Court Clerk F. W. Richardson and Commonwealth's Attorney C. V. Ford were unsuccessful in attempts to have the will returned to the Fairfax Courthouse. After J. P. Morgan's death in 1913, the Falls Church Chapter, National Society of the Daughters of the American Revolution, chaired by

Richard Ewell Thornton, great-great-grandson of Richard Ratcliffe, was state senator from 1908-1919 for the 14th Senatorial District of Virginia. He and his wife, Sue Contee Thornton, entertained William Howard Taft in Fairfax when the president was on his way to Manassas to celebrate the Peace Jubilee on July 21, 1911. The photo was taken at the Thornton home on Little River Turnpike, which was next to Ratcliffe Park and the Fairfax Museum and Visitors Center. Courtesy of Bankhead T. Davies

Regent Mary Grimsley (Mrs. John S.) Barbour, began a new campaign by writing a strong letter to Morgan's son requesting the return of the will. The subject became a matter of concern to individuals and organizations outside of the County's borders until finally, by the time the will was returned to Fairfax County Court Clerk Richardson on October 14, 1915, the effort had been reinforced by the Virginia legislature, the Governor, Virginia's Attorney General, the State Supreme Court, and the U. S. Supreme Court.[28]

There were two Fairfax County Fairs, one for whites and one for blacks, held intermittently for many years, usually at harvest time in the fall.[29] Despite poor weather conditions for the third year in a row, Editor S. R. Donohoe reported at length in his *Fairfax Herald* in October 1914 about the many compliments offered by visitors from near and far concerning the Fair's exhibits. Some were pronounced superior to equivalent exhibits at the Richmond State Fair. One gentleman who traveled all over the country for the Southern Railway stated that it was the best county fair he had seen, with an attractive setting, good order and exhibits, and an animated spirit among the participants.[30]

The favorite feature of the Fair, according to the writer for the *Herald* in 1914, was the showing made by the schools. In spite of inclement weather, a large group marched in the school parade, and presented exhibits in the school. Adult exhibits singled out for special praise were fruit (especially apples), garden produce, corn, flowers, and various farm animals. A popular principal speaker at the Fair was U. S. Vice President Thomas R. Marshall.[31]

The Fairfax County Colored School Fair Association put on their first annual fair in 1915. A program which has survived from their Sixth Annual Fair in October 1920 shows extensive participation from all portions of the County. It was held on the Fairfax Court House Fair Grounds. The many featured departments of the Fair included Literary Work, Domestic Science, Domestic Art, Manual Training, the Home, Agriculture, Live Stock, Trades, Corn, Tomato and Potato Clubs, and special prizes for pupils of the public schools. The President and Supervisor of the festivities was A. T. Shirley of Herndon; First Vice President, Mrs. Mary E. Holland, Accotink; Second Vice President, Mrs. F. A. Ransell, McLean; Treasurer, Mrs. L. H. Jackson, Barcroft; and Secretary, William A. West of Vienna.[32]

Special prizes were given for classroom projects, sewing and handicrafts, and a one-dollar prize was

An automobile with a Maryland license tag got bogged down on an unsurfaced muddy road near Fairfax in 1911. Car and passengers were captured on film for the Virginia Department of Highways.

The school population had grown to the extent that a brick addition was built on Fairfax Elementary School in 1912. It was of hipped-roof design and placed in front of the first unit of the school built in 1873, and perpendicular to it. From the postcard collection of Tony Chaves

offered to the best school pupil's essay on "The Progress of the Colored People of Fairfax County." Regular prizes were promised for a dozen different essay subjects written by school children, and categories for the prettiest jars of jellies and preserves and cans of pickles, fruits and vegetables. Cakes, pies, breads, cookies and candies were judged for awards as were hand and machine-made articles and manual training projects, vegetables, livestock and corn, tomato and potato clubs for boys and girls and community exhibits.[33]

The advent of the First World War caused an expansion of the Federal government bureaucracy in the United States. Support services were needed for the rapidly increasing population, and women began to fill positions, some for their first jobs outside the home. They came from nearby towns such as Fairfax and counties in northern Virginia and from all parts of the country as well. Men, both black and white, enlisted in the military services from their rural homes in and around the Town of Fairfax. Some women joined the war effort as volunteers, working with the Red Cross.[34]

One of the devastating effects of the First World War was the influenza epidemic of 1918, which was experienced nationwide. It began as an epidemic in Virginia at Camp Lee near Petersburg on September 13, 1918. Within a month, more than 500 had died there. The worst of the contagions was over by November, but the total number of deaths from it in the state was 11,641. The three counties hardest hit in Virginia were Warwick, Fairfax and Prince William. The flu epidemic killed more Americans than World War I.[35]

Early in 1919, local commissions, consisting of a chairman and two associates, were established in each county and city in Virginia to collect in their respective communities' records of military and civilian activities relating to the World War. In Fairfax County, Wilson M. Farr of Fairfax was chairman; Mrs. G. L. Stuntz of Vienna and Rev. William C. Torrence of Herndon were the two associates.[36]

With the World War over, the country and county turned attention back to domestic concerns. One major need was for highways, generally financed in Virginia by county bond issues until 1919, when the state highway system was established. Road building thereafter seemed assured with funding from both state and federal appropriations.[37] A name closely linked with roads was that of State Senator Harry F. Byrd, whose rise in power and popularity within the Commonwealth had begun. In 1918, a legislative commission on roads to which Sen. Byrd had been appointed recommended that the state constitution be amended to permit the authorization of highway bonds. In 1920, Sen. Byrd not only voted against this amendment, he stated his firm opposition to issuing general obligation bonds for *any* purpose; "pay-as-you-go" became Sen. Byrd's strong career motto. Virginia's roads, however, were atrocious at the time. The road bond referendum passed in Virginia in 1920.[38]

A statewide referendum on the 22nd of September, 1914, establishing prohibition in Virginia, was passed 94,000 to 63,000. It was up to the General Assembly of 1916 to establish the exact prescription to make the

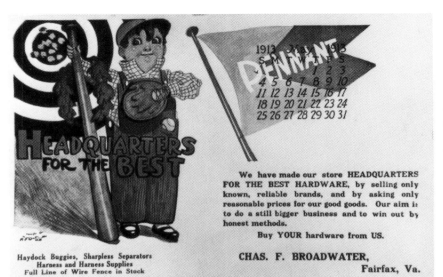

Merchant Charles F. Broadwater used postcards to advertise his hardware store in Fairfax in 1913. It was still the period of the horse and buggy, of dairy cattle and farms protected by wire fencing. Courtesy of Randolph Lytton

law effective. When finally passed, the legislation permitted every householder "to obtain from outside the state one quart of liquor, three gallons of beer, or one gallon of wine per month."[39] When national prohibition legislation in the form of the Eighteenth Amendment was passed in 1920, it prohibited Virginians the monthly allowance of alcohol allowed by the state's legislation. "The moonshiners and bootleggers moved in at once," according to Virginius Dabney. "Thousands of otherwise law-abiding citizens began violating the law."[40]

The Nineteenth Amendment to the United States Constitution granting women's suffrage was ratified by Congress and a sufficient number of states in 1920, although the Virginia Assembly did not ratify the amendment until 1952.[41]

During and after the First World War, the Federal government had increased in size, and many among the federal bureaucracy found the Town of Fairfax a congenial commuter community. Federal employees sent their children to school in the federal city via the trolley. But the maintenance of sidewalks leading to the station was inadequate. A local resident complained in a letter to the editor of the Herald:

The condition of the walkway along Cedar Avenue, near the railroad station, is a disgrace to the town and its officials. Weeds, shoulder high, fill the walkway and make its use disagreeable in good and impossible in wet weather. The stoppage of the roadway about fifty feet from the station is also a great inconvenience to those who use the station, from the eastern section of the

town, and it is hoped that the Town Council, at its next meeting, will take steps to give some relief. One of the Sufferers.[42]

Some parts of the main street through Fairfax were reportedly several feet above the sidewalk while other parts were several feet below. Major work on both roads and sidewalks was needed before drivers and pedestrians could travel in comfort and safety.[43]

The unpaved roads in Town frequently needed attention. A petition from the local black population was presented to the Town Council asking that some work be done on School Street leading into their subdivision and that two street lights be installed. The Council allowed $50.00 for gravel, with the under-

The Barbour House, moved a half block south in the 1970s from its original location, is now at 4069 Chain Bridge Road. It was built between 1910 and 1915 as a residence by attorney John S. Barbour, who had moved to Fairfax from Culpeper. The architectural style is Colonial Revival and two wings were added in 1978. It is now used as a restaurant. Courtesy of the Fairfax County Public Library Photographic Archive

The Southern Railway had photos made of all of their railroad stations following the First World War. This picture of Fairfax Station was made in 1919, just as the availability of automobiles, trucks and buses was beginning seriously to interfere with railroad passenger and freight business. Courtesy of the Fairfax County Public Library Photographic Archive

standing that the colored citizens would do the work. One light was ordered for the street, all work to be supervised by the Council.[44]

The publisher of the *Fairfax Herald*, Capt. Stephen Roszel Donohoe, who had frequently commented on the need for attention to these matters died in 1920. Donohoe had been born in Loudoun County, Virginia. He had published two papers elsewhere in Virginia when he moved to Fairfax in 1882 and established the weekly *Fairfax Herald*. Serving at different times in elected or appointed positions on the state level, Capt. Donohoe was a well-known and well-respected Democrat. His two daughters, Mrs. George B. Robey and Mrs. F. S. McCandlish, were also residents of the Town of Fairfax. Donohoe was succeeded as editor by William Francis Carne.[45]

H. B. Derr, the County's agricultural extension agent, highlighted the changing times in his 1923 annual report. "When Washington and Alexandria were full of fine horses, Fairfax County made considerable money supplying the market with timothy hay. But our average farmer should think that automobiles do not eat hay consequently they should adapt themselves to the changing conditions."[46]

Perhaps in reaction to changing values, the local chapter of the Ku Klux Klan gained visibility when a new and larger brick elementary school with large white columns was built in 1925 next to the earlier 1873 school on Little River Turnpike (Route 236).

The group, which called itself the Cavaliers of Virginia, Inc., bought the old school building the following year. The front section on the first floor was used as a shop in which to print the weekly newspaper, the *Fairfax County Independent*, and the large room on the second floor was used for meetings.[47]

The original Ku Klux Klan had sought to redeem the South from Northern Reconstruction efforts after the Civil War, but in 1915, a new Klan, adopting many of the symbols of the earlier organization, was founded and was actively represented by a local chapter. Local Klansmen no doubt saw themselves as defenders of traditional moral values in the community. In 1923, the *Fairfax Herald* reported that "While the Rev. J. C. Thrasher, of the M. E. Church, South [of Fairfax] was delivering his farewell sermon, ten robed and hooded members of the Ku Klux Klan entered the church and presented the pastor with a purse containing $50 in gold. Mr. Thrasher," the paper explained, "was much beloved by the people of the community." Fairfax County Agricultural Agent H. B. Derr acknowledged that Klansmen were often "the drawings cards" at agricultural fairs and at gatherings for "community betterment."[48]

At the March 1925 meeting of the Fairfax County School Board, the contract for the construction of the Fairfax colored school on School Street was awarded to Mr. E. W. Detwiler, of Clifton, on his bid of $3,780. Cards of thanks were later published in the *Fairfax*

The photo shown here indicates the heavy equipment that was used to put a hard surface, for the first time, on Lee Highway near Blake Lane just east of Fairfax Circle. Photo taken in 1924, courtesy of Lee Hubbard

The Prichard House at 3820 Chain Bridge Road was built in 1916 by Fairfax Sheild McCandlish, a prominent local attorney. It is significant as an example of early 20th century domestic architecture in the popular Colonial Revival style. Courtesy of the Fairfax County Public Library Photographic Archive

An ornate hearse graced Reed & Money's advertisement in the Fairfax Herald *in 1917. O. B. Campbell was the company's manager. Courtesy of the Virginia Room, Fairfax County Public Library*

OLD FAIRFAX HERALD PRINT SHOP   Friday, February 23, 1917.

Herald by the Fairfax Colored School League expressing appreciation for friends both white and black who assisted with a recent fund drive in order to clear up the land title for the school to be erected in the summer.[49] Fundraising efforts continued the following year: "Troupe E of the Fairfax Colored School League will give an attractive program at the colored school house on Fri eve Nov. 19, 1926, at 7:30 PM. Old fashioned costumes will be worn, portraying the life of colored people two generations ago. The program will consist of recitations, camp meeting hymns, etc. The proceeds will be for the benefit of the school."[50] The school was active in community service as well, winning first prize among all the county's black schools in 1927 for having sold the largest number of tuberculosis seals.[51]

The earlier Fairfax colored school building, located within Fairfax Cemetery, was sold at public auction in April 1927 by Mr. James U. Kincheloe, who acted as auctioneer. Mr. F. S. McCandlish was in charge of the sale, and the lot and structure, a frame one, was purchased by the Fairfax Cemetery Association on a bid of $170.[52]

The colored school on School Street often served as a center for its community, as was evident in a September 1935 *Fairfax Herald* news item: "The colored residents of Fairfax very successfully went theatrical last week when Thursday last they produced a play 'The Old Folks Wedding' in the colored school

auditorium, which was a success both from an amusing standpoint as well as financial. The audience attending filled the auditorium, and included a number of white persons. The action in the play was well done . . . and Ellen Gray was director of the performance."[53]

The list of officers and directors of the National Bank of Fairfax demonstrated in 1925 the gradual transition taking place from a predominantly rural community to a bustling urban center. Dr. F. M. Brooks, who owned a farm between Fairfax and Fairfax Station and had a medical practice, was president of the board of directors. A Fairfax attorney, Thomas R. Keith, was first vice president; R. E. Thornton, senior judge of the Circuit Court, was second vice president; Wilson Farr, Commonwealth's Attorney, lawyer and dairy farmer, who lived at "Five Chimneys" on Main Street, was a director, as was M. D. Hall, superintendent of schools; and F. W. Richardson, county court clerk. Other directors from outside the town boundaries were F. W. Huddleson, county treasurer and owner of a dairy farm west of Fairfax on Route 50 near Chantilly; Dallas Berry, a farmer on Route 7 west of Tysons Corner; Dr. Ford Swetnam of Fairfax Station; Douglass S. Mackall, attorney from Langley, Richard Farr, farmer, and M. E. Church, pharmacist, real estate agent and entrepreneur of Falls Church.[54]

It was probably of interest to many town citizens in 1926 to hear that a number of local worthies had been

A modern building for the times was built for the growing elementary school population of the Town of Fairfax in 1925. Made of brick with a two-story, white-columned portico, the building now is used by "Gold's Gym." From the postcard collection of Tony Chaves

Katherine (Kitty) Pozer was born in Georgia, daughter of the Reverend Robert S. and Dr. Kate Waller Barrett. During World War I, Kitty drove an ambulance with the Canadian Ambulance Service in London. She married Major Charles H. Pozer, a Canadian Engineer Corps officer, during the war. She and her husband moved into the historic Ratcliffe-Allison House in Fairfax, then called Earp's Ordinary, on her mother's death in 1925. The photograph was taken about 1918. Courtesy of the City of Fairfax

Washington Inn, Fairfax, Va.   Built 1792

In the early 1920s, legends grew around the brick house which had been owned by the Ratcliffe and Allison families. It was said to have been built in 1792 and that General George Washington had stayed there during his lifetime. It was erroneously called Earp's Ordinary or the Washington Inn, where tea was graciously served by owner Kitty Pozer to her visitors. In recent times, architectural historians have determined that the Earp family never owned this particular property and that the oldest section of the house was built between 1805 and 1813. Mrs. Charles Pozer donated the house to the City in 1973. From the postcard collection of Tony Chaves

drinking illegal ardent spirits at Lewis F. Ellis's barber shop. The sheriff had come over from the Courthouse and arrested the barber, who was indicted.[55] Obviously, not all of the alcohol in the barber shop was in the hair tonic bottles. "During the prohibition era, Virgil Williams was the prohibition officer and was an enforcer, confiscating cars of those seized with bootleg whiskey in their cars. These cars were sold at public auction at the Courthouse at regular intervals."[56]

Electricity and movies came to the Fairfax Town Hall on a regular basis in the 1920s. Norman Cobb was the projectionist. Carl Allensworth, who had been blind since infancy and had attended the School for the Blind in Staunton, Virginia, played the piano to accompany the silent films. Even though the music did not always match the action on the screen, he was said to get along very well with his white cane, taking the "Toonerville Trolley" to Fairfax from Vienna when he had a movie playing date.[57]

After the Labor Day weekend in 1928, a growing problem was noted in the *Herald*. "Judging from the number of automobiles that rolled over the roads through Fairfax from Saturday noon until Monday night, there must have been but few people left in Washington and Alexandria . . . traffic the heaviest in years."[58]

Prominent visitors came to Town from time to time. President and Mrs. Calvin Coolidge visited Fairfax Courthouse while on their way to visit "Oak Hill," once the home of President James Monroe on Route 15 in Loudoun County. Representative R. Walton Moore and County Court Clerk F. W. Richardson showed the distinguished guests the wills of George and Martha Washington and other old records. The Coolidges' pictures were taken beside the Marr Monument. The clerk presented Mrs. Coolidge with a printed copy of General Washington's will. President Coolidge also made a "cameo appearance" in a movie, *The Road to Happiness*, being made mostly in Fairfax County at the time by the Ford Motor Company.[59]

Undocumented tradition in the Fairfax Volunteer Fire Department is that a Fire Brigade was organized about 1900. The Town Council purchased a few fire extinguishers in 1909.[60] A hand-drawn, two-wheel chemical wagon with chemical tanks and 50 feet of hose with a nozzle was the first piece of equipment. An exact replica of this device is on display in the County Fire Department museum in the Massey Building. The FVFD, Inc., was formally chartered under the statutes of the Commonwealth of Virginia and incorporated on April 7, 1928. By 1930, the fire company had 35 active members on its rolls, a large portion of whom were active firefighters.[61]

This 1927 aerial view of the center of the Town of Fairfax was the first one known to have been taken from a plane. Buildings are shown at the period prior to expansion. The Courthouse is still a small building; the Willcoxen Tavern is across Main Street and the Fairfax Garage west of the tavern had not yet burned. Courtesy of Scott W. Boatright

Commenting on the Town of Fairfax in 1929, the *Industrial Directory of Virginia* painted an entirely new portrait of the County seat compared to the picture at the turn of the 20th century. Communication facilities—telephone lines, the electric trolley, and radio transmissions—had multiplied. Cars, buses, trucks and trolleys, electrical power and improved roads had transformed the community. The Directory reported:

The dairy industry is conducted on an extensive scale. The Washington market is an impetus to the dairy business, poultry raising and market gardening. The raising of cattle, sheep and hogs engages the attention of many farmers. Fairfax, the county seat, is located about the center of the county, connected with Washington and Alexandria by electric line and improved highways . . .

this is a thriving inland village and charming residence Town. Industrial operations in the county are represented in paper, pulp-cutting, flour and feed mills.[62]

Diversions, new and old, remained available. Ice cream socials were sponsored by various organizations and merchants; there were Sunday School picnics, Easter egg hunts and church suppers. Road tent shows occasionally came to Fairfax. Firemen's carnivals provided games of chance and dancing for amusement and fund raising. Residents of the Town enjoyed the Willard estate (Layton Hall), which during the 1920s was still a large property, beautifully maintained. On a weekend you could meet your neighbors strolling along its streams and through its fields. Children used the property for fishing, swimming, sledding and

The eight gentlemen shown were photographed during the last meeting of the Marr Camp of Confederate Veterans in Fairfax, about 1928. Seated in front, left to right, are James H. Wiley, Charles E. Davis, Robert Wiley, J. Nelson Follin and John P. Chinn. Standing in back, same order, Thomas H. Lee, Charles F. Russell and George K. Pickett. Courtesy of Lee Hubbard

football. There never was a "Private, Keep Out" sign posted. Like a lovely, private park, it was a loss to the community when it was sold and developed.[63]

According to the 1930 census report, the population of the Town of Fairfax on April 1, 1930, was 634-118 people more than the official count of 516 on January 1, 1920. There were six farms enumerated within the Town limits. The Town Council felt the pressure of the burgeoning population. They ordered that all subdivision plats laid off in the Town of Fairfax must be submitted to the Council for approval. Streets in subdivisions must be at least 40 feet wide and alleys no less than 12 feet wide.[64] The Council agreed to sign a contract with the J. B. McCrary Company, municipal engineers of Atlanta, to make a survey of the Town for both water and sewer service in October 1928.[65] Delegates from the Garden Club asked the Town to keep the streets clean. A Council committee was asked to report on the advisability of approving a central system for water and sewer service.[66]

A representative from the Fairfax Volunteer Fire Department, Incorporated, requested an appropriation in February 1929 for the laying of pipe from the stream at the foot of the cemetery up Main Street to the corner of Payne Street to provide for any fire emergency in the center of town. A motion was carried that the Town purchase 500 feet of hose at a cost not to exceed $500 instead of the iron pipe requested.[67]

At a special meeting of the Council, it was decided that water bonds were to be sold not exceeding the value of $100,000. The water system was to consist of a well or wells, electric pump or pumps, pump house

and water towers or reservoirs to be located on the land of Albert R. Sherwood. The bond issue for the central water system was approved by the voters on November 6, 1930, according to Town Council minutes. The first sewerage system was to consist of a treatment facility along the creek behind the Old Post Estates.[68]

The *Herald* indulged in a little nostalgia:
The Town Pump, for many years an institution in Fairfax, and used by many residents of the town—is no more. At a recent meeting of the Board of Supervisors an order was entered authorizing the filling up of the well from which men, now gray-haired grandfathers, drank cooling water in the hot days of many summers. . . . It is to be regretted. A town pump is always an institution in a country town like Fairfax. . . .[69]

One of the most memorable events in the Town's history occurred on Saturday, September 14, 1929. At the Fairfax County Fair, a complement of uniformed guards and the uniformed Ballston Klan Band No. 6 regaled the crowd with several selections at the midway before marching to the grandstand. The speaker of the evening was a Judge Connaughton, a member of the legal staff of the Knights of the Ku Klux Klan. He reportedly received frequent applause during his speech. At the conclusion of the address, the lights went out and a fiery cross blazed forth, followed by a solo, "The Old Rugged Cross," sung by a robed Klanswoman. A fireworks display ended the program.[70]

In a 1928 Fairfax County Chamber of Commerce publication, Historic, Progressive Fairfax County, *were included advertisements for the Black Lantern Inn at Little River Turnpike and Lee Highway, encouraging motorists to take rooms and meals at the new tourist facility. M. E. Church, president, also encouraged readers to continue their patronage of his Arlington & Fairfax Railway Company to increase its revenues in northern Virginia and thus benefit the economy. Courtesy of the Fairfax County Public Library Photographic Archive*

The Town pump, in the Courthouse Park, served thirsty travelers and visitors to the Towns of Providence and Fairfax for many generations. It was referred to as "an institution in a country town like Fairfax," when it was filled up due to pollution in 1929. Courtesy of the Fairfax County Public Library Photographic Archive

A Ku Klux Klan funeral ceremony was photographed at Fairfax Cemetery about 1929. Courtesy of the Fairfax County Public Library Photographic Archive

A raging fire broke out in the Fairfax Garage on Main Street when that Klan Day, 1929 was being observed at the annual Fairfax County Fair nearby. An estimated crowd of 5,000 people, many of whom were already on the Fair Grounds, tried to get to the scene of the fire. The newspaper account reported that only the efficient and skillful handling of the traffic by the Klan guards at the fair gate prevented complete confusion and congestion in the tie-up of all traffic.

The Town of Fairfax was reported in the September 20, 1929, *Herald* as rapidly recovering from the disastrous fire of the previous Saturday night. The Fairfax Garage building was destroyed and for a time the Come Rite Inn and the law office of John W. Rust were threatened. Firemen on surrounding rooftops were able to confine the fire by using chemicals to extinguish sparks that fell on the roofs. The siren of the Fairfax Fire Company was sounding the alarm when the fire destroyed it.

The loss of the contents of the garage was estimated at $14,000, with $8,000 insurance on the building which was owned by the estate of the late Lehman H. Young. It was fortunate that the establishment's new Ford cars were all out at the Fair, on exhibition, so that just five used cars were lost in the fire. Two privately owned autos which were at the garage for repair were also destroyed.

R. R. Farr and Mayor Tom Chapman, who had offices in the second story of the garage building, lost practically everything, but had some insurance coverage. On Monday afternoon, the safes of the Fairfax Garage Company and of Mayor Chapman were found cool enough to open. There was only a little scorching on the edges of their papers. The Town records were almost a total loss. The law libraries of Rust and Richardson had been moved across Main Street to the Courthouse grounds and were undamaged.[71] The records of the meetings of the Council of the Town of Fairfax for the months of July, August and September were destroyed. Other Town Council records were lost.[72]

Another loss came in 1930. Willcoxen Tavern, also known as the Union Hotel and the Fairfax Hotel, was demolished so that a new building for the National Bank of Fairfax could be erected in its place. Some of the materials including bricks, doors and mantel pieces, were salvaged and incorporated in 1932 into a new structure called "Flint Hill," the family residence of Helen Hill Miller, author, and Francis Pickens Miller, politician, and later a candidate for the United States Senate. The building was moved intact across Chain Bridge Road in 1986, where it became the administration building for the Flint Hill School.[73]

Ground was broken for the Lee Highway bypass around the Town of Fairfax in 1931. Will Pobst, owner of Cloverdale Farm, tipped the first shovelful of dirt at the Fairfax Circle construction site. The new road, when completed, met Lee Boulevard (now Arlington Boulevard) at Fort Buffalo (now Seven Corners). Present at the ceremony were State Senator-elect John W. Rust, Frederick W. Richardson, Robert D. Graham, Rufus Pobst and daughter Shirley (now Young), Stewart Preece, Robert McCandlish, and John R. Olcott of the Northern Virginia Construction Company, who with others composed the throng of spectators. A Washington Star staff photo

6.
Cows, Corn and Commuters, 1931-1960
by Nan Netherton

airfax County's dairy industry was faced with a dilemma in the early 1930s. After years of leading the Commonwealth of Virginia as the number one producer of dairy products, its main market for milk was Washington, D. C. A new requirement in the neighboring jurisdiction called for a minimum of four percent butterfat, a standard which the champion Holsteins of Fairfax could not meet. With advice from County Agricultural Extension Agent H. B. Derr, dairy farmers, including those in the Town of Fairfax, switched to crossbreeding with Guernsey and Jersey animals for richer milk. Derr also mentioned in several reports that corn was the second most important product in Fairfax.[1]

For a number of years in the 1930s, the Fairfax County 4-H Club rallies presented large pageants in which each separate club in the County took part. Large crowds of well wishers attended to enjoy the efforts made by the boys and girls who composed the membership. The 1930 pageant was held at the County fair grounds (now the location of Paul VI High School) on May 3, with an audience estimated at from 2,500 to 3,000 people to see "Sally Fairfax's Wish." There were 396 club members from 19 clubs and the Fairfax club won the prize for having the largest number of adults from their own community in attendance.[2]

The Fairfax fair grounds were also the scene of the 1931 rally, on May 2. Nineteen County clubs were represented. This time, 4-H demonstration contests were held, interspersed with dramatizations of folk songs and favorite old, familiar ballads such as *East*

Side, West Side; *School Days*; and *Aunt Dinah's Quilting Party*.[3]

After lunch on May 14, the 1932 Fairfax County 4-H Club rally was held on the lawn in front of the white-columned Fairfax School (now "Gold's Gym") to view the "Life of a Fairfax Man." Players from the various clubs, 350 in all, took part in costumes in the pageant to show that the characteristics of George Washington were the 4-H Club ideals of the present. A crowd of 500 people looked on as members acted out examples of incidents in Gen. Washington's life which illustrated the theme.[4]

A bond issue for a water system in the Town of Fairfax was approved by a wide margin in November 1930. A suitable lot near the center of Town was sought by an appointed committee. The McCrary engineers' estimated cost for the system was $46,980.24, and the contract was to be inspected by three Fairfax lawyers before approval. Mayor Chapman was authorized to seek bids for digging wells. F. N. Haigman, Jr., was awarded the contract to dig the well and the J. B. McCrary Corporation of Atlanta was awarded the contract to construct the Town water system.[5]

Construction work began in November 1931 on the new road (Route 50) connecting Lee Highway (Routes 29 and 211) at Hatmark (near Fairfax Circle) with the highway at the Black Lantern Inn (Kamp Washington) just west of Fairfax at the Little River Turnpike (Route 236). State Senator-elect John W. Rust and quite a number of Fairfax residents witnessed the movement of the first load of earth by a large power shovel. The

In the 1920s and 1930s, travelers' accommodations began to provide services to the motoring public. The Cloverdale Farm Modern Tourist Home, operated by the Pobst family, at Fairfax Circle—"off the noisy highway"—offered their hospitality at the intersection of Lee Highway and Lee Boulevard. From the postcard collection of Tony Chaves

Early in the 1900s, the old Willcoxen Tavern, which had served the public for over 100 years, was operated by C. P. Henry, Manager. On a postcard printed in the early part of the 20th century, the building had reached resort status. It was described as "A clean, comfortable, commodious, country colonial inn, located in beautiful and historic Fairfax, Va. 20 miles by trolley from Washington, D. C. A homelike and delightful resort for week's end, month's end or season's end." From the postcard collection of Tony Chaves

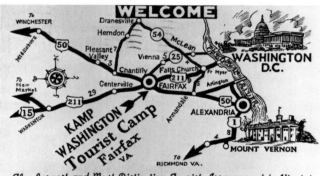

The Kamp Washington cottages were advertised as "modern and semimodern," cool and shady and located on beautiful grounds. The owner declared his tourist camp at the intersection of Lee Highway and Route 50 to be "The Largest and Most Distinctive Tourist Arrangement in Virginia." From the postcard collection of Tony Chaves

Postcards widely circulated as advertisements by Kamp Washington owner Warren W. Stoner, invited tourists to "Make this camp your home while visiting the Washington Bicentennial 1732-1932." There were 30 cottages, beautiful grounds and reasonable rates. From the postcard collection of Tony Chaves

Manuel's Tourist and Trailer Park was located two miles west of Kamp Washington on Route 211 in the 1930s and 1940s, C. Manuel, proprietor. From the postcard collection of Tony Chaves

actual "cut-off" road through the fair grounds and a number of farms, two and one-half miles in length, had been budgeted for about $85,000 in state funds and was expected to be completed in 120 days.[6]

Truro Episcopal Chapel was built in 1933, patterned after Payne's Church, built in 1768. Payne's was destroyed during the Civil War in 1863.

Fairfax County School Superintendent W. T. Woodson appeared before the Town Council and stated that it was possible for the County to obtain a central high school in the Town of Fairfax from a federal loan and asked the Council to donate 12 acres to the County School Board for the school building and playground. A bond issue would have to be voted on by the citizens of the Town, but a permanent committee was appointed, and the Council was asked to find a suitable location at the lowest possible cost.[7]

An Act of the General Assembly was approved September 12, 1933, abolishing town and other separate school districts and boards in four Virginia counties, including the school district of the Town of Fairfax. The county became the unit for the entire county, including incorporated towns, except for Falls Church.[8]

Mayor Chapman was instructed to write a letter to the Fair Association asking to purchase part of the Fair Grounds for school purposes, offering $5,000. The Town Council agreed to supply part of the $5,000 purchase price for part of the Fair Association land inside the corporate limits, believing it to be in the public interest and to the advantage of the Town for the construction of a high school. Land was purchased and Fairfax High School was built and opened for classes February 1935.[9]

After years of prohibition of alcoholic beverages in the nation, the law was repealed. According to Virginius Dabney, with repeal in 1933, ended was "the era of the amphibious statesmen—that notorious species which voted 'dry' and drank 'wet.'"[10]

A delegation from the Garden Club visited the Town Council in reference to the beautification of the Town in November 1933. The Mayor appointed a committee of the Council to confer with a committee of the Garden Club whenever any trees were to be cut down.[11]

Planning to make use of the building more convenient, the Garden Club requested that the Town supply free water to Willard Hall. The Council agreed to provide the water if the Garden Club would pay for tapping and running the line to the Hall.[12]

Truro Chapel was named after the colonial church parish of the same name, which once included Fairfax and Loudoun counties and the Town of Alexandria. The chapel was a 1933 replica of Payne's Church, constructed on the Ox Road in 1768. It is a successor to the wooden Zion Episcopal Church, first built in the Town of Providence in 1843, destroyed during the Civil War, and rebuilt in 1874. Courtesy of the City of Fairfax

Dr. Gunnell's house, where Mosby captured General Stoughton in 1863, became the Episcopal Church Rectory after the Civil War. A balancing wing was added to the Rectory in 1911. The Rectory is on the National Register of Historic Places. It is located at 10520 Main Street. Courtesy of the City of Fairfax

An unwelcome announcement appeared in the *Herald* in December 1933. The grand jury in the United States Court in session in Alexandria returned an indictment against Miss Ludema Sayre, on a presentment for having been short $3,372 in her accounts as postmaster of Fairfax. There were five counts in the indictment. Miss Sayre was succeeded as postmaster July 1 by Lewis M. Coyner. The trial of Miss Sayre was set.[13] Miss Sayre was a community leader, farmer, Girl Scout leader, Centreville Grange member, Women's Market (co-op) member, Chamber of Commerce director, and the Fairfax Town postmaster. The sad story appeared in the *Herald*:

> Miss Ludema Sayre, former postmaster of Fairfax, in the U. S. Court at Alexandria, Friday last pled guilty to an embezzlement indictment and was given a suspended sentence of two years.
>
> Miss Sayre took the money while in charge of the post office here. She is to report to the probation officer every two weeks, wherever she may reside. Rev. Herbert A. Donovan is probation officer for this county, and Miss Sayre will report to him as long as she resides in the county.[14]
>
> Miss Sayre, formerly postmaster at Fairfax Courthouse, returned to her home in Los Angeles, California, having arrived there on Christmas Eve. Her many friends in this part of the world will miss her.[15]

At the meeting of the Fairfax Bar Association held in the office of George B. Robey in January 1932, Frederick D. Richardson was elected president; F. S. McCandlish, vice president; John W. Whalen, treasurer; and Paul Brown, secretary.[16] The Fairfax Bar Association was considering taking action in December of 1935 on the coming retirement of F. W. Richardson, January 1, from the office of clerk of the court. He had served in that capacity for years, aiding most of the members of the Fairfax Bar Association, and it was felt that the Bar should express public appreciation on his retirement.[17]

The State Corporation Commission notified the Town Council that the Arlington & Fairfax Railway had applied for a permit to abandon its service from Vienna to Fairfax. The Arlington & Fairfax Motor Transportation Company had applied for a permit to operate motor buses between Vienna and Fairfax.[18]

The Town was feeling uneasy about animals which were out of control. George Hunter had to be asked to cease allowing his horses to roam at large in the town. The Council voted to authorize the County Game Warden to enforce the dog laws in the Town. Miss Ida Jones and Mrs. Thomas P. Chapman, Sr., complained about the noise made at night by Joseph Bennett's gaming roosters (fighting cocks) to the extent that the two ladies were unable to sleep. The mayor and clerk were directed to ask Mr. Bennett to abate the problem or the Council would be compelled to consider some action.[19]

The Town Council passed a resolution adopting the offer of the United States to the Town of Fairfax, Virginia to aid by the way of loan and grant to finance the construction of a sewer system for the Town. The government grant was to be 45 percent of the cost of the project, not to exceed $45,000, and the Town of

The National Bank of Fairfax opened its doors in 1931. Shown in this 1932 photo are Wise Kelly on the right, later president of the bank; and Stacy Sherwood on the left, later a bank officer. Standing in the doorway is Claude Beach. Courtesy of Lee Hubbard

Fairfax was to sell $55,000 worth of bonds to purchasers other than the United States. The bonds were to be negotiable, general obligation, serial, coupon bonds in denominations of $1,000, four percent interest per annum payable semi-annually on April 1 and October 1. There were five votes in favor, none against. A. G. Pinkston & Company was awarded the construction contract.[20] A resolution was passed by the Council to request a further allotment of $20,000 to allow for the construction of a sewer in the colored settlement south of Jones Street on Payne Street.[21]

The Fairfax Town Council signed a contract with the National Bank of Fairfax in 1935 when a bid was submitted by the bank's attorney, Maj. R. R. Farr. An ordinance was adopted by the Council authorizing the issuance of $55,000 worth of bonds of the Town, maturing over 30 years' time, paying three and one-half percent interest. Sewer bonds were printed, signed by Town officials, and turned over to the purchaser, the National Bank of Fairfax, in 1936.[22] The sewer system was completed June 1, 1937. The assessed value in the Town was figured as $527,892.00 by the tax consultant, Miss Ruth Sherwood, in April 1938.[23]

The National Bank of Fairfax was built on the land where the Willcoxen Tavern had stood for more than 100 years, on Main Street, the Little River Turnpike. The bank was founded in 1902 in the old clerk's office near the Fairfax County Courthouse. Courtesy of the City of Fairfax.

Residents of the colored section in the southern part of the town requested gravel for their street which led west off Payne Street. The Council ordered 25-30 loads of gravel to be spread by the residents, the Council to pay for the gravel after it was delivered.[24]

A new medium of communication was rapidly becoming popular with Fairfax residents of Town and

Before the first firehouse shown here was built, the fire truck was parked at Cooper's wagon shop on Main Street behind the Courthouse. The building was unheated and in the cold of winter, the radiator froze and the engine cracked. The apparatus was then parked at the Fairfax Garage. This building was constructed on Mechanic Street (now University Drive) across from the Town Hall in 1932. Courtesy of the Fairfax Volunteer Fire Department

The Fairfax Volunteer Fire Department baseball team posed for this formal photo about 1938. Standing in the back row, left to right, are Charlie Mundy, Dick Adams, Bruce McClure, Pete Keys, Stuart Bryce, Ambrose Carrol and Redmond Simpson; middle row, same order, Jim Mahoney, Roy Hollis, John Mahoney, Council Sutphin, Aubrey Sutphin, and Tom Mahoney; front row, Maurice Williams, ? King, Gordon Riggles, Richard Nevitt, Tab Wells, and Davis Mohler. The batboy in the front is Moncure "Snuffy" Smith. Courtesy of the Fairfax County Public Library Photographic Archive

County. In 1936, County Agent Derr reported, "We find we can reach twice the number of farmers in the county with the radio than we can with the county paper."[25]

Citizens of the Town of Fairfax did not forget their neighbors in need during the Great Depression in the dark years of the 1930s. School teachers acted as a social service agency. If a child or a family had a need, this fact was brought to the principal's attention and the Parent Teachers Association responded. Clothing and food were provided. Holiday food collections and clothing and toy drives were annual events.[26]

The Fairfax Elementary School lunch program began in 1937 or 1938. The national school lunch program had begun in 1935 when top government officials realized that many potential American servicemen were unable to pass military physicals because of malnutrition. A national program was developed and on August 24, 1935, a public law was passed to encourage foreign and domestic consumption of agricultural commodities.[27]

Tom Chapman, deputy clerk of courts, was PTA president of Fairfax Elementary School and was followed in office by Helen Friedlander, mother of five healthy, hungry boys. A space for a cafeteria was found in the basement and cafeteria workers were hired, menus planned, and Helen and others began making regular trips to Fairfax Station to pick up

surplus food delivered by the trains and taking it back to the school.[28]

The school lunch project was so successful nationwide that it was made a permanent program by Act of Congress in 1946. Upon signing the bill, President Harry S. Truman stated: "In the long view, no nation is any healthier than its children or more prosperous than its farmers; and in the National School Lunch Act, the Congress has contributed immeasurably both to the welfare of our farmers and the health of our children."[29]

In January 1940, John Connolly purchased 200 acres of land near Fairfax Circle on Old Lee Highway from Everett Swayze and Marie Swayze Gibson. He acquired 62 additional acres from adjacent landowners. The land was purchased and designed as a golf course by the Fairfax Country Club. In the 1950s, the Army Navy Club offered to purchase the land, then bought another piece of property in Chantilly in 1956. The plan for Dulles Airport included that parcel so the government purchased it in 1958, and the Army Navy Country Club purchased the Fairfax Country Club after all.

Meantime, in 1948 a group of townspeople purchased part of the old Hope Park plantation, the Haight farm on the Old Ox Road (Route 123) south of town. It was initially called the Courthouse Country Club. When the old Fairfax Country Club changed its name to Army Navy in 1958, Courthouse became the Country Club of Fairfax.[30]

Taylor's Pharmacy on Main Street became Ellicott's Dry Goods Store and F. W. Jones' 5¢ to $1.00 store. Standing on the sidewalk in front of them is Miss Jennie Moore, one of R. Walton Moore's three sisters, in this photo taken about 1940. An ice cream truck is making a delivery to Ramsay Taylor's Pharmacy on Main Street at Mechanic Street in the 1920s in this photo. Mechanic Street is now University Drive and Taylor's Pharmacy is now Picco's Restaurant. Miss Jennie Moore's picture courtesy of the Fairfax County Public Library Photographic Archive; Taylor's Pharmacy picture from the postcard collection of Tony Chaves; Ellicott's Store photo courtesy of Lee Hubbard

The Honorable R. Walton Moore wrote his memoirs in 1939. He was proud of the number of notable people he had entertained in the Town of Fairfax. The Mount Vernon Ladies' Association of the Union had been guests of R. Walton Moore at his home and were given the opportunity to see the original wills of General and Mrs. Washington. For a number of years, seniors at the Madeira School were entertained at his home and Walton Moore always took them to the record office to see the Washington wills. Moore and his sisters often had distinguished visitors both domestic and foreign to dinner at their home in Fairfax, and before the guests left, Moore would take them to see the old records and portraits of historical figures in the Courthouse. His guest list included ambassadors, Supreme Court justices, senators, congressmen and college presidents. The Moore sisters, Maggie, Helen and Jennie, for some years held a May garden party at their home in Fairfax which was attended by hundreds of visitors.[31]

Early in 1939, an obituary appeared in the *Herald*. William F. Carne, for nearly 25 years editor of the *Fairfax Herald*, died at his home in Fairfax following a long illness. He was born in Alexandria, October 4, 1866, and was educated at the old St. Johns Academy in that City. He worked for Capt. S. R. Donohoe when he was editor of the *Alexandria Times*, and worked on numerous other newspapers before buying the *Fairfax Herald* in 1916 from Capt. Donohoe. He had one son, William L. Carne. An *Alexandria Gazette* editorial on December 6, 1939, stated that the *Fairfax Herald* ". . . was and still is the organ and spokesman of the community."[32]

In 1940, the Fairfax County Board of Supervisors decided to establish a County police department which had jurisdiction in the Town of Fairfax until the Town became a city in 1961. The first major case the new department investigated was the Holober murders, which occurred at a nudist camp near present-day Reston in 1949, attracting national publicity. Fairfax was congratulated for its speedy solution of the crime.[33]

During the decade between 1940 and 1950, the county's population more than doubled, from 40,929 to 98,557. Without regulations for planning and zoning, subdivisions grew like weeds on the large farms where once cattle had grazed and corn had grown to produce up to 90 bushels per acre.

With the increase of people who bought and lived in those houses, taking care of their needs grew more and more difficult. Water and sewer service barely kept up with the demand. The mayor suggested that the Town obtain a place where it could dump its tin cans and trash and also another lot on which to drill another well. When the Town had large farms, there was always a corner to use for a small trash dump that Virginia creeper, poison ivy and honeysuckle would gradually cover, but that was not possible on small house lots of about one-quarter acre.[34]

Kitty Pozer, one of Dr. Kate Waller Barrett's daughters, lived with her husband, Charles, in the Ratcliffe-Allison House (then called "Earp's Ordinary"). She appeared before the Town Council in 1940 to ask for a study of the zoning question because some sort of zoning regulations were going to be needed in the near future.[35]

The Fairfax High School had been opened for classes in February 1935; Oakton seniors of the Class of 1935 graduated at Fairfax High. Its new auditorium opened in 1940 with the theatrical production of "As the Clock Strikes," given by the Court House Players, directed by Muriel Gilbertson. Productions by the Barter Theatre followed, as did many county-wide meetings.[36]

Visitors and townspeople could drop in at the friendly eatery, the Come Rite Inn (on Main Street), for a cup of coffee and a piece of pie or a meal between 7:30 a.m. and 11 p.m. and expect to receive "clean, prompt, efficient service from Elmer Dove, proprietor." Martha Dove also took her stint as the proprietor.[37]

For more formal settings, one could stop at Kitty Pozer's Washington Inn to see antiques, buy gifts, have a light lunch or afternoon tea at "Earp's Ordinary."[38] The best-known inn in the Town was the Black Lantern Inn, on Route 236, the Little River Turnpike, near the tourist court called Kamp Washington. Not only were Inn owners Elvira and Marguerite Merigold proprietors of an official AAA-approved tourist court, they were 15 miles from Washington and one mile west of Fairfax Courthouse, Virginia, at the fork of Lee Highway and the Winchester Road (Route 236), in a convenient location for the traveling public. They offered complete meals from one dollar up, including chicken and old Virginia ham. There were tourist rooms equipped with running water, baths and electric lights.[39]

With the nation's concerns due to wartime preparedness, the Fairfax Volunteer Fire Department had difficulty filling its ranks in 1941 because of the military draft. Many members of the County fire departments had entered the army under the draft law,

Routes 29-211-50 — Junction of 123 & 211
FAIRFAX, VIRGINIA

The Tastee 29 Diner at 10536 Lee Highway opened as a restaurant about 1940. The diner remains architecturally significant as a type of construction. It still has a high degree of integrity of design features typical of the early 1940s. An early postcard advertised it as "The Gateway to the Skyline Drive." In November 1992, it was entered in the National Register of Historic Places. From the postcard collection of Tony Chaves

and this had resulted in a rather serious situation as far as the fire companies were concerned. While the remaining members of the companies would undoubtedly continue to render the best service in their power, they naturally felt the handicap of having lost so many men. Under the circumstances, the people of the County were asked to cooperate with the firemen by endeavoring to keep calls to a minimum, and by making efforts to extinguish small fires themselves. Most of the County firemen were within the draft ages, and six members of the Fairfax company had already entered military service.[40]

One certainly could not classify Fairfax as a sleepy little town. Mayor R. R. Farr was elected to the Virginia House of Delegates and offered his resignation as mayor of the Town since he could not hold two elective positions at the same time. On December 2, 1941, attorney John H. Rust was appointed mayor to fill out Farr's unexpired term.[41]

Rust was mayor when World War II broke out on December 7, and the next spring when elections for mayor and councilmen were held, Rust went to the polls and asked the voters to elect Robert Graham, since Rust had decided to join the armed forces. Graham was elected and served throughout the war as mayor of the Town of Fairfax.[42]

The pressure of the need for housing by incoming Federal government personnel hired to help with the war effort made the working farms in the Town of Fairfax look like prime subdivision development property. There were no subdivision or zoning laws to assure orderly planning then. These laws were later established as town ordinances.

Attorney John H. Rust, in a celebratory mood, stands here with his wife, Jeanne Johnson Rust. She wrote the book, A History of the Town of Fairfax, *published in 1960. Courtesy of John Rust*

According to City records, the Westmore neighborhood was established in 1929 and building continued until 1967. In the early 1940s, house prices ranged from $2,990 to $5,000 in Westmore.

This two-bedroom, one bathroom pre-fabricated house at 4100 Chestnut Street featured hardwood floors and wallpaper in all rooms at a cost of $8,950 in the fall of 1949. Note the mud yard and street and woods in the back of the house.

The neighborhood's greatest growth occurred in the early 1950s, as a Levittown-style development of starter homes for World War II veterans. Courtesy of the photographer, Glenn Moore

Practical matters continued to require the Town Council's attention. An ordinance was passed stating that "It shall be unlawful to maintain and operate within the limits of the Town of Fairfax, Virginia, places commonly known as 'Automobile Graveyards.'"[43] The Council received a proclamation from the governor that all departments and agencies of the Commonwealth were to observe Eastern Daylight Saving Time from August 10 to September 28, 1941.[44]

President Franklin Roosevelt established the High School Victory Corps on September 25, 1942. It was a national voluntary organization for secondary schools for the purpose of mobilizing high school youth for more effective preparation for and participation in World War II.

High school students were asked to (1) enroll in physical fitness programs; (2) choose studies with immediate and future usefulness to the war effort; (3) participate in at least one important or recurring wartime activity or service such as war bond and stamp sales, Red Cross activities, air raid warden service, airplane spotting, letters to men in the armed service, USO service, health department clinic work, farm aid, salvage campaigns, care of children of working mothers, gardening, school janitorial assistance, book collecting for servicemen, Ration Board assistance, public library work, first-aid work, and collection of first-aid supply kits for the Virginia Reserve Militia. In addition to general membership, five special divisions were provided: Air Service (Air Corps); Land Service (Army); Sea Service (Navy); Production; and Community Service.[45]

Students were encouraged to be participants on the local level. The Fairfax High School Government Association was established between 1942 and 1943. The constitution was written for the purpose of providing a substantial self-government; developing a cleaner, stronger, and more democratic code of living in each individual; and to insure justice to the student body.[46]

Consolidation of the County high schools, principally due to Superintendent W. T. Woodson's efforts at total consolidation at all levels, enabled Fairfax High to have a large student population with a variety of talents. According to the annual in 1943: "Our band had a very successful year and has been received with much enthusiasm. . . . It has been a great help in boosting ye olde school spirit. . . . Future plans include . . . purchasing of uniforms and a corps of majorettes. . . . Several new instruments were obtained during the last year, including a big bass horn which is three sizes larger than the boy who plays it."[47] As for direct support of the war effort, in February 1944, $50,000 in war bonds and stamps were sold at the Fairfax High Bond Rally featuring outstanding citizens and servicemen.[48]

Great secrecy and heavy security surrounded the Willard mansion, Layton Hall, from late 1943 to the end of World War II. Experience with bad recruitment led the Office of Strategic Services to establish an assessment program beginning in November 1943. "The locus of the undertaking was a country estate forty minutes outside Washington, a farm with rolling meadowland and self-respecting shade trees, massive barn and satellite sheds and kennels, which provided ample space for setting up all sorts of stressful situations, indoors and outdoors, to test the intelligence and stamina of the candidates. This was known as 'Station S' (for secret)." In groups of about eighteen men, the duration of each testing period was three days. Layton Hall was an important training center, but not listed by name, only by the term "Station S" in the Town of Fairfax. It was the first attempt in America to design and carry out selection procedures to assure (by psychologists and psychiatrists) the merits of men and

Layton Hall, the old Willard home, was one of eight training centers throughout the world during World War II for assessment of men by the Office of Strategic Services (OSS). The organization was renamed the Central Intelligence Agency (CIA) after the war. The center was known as "Station S" in the Town of Fairfax. Courtesy of the Fairfax County Public Library

women recruited for the Office of Strategic Services. There were eight assessment stations throughout the world.[49]

The Fairfax High School was a unifying influence on the townspeople of Fairfax, man, woman and child. Not only did regular school activities and special events draw people together, but the annual book published was a major project for the student editorial staff and faculty advisors. The enrollment and teaching staff had grown since 1935 from 468 students and 14 faculty to 927 students and 42 faculty in 1945. A bit of school history appeared in the 1945 annual: "Plans for a Fairfax High School Yearbook originated in the minds of a few students from Clifton High School, who with some paper, pictures, and paste had made a yearbook—a yearbook of which they were very proud. They carried their ideas into Fairfax High School in the fall of 1935 where they formed a group and called themselves a Yearbook Staff."[50]

Since at least 1891, circuses and traveling shows of different kinds have toured or been sponsored by organizations in the Town of Fairfax. Not all of the events were announced in the *Herald* newspapers, but some which were show an interesting style of announcement and assortment of entertainment for almost 70 years. One example appeared in the *Herald* in 1891: "Flaming posters announce that Wm. Main & Co.'s show will exhibit here on Thursday next, the 23rd instant. Of course all the small boys as well as the grown people will see the show."[51]

The following large 7"x12" ad in the *Herald* had lots of "white space" and large type so everyone could easily read it. "Franconia Volunteer Fire Department presenting James E. Strates Shows May 11, 12 and 13, 1939; Fairfax County, near Alexandria City Limits; Roberts' Show Grounds; 18 Thrilling Rides, 15 Big Shows; Featuring Miss Billy Smithly and her Nubian Lions in Lion Autodrome. Saturday, Kids' Day, Free Gate. All shows, all rides, 5 cents until 6 p.m. Gen'l Adm., 10 cents."[52]

Another large display ad appeared in the *Herald* in 1945: "Donkey Baseball circus—Hilarious Entertainment cosponsored by American Legion, Billy Mitchell No. 85 vs Fairfax Post No. 177 at Ballston Field, Arlington, Sept. 9, Fairfax Fair Grounds, Fairfax, Sept. 16, 1945."[53]

This news item appeared on page 1, "above the fold," in 1960: "The Fairfax Lions Club will sponsor a circus at Fairfax Circle and R 237 Saturday of this week. Two performances will be given and the proceeds will be used for the club's sight conservation program."[54]

On Monday, December 1, 1947, the Fairfax Theatre (now the location of Ourisman Fairfax Toyota), located on Lee Highway near the intersection with Route 123, had a gala opening to a capacity crowd of about 1,500 people. Town and County officials were present to extend a welcome to the new Town enterprise. The Honorable Paul E. Brown, Judge of the Circuit Court, was Master of Ceremonies. Mayor Robert D. Graham made a speech of welcome and several other notables also spoke, including W. T. Woodson, Superintendent of Schools, speaking on the educational value of motion pictures, and former Senator John W. Rust and Senator Andrew W. Clarke. The full program included newsreels, comedies, and the feature, "Variety Girl," starring Bob Hope and Bing Crosby. The theater was fireproof, and air conditioning was promised for the following summer. Old residents who attended compared the modern talking film with the old silent films, which were shown by Norman Cobb at the Town Hall more than 20 years earlier.[55] The *Herald* had written in 1925: "Mr. Cobb deserves the support of the people of Fairfax and vicinity and it is hopeful that they will patronize his show instead of going into Washington to be amused."[56]

Discussion about the Town taking out liability insurance to protect it against any suits for damages resulted in Mayor Graham agreeing to get figures from his insurance company and report. Payment was later authorized for liability insurance premiums for the Town.[57]

Vehicles, both moving and parked, had caused endless problems during the decade. In addition to prohibiting the operation of automobile graveyards within the Town's boundaries,[58] the Council had written an official letter to the Fairfax County Board of

The Fairfax Theater opened in 1948 on Lee Highway near its intersection with Route 123 to a capacity crowd of about 1,500 people. Town and County officials were present for the occasion and Judge Paul E. Brown was Master of Ceremonies. Superintendent of Schools W. T. Woodson spoke on the educational value of motion pictures. Former Senator John W. Rust and Senator Andrew W. Clarke were also present. The film advertised on the marquee, West Side Story, *was released in 1961. The theater building is now used by Ourisman Fairfax Toyota. Courtesy of the artist, Jackie Cawley*

Supervisors asking that County employees park in the lot behind the Courthouse designated for the purpose, instead of on the Town streets.[59]

An ordinance had been passed in 1946 to require taxicab operators to buy permits with annual fees.[60] An ordinance effective in 1948 regulated vehicular parking on Little River Turnpike, Payne Street (now Chain Bridge Road), Mechanic Street (now University Drive), Sager Avenue, West Street, North Street (once known as "Lovers' Lane"), and East Street.[61] A parking meter manufacturer's representative demonstrated his company's equipment and the Council placed an order for meters. After they were installed and operating, a Town resident spoke in favor of the new parking meters, stating that they were "a real mark of progress in the Town."[62] Finally, a Town ordinance was adopted entitled "Traffic Code of the Town of Fairfax."[63] To complete the modern improvements, the Council agreed to request from the Virginia Department of Highways a stop-and-go light at the downtown intersection of Routes 123 and 236.[64] The request was denied in 1949 due to lack of sufficient traffic.

After Mavis Cobb and her brother, Norman Cobb, requested approval to receive sewer and water service for Cobbdale, a 90-acre subdivision just outside the town on Route 123 toward Oakton,[65] the Council realized that the volume of applications was so high, it was time to pass a subdivision ordinance. It had been urged by County Purchasing Agent R. M. Loughborough, who was working on the same ordinance for Fairfax County, that the Town Council consider the same action.[66] By December 1947, the Town ordinance was in readiness.[67]

It is easily understandable that a resolution was carried in Council that a Mayor's court be established for the purpose of enforcing all ordinances and codes of the Town, effective September 15, 1949.[68] In this duty he would be assisted by Deputy Town Sergeant H. F. Mayberry who had just been appointed in March. Two improvements were to be made: an emergency telephone was to be placed on an iron post near the Courthouse wall, and a radio was to be purchased and installed in the Town police car.[69]

Elvira and Marguerite Merigold must have been relieved when their request for a sewer tap for the Black Lantern Inn was granted in September 1949.[70] The very next month, a referendum was proposed for a bond issue of $300,000 to construct a sanitary sewer line on the Accotink Water Shed in the Town of Fairfax and for the construction of a modern disposal plant for the town. The ordinance was adopted on December 7, 1949, with a special election to be held on April 17, 1950.[71] The bond issue was approved.

The Virginia Department of Health and officials at Fort Belvoir were relieved because the old sewage plant had been depositing polluted effluent into

The Court House Market was built on the corner of Chain Bridge Road and School Street in 1948 by Warren "Chick" Morarity. It has served as a friendly neighborhood market ever since. Courtesy of the Fairfax County Public Library Photographic Archive

Accotink Creek, flowing down to Fort Belvoir's raw water intake. Better days were ahead.[72]

A rite of passage which had been experienced and enjoyed by young boys between the ages of 10 and 12 for decades was threatened with extinction at the December 1949 Council meeting. Local boys had been delighted to obtain a rifle of their very own to use for target practice and, later, for hunting small game for the dinner table. But with the growing congestion in the Town and the closer and closer proximity of the dwellings, it became a dangerous sport for the experienced and inexperienced alike. Citizens appeared to oppose the "pernicious" use of firearms by children of the Town. One resident stated that someone had shot a beebee through his window and he inquired what could be done about the unauthorized use of firearms in the Town.[73]

According to federal census figures, the population of the Town of Fairfax was 1,946 in 1950. Ten years later, the Town's population had multiplied seven times—to 14,045, including the newly annexed land, according to the City status order of June 30, 1961.

The Mayor and members of the Town Council were faced with a thousand and one problems and much of the time, they coped admirably and in a pleasant, friendly manner, as evidenced in the hundreds of pages of Town minutes which have been preserved in the Office of the City Clerk.[74] One of the necessary tasks was to have a survey of the Town made. Joseph Berry's firm completed field work on the requested survey for a map of the official Town boundaries in 1951. Necessary office space was rented in the new firehouse for the police department, the town clerk and a council chamber.[75]

A letter was read to the Council from the University of Virginia relative to the proposed new Town charter. The University of Virginia was requested by letter to assist in the preparation of a new charter for the Town of Fairfax. After two years, the Council in a special meeting decided to try to amend the old charter rather than adopt the new one which was severely criticized in the meeting.[76]

There were numerous questions that the Mayor and Councilmen had to answer over the years. They included applications for subdivisions, acceptance of private streets into the Town's street system, public bus transportation, street lights, sidewalks, walkways, school property safety, water supply, sewage disposal, trash and garbage removal, auto speed control, and street repairs. With increasing interest in business and commercial development, the Council joined the Chamber of Commerce with a $100 donation in 1954.[77]

Discussions continued for months while the Council came to agreement concerning the subdivision ordinance. It was eventually released for publication in the *Fairfax Herald* for four consecutive weeks in May 1953.[78]

An ordinance was adopted establishing a town planning commission.[79] Another ordinance set speed limits based on the State Highway Department's recommendations. Townspeople were concerned with the frequent speeding of cars and trucks through the Town.[80] Because of the possibility that in the future, Fairfax County might levy an automobile license tax on Town residents, the Council adopted a motor vehicle license ordinance for the Town.[81] A department of streets was established by ordinance to service the approximately 15 miles of paved streets within the Town's corporate limits. Those streets had been

maintained in part by the Virginia Department of Highways funds to defray costs at the annual rate of $300 per mile.[82]

Ordinances and codes were adopted to regulate activities in the Town. Among them were: the building code[83] and the zoning ordinance. Edgar Prichard was appointed zoning administrator and later chairman of the board of zoning appeals.[84] Ordinances were adopted to award the franchise to Virginia Electric and Power Company to furnish electric power and maintain the electric system in the Town[85] and the franchise to Washington Gas Light to supply natural gas to the Town.[86] When measurement of water consumption became necessary, the Council directed that water meters be installed on all of the Town wells to establish a system of records.[87]

The Town Council approved the Town's planning commission request that the Fairfax County board of supervisors include the Town of Fairfax in its master plan at no cost to the town. It was reported at the Council meeting of May 5, 1954, that the Fairfax County board of supervisors agreed to include the Town of Fairfax in its master plan as long as it did not delay completion of the County master plan.[88]

Planning consultant Francis Dodd McHugh for the County and Herbert Schumann of the County planning office were present in November to ask for suggestions before they began the master plan for the Town, which they believed should include:

(1) Highways in relation to the Town;
(2) A study of the downtown, including off-street parking;
(3) A future general land use plan;
(4) Public incentive facilities such as parks and schools;
(5) A plan for a water supply.[89]

In an unusual announcement, Mayor John C. Wood paid tribute to Councilman Albert R. Sherwood and expressed the appreciation of the Council for his 41 years of service during which Sherwood had missed only five meetings. A bronze plaque was ordered with an inscription to honor Mr. Sherwood's services.[90]

In response to a request by Bill Sheads on behalf of the Fairfax volunteer fire department, the Council appropriated $3,834 toward the purchase of a new ambulance for the rescue squad in 1956.[91] As the business of the Town continued to increase, the Council deemed it necessary to upgrade the position of Town engineer to a new designation of Town manager. The job description had yet to be prepared, but Glenn Saunders, Jr., was appointed the first to serve in that position, as of September 1, 1956.[92]

Examples of other Town concerns addressed by the Council included a plethora of actions. The group entered into the Virginia Retirement System in 1952 in order to participate in Title II of the Social Security Act for the employees of the Town.[93] In 1955, the

The Chilla-Villa Motel on Route 50 in Fairfax was advertised in the 1950s as being "new and extremely modern." The owners and operators were Mr. and Mrs. P. E. Myers and Donald Myers. Numerous other motels have been built since between Fairfax Circle and Kamp Washington. Courtesy of Randolph Lytton

Council decided to bond the Town treasurer for faithful performance of duty as well as for honesty.[94]

The Fairfax Cemetery Association and Council agreed in 1960 to turn the operation of the Fairfax Cemetery over to the Town which would operate it under a division of cemeteries and parks.[95] In the same year, the names of two important streets were changed. North East Street came Old Lee Highway and Schuerman Road became Pickett Road.[96]

In addition to the many relatively small housekeeping chores that took up the Town Council's meeting time between 1950 and 1961, there were four major concerns which exerted strong influences on the future development of the Virginia town. They were schools, the water supply, the sewer treatment plant, and a vital annexation suit.

During the decade of 1951-1961, services in the Fairfax County public schools were increased. Homebound-student teachers and classroom teachers increased with the school population. Special teachers in art, music, reading, speech, science, foreign languages and psychological services, provided expansion in the overall school program. The Belle Willard School in the Town of Fairfax, constructed in 1957, served the orthopedically disabled children in grades 1 to 8. After considerable study by County organizations working with the school board and staff, the decision was made to reorganize from seven grades of elementary school and five of high school (7-5), to six grades of elementary, two of intermediate, and four of high school (6-2-4). This plan was implemented in the school year 1960-61 with the opening in Fairfax County of nine new 1,000-student intermediate schools for grades 7 and 8.[97]

The yearbook or annual of Fairfax High, *Fare Fac Sampler*, was well-designed. Awards won by the publication during 1953 were the National Scholastic Press First Place Honor Rating and the Honor Award from the Southern Scholastic Press Association. This latter award was the highest award received by a Fairfax County school.[98]

The 1954 edition of the *Sampler* had a double-page dedication to Philip James Fuller, long-time chairman of the Music Department and Fairfax High bandmaster, for his inspiration, encouragement, friendship to the students and faculty and his fostering of respect and pride in Fairfax High School. There were 1800 students, grades 8 to 12, at Fairfax High in 1954. Steel quonset huts provided the necessary extra classroom space.[99]

Dorothy Farnham Feuer was a musician who lived in the Town of Fairfax. She was a fine violinist who wanted to play in a community orchestra. Since there was no such organization in the Town or County at the time, she and other members of the Fairfax Woman's Club, music teachers in the schools, and adult musicians in the community worked together. She founded the Fairfax Symphony Orchestra in 1956, with Philip Fuller as its first conductor. Later, the Northern Virginia Youth Orchestra was founded in her honor, and a number of Fairfax High musicians have enjoyed the opportunity to play with the talented group.[100] Her work helped to stimulate string programs in the public schools.

In an effort to forestall the integration of public schools in Virginia, open to all students, a Virginia constitutional convention met on March 5, 1956. Members voted unanimously to legalize tuition grants. The name of the movement, "Massive Resistance," came from a statement by Harry F. Byrd that "massive resistance is the best course for us to take." Fairfax County citizens organized to "Save Our Schools." In 1959, the Virginia Supreme Court of Appeals outlawed the public school closings that resulted from massive resistance and ordered that the State must support free schools, including those which were integrated.[101]

A 1957 fiscal summary demonstrated with pie-charts the County's tax dilemma of the times: all real estate and personal property taxes collected by Fairfax County represented 62.9 percent of its total revenues; the school system represented 63 percent of its total expenditures.[102] In regard to higher education, the Town expressed its strong wishes more than once. In 1954, the Council resolved that the Town of Fairfax go on record as being in favor of the Board of Supervisors of Fairfax County buying the Willard tract and the University of Virginia establishing an extension school there.[103] In 1954, a resolution was approved to request funds from the state legislature for the university site.[104]

Even though the Town drilled a number of deep wells and leased others, water was still in short supply. Councilman Albert Sherwood suggested that the Council acquire approximately 10 acres of land somewhere on Difficult Run between Route 211 and Waples Mill, and thus endeavor to move into another watershed in 1952, for an adequate Town water supply.[105] In the meantime, the Council arranged to lease the well at the Fairfax Theatre on Lee Highway near Chain Bridge Road, which had a flow of approximately 160 gallons per minute. It was leased on a yearly basis at $50 per month by the Council.[106]

Ironically, there were times during each year when the Mayor and Town Council members had more water than they knew what to do with. That was when a gully-washer of a Virginia rainstorm flooded the streets, ditches and low places. In September 1952, storm drains were inadequate and water stood in deep puddles for some time after the heavens had opened up.[107]

The Town engineer was asked to write a letter in 1954 to the governing body of Falls Church to determine if Falls Church would furnish a water supply for Fairfax and, if so, under what conditions. A letter was promptly returned from the Falls Church Water Department proposing a choice of three plans to construct a water line from the City of Falls Church to Fairfax Circle. A study committee was appointed, but later the Council decided to continue its search elsewhere.[108]

Water usage was increasing for a new reason—swimming pools. The Town engineer was instructed in February 1955 to find out how the owners of the Anchorage Motel on Route 50 planned to fill a large swimming pool under construction on their property.[109] A few months later, the Fairfax Community Swimming Pool, a private corporation, requested that the Town permit the corporation initially to fill its pool free of charge. The Council decided that a fee of five dollars would be charged, regular water charges to be made after the first filling.[110]

Adoption in 1956 of an ordinance by the Council declared the expediency of borrowing the sum of $4,500,000 by the Town of Fairfax and the issuance of revenue bonds for the purpose of providing a supply of water. At that time, water came from several town wells. The water table in the area was dropping lower annually, and the health and welfare of the town required a new source of water. The new supply would soon be available from Goose Creek in Loudoun County. On April 5, 1956, the bond referendum was passed.[111] The Council determined that they should enter into signed agreements with the Board of Supervisors of Loudoun County and the Loudoun County Sanitation Authority regarding the Town's Goose Creek water project.[112]

A contract was awarded for building a dam and impounding reservoir for the Goose Creek Water Project to Lewis Construction Associates of Goldsboro, North Carolina for the price of $563,192. The estimated time for the job completion was 510 calendar days. The Mayor and Town Clerk were authorized to execute a contract with the Town of Herndon for the purpose of purchasing water from the Town of Fairfax.[113]

Still another arrangement had to be made. The Council wished to construct a certain portion of the transmission main along the right-of-way of the Washington & Old Dominion Railroad. The Town accepted and executed the easement agreement as proposed by the W&OD Railroad. Water filters at Goose Creek were to be used to purify 3,000,000 gallons per day.[114]

The proposal of Lewis Construction Associates for the construction of a canoe platform at the Goose

The Anchorage Motel and its grand swimming pool were built near Fairfax Circle on Routes 50, 29 and 211 in 1955. It was "state of the art" in motels of the period. Before TV and air conditioning had become generally available, it advertised on its postcards: "One of America's newest and most modern motels. Beautifully furnished and decorated. Fully 'air conditioned,' TV in each unit, tile baths, tubs and shower, wall-to-wall carpeting, filtered swimming pool, restaurant nearby." Courtesy of Randolph Lytton

Creek Dam for $300 was accepted. Thus a facility to make recreational use of the reservoir lake was made available in 1961.[115]

The Council contracted for a trunk sewer to be constructed along Accotink Creek to the Fairfax Pumping Station by S. J. Bell Construction Corporation for $44,719. No one outside the corporate limits of the Town of Fairfax was to be permitted to connect to this South Fork Interceptor Sewer until arrangements for financing additional sewage treatment facilities had been made.[116] The Town Manager reported on the inadequacy of the sewage treatment plant then in use. A new filter unit was authorized to be installed immediately and later used when the new treatment plant was built. A Council action authorized the Town Manager to apply for a partial federal grant for sewage treatment works under the Federal Water Pollution Control Act. If approved, the Town of Fairfax would pay the remaining cost of the approved project.[117]

In December 1956 the sewage treatment plant's capacity was 500,000 gallons per day. The pollution load in Accotink Creek affected the raw water supply at Fort Belvoir downstream. Contract No. 1 of the new Sewage Treatment Plant was awarded to the English Construction Company, at a cost of $69,700 for the new plant which had a capacity of 2,000,000 gallons per day. Building began in 1957 for this

Josiah S. Everly was founder of the Everly Funeral Home, a family business, in Fairfax. He was successor to E. W. Groff, whose residence and place of business on Main Street he purchased in 1946. Photo taken in 1955 courtesy of the Fairfax County Public Library Photographic Archive

facility with four times the capacity of the earlier one.[118] Eventually, due to environmental concerns, it became necessary to connect the sewer mains to the Lower Potomac Treatment Works near Telegraph Road and U.S. Route 1.[119]

Attorney John H. Rust, Sr., was directed by the Council in 1953 to investigate the question of annexation of additional land by the Town and to prepare a written report of his findings. Mr. Rust soon presented the report he had prepared entitled "Annexation—what it means to the Town of Fairfax." In 1958, adjacent territory proposed to be annexed by the Town of Fairfax contained 5,070.15 acres.[120]

The Town had been incorporated in 1892 with an area of 1,626 acres, and no land had been added since, although the population had tripled in the past seven years. The Town was almost completely built up, with little land remaining for expansion, and unless additional land was acquired, the Town would cease to grow. The little municipality was at the time providing water or sewerage service or both to 70 percent of the people living in the area sought to be annexed.[121]

The annexation suit of the Town of Fairfax was completed when a special court of three judges awarded the Town about 40 percent of the territory sought in the petition. The approved 2,224 acres included about 3,000 persons. All of the commercial property between Kamp Washington and Fairfax Circle was included.

The three-man court which heard the case included Judge Paul Brown, senior judge of the circuit court; Judge Hamilton Haas of Harrisonburg; and Judge Temple of Prince George County. Fairfax County was represented by Robert Fitzgerald, Commonwealth's

One of the earliest efforts at recycling materials involved collecting used newspapers and selling them by the pound to scrap merchants, who took a variety of used reusable materials for resale. During the 1950s, the Town of Fairfax, like many other local communities, had regular paper drives, modest proceeds from which benefitted Scout troops, citizens associations and other worthy causes. Courtesy of the City of Fairfax

Attorney, and Frank Ball of Arlington, and attorneys for the Town were Calvin Van Dyck and Edgar A. Prichard.[122]

Fairfax County lost its annexation defense when Virginia's Supreme Court of Appeals held that the best interests of the Town of Fairfax required the annexation, effective December 31, 1959.[123] On page 1 of the *Fairfax Herald* on January 8, 1960, the following letter from the Mayor was printed "above the fold":

WELCOME TO THE TOWN OF FAIRFAX

Dear Citizen: As of January 1, 1960, you will be a resident of the Town of Fairfax. On behalf of the Town Council and administrative officials of the Town, I want to take this opportunity to welcome you. We are proud of our Town and its past history and accomplishments. With your help, we can expect even greater things in the future. Once again, welcome to the Town of Fairfax. Sincerely, John C. Wood

A new government center for the Town of Fairfax was being seriously considered in May 1960, and a loan of $15,000 was secured from the Community Relations Administration for preliminary planning. The new building was expected to cost about $600,000, and the town hoped to start building in about six months or as soon as the necessary funds were raised.[124]

On May 3, 1961, the Town Attorney was "instructed to institute and prosecute in the name of and for the Town of Fairfax, any and all legal proceedings necessary to have the Town declared by proper decree of the Circuit Court of Fairfax County to be a community of five thousand (5,000) population or more, and further declared to be a City of the Second Class." It became an independent City of the Second Class on July 1, 1961.[125] A regular meeting of the City Council of the City of Fairfax was held on July 5, 1961. The City Engineer presented the bids for the new City Hall. The contract went to E. H. Glover, Inc.; the bid was $587,570.[126]

Like many children her age, Karen Ann Moore of Westmore enjoyed riding on special occasions at Bernie's Pony Ring at Fairfax Circle. Shown in the background of this 1960 photo are the Howard Johnson's Restaurant on the hill and the Esso station. The Texaco station is still there. A McDonald's occupies Bernie's property now. Photo by Glenn Moore, courtesy of the Fairfax County Public Library Photographic Archive

Some City of Fairfax Churches

Christ Lutheran Church
3810 Meredith Drive

Church of the Apostles
3500 Pickett Road

Congregation Ahavat Israel
9932 Main Street

Fairfax Baptist Church
10830 Main Street

Fairfax Christian Church
10185 Main Street

Fairfax Kingdom Hall of Jehovah's Witnesses
3701 Jermantown Road

Fairfax Presbyterian Church
10723 Main Street

Fairfax United Methodist Church
10300 Stratford Avenue

First Church of Christ, Scientist
3725 Old Lee Highway

Greater Pentecostal Temple of Christ, Bible Way, W.W.
4340 Ox Road

Mount Calvary Baptist Church
4325 Chain Bridge Road

Northern Virginia Mennonite Church
3729 Old Lee Highway

St. Leo the Great Catholic Church
3700 Old Lee Highway

Truro Episcopal Church
10520 Main Street

Fairfax Baptist Church

Fairfax Presbyterian Church

Fairfax United Methodist Church

Mount Calvary Baptist Church

St. Leo the Great Catholic Church

Truro Episcopal Church

© City of Fairfax 1973

The City Seal, adopted in 1973, was designed by the College of Arms, London, England, as a result of the work of the 11-member City Seal Commission chaired by Will Carroll. The soldier in the seal represents Captain John Quincy Marr, the first Civil War officer casualty, who was killed in the skirmish at Fairfax Courthouse in 1861. The English character represents Thomas, 6th Lord Fairfax, from whom the City derives its name. The main body of the shield is that of the family of the Lords Fairfax of Cameron; the lion symbolizes the defending of the City; and "Fare Fac", meaning "speak-do" (or "say it and do it") is the motto of the Fairfax family. The griffin, half eagle and half lion, symbolizes the founding of the Virginia Colony by England and the alliance between America and England. The griffin's seated position is emblematic of a democratic people seated in Council amicably settling their mutual problems. Courtesy of the City of Fairfax

7.

From Sleepy Town to Vibrant Small City, 1961-1968

by Peggy Talbot Wagner

The Town of Fairfax had been "moving steadily towards city status"[1] for at least ten years. As early as June, 1957, the Town Council had hired New York consultants to begin an annexation study which included a component regarding possible city status. That study resulted ultimately in court approval of the annexation of 2,224 acres of County land, more than doubling the Town's area and increasing its population to 11,500. Thus began the emergence of the City of Fairfax and the beginning of a decade when two strong leaders—Mayors John C. Wood, favoring independence, and Edgar A. Prichard, supporting regional cooperation,—would define and influence the issues that determined the City's course far into the future.

The irony of the competition between these two leaders was the number of parallels in their lives and careers. Both received their law degrees at the University of Virginia Law School and subsequently came to Fairfax to practice law. Both served as president of the Fairfax Bar Association; both were City Council members and both were elected Mayor; both were members of the George Mason University Board of Visitors, and both served as Rector; both were members of the GMU Foundation; both were members of boards of the same two banks; and both were members of Truro Episcopal Church.[2]

Simultaneously, both Falls Church and Alexandria were initiating annexation suits against Fairfax County. Beleaguered by the prospect of a continuing fragmentation of its territories by smaller jurisdictions,

the County began exploring the possibility of consolidation with Clifton to form a city which, under Commonwealth of Virginia law, would be legally immune from annexations. Such a move would swallow up Fairfax and neighboring towns into the vast, largely undeveloped Fairfax County.[3]

The Town Council, led by Mayor Wood, began a campaign to preserve the Town's political integrity and its ample assets which had been paid for by Town residents. Mayor Wood had a vision of a "tax-free zone" for the Town residents, that would be financed by the sale of utilities and other types of venture funds.[4] The construction by the Town in the mid-1950s of a dam and modern water treatment plant at

John C. Wood, the first Mayor of the City of Fairfax and earlier Mayor of the Town of Fairfax, served a total of 11 years (1953-1964) in that office. His major accomplishments were establishing the City's water supply system; achieving the City's independent status; ensuring the City's economic stability; and influencing the location of George Mason University at the City's southern border. Mayor Wood died in August, 1994. Courtesy of the City of Fairfax

The City Hall, located at 10455 Armstrong Street, was completed in 1962. A construction contract was awarded on July 5, 1961, at the City Council's first meeting after receiving City status. Courtesy of the City of Fairfax

Goose Creek in Loudoun County at a cost of $4.5 million and a subsequent expansion program were important steps toward realizing Mayor Wood's dream. The Town also enjoyed "one of the healthiest tax bases in the area."[5] "The Town Council felt that Fairfax residents would not have an adequate voice in the proposed city, and that the Town's assets would be spread throughout the new city instead of benefiting only the citizens of the Town of Fairfax."[6] The only legally available option to protect Town interests was to seek city status.[7] The Town Council, through a unanimous resolution adopted on May 3, 1961, instructed the Town Attorney to pursue legal proceedings toward the Town's status as a city of the second class.[8]

The Fairfax County Board already had announced its intention to become a city by merging with Clifton, a move that would have resulted in the second largest city in the United States. Circuit Court Judge Paul E. Brown signed the court order authorizing the County and Clifton to proceed with steps toward a consolidation referendum. Following directions adopted by the Town Council on June 21, 1961, (with an abstention by Councilman Prichard)[9], the Town Attorney appeared before the same judge to obtain city status for the Town. The Court entered the order June 30, 1961. Fairfax County had lost its bid to guarantee its territorial integrity, and Fairfax Town had become a City of the Second Class."[10] Frank Gooding, Deputy Circuit

Court Clerk, did not report immediately the filing of the documents. Finally learning of the documents, Ann Wilkins, Chairman of the Board of Supervisors, was provoked that the Supervisors had not been notified immediately. When asked by reporters why he had failed to notify the Board earlier of the papers, Gooding replied, "Nobody asked me."[11]

On July 5, 1961, at the first City Council meeting, voting precincts were established, three people were appointed to the City's School Board, and a contract was awarded for building the new City Hall to be located on City-owned property on Armstrong Street. In the August meeting, the new City Council determined a list of services to be contracted with the County to supplement those already provided by the City.

The City, when a Town guided by Mayor Wood, had invested in substantial infrastructure and had in place an impressive public works program run by a small staff. Since 1957, the Town had operated its own refuse collection and street construction, resurfacing and sweeping programs. The Goose Creek Water Supply Project in Loudoun County, approved in 1957 and nearing completion, allowed a yield of 3.5 million gallons of water per day.[12] The project would supply water to the City as well as the Town of Herndon and the Loudoun County Sanitation Authority—a profitable proprietary arrangement. A new sewage treatment plant with a capacity of two million gallons per day located on Pickett Road was completed in 1958, and 57 miles of sanitary sewer lines were in operation

The City's Goose Creek Reservoir in Loudoun County, Virginia, approved in 1957 and completed in the early 1960s under Mayor Wood's leadership, has a 200-million gallon capacity. Courtesy of the City of Fairfax

Contractors laying water pipeline along the south side of Main Street (Route 236) across from Railroad Avenue in conjunction with the widening of Route 236 in the late 1960s. Courtesy of the City of Fairfax

Shown in March, 1954, the City's two-million gallon sewage treatment plant was completed in 1958. The sewage treatment plant was formerly located on Pickett Road at the site of the present-day City Property Yard. The City abandoned its sewage treatment plant in the late 1960s when it joined the area-wide sewage treatment program with Fairfax County. The photo left shows the chlorine contact tank in the right foreground and Pickett Road just beyond the building. The photo right shows the trickling filter in front of the building and old Pickett Road in the wooded area to the left. Courtesy of the City of Fairfax

by 1961. By 1975, 90 miles of sewer lines were in place.[13] Police and volunteer fire protection, snow removal, street lighting and street signs were provided. An administrative staff of only seven individuals oversaw all programs except fire protection for the community of almost 15,000 people.

Although the new City was surprisingly well prepared to take on its new responsibilities, there were a number of functions that, costwise, would be beyond the financial capability of a small jurisdiction. The Council had decided to continue with the Fairfax County school system on a tuition per pupil basis until permanent arrangements could be made. Additionally, court functions; sheriff and jail; maintenance for school buildings and grounds; public assistance and welfare; health; library; fire protection to complement the volunteer program; and sanitary land fill were services only a large government organization with substantial resources could provide readily, and many of them were not permitted by State Code to be undertaken by a city of the second class.[14] On October 4, 1961, the City contracted with the County for these services, which were estimated to cost less than $50,000.[15]

In subsequent meetings, the Council approved additional equipment and projects for the public works operation, refined the water and sewer systems, initiated the study of a separate school system and

approved rezonings.[16] The application of American Oil Company to rezone to Industrial over 116 acres of land bordered by Little River Hills subdivision on the west and Pickett Road on the east was opposed substantially by City residents, nearby Mantua Subdivision in Fairfax County and the Fairfax County School Board. The rezoning would allow the development of an oil storage and distribution facility by four oil companies, American Oil Company, Texaco, Gulf Oil and Cities Service.

The Planning Commission unanimously recommended approval to the City Council, and fifteen days later, the tank farm rezoning, with a two-acre reduction in size, was unanimously approved by the City Council. The Council would spend the next year fighting a suit challenging the rezoning filed jointly by Little River Hills, Mantua Subdivision, the Fairfax County Board of Supervisors and the Fairfax County School Board.

The court action, referred to as "an intensive year-long war which has been waged against the oil tanks"[17] featured expert testimony. Mantua Subdivision alone raised a $5,000 war chest to finance full-page newspaper ads, a "satirical Oil Dump Coloring Book"[18] and helicopter flyovers to photograph the tank farm site and surrounding residential areas. Opponents to the tank farm alleged "the City rushed into the zoning in a desperation move to broaden its tax base."[19] They

This 1956 GMC foam unit truck was owned by the Pickett Road tank farm until after the mid-1960s when it was donated to the City of Fairfax Fire Department. The trailer attached to the rear of the unit hauled booms that had to be manually raised to reach the top of tanks for spraying the fire-fighting foam, a fearful and dangerous operation. According to James E. Anderson, one of three paid battalion chiefs on the City's first career staff roster in 1977, this foam unit remained in service for about 10 years when it was sold in order to purchase a 1978 Seagrave model (subsequently sold and replaced by the current unit.) Courtesy of the City of Fairfax

concentrated the legal challenge on issues of incompatible use; adverse effects on nearby residential properties, including Fairfax County's W. T. Woodson High School; and safety and environmental dangers. Oil leakage was not mentioned. A raucous crowd applauded the final emotional arguments of the plaintiff's attorney, but Circuit Court Judge Albert V. Bryan, Jr. upheld the City's rezoning for the tank farm on the basis of the evidence he heard during the trial.[20]

The School Board, in 1963, was appointed to the dual role as Recreation Committee. A subcommittee was formed to administer all recreation programs and facilities and to explore and recommend specific sites for parks and playgrounds.[21] The committee's work resulted eventually in specific recommendations for the acquisition of park land, a program that was substantially furthered under Mayor Prichard's leadership in the mid-sixties. The active School Board also joined the Council in April, 1964, in a motion to acquire the necessary school buildings and begin the planning operation of the City's own education system.[22]

Action was initiated with VDOT in 1963 to widen the remaining two-lane portions of the east-west corridors, Routes 50 and 236. The Council also approved the construction of an extension of what is now University Drive from the center of the City to City Hall at Armstrong Street, a 30-foot wide 1,100-foot segment, at the cost of $10,000.[23]

Led by Mayor Wood, a resolution was adopted in 1963 requesting the Governor to facilitate the construction of George Mason College of the University of Virginia on land given by the City for that purpose. Citizens had committed $714,000 toward the establishment of the college to cover the cost of the acquisition of 150 acres of land located in the County at the City's southern boundary and provision of utilities to the site.[24] Mayor Wood expected the two-year liberal arts college to expand into a four-year college within a relatively short time.[25] The college opened on the donated land with a four-building complex in September, 1964, (shortly after Mayor Wood's term ended) with seven full-time and 18 part-time professors and 343 students. By 1966, George Mason became a four-year college as predicted, and the campus, in 1976, expanded to 600 acres in size. In this extraordinary educational venture, Mayor Wood was the trailblazer in the City's first successful economic development thrust.

In 1964, the Council authorized the sale of government bonds using sewage treatment plant funds, the water reserve fund and a loan from general funds for the purpose of financing the filter expansion at Goose Creek.[26] This was done with the help of a minor loan that was paid back before the end of the year.

Between April 17, 1963, when the apartment zone was approved, and August 19, 1964, 20 apartment projects were approved through rezonings. Most of these apartments remain today, rounding out the City's housing stock by providing economical housing.[27]

Edgar Prichard challenged Mayor Wood in a spirited election campaign in which some of the political issues resounded decades later. Generally, the competing political visions concerned the appropriate

The filter gallery at the Goose Creek water treatment plant in Loudoun County, Virginia. Courtesy of the City of Fairfax

Edgar A. Prichard served as the second Mayor of the City (1964-1968.) Mayor Prichard spearheaded the adoption of a formal planning program; guided significant public safety and road improvements; and furthered the acquisition of park lands and City-owned school facilities. Courtesy of the City of Fairfax

extent of the City's future cooperation and partnership with the County. Specific issues were the concept of maintaining the County's presence in the center of the City, the scope of the City's water service in the County, and the extent of the County's role in providing school services to City children.[28]

Councilman Edgar Prichard and an almost entirely new Council were elected to office in 1964. Mayor Prichard praised former Mayor Wood's service to the community but resolved that, in the future, the policy of the City would be to reconcile the City's many differences with the Fairfax County Board of Supervisors, to put the finishing touches on the multi-faceted contract with the County, and to continue the County's role in the operation of the City's schools, while at the same time adhering to the decision to purchase the school facilities themselves. The City Council and the new Mayor devoted themselves to these policies during Mayor Prichard's first term.[29]

In 1966, as a result of a controversial apartment rezoning proposal near Mosby Woods, the Council approved a compromise which included a new townhouse ordinance, as well as the townhouse development known as Cambridge Station. Shortly thereafter, the Council also approved Courthouse Square, on University Drive near City Hall, and The Mews, between University Drive and Chain Bridge Road. Other townhouse projects followed.[30]

Planning-related projects were high priorities of the Prichard administration. In 1964, "a uniform house numbering system was adopted by the City, which was coordinated with the system adopted at the same time by Fairfax County."[31] The first staff horticulturist was employed to oversee the City's beautification and landscaping program. The first Planning Director was

hired in October 1965, and a $10,000 contract was let with the County Planning Office for the preparation and printing of the first City Comprehensive Plan. The contract was later modified to include active participation by the City Planning staff and Planning Commission. The Planning Commission's recommended plan featured an inner beltway around the core of the City and an increase in land specified for multi-family use. These two features were removed when the City Council adopted a revised plan on June 18, 1968.[32]

The new Planning Department included the first full-time Zoning Administrator for administration and enforcement of the Zoning Ordinance. As part of the Zoning Ordinance revisions approved by the City Council on November 18, 1964, the Old and Historic Fairfax District was established in the center City, and the Board of Architectural Review was charged to foster appropriate construction of new structures and restoration or demolition of historic buildings in the new District. Flood plain regulations, which were adopted in 1965 to protect new construction from flooding, served additionally to preserve open space

Mayor Edgar A. Prichard and Ludlow "Pete" King, builder-developer, admire signage for Courthouse Square, the second townhouse project approved under the new Townhouse Ordinance adopted in January 1966. Located diagonally across from City Hall, the project featured 40 units at prices that have quintupled in value. Courthouse Square remains an attractive, well-kept community. Courtesy of the City of Fairfax

and set aside land for recreation, a goal that had become increasingly important to the City Council.[33]

In December 1965, the Council, with the help of Federal funds, acquired a 45-acre site for the first municipal park, located between Old Lee Hills and Little River Hills. The park was named Daniels Run for the creek running through its middle. The Council adopted a master plan for its development in 1967, and the park was later expanded to 48 acres.[34] By June of 1965, the City was operating seven summer playgrounds.[35] In Mayor Prichard's second term, a 13-acre site for park land on Old Lee Highway was acquired and development plans were created. The park, opened in July 1968, was named for the late Judge E. Calvin Van Dyck, former City Attorney. Its land area was increased in September 1968, through a land-swap that allowed an expansion of St. Leo's Church School.[36]

At the same time, private residential and commercial expansion was underway, keeping the City staff busy reviewing building permits and site plans. Construction of the apartment projects approved in Mayor Wood's two terms exceeded $2.5 million in value. Among the new commercial projects were a community shopping center, a 1,200-capacity theater and new bank administrative offices. Combined with school and church construction, new buildings in the City totaled $7.1 million in 1964-65. Commonwealth Doctor's Hospital, an 80-bed medical and surgical hospital with an expansion capability of 400 beds, approved by the Board of Zoning Appeals in October, 1964, was completed in 1967.[37]

A controversial agreement, later known as the "Peace Treaty," to resolve outstanding issues with Fairfax County, was approved unanimously by Council in April 1965, and endorsed by the School Board.[38] The agreement included an area-wide sewage treatment program allowing abandonment of the City's own treatment plant by 1968; retention of the County's government facility in the center of the City; and alternatives for City or County operation of the school system with the purchase of five County-owned schools within the City boundaries. The package required a payment of an estimated $4.9 million to Fairfax County subject to a referendum regarding City acquisition and operation of schools. Former Mayor Wood opposed the agreement and ran for Mayor as a write-in candidate in May 1966. Mayor Prichard was reelected by a margin of 100 votes.[39] The issues were

Workmen install the sewage lift station to serve the School Street area in the late 1960s. The station lifted sewage by way of a force main to the City's gravity system. Courtesy of the City of Fairfax

settled, at least temporarily, by referendum in July 1966, when voters rejected both bond referendums for acquisition and City operation of schools and school construction by a better than two-to-one vote.

The first City-built and owned school, already completed in the spring of 1965, was John C. Wood Elementary School, named for the former Mayor.[40] The school, located on Old Lee Highway, was planned as a 16-room, campus-style building to serve over 400 students with an expansion capacity of up to 600.[41] Although initially there were insufficient funds to construct a cafeteria, a tax windfall enabled by a semiannual tax collection policy permitted its construction in 1965. Still another addition to the school was approved by the City Council in 1967. In October of that year, the County Board of Supervisors agreed to sell to the City the one-year-old Jermantown Elementary School. The building sat on 11.6 acres of land that increased the City's recreational capability by providing additional playing fields.[42] The City now owned three schools, since the Fairfax Elementary School had been transferred to the City earlier.

As a prelude to Fairfax County's condemnation and/or purchase of land surrounding the County Courthouse to accommodate its new government complex, the City instituted a moratorium on all rezonings in the area.[43] This fact angered property owners, who claimed the zoning freeze depressed the market value of their land. Colonel Edward Offley, an "89-year-old retired Cavalry officer, last owner of what was originally the Richard Radcliffe [sic.] farm . . . threatened suit against the county when his application for a change of zoning from residential to commercial was turned down."[44] Fairfax County had also threatened Colonel Offley with a condemnation, but the parties eventually reached an out-of-court agreement on the five-acre property resulting in its peaceful transfer to the County.

The January 1966 agreement ceded the center City land to Fairfax County for its government center and guaranteed that the County government would remain in the City. The County gained jurisdictional rights in the property area within the "hole in the center of the donut." Everything that occurs within City boundaries around the "hole" is controlled by the City, including construction and maintenance of public infrastructure.[45] The agreement included the County's legal authority to approve land use, zoning and construction standards in the middle of an area of the City crucial to the success of its economic viability, the preservation and enhancement of its historic properties, its streets and traffic circulation. The County's first use of this authority was to plan and construct a 13-story administrative tower on the property.

The continuance in the City of the County government facilities attracted construction employees, a large County work force and legal professionals who would patronize City shops, restaurants and services, spawning the need for additional construction and renovation work. As the size of the County work force outgrew the available space, City buildings were rented for the spill-over needs. All these spin-off activities boosted the City's economy. Retaining the County government center would continue to have a far-reaching effect on the City's future, as would the area-wide sewage treatment program, another facet of the 1965 City-County agreement. The new County sewage facilities treated the combined sewage of the Accotink and Pohick watersheds, allowing the abandonment of upstream plants, including the City two-million-gallons-per-day treatment plant built in 1958.

The 13-story Massey Building on Chain Bridge Road, completed in September 1969, served as Fairfax County's administrative center until May 12, 1992, when the new Fairfax County Government Center opened in Fair Oaks. The Massey Building now houses the Fairfax County Public Safety offices. Courtesy of the City of Fairfax

The 1965 agreement finally resolved the "border war over water service"[46] that resulted from the litigation against the County concerning service to Reston. It was agreed that the County would purchase water directly from the City for provision to Reston for a limited number of years. In addition, the City supplied water to Herndon residents and, by wholesale contract, to the Fairfax County Water Authority and the Loudoun County Sanitation Authority. In May 1965, the voters approved the sale of water bonds for the expansion of water storage at the dam site on Goose Creek, and a month later construction started on the 3.5-mile-long water main on Main Street between Pickett Road and Jermantown Road.[47] By 1995, 172 miles of water main lines would be in place, 80 percent of which were installed before 1973.[48] A little over a year later, another water bond was issued to supplement Federal funds for another expansion of the system. This project, a 1.3 million gallon reservoir and a new pumping station along Beaver Creek in Loudoun County, was initiated to avoid future water shortages such as the one the previous summer that had resulted in a water shortage for City residents and other customers.[49]

Concurrently, the City was addressing the deficient road system. Improvements to Lee Highway and

The water treatment plant and settling ponds in Loudoun County are key parts of the City-owned water system serving City residents and other customers. Courtesy of the City of Fairfax

portions of Chain Bridge Road began in 1965, enabling the roads to serve as arterial connections to Interstate Route 66. Lee Highway was widened to four lanes with a landscaped median strip, turning lanes and new signalization. The traffic pattern at Fairfax Circle, the highest accident location in the City, was improved by a change in the traffic pattern and installation of traffic signals. The City's share of the cost of these projects was 15 percent, with State and Federal funds covering the balance.[50] To enhance safety on the roads, a street lighting program was initiated with plans to expand the system annually until all commercial areas were lighted.

Widening to four lanes was approved for a two-mile segment of Main Street, from Old Lee Highway to the western edge of the City. Grave concerns were expressed by the Fairfax County Historic Landmarks Preservation Commission. The proposal would bring the highway within ten feet of the historic Courthouse, built in 1800. "All the trees would go and there would be a 15-foot high wall with a sidewalk on top between the Courthouse and the highway. It would stick up like Mount Everest,"[51] claimed Bayard Evans, Chairman of the Commission. Although the Virginia Department of Transportation was asked to use State

funds to build a bypass around the historic section of the City, construction proceeded instead with the widening.[52] This problem was mitigated later by the construction of a one-way pair (eastbound traffic only on Main Street and westbound traffic only on North Street) around the historic downtown area that slightly reduced the width of Main Street adjacent to the Courthouse.

By the mid-1960s, the City's population had grown to over 22,000 people and vehicular traffic had increased dramatically. These increases necessitated changes in the public safety program to meet public needs. The police department, which almost doubled in size in the mid-1960s, underwent an overhaul. Obsolete vehicles and uniforms were replaced, and an intensified training program was inaugurated. New radio and direct telephone communication systems were provided, serving both the City and nearby jurisdictions.

At the same time, the Volunteer Fire Department, having occupied its new headquarters station on University Drive in May 1965, installed a telephone alerting system. Special equipment was installed in the homes of volunteer firemen through which fire warnings could be transmitted from the central fire control

The 1964 Police Department poses with (top row, left to right) City Manager William M. Zollman, Jr., Council members Philip D. Fisher, Ruth G. Bradford and A. Howell Thomas, Mayor E. A. Prichard and Council members Arthur J. Lamb, John W. Russell and George A. Hamill. Serving a population of over 22,000, the Police Department was upgraded with intensified training and new public safety equipment and had nearly doubled in size by the mid-1960s. Courtesy of the City of Fairfax

headquarters, thus virtually eliminating the use of audible sirens. The services of a County Fire Marshal were acquired by contract with the County, permitting more fire prevention activity. A regular training program was provided by the Fairfax County Fire Training Center.[53]

In February 1968, after serving two terms, Mayor Prichard announced that he would not stand for reelection. He said he was convinced that the "City was well established, had mended relations with Fairfax County and was on the path of sound fiscal and personnel policies."[54] During his tenure, he had not collected his annual $5,000 salary as Mayor nor his stipends as a Council member because he considered the jobs part of his service to the City.[55] His "Clean Slate" Council had accomplished the stated goals of its original campaign and had been awarded recognition by the League of Women Voters for facilitating participation of citizens in their government through the use of regular newsletter mailings

and improved communication measures at City Council meetings.[56]

At its last meeting in 1968, the City Council adopted an amended version of the Comprehensive Plan initiated in 1965. The Council had deleted a key provision—the inner beltway that was proposed to bypass the center city. Further, almost all the land designated for apartment development in an earlier Planning Commission version had been deleted in favor of a lower density residential designation, a move that was expected to reduce future population densities by up to 4,000 persons. Both actions favored protection of the single family neighborhoods from intrusion by roads and high density development.[57]

George Hamill was elected mayor on June 11, 1968, after a low-key campaign.[58] Through his term and those of mayors to follow, the City continued to build on the foundation well laid by its first two leaders and to fluctuate between their respective policies of total independence and regionalism.

Fire fighting equipment with volunteer firefighters outside Fire Station #3, which opened on January 16, 1965. Courtesy of the City of Fairfax

Officer Rita M. Marinoble became the first woman to join the City's 47-member police force in July, 1972. After training at the Northern Virginia Police Academy, Officer Marinoble served in the Police Department for a few years. Courtesy of the City of Fairfax

Firefighters tow an old fire pumper wagon in the 1992 Independence Day Parade. Courtesy of the City of Fairfax

Fire Station 33 on Lee Highway and Volunteer Fire Station 3 on University Drive were both significantly upgraded and expanded to meet current needs as part of the 1993 bond issue referendum. Each station can now accommodate female firefighters in private quarters. Fire Station 3 was expanded to include administrative offices for the career Fire Chief, his administrative staff and the volunteer officers. Courtesy of the City of Fairfax

This aerial photograph shows special equipment owned by the City of Fairfax in the 1960s. Shown from left, clockwise, are a pumper truck, cherry picker, crane, street sweeper, sanitation truck, road grader, pick-up truck, police car, paint striping machine and police van. Courtesy of the City of Fairfax

8.

The Changing Face of the City, 1968-1978
by Peggy Talbot Wagner

By 1968, the City's population had grown so rapidly that elected officials focused much of their effort on deciding what kind of a community the City should be and how it should look. The planning efforts set the stage for a confrontation between the goals of the development industry and the desires of many homeowners, whose views were in stark contrast. The years between 1974 and 1978 saw a resurgence of the zeal for City independence that Mayor John C. Wood had kindled in the City's first years. The champions of this citizen movement were a Council majority and a Mayor who boldly defied Fairfax County and the region to pursue the independent policies they thought best for the City. In the end, though, the silent majority voiced its opinion with votes, and the political pendulum swung again toward a cooperative relationship with its next-door neighbor, Fairfax County, and the region, the philosophy that had been espoused by Mayor Edgar A. Prichard.

In the June election of 1968, George Hamill was elected mayor in a contest in which there were no divisive campaign issues. Mayor Hamill's first term was marked by many ceremonial events over which he presided with a flair and a smile, and with the creation of important advisory committees.

The City Council in February 1969, appointed a Policy Advisory Committee headed by Dr. C. Barrie Cook. The Committee's final product, Community Goals Study, was to address a full range of City concerns to ensure that the City's short-range program was consistent with long-term goals. In December

George A. Hamill, Mayor from 1968-1970, fostered citizen participation through the establishment of a Policy Advisory Committee that produced a long-range Community Goals Study and permanent advisory committees serving the Mayor and City Council. Courtesy of the City of Fairfax

Councilman Henry A. Minor, the City's first black councilman, was elected in 1968 and served until March, 1970, when he moved from the City to nearby Vienna. Courtesy of the City of Fairfax

The old Mount Calvary Baptist Church, shown in this photo, was located along Chain Bridge Road opposite Armstrong Street. It was demolished in 1967. Courtesy of the City of Fairfax

1970, after 70 citizens had spent 4,500 man hours in preparation, a goals statement was released supporting moderately priced housing, a City welfare department and regional health programs. Rapid transit, the acquisition of additional park sites and stream beds, and a community school system were also highlighted.

During Mayor Hamill's first term, in addition to the initiation of the Policy Advisory Committee, the Economic Development Committee and the Park and Recreation Advisory Board were created. The Mayor said he had promised more citizen involvement through active advisory committees and said that he was "proud of our record of 8 specific promises made and 7 fulfilled,"[1] as he announced that he was running for a second term. Other achievements, he said, were continued leadership in school matters; continued cooperation with Fairfax County; staff study of all aspects of the City-County Agreement; and increased support of the City Fire Department, among others. In

a three-way race with Nathaniel F. Young and Walter J. Stephens, Jr., in early June 1970, Mayor Hamill was reelected.

In a surprise move eight days after the election, Mayor Hamill resigned. He explained, "I just goofed when I decided to run. I should not have done it . . . the city is not going to suffer, the citizens elected a good council. . . . Both my business and my family have suffered from my political career and . . . I just threw my hands up and called it quits."[2]

Councilman John Russell, who had seniority on the City Council, was appointed to replace Mayor Hamill after a lengthy and well-attended Council session. A crowd of about 100 citizens cheered when Russell was appointed at 10:30 p.m.[3]

In February 1972, Miller and Smith, a northern Virginia development firm, filed an application to rezone the 35-acre parcel known as the Disc tract, formerly part of the Willard family's Layton Hall

John W. Russell served as Mayor from 1970-1974 and again in 1982 and 1983, when he was elected to the Virginia Senate. Under his leadership, the Council voted to increase the funds for capital improvements in the schools. Courtesy of the City of Fairfax

estate, bordered by four streets (University Drive, Layton Hall Drive, Old Lee Highway and North Street). About 120 residents, organized as the "Citizens for a Sensible City," opposed the rezoning.[4] Supported by the group of citizens opposing the Disc rezoning, a slate known as Fairfax Citizens for a Livable City (FCLC) announced candidacy for five Council positions. Mayor Russell announced for reelection with the incumbent Council. The campaign issues centered around the Center City Plan, the Planned Development Ordinance and the Disc tract development. When the election was over, the six incumbent Councilmen had been defeated. The five Livable City candidates, plus Nat Young, who ran outside the slate, were elected along with incumbent Mayor Russell, who ran unopposed.

John T. (Til) Hazel, attorney for Miller and Smith, withdrew the Disc tract rezoning application. He then submitted a plan for a 10-acre shopping center with buildings and pavement covering about 95 percent of the site, a plan that was permitted by right under the site's current commercial zoning. The plan was opposed by some of the new Councilmen, and by late November, the new plan was also abandoned. The developers then approached the City Council with a modified mixed-use application for Council approval.[5] Despite the applicant's meeting and even exceeding recommendations, the Council was split down the middle on the issue. The Mayor declined to participate. Without the Mayor to break the tie, the rezoning application failed on a tie vote.

That same night, the City Council adopted a three-month building moratorium to allow the Center City Plan to be completed. Lindsay Santmire, the Planning Director, told reporters, "The moratorium ordinance will require them (Miller and Smith) to go before the council for a building permit . . . But they could go in and cut trees and start grading the land while they are waiting for a building permit."[6]

Within a day, a demolition crew began felling trees. Frantic meetings called by City officials were held to persuade the developers to stop the clearing and rethink their application; 85 percent of the site was cleared of trees.[7] It was agreed that the developers would halt further tree cutting and the Council would consider the matter again. On December 19, the Council unanimously voted to deny the application resubmitted by the disgruntled developers in its

This cartoon appeared on December 14, 1972, in the Virginia Sentinel *after the Disc Tract, formerly part of the Willard family's Layton Hall Estate, was stripped of trees despite the City's objections. The well-known northern Virginia attorney, John T. "Til" Hazel, represented the developers, Miller and Smith, who were frustrated at City Council's denial of the project after they had substantially reduced the density of the planned commercial and residential development to meet Planning Commission conditions. Graphic from* Virginia Sentinel

Payne's Boarding House, located on the northwest corner of Chain Bridge Road and Judicial Drive (formerly Jones Street), as it appeared in July 1967, before it was demolished. It is remembered that unmarried women school teachers boarded in this house. Courtesy of the City of Fairfax

original version. The development on the Disc tract, however, took years to finalize. The Disc tract eventually was developed as Courthouse Plaza Shopping Center.[8]

An 11-member Center City Commission headed by Peter Max recommended that the center city be designated predominantly for office and retail uses with its outer rim devoted to residential, transitional uses. The Center City Plan eventually was adopted in a modified version in May 1973. However, the rezoning controversies continued.

A number of hearings had yielded no decision concerning a mixed-use development proposal for the Orr property on Old Lee Highway across from the Army Navy Country Club. The Orr tract rezoning— Great Oaks—was approved after extensive plan tweaking and intense negotiations.

While property owners near the Orr and Disc tracts spoke against a concentration of more residential development near their holdings, those near the City's western border were vocalizing against a proposed commercial use, a Hechinger's store proposed for the corner of Jermantown Road and Route 50. After three years of legal maneuvering, the Virginia Supreme Court overturned the City's denial of the rezoning of the Hechinger property.

Added to the political climate surrounding so many development issues was the chasm that had developed between Mayor Russell and the Livable City Councilmen. As early as November of 1972, the Mayor had said, "Right now I have little or no influence on the Council. . . . Somehow my job as mayor has changed, my heart isn't in it like it was before. But I'm not quitting, I'm a fighter."[9] In March 1974, John Russell decided not to run for Mayor again, stating "under current conditions, I simply do not now fit in."[10]

Aerial photograph showing the Assembly Townhouses located just south of the City's northern boundary and Route I-66. The Assembly features 75 units built in the early 1970s by W. Rembert Simpson who served the City as Public Works Director in the early 1960s, Councilman from 1968 to 1972 and in the 1990s as Chairman of the Board of Zoning Appeals. Courtesy of the City of Fairfax

The Mosby Woods neighborhood is located on the north side of Routes 29, 211 and 50 with the main entrance on Plantation Parkway. The principal building period for the various designs of residences was 1961 to 1967. Courtesy of the City of Fairfax

Of the five Livable City Councilmen, four were running for Council and one, Dick Rucker, for Mayor. Shortly before the election, it became apparent that the FCLC was now perceived as the establishment and was on the defensive. Four of the FCLC candidates were defeated in the election. Nat Young defeated Dick Rucker to become the Mayor. Of the FCLC candidates, only Dr. Frederick McCoy and newcomer Susanne Max, who had led the FCLC movement in 1972, were elected to Council.

The "Livable City" Council left a legacy which still guides the City as the end of the century approaches. It revised the planned development ordinance, adopted a plan for the Central Business District, and adopted erosion and tree protection laws and tax relief for the elderly. It reorganized the Economic Development Authority and adopted requirements for new construction in certain parts of the City to receive approval from a newly-appointed Board of Architectural Review.[11]

Nathaniel F. Young, Mayor from 1974-1978, championed the concept of an independently run City capable of providing all necessary services to its citizens. The Fairfax City Express bus service was initiated during his tenure. Courtesy of the City of Fairfax

Nathaniel "Nat" Young was elected Mayor during the Watergate crisis when voters were focused on political integrity. His campaign had stressed honesty, fiscal responsibility and responsiveness to the City's citizens. He expressed a desire to curb growth and governmental bureaucracy and stated that the City-County contract was lopsided in favor of Fairfax County. He believed laws like the Tree and Architectural Control District ordinances intruded upon the rights of others. When he took office, he was described as the "Home Town Mayor. . . . Fond of recalling the days when Fairfax 'had more cows than people' and a habitual user of words like 'shucks,' 'doggone,' and 'durn tootin,' Young offered voters an old-timey, folksy image in a year when nostalgia . . . [was] the hottest thing."[12]

The essence of Mayor Young's political philosophy was distilled early in his second term when Fairfax, a federally designated Bicentennial City, was jointly celebrating the nation's 200th birthday and the City's 15th anniversary on Independence Day. Mayor Young greeted the crowd on that occasion from a hot air balloon; he was dressed in a shirt with red, white and blue ruffles garnished by a red, white and blue corsage. He led the crowd in singing Happy Birthday to America and to the City of Fairfax.

Mayor Young was reelected without opposition in 1976. The *Northern Virginia Sun* described him as "a combative and aggressive public official."[13] In his first term, after a barrage of angry accusations in which the Mayor played a major part, the City in a successful law suit blocked a subsidized housing project proposed by Fairfax County in a location adjacent to the City's southwest corner.[14]

When the Fairfax Hospital Association (FHA) announced plans to purchase the Commonwealth Doctor's Hospital, so advantageously located in the City, Mayor Young blasted the plan.[15] Believing the transaction would increase patient costs, decrease the quality of care and possibly result in the loss of the

This photograph shows heavy traffic at the intersection of Routes 29 and 50 near the old Exxon Station at Kamp Washington in the 1970s during the fuel shortage. Just beyond the station is a sign for Super Giant (now located at Route 50 and Jermantown Road). Courtesy of the City of Fairfax

hospital, he led the City's move to join a group of doctors in an anti-trust suit to prevent its sale.[16] The suit failed, and the sale was completed.[17] As feared, the hospital was relocated to Fair Oaks, and the facility was converted to a nursing home, Commonwealth Care Center, by 1986. Through persistent negotiations by the City, FHA did agree to retain an emergency service, ACCESS Emergency Care, in the City.

In 1976, a referendum issue to authorize the City's sale of bonds for capital improvements at Westmore and Jermantown Elementary Schools was to be considered along with the May 1976 City Council election. The referendum was defeated. The defeat of the school bond referendum began another barrage of citizen debates on the City operation of an independent school system.

On another front, in December 1976, the City filed a lawsuit against numerous defendants, including Washington Metropolitan Area Transit Authority (WMATA) and its member governments, "seeking to force construction of a rail line terminating at Vienna"[18] as called for in earlier agreements. In the face of cost overruns on the new Metrorail system, the system terminus at Vienna was proposed to be delayed by WMATA. The plan instead was to end the line at the Glebe Road (Ballston) station in Arlington, thus completing only 60 miles of the planned 100-mile route. The City of Fairfax had already contributed $1.9 million to Metro with the understanding that a station would be built in a location convenient to City riders one-and-a-half miles from the City's border. "They are truncating it," Young said of the Metro

Greg Schmitz and Alexander Rhue put the finishing touches to the new entrance to Westmore School just in time for its 35th birthday in 1988. Courtesy of the City of Fairfax

Former City Treasurer Frances L. Cox with Charles "Chuck" Robb, later elected Governor of Virginia, and his wife, Lynda Johnson Robb, campaigning in the 1977 Independence Day parade. Courtesy of the City of Fairfax

proposal. "We are saying that you can't do that. . . . They look at us, and because we are such small peanuts in the system, they say, 'Go away boys, don't bother us.' We're standing up for our rights. They can't ignore us."[19]

When the Metro Board decided to stand by its interim plan for a 60-mile rail system, construction had to be suspended for almost two years until a final court judgment was rendered. In 1977, the U.S. District Court gave Metro six weeks to amend its interim plan to include the Vienna station or pay the City of Fairfax $1.9 million.[20] In September 1978, the court overturned the $1.9 million award to the City, indicating that Metro had not abandoned, but only delayed, the extension of the rail service to Vienna.[21] The City was invited to return to court if the station did not materialize.[22] Although City officials were skeptical the station ever would materialize, the ground breaking for the Vienna Metro Station finally occurred in September 1982. The CUE bus service (City University Energysaver) has provided service to the station since its opening in 1986.

In a move to reduce payments to Metro, the City Council in November 1977 voted to leave the Metrobus system by January 1978. The City Manager had informed the Mayor and Council that the City's Metro deficit would increase in one year from $80,000 to $280,000 and indicated that the Metrobus service

was not efficient for City riders anyway. The Council decided to hire a private company that would provide direct rush hour bus service, door to door, at less cost.[23] Riders from adjacent communities were worried about how their bus service to and from Fairfax would be affected. To avoid inconvenience to its own residents, Fairfax County, at Metro's suggestion, agreed to subsidize the Metrobus route through the City.[24]

In March 1977, the Fairfax County Board of Supervisors adopted a resolution to renegotiate all its service contracts with the City of Fairfax. Spurred on by the desire for a City-run fire department, the battle was on, and the bid for independent schools quickly became its nerve center.[25]

While 40 or more citizens turned out to tell Council members "to act like gentlemen in their dealings with Fairfax County in the recent dispute over renegotiating the school service contract,"[26] others were campaigning citywide for a referendum to settle the independent school system issue once and for all. In May 1977, about 175 individuals, more than half of whom opposed independent schools, packed a public hearing on the issue.

In June, the City School Board voted down the proposal for a referendum for independent schools, and former Mayor John Russell, who had been appointed to the School Board to bolster the issue,

Public Works paving crew installing curb and gutter along a City street, about 1978, as part of the City's annual residential sidewalk-curb and gutter improvement program. Courtesy of the City of Fairfax

The City paving crew operating a power roller on a residential street as part of its programmed annual repaving program in November, 1984. Courtesy of the City of Fairfax

resigned. Mr. Russell said that the Board, while appearing in public to support City-run schools, had an "entirely different attitude behind closed doors."[27] His remarks about the poor quality of teaching under the County contract, which opinion was shared by a faction in the City, drew angry retorts from the president of the Fairfax Education Association.[28]

A citizen group, CARE (Citizens' Action for Responsive Education), was formed in June to promote an independent school system. Its chairman, Diana Thomas, indicated that the campaign would become an election issue the following spring, and in September a petition with 1,400 signatures was presented to the City Council requesting a 1977 referendum on independent schools.[29] The Council declined to schedule a referendum, in effect delaying a decision until the outcome of the contract negotiations was known.

But the City-County contract negotiations were not going well. The County had thrown up its hands earlier when meetings of representative members of the County Board and the City Council had proved fruitless and subsequently had turned over its negotiating authority to the County attorneys. At first balking at the new format for negotiations, the City finally chose the City Manager and the City Attorney to represent its interests. The sessions went poorly. In seven months there had been no progress and at one point, the County Attorney left the City Manager's office in a huff, claiming that he had been treated rudely. That version was contradicted by Mayor Young, who said the County representatives had left with a threat regarding higher contract costs to the City.[30]

Having been negotiating with Fairfax County for months to amend the Fire Protection contract to

The Duncan Chapel Methodist Church on Chain Bridge Road and Courthouse Drive in 1967. The building was used to house the Fairfax County Public Library and the Planning Office when it was no longer used by the Methodist congregation. It was demolished in 1970. Courtesy of the Fairfax County Public Library Photographic Archive

establish its own fire department, the City in November sent the County a new set of proposed terms for consideration. Although Mayor Young considered the terms generous, the County Board emphatically did not agree and voted to end all contract talks with the City because it felt that meaningful negotiations had become impossible. In mid-December the County billed the City for an additional $2.0 million over the existing $8.6 million the City had already agreed to pay for the year. The accompanying letter from County Board Chairman John Herrity told the City if the additional cost was not agreed to by March 15, 1978, all the County contracts would be canceled. The School Operation contract, the first to go, would expire on July 1, 1979. Further, Herrity said, "The Board of Supervisors will not agree to permit the City to pick and choose between the services included. . . [the charges] are designed to assure that all costs of such services to the County taxpayers are shared fairly by the taxpayers of the City."[31] Mayor Young replied that in order to pay the additional $2.0 million, the tax rate would have to be raised by 33 cents. "The assumption is that we have nowhere else to go and that isn't so . . . the or-else isn't that horrendous. This is not negotiation. This is dictation."[32]

A flurry of news articles, in turn, heaped criticism on the City or, alternatively, praised its tenacity in holding fast to its rights against its more powerful opponents. Charges and counter-charges were exchanged between the City Council, who believed the County was responsible for the contract predicament, and the County and some City residents who blamed the City for the problems.[33]

By the new year the political climate was becoming more intense. Over 200 people crowded the council room and 45 of them had signed up to speak about the contract negotiations at the emotional seven-hour City Council meeting on January 3, 1978. The views were sharply divided, but former mayor and current School Board Chairman George Hamill seemed to sum up the Council's majority consensus by testifying that "there is no way that the City Council or the City . . . can ever again be assured that the contract will not again . . . be unilaterally changed to suit the county's purpose."[34] In a vote taken just prior to adjournment at 3:15 a.m. on January 4, the Council voted to accept the County's termination of the school contract, but left the door open for future negotiations.[35]

This decision mobilized the forces favoring the County school contract. A petition calling on the City Council to reopen the school contract talks was delivered to the Council meeting on January 17. Proponents had every reason to believe that the Council would view their demand favorably since 4,272 residents (compared with 9,300 registered voters) had signed the petition. In a tie vote broken by the Mayor, however, the presentation of the petition was delayed to the end of the meeting by the Council.[36]

When finally the petitioners were permitted to speak, reality had sunk in. The speakers spoke sadly about having been relegated to the end of the meeting and about the "frightening reality that a wall is being erected around this City to keep its citizens from day-to-day contact with their historical neighbors. . . ."[37] After the meeting, which ended at 1:50 a.m. the following day, the Mayor and Councilmen who supported independent schools discounted the significance of the petition, indicating that they believed the petition signers had been misinformed. There were even some claims that Fairfax County may have orchestrated the whole crisis.[38]

Subsequent efforts by two state legislators, Senator Adelard Brault and Delegate Vincent Callahan, to encourage fruitful renegotiations between the City and the County failed.[39] A public meeting on January 10, 1978, called by the three Council members supporting the County contract, was boycotted by the Mayor and three Council supporters of the independent school system. The Council members in attendance carried on anyway with Councilman Lee Wigren wielding a megaphone to address the outdoor crowd. The City-County Agreement, particularly with reference to schools, had now become the major political issue for the upcoming May elections. "One observer predicted the election will be 'one hell of a humdinger' compared with recent city elections that have varied 'between dull and abysmally boring'."[40] In a news article, former Mayor Wood stated he didn't think "that regionalism stuff is worth a hoot,"[41] while former Mayor Prichard indicated the problem was "a matter of power and personalities rather than issues and ideology."[42]

Councilman Fred Silverthorne had announced in early August of 1977 that he would be running for Mayor in the spring. He had said, "If Mayor Young, who favors independent schools, brings it up as an issue, then I think the people of the city, who are opposed to independence, will decide the election."[43] He was right. In a record turnout of almost 50 percent of all registered voters, Frederick W. Silverthorne received 55 percent of the vote to become Mayor. All the incumbent Councilmen who supported independent schools were defeated while County contract supporters, newcomers and incumbent Council members alike, garnered between 50 and 60 percent of the vote to become Councilmen.

The thaw in the frigid City-County relationship began shortly afterward. Ellen Wigren, wife of then Councilman Lee Wigren, now deceased, recalls standing in line for breakfast while attending a Virginia Municipal League convention in Roanoke. "Lee and I stood next to Fairfax County Supervisor Jim Scott in line. Lee and Jim, who were long-time friends, began chatting about the gulf in the City-County negotiations, agreeing that the matter should be handled as rational human beings. The discussion continued through breakfast, and before I knew it we were racing back toward Fairfax to continue the discussions instead of remaining in Roanoke where I expected to visit with family members."[44] The dialogue continued in the Wigren's living room, prefacing an amiable conclusion of the bitter contract disagreements.

In October, the official City and County representatives hashed out a new contract, later ratified by both jurisdictions, at a friendly breakfast. A permanent negotiating committee for discussions on topics of mutual interest was appointed.[45] The City's declarations of total independence had given way to the promise of a new era of regional cooperation.

Councilman Lee Wigren stood on the steps of Fairfax City Hall on January 10, 1978, and addressed, through a "bull horn," the crowd of City of Fairfax citizens. They had come to attend a public gathering regarding the City-County schools contract issue. Courtesy of Ellen Wigren

William A. Jackson, Crew Supervisor, (left) and other Public Works employees load a sanitation truck in 1987. Mr. Jackson received the 1992 Fairfax Award, the highest employee award given by the City, for his outstanding service to City residents. Mr. Jackson, the City's first 30-year employee, was so well known and admired by City residents that his personnel file was packed with letters of praise and commendation. His retirement party in 1993 was full to overflowing with guests in large part because of the many Fairfax residents who attended to lavish praise on the quality of his service to the City. Courtesy of the City of Fairfax

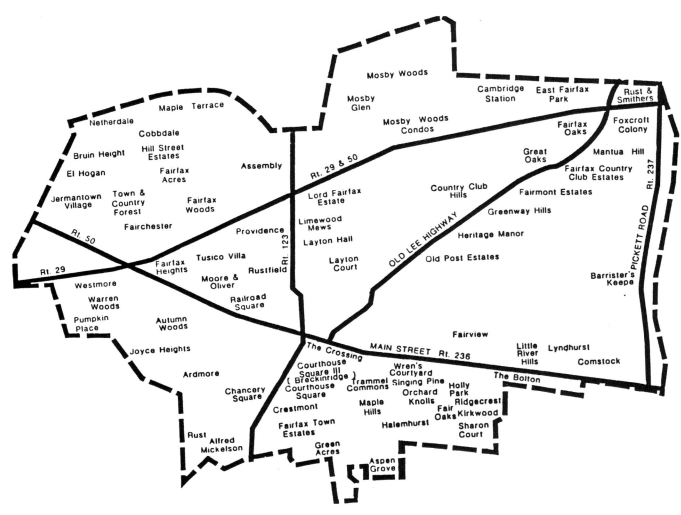

City of Fairfax neighborhoods, 1996. For years of construction, see Appendix J. Courtesy of the City of Fairfax

9.

Two Decades of Progress and Change, 1978-1996
by Peggy Talbot Wagner

The working relationship with Fairfax County restored, the succeeding City of Fairfax administrations dealt with numerous issues between 1978 and 1988. No firm decision had been reached about acquisition of the school buildings located within City boundaries. Public transportation was needed to assist the City's commuter population; traffic bottlenecks within City boundaries were intensifying. Decisions had to be made about the disposition of City-owned buildings and the recognition and preservation of historic properties. "Citizen complaints" had to be met with action, often of the legislative variety. It was time to look backward as well as forward to inventory the progress and identify the needs of the City on every front, a process often both dictated and facilitated by numerous turnovers in top level leaders.

Noteworthy achievements, many reflecting the goals of the 1988 Comprehensive Plan and the recommendations of a newly-appointed City-wide study commission, were to occur in the '90s under the proactive leadership of Mayor John Mason. The City needed first, however, to resolve compelling problems not of its own making. The poor economic climate, exacerbated by Fairfax County's move of its administrative offices out of the City, initially monopolized the attention of the City Council. Then a major oil leak emanating from the tank farm at the City's eastern border dominated newspaper headlines for over three years and forced the dedication of massive City resources and manpower to lead the clean-up and restitution efforts. In late 1992 and early 1993,

however, through the determination of the Mayor and City Council, the launching of a major economic development program and the appointment of the 2020 Commission began to pull the City forward into an era of creative initiatives. These resulted in the rebirth and refinement of many earlier ideas and stimulated an exciting period of new vision, revitalization and confirmation of small-town ideals for the City of Fairfax.

The decade of 1978 to 1988 saw a number of dramatic turnovers in individuals, both elected and appointed, serving the City. In addition to the changes resulting from the two-year elections of the Mayor and City Council, the reorganization of a department; resignations; the 1981 Treasurer's election; and a conviction and prison term resulted in new faces and new ways of doing things in City government.

Because of a 1979 law that "put the volunteer chief in charge of all city firefighters,"[1] the City's highest paid career firefighter, Harold E. Dailey, was serving as the number two man under Volunteer Fire Chief Charles Seay. This division of authority had resulted in disputes between volunteers and the 39 paid firefighters.[2] When the Council decided to rectify the situation by adopting a new ordinance, Chief Seay submitted his resignation and a new volunteer, James McGrath, was elected replacement chief by the volunteers. Although the new ordinance was never considered, the Council was concerned that the new chief could not be equally responsive to both the volunteers and the City Manager.[3] In a compromise move, City Manager Edward A. Wyatt appointed

Some of the extensive damage done in the City of Fairfax during Hurricane David is shown here. After it passed through the area on September 4, 1979, Williamsburg Square off Route 236 looked like this. Photo by Martin Mooney, courtesy of the Fairfax County Public Library Photographic Archive

A Dial-A-Ride bus parked in front of City Hall. Dial-A-Ride buses, responding to telephone requests for rides on random routes, operated for 11 months in 1974-1975. Although the first three buses were purchased with a grant from the Northern Virginia Transportation Commission, the service was terminated by City Council in April 1975, because its cost to the City ($450 per day) far exceeded its earnings ($50-60 per day.) The Fairfax City Express, a service for commuters traveling between the City and the Pentagon and the District of Columbia, operated from the late 1970s until 1986. Courtesy of the City of Fairfax

Dailey as chief of both the paid and volunteer firefighters with a volunteer second in rank.

The City Council faced a reevaluation of the Fire Department structure by early 1985 when Chief Dailey announced his resignation after holding his position for only about a year. After the City Council adopted an ordinance redefining the authority of the Fire Chief to provide total control over both the paid and volunteer fire forces, Chief Dailey withdrew his resignation[4] and remained with the City until his retirement in June 1990.

In November of 1981, Frances Cox, the city treasurer for 20 years, was defeated for reelection by Ray M. Birch.[5] Cox had been the subject of criticism from various sources for two years, and her defeat was not a surprise. But within weeks after his election, Birch resigned, stating that the treasurer's office was in such disarray that he could not perform his duties.[6]

Acting Treasurer John Coughlan, who was appointed pending a new election, conducted an investigation which led to Cox's indictment, trial and conviction for embezzlement. She served a jail sentence of

Frederick W. Silverthorne, Mayor from 1978 to 1982, oversaw the restoration of friendly relations with Fairfax County, resulting in the cooperative administration of County contracts for the operation of schools and other services. Courtesy of the City of Fairfax

George T. Snyder, Jr. served as Mayor from 1984-1990. Credited with ability to achieve consensus among City Council members, Mayor Snyder led the adoption of comprehensive transportation plans, the expansion of the CUE Bus service and completion of traffic circulation initiatives on major City streets. Mayor Snyder died in November 1995. Courtesy of the City of Fairfax

over three months. In November 1982, Stephen L. Moloney, a CPA and IRS program manager, was elected in a five-way contest for the position.[7]

Frederick W. Silverthorne served as Mayor from 1978 until 1982. He led the restoration of friendly relations with the County including the ratification of new contracts and County operation of City schools.

John W. Russell, having served two earlier terms from 1970-1974, was elected again in 1982. He resigned from office when elected to the State Senate for a four-year term in November 1983. Under Mayor Russell, the Council voted to increase the funds for capital improvements in the schools.

George T. Snyder, Jr., who was appointed to serve an interim term as mayor to replace Mayor Russell in 1983, was elected in 1984 and served until 1990.[8] Although Mayor Snyder stated when originally appointed that he was not interested in running, he announced that because of citizen encouragement he would stand for election in 1984. Two Councilmen then called for his resignation, believing that Mayor Snyder as incumbent would have an unfair advantage.[9] Four members of the Council supported Snyder's decision, however, and he was elected to office by a majority of 57.8 percent of the voters.[10] Councilman Robert F. Lederer, Jr., "credited Snyder's mayoral appointment in 1983 as one of the City's turning points. 'It helped define who we are today'."[11]

The Mosby Woods Boundary Adjustment of December 31, 1980, maintained the City's population level above the 20,000 mark and unified a subdivision community. Prior to the adjustment, Mosby Woods had been divided by the City-County line with about two-thirds of the community located in the County.[12] Dale Lestina, the leader of Mosby Woods' successful

bid for inclusion in the City, later recalled "the boundaries went through some people's houses. So some people ate dinner in the county and slept in the city without ever leaving the house."[13]

In the following decade, the City and County ratified additional boundary adjustments. In 1991, Pumpkin Place on the City's western boundary, Maple Terrace on its northern boundary, and the Greater Pentecostal Temple of Christ with adjacent home on Ox Road came into the City along with a few homes built in Mosby Woods after the earlier adjustment.[14] In January 1994, Aspen Grove, a townhouse community including a historic home of the same name off Roberts Road, became part of the City. Additionally, minor corrective adjustments were made which moved a portion of the Barcroft Bible School property east of Pickett Road and a lot on Burke Station Road into Fairfax County.[15]

Six new City of Fairfax entry signs designed by the City Planning Office were erected at locations on principal streets at the edge of City boundaries in 1984-1985. The old original signs were converted to display boards for service club signs. Courtesy of the City of Fairfax

The Fairfax Cemetery, located at 10565 Main Street, has historical significance as a post Civil War cemetery. A historic survey commissioned by the City in 1989 indicates that the cemetery dates back to 1865-1870 and was first supervised by the "Ladies Memorial Association" for Confederate States' soldiers who were buried in Fairfax County. An obelisk in the center of the cemetery commemorates the Confederate dead. A plaque nearby indicates that a few Union soldiers are also buried in the cemetery. By 1875, the cemetery was run by the Fairfax Cemetery Association when it presumably became a cemetery for civilians. In 1965, the City of Fairfax assumed the operation and care of the Fairfax Cemetery. Courtesy of the City of Fairfax

The Jermantown Cemetery, located at 11085 Main Street, has historical significance as the only known black cemetery in the City of Fairfax. A survey commissioned by the City in 1989 revealed that the deed to the land dated August 14, 1868, records the owner as "Colored Burial Sons and Daughters of Benevolence of Jermantown." At the time of the survey there were 40 grave-stones, but several new markers have appeared since then. Evidently the cemetery was used for burials of former slaves who were denied burial in the Fairfax Cemetery. Courtesy of Peggy Talbot Wagner

In January 1979, a long-standing goal of two decades of elected leaders was finally met. A bond issue for $1.57 million was approved by voters for the acquisition of Layton Hall, Westmore and Green Acres elementary schools and Sidney Lanier Middle School.[16] The City now owned and controlled the physical plants for all public schools located within its boundaries.

By 1982, it was clear to the School Board that because of declining enrollment at the John C. Wood School, its elementary students should be reassigned to another school and an alternate use found for the structure.[17] To alleviate overcrowding of staff accommodations in City Hall and centralize Public Safety functions, it was decided in 1983 to close the school operation and relocate the Police and Fire Departments to the facility[18] along with the Department of Parks and Recreation. Several of the school's former classrooms and its multipurpose room are used for the City's adult education, senior citizen programs and other community activities.

In December 1985, and February 1986, respectively, the City Council voted to sell the Fairfax Elementary School to a private owner for redevelopment as an office complex and to rezone the property for commercial use.[19] The adjacent Old Elementary School building was retained for future renovation and subsequently became the permanent home for the Fairfax Museum and Visitors Center.

Old Town Hall was presented to the City of Fairfax in September 1982 by a nonprofit board of trustees that had guided its care for several years. In the five years prior, private and public funds had been spent on renovations for the building that formerly had been a private facility rented for social and political affairs. The trustees continued to meet as a government board, studying ways to raise money for renovation.[20] By summer 1983, the group was encouraged by the City to become a charitable corporation, Historic Fairfax City, Inc., with George Hamill serving as its first president.[21] The Historic Fairfax organization proved to be an active support group for the preservation and utilization of several historic structures located in downtown Fairfax, including the Ratcliffe-Logan-Allison House (formerly known as Earp's Ordinary).

One of the most notable achievements of Historic Fairfax, under the strong volunteer commitment of John Gano, president from July 1989 until March 1996, was the interior renovation and restoration of the Old Fairfax Elementary School to house the Fairfax Museum and Visitors Center. The Museum was opened to the public on July 4, 1992.[22] Under Gano's leadership with assistance from John and Jeanne Rust and many others, private funds were raised in addition to public funds authorized by City Council for the project. An interesting collection of historic relics and artifacts has been assembled under the leadership of Daryl Humrichouser, the Museum's first director/

curator.[23] She is assisted by a large staff of volunteers. The City Council was so impressed with the success of the project that it designated July 14, 1992, as "John H. Gano Day."[24] With the help of funds from a bond issue passed in 1993, the Museum expanded its usable area in 1995 when the second floor was renovated to provide office and storage space, new display areas and a fire escape. This section was opened to the public in February 1996.[25]

In 1986, the City published a manual, "Historic District Guidelines," to inform developers and architects of the City's expected standards for architectural details and materials for construction and renovations in the locally designated "Old and Historic District." The City Council, increasingly interested in its historic properties, also charged staff in the mid-1980s with the task of preparing the nomination of the downtown area to the National Register of Historic Places. With the assistance of the City's professional consultant, the nomination was filed with the Commonwealth of Virginia Department of Conservation and Historic Resources, subsequently approved for the Virginia Historic Landmarks Register and recommended to the U. S. Department of Interior for inclusion in the Register. On August 27, 1987, notice was sent that the City of Fairfax Historic District had been entered officially into the National Register of Historic Places. The District is located on 35 acres and contains 52 buildings, 35 of which are considered contributing structures.[26] (Please see appendix for full listing of included structures.)

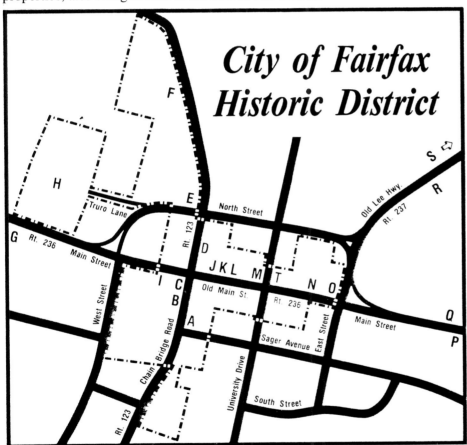

City of Fairfax Historic District

Chain Bridge Road		Address	Year
A	Oliver House	4011	1830
B	Fairfax Courthouse	4000	1800
C	Marr Monument	4000	1904
D	Ford Building	3977	1835
E	Moore House	3950	1840
F	Donohoe House	3920	1880

Main Street			
G	Confederate memorial	10565	1890
H	Truro Rectory	10520	1833
I	Old Fairfax Jail	10475	1885
J	Hav-aBite	10416	1895
K	T.T. Reynolds	10414	1895
L	Fairfax Hay and Grain	10412	1900
M	Fairfax Herald	10400	1900
N	Earp's Ordinary	10386	1805
O	Draper House	10364	1830
P	Old Fairfax Elementary	10231	1890
Q	Farr Homeplace	10230	1870

Old Lee Highway			
R	Grandma's Cottage	3901	1865
S	Blenheim	3610	1850

University Drive			
T	Old Town Hall	3999	1900

A map of the City's historic structures shows the City's Historic District (entered into the National Register of Historic Places on August 27, 1987) with its boundaries outlined in broken lines. The structures shown outside the boundaries, although historic, are not included in the official National Register District, with the exception of the Old Fairfax Elementary School (letter "P") which was admitted to the National Register in November 1992, along with the Tastee 29 Diner located on Lee Highway. The old Fairfax Elementary School, with interior renovations and exterior restoration, was opened on July 4, 1992, as the Fairfax Museum and Visitors Center. Courtesy of the City of Fairfax

The Gunnell House, 10520 Main Street, was built about 1835 with a 1911 addition. Designated as a highly significant structure in the City's 1987 National Register Historic District, it is currently owned by the Truro Episcopal Church and has been used as a rectory. It was owned by Dr. William Gunnell when John S. Mosby captured Union General Edwin H. Stoughton at the residence during a Civil War raid, March 9 and 10, 1863. Courtesy of the City of Fairfax

The Moore/McCandlish House (c. 1840) located at 3950 Chain Bridge Road was rehabilitated in 1985-1986 to serve as an office building. Included in the City's 1987 National Register Historic District, the house is considered significant for its architectural character and its important association with R. Walton Moore, a well-known politician in the 20th century. Courtesy of the City of Fairfax

The Sauls House at 10381 Main Street, built in about 1892, is listed in the City's 1987 National Register Historic District because of its fine architectural qualities. It is now part of the commercial complex, Victorian Square, rehabilitated by Bob Lewis in the late 1980s. Courtesy of the City of Fairfax

As a result of a citywide inventory conducted for the City in 1990, the Council submitted two more historic property nominations for State and Federal recognition. Both the Old Fairfax Elementary School (Fairfax Museum and Visitors Center) and the Tastee 29 Diner were added to the National Register in November 1992. It was noted that the Diner was "only the fifth [diner] in the nation and first in the south to be honored as a historic landmark."[27]

The City attained Certified Local Government (CLG) status from the Virginia Department of Historic Resources in October 1990, one of only ten Virginia jurisdictions to achieve that distinction by 1990. The CLG designation enables the City to compete for financial assistance for projects that enhance the City's heritage projects. In addition to a $7,195 grant in 1991 to prepare the National Register nominations for the Old Elementary School and the Tastee 29 Diner, the City has received funds for preparing and distributing an annotated map of historic sites, preparing design guidelines for the Old Town Fairfax Historic and Transition districts and conducting a citywide archaeological assessment.[28]

Ridership on the Fairfax City Express, a contract bus service providing public transportation to the Pentagon and Washington, D.C., reached its peak in August 1983, with 22,289 riders. The program was discontinued in June 1986, in order to help facilitate the revamping and expansion of the CUE Bus service partly financed by a $65,000 grant from the Commonwealth of Virginia.[29]

The original CUE Bus program, jointly funded by the City and George Mason University, had been inaugurated on August 18, 1980, to provide local service for City residents and University staff and students.[30] With expanded routes and six additional buses, the revamped CUE Bus program was designed to provide adequate service between the City and University and the Vienna Metro Station, which opened on June 7, 1986. "In its first full year of operation as a feeder network to the . . . station, the . . . bus system carried almost a half million passengers."[31] A new bus route was added in early 1987 to further improve service to the Metro station. In a measure to cut waiting time by half, the City purchased five new buses in 1990, nearly doubling the size of the fleet.[32] By 1994, ridership on the CUE bus had reached 858,000.[33]

"Ten years after the City requested the Virginia Department of Highways and Transportation to improve Pickett Road, construction began in 1983"[34] and was completed in June 1986. This project transformed what was still a one-lane gravel road in the early '70s, to its present-day four-lane configuration. For years, elected officials had been pressured by citizens to retain a rural atmosphere on the road. It was not until February 12, 1980, after favorable public input, that the City Council officially endorsed the plan for widening Pickett Road between Routes 236

Pictured above is Maureen Kelly, millionth rider of the CUE Bus system in 1988. A 17-year-old from Merrimack, New Hampshire on vacation with her family, Kelly won a gift certificate from Wild Oats for her record-setting ride. One of her stops was at the Fairfax Museum and Visitors Center. In the drawing for consolation prizes donated by local merchants, the winners were John Tate (a gift certificate from The Cellar), Hans Beckel (a gift certificate from The Ship's Hatch), Ralph Mosely and Keith Hamilton, Jr. (gift bags from the Chamber of Commerce) and Veronica M. Amadaor (passbook for a month of free rides on the CUE Bus). Photo by Richard Mason, courtesy of the City of Fairfax

When Paul Christy climbed on the CUE Bus during the morning rush hour on December 12, 1994, he became the 7 millionth rider on the City's CUE Bus system. Christy, who was riding to the Vienna Metro Station to get to work, received a pass to ride the CUE Bus free through 1995 and a gift certificate for Artie's restaurant. Courtesy of the City of Fairfax

Gateway Regional Park was opened to the public by the Northern Virginia Regional Park Authority on June 3, 1995, "National Trails Day." The park serves as a trails "crossroads," linking the nearby Washington & Old Dominion Railroad Regional Park Trail/City of Fairfax Connector Trail with the City of Fairfax trails network. Benches, a water fountain, area maps and interpretive signs are located in and around the pavilion to serve the users of the park. C. Barrie Cook, M.D. and Arthur F. Little represent the City of Fairfax on the Northern Virginia Regional Park Authority Board. Courtesy of the Northern Virginia Regional Park Authority

and 50, which "Mayor Frederick W. Silverthorne hailed as 'the end of a narrow, dangerous road',"[35] and James R. Shull, Public Works Director from 1972 until 1989, recently characterized as "the 'project of his career,' having lasted almost his full tenure with the City."[36]

In 1983, improvements were made to selected portions of Chain Bridge Road near West Drive, Commonwealth Hospital, Armstrong Street and Judicial Drive. Picturesque Rust Curve, on Chain Bridge Road, remained undisturbed.[37] By 1986, additional lanes added to the section between Route 50 and Interstate 66 eased traffic flow on northern Chain Bridge Road.[38] In 1993, the section of the road located between Judicial Drive and University Drive (just south of the City's boundary) was widened to four lanes with a landscaped center median strip.[39] This relieved traffic congestion and provided an attractive southern entrance to the City.

The importance of transportation issues during the administration of Mayor George Snyder was underscored with the adoption of a Comprehensive Transportation Plan in 1987 prior to the adoption of the new Comprehensive Plan in 1988. The Plan highlighted the need for bypass routes around the City and provided a blueprint for recommended transportation improvements and policies throughout the City. Transportation measures adopted prior to that Plan included an intersection improvement program beginning in 1985 to enhance traffic flow at Jermantown Road and Main Street, Main Street and Lee Highway,

and Lee Highway and Chain Bridge Road. A one percent restaurant tax to fund the ten-year transportation plan was approved the same year. Starting in 1986, a computerized traffic signal system was initiated and ultimately installed throughout the City. The City continued with its infrastructure rehabilitation program throughout the decade, including the repavement of streets and repair of brick sidewalks.[40] The brick sidewalk project sparked substantial redevelopment in the downtown area.[41]

By 1995, the City, administering its own road improvement and maintenance program under Virginia law, had amassed 15.7 miles (55 lane miles) of arterial roads and 51.2 miles (103.4 lane miles) of collector and local roads.[42]

Beginning in 1985, in response to public demand, the City Council began comprehensive revisions to the Zoning Ordinance with the appointment of the Zoning Review Committee (ZRC). Headed by Councilman Robert F. Lederer, Jr., the committee was composed of Council and Planning Commission representatives. Within the next few years, significant revisions recommended by the committee and adopted by Council included regulations governing the construction and demolition of buildings in the Old and Historic District; strengthening required on-site parking and landscaping specifications; modifying

In the early 1970s, a City worker operates the vacuum on the leaf machine truck during the City's annual fall leaf removal program. Courtesy of the City of Fairfax

William Jackson, Cecil Steele (now deceased) and other public works employees unload linden trees scheduled for planting in the median strip on Lee Highway (May, 1969). The tree planting program, started in the 1960s and continuing today, has resulted in numerous Tree City U.S.A. awards for the City. Courtesy of the City of Fairfax

density formulas; stipulating minimum open space and upgraded landscape standards for commercial projects; increasing control of commercial signage; requiring underground utilities for new construction; and protecting trees.[43]

The Highway Corridor Overlay District adopted on November 8, 1988, enabled additional scrutiny of proposed development within defined areas along the major corridors for "the prevention or reduction of traffic congestion and the facilitation of well-conceived, coordinated development."[44] Many of the zoning measures adopted during the period were

unique to the City, and other jurisdictions used the measures as a model for their own zoning revisions.

Rezoning activity was unusually heavy during the decade, particularly from 1982 through 1987 when commercial requests were at their peak. Between 1978 and 1988, 88 requests for rezonings were received by the City, of which 52 were approved and the remainder withdrawn or denied.[45] Some Council members and Mayor Snyder, who believed that the residential character of the City was being threatened, were particularly concerned about rezonings from residential to commercial designations, and prided

Several historic buildings on Main Street in the heart of the City's 1987 National Register Historic District are shown, left to right: the Friendship Grill (now Hav-A-Bite Restaurant), 10416 Main Street; Nickell's Hardware store built in 1895 (now T. T. Reynolds Restaurant), 10414 Main Street; Fairfax Hay & Grain Store building erected in 1900 (now Executive Press), 10412 Main Street; office building constructed in 1936-1938 and operated as a grocery store into the 1940s with Colonial Revival detailing added in 1966 (now Security Systems Unlimited), 10410 Main Street; and Old Fairfax Herald and Print Shop building, an important landmark in the district because of its association with the Fairfax

Herald, published from 1882 until 1971, 10400 Main Street. The Fairfax Herald was established by Captain S. R. Donohoe who in 1904 moved to this small one-story building. This group of buildings is important to the historic district because it illustrates the character, building type and scale of the commercial core of Fairfax in the late 1890s and turn of the century. The commercial building displaying the Alibi Restaurant sign (at the far left) is considered a non-contributing building because it is less than 50 years old. Courtesy of the City of Fairfax

themselves on never having voted for a commercial rezoning. Actual construction of commercial projects, however, reached a peak in both 1987 and 1988 with building starts of 1.8 million square feet in each of those two years.[46] During the decade, six low-rise office buildings sprang up on Judicial Drive. Other new construction resulting from rezonings included six new restaurants, five of which were of the fast food variety. By 1994, 106 restaurants were operating in the City. A new apartment complex, Providence Park, was the first multi-family project to be built in over 20 years. Residential projects included an upscale

The four-story, 61,000-square-foot award-winning Foster Building at 3975 University Drive at the intersection with North Street includes offices occupied by the Central Fairfax Chamber of Commerce. The building was completed in 1985. Courtesy of Foster Management, Inc.

This photograph shows a corner of the five-story "9900 Building" located in the Fairfax Square Professional Center on Main Street. The "9900 Building" and the Center have received many awards for their design and appearance. Courtesy of Van Metre Management Company, AMO

residential condominium community, Rustfield, and a low-density townhouse project, Fairfax Oaks. Mixed-use projects included Railroad Square, a mixture of apartments and commercial space, and Commonwealth Park, serving University students and staff with piggy-back apartments and an office building.

Although the period yielded a significant amount of new commercial space, the total acreage rezoned from residential districts to commercial districts amounted to only about one per cent of the City's total acreage.[47] Furthermore, commercial uses have continued to account for a hefty portion of City tax revenues, consistently allowing the City to set real property tax rates that are among the lowest in the northern Virginia region. By the fiscal year 1991-1992, 59.4 percent of all City revenues were generated by commercial uses compared to 40.6 percent from residential sources.[48]

Good communications became a hallmark of the eighties. A city information newsletter, more recently known as *Cityscene*, has been mailed to all residents and businesses for years. To complement citywide cable TV hook-ups with Media General Cable of Fairfax, the City inaugurated City Screen 12 on April 1, 1985, enabling a continuous bulletin board display of government information and public service announcements on local TV screens. The first live coverage of City Council meetings occurred on January 27, 1987.[49]

Town meetings sponsored by Mayor Snyder and the City Council, starting in September 1984, have promoted public input into vital issues. Many citizens actively participate by speaking before the City Council.

Donna Ruggiero Monacci, Cable TV Specialist, operates a video camera at a City Council meeting. The first live coverage of a City Council meeting occurred on January 27, 1987, when the Community Relations Office inaugurated Cityscreen-12, the City government access channel on the Media General Cable system. Courtesy of the City of Fairfax

In 1986, the City celebrated its 25 years of incorporation and reviewed its progress at City Hall with a Jubilee celebration. The party featured a parade of past and present City leaders, a memorabilia display, the City Band and a giant birthday cake.[50] In the City's 25 years the population had leveled at 20,537 by 1980, a 15 percent decline since 1970 but about a 65 percent increase since the City's incorporation. The composition of City residents reflected "nationwide trends of an older population, a lower birth rate and an increased number of widowed, separated or divorced households. By 1980, the City was 90 percent developed."[51]

The 1988 City of Fairfax Comprehensive Plan essentially set the stage for the decade of the nineties. After a citywide questionnaire and numerous work

sessions and public hearings by the Planning Commission and City Council, the plan was approved by the Council on November 29, 1988.[52]

The 1988 plan, which presented the City as the historic and geographic crossroads of northern Virginia, sought "the preservation and enhancement of the City's residential quality of life and distinctive identity."[53] The goals for preservation and enhancement of the City's existing housing stock and for "move up" housing resulted in major housing studies and programs and influenced residential development trends well into the nineties. Its goals for Old Town Fairfax resulted in entrepreneurial steps never before pursued. Its focus on community appearance spurred the creation of more exacting standards for commercial development and preservation of historic properties. The Plan prompted increased cooperation with neighboring jurisdictions and George Mason University for the purpose of jointly resolving transportation, educational and other issues of mutual interest. The City entered the decade of the nineties with a mission to refine and enlarge the focus appropriate for a maturing community.

In November 1989, Mayor George Snyder announced that he would not seek reelection in 1990 because he had accepted a demanding new job. He had been "overwhelmingly reelected . . . in the elections of 1984, 1986 and 1988."[54] He had been named "Most Effective Politician" in the area served by the Fairfax Connection for three years running,[55] a tough act to follow. In his campaign for Mayor in early 1990, John Mason promised to "continue the low-key, consensus-building political style of Snyder. . . .

A public works crew plants flowers at the intersection of North and Main streets as part of the City's annual summer landscaping program. Courtesy of the City of Fairfax

John Mason has served as Mayor from 1990 to the present. The first four-term Mayor in the City's history, Mayor Mason has provided strong leadership in developing initiatives to strengthen the economy, upgrade housing, address capital needs, improve community appearance, encourage the arts, and further regional cooperation. Through the 2020 Commission appointed during his term, the City Council focused on the long-term future needs of the City. Courtesy of the City of Fairfax

While I have a reputation for attention to detail, as a mayor one has to step back from that and look towards achieving consensus."[56] The newly elected Mayor Mason "predicted that tougher economic times, spurred by a softer real estate market and the exodus of office tenants from downtown buildings when Fairfax County moves to its new Fair Lakes headquarters, will demand aggressive leadership from the mayor's office."[57]

It was predicted that the entire decade of the nineties might well be austere. Early in the new decade, the 1990 City budget that proposed a "mere 4.1 percent increase. . . . 'Hold the line is an old refrain, but it's sincere' said [City Manager] Wyatt, who peppered his budget message several times with words like 'caution' and 'alarm'."[58] The newspapers printed news about business closings, the effects of the weak economy, State budget cuts and speculation about the timing of a possible recovery of the economy.[59] But news of another kind was about to claim the lion's share of City Council attention. The new Mayor was about to be tested not with "fire" as had been predicted in litigation against the tank farm rezoning, but by a major oil leak first reported in 1990.

The first news reports of "the leak" did not predict its magnitude. The simple headlines "Fuel depot can't find source of leak" and "Size of Fairfax City spill unclear"[60] did not begin to suggest the months—and years—of tracing, monitoring, recovering, defending and compensating for the leak of "an estimated 100,000 to three million gallons of oil into the soil"[61] by Star Enterprises, regional distributor for Texaco, Inc.

Before the headlines would subside, the U.S. Environmental Protection Agency, Fairfax County, the Citizens for a Healthy Fairfax formed by residents of Mantua and Stockbridge Subdivisions, the Virginia Department of Environmental Quality, the Virginia Legislature, the Virginia Governor, the Governor's Advisory Commission, two U.S. Congressmen and countless others would become involved. The City Fire Department would assign two staff members to provide daily technical direction and coordination. A technical committee with Fire Department representation would meet twice a day at the Tank Farm, and a City staff "Tank Farm Task Force" would meet weekly to assess progress and coordinate departmental involvement.[62] Star Enterprises is engaged in a four-phase program to stabilize and remediate the petroleum.

James R. Shull, public works director of the City from 1972 until 1989, standing at the Tedrich Boulevard entrance to Daniels Run Park. This is one of several neighborhood entrances to the park located between Old Lee Hills and Little River Hills. Originally composed of 45 acres purchased in December, 1965 with the help of federal funds, the park was expanded under the guidance of Jim Shull to 48 acres some time after the City Council adopted a master plan for its development in 1967. Running through its middle is Daniels Run for which the park is named. With the exception of well-kept hiking trails, the park is maintained in its natural wooded state. Photo by Peggy Talbot Wagner

Mayor John Mason wasted no time in setting up the framework for the goals articulated in his 1992 election campaign. He had credited the previous Council with dealing "successfully with a series of difficult challenges, including balancing the city's budget in a recession and overseeing the cleanup of a petroleum leak emanating from the Pickett Road tank farm."[63] The City was also satisfactorily negotiating a compromise with Fairfax County to modify plans and eliminate certain features for its planned jail expansion on Judicial Drive behind the Judicial Center.[64] It was now time to enlarge the agenda with a full-blown economic development thrust and to involve a broad spectrum of residents in goal setting for the year 2000 and beyond. A month after the election, the mayor announced that "the Council has reaffirmed with [City Manager Robert] Sisson the number one goal [of] reorienting the entire City staff to work toward economic development."[65]

There was good cause for the focus. Commercial vacancy rates were high throughout the region. A 20.5 percent vacancy rate was reported by the City in June

1992. As of July 1st, the City had 758,000 square feet of available office space, a status attributed by the newly appointed Economic Development Coordinator to the County's move out of the City.[66] The County move had been well anticipated, however, since the mid-eighties with the City Council and others taking steps to counter, and even capitalize on the move.

In the next three years, the City Council with help from business owners pursued several other initiatives to accelerate "the pace of economic development in the city."[67] In 1992, an economic consultant was hired[68] and the Council approved ordinance revisions to ease commercial signage restrictions and to relax parking restrictions for downtown businesses.[69] The combined public and private efforts yielded some early short-term benefits. By the end of 1992, Executive Director Mary Esther Obremsky of the new Downtown Fairfax Coalition expressed satisfaction that "15 new retail businesses opened that year."[70]

An economic development summit of the City Council, business leaders, consultants and City staff members convened in early 1993 to review steps already taken and solidify long-term planning.[71] In September of 1992, the City Council had appointed the 2020 Commission "to design a 20- to 30-year plan designating the city's direction . . . [and strategies for] all city issues from education to public services and utilities."[72] Mayor Mason's election goals were well underway in the first year of his second term.

In 1992, Dale Lestina, the citizen who successfully led the campaign for sound barriers to buffer Mosby Woods from traffic noise on Route I-66, was appointed as chairman of the 2020 Commission.[73] Initially, 84 individuals were appointed, but the size of the Commission quickly escalated to 112 members because of the keen interest of City residents in the scope of its work. Twelve subcommittees studied and produced 136 recommendations on important City issues.[74] Anxious that the report would not sit on a shelf and die, the City Council directed that a summary of the report be sent to every household in the City and that staff recommendations to the Council be justified with those of the 2020 Commission.[75] Several of the Commission's ideas were incorporated into City projects and programs.[76]

Because of the declining economy and the desire to keep taxes low, several capital projects to improve or upgrade City facilities were placed on the back burner for several years. In the fall of 1993, the City Council, in order to catch up with maintenance and improvement projects, approved six proposals (property yard; the fire stations; transportation; Old Town historic properties; storm water management; and Goose Creek Reservoir) for inclusion in a $9,570,000 bond issue referendum that passed overwhelmingly. Work on the projects is currently underway or complete.[77] Among the more visible of the finished projects are the attractive new facades, landscaping and additions designed and constructed to meet the current needs of Fire Station 33 located on Lee Highway and Volunteer Fire Station 3 on University Drive.

In 1996, construction was completed to correct structural defects and meet code requirements on the Sisson House located next to City Hall.[78] The house,

A wedding ceremony was held at the historic old Robert Sisson home, restored for use as a City office building, on Chain Bridge Road on May 7, 1995. The celebrants were, left to right, Marilyn Salak; Peter McCahill, groom; Jackie Henderson, city clerk; Phylis Salak, bride; who served as General Registrar at the Sisson House for many years; Alan Jacobs; Ann Jacobs; Matt Stuckey; Hope Salak; Scarlet McCahill; Paula Salak; and Wesley Salak. Courtesy of Phylis Salak and Peter McCahill

dating back to the 19th century[79] and once occupied by the stage coach driver coincidentally sharing the same name as the current City Manager, Robert Sisson, provides offices for the School Superintendent and the City Electoral Board and Registrar.

The bond issue for stormwater management did not begin to cover the estimated cost of "almost $9 million in identified, needed major . . . projects."[80] For several years the City Council had been exploring ways to finance these projects. An answer came in the Council-approved 1996-1997 budget that included a provision to dedicate two cents of the annual real estate tax rate to the completion of prioritized stormwater projects. It was estimated by City Manager Sisson that the process will take approximately 20 years for completion.[81]

The goal of the 1988 Comprehensive Plan to "preserve and enhance the existing housing stock"[82] began to take form in October 1992, with "plans . . . to begin a partnership between government and private business to encourage home improvements in the city."[83] The concept developed into a full-blown award-winning housing program[84] that includes home equity loans, tax incentives and many other special features. The programs's 1995 and 1996 annual "Citywide Spring Tour of Homes" showcased 19 of the newly rehabilitated homes along with four new home developments.

Although major commercial construction has subsided since building permits were issued in 1990

for Montgomery Ward on the City's western boundary and Jennings Storage at the eastern boundary,[85] several residential projects have been built recently or are now under construction. Comprising a total of 446 new dwelling units, they include 139 single family homes, 217 townhouses and 90 condominiums. Over two-thirds of these homes are "located within a half mile of the historic downtown area."[86] Mayor Mason said, "We've taken deliberate steps to tackle [housing] with a two-pronged approach. We want residential development and we're working on our existing housing with the home pride program."[87] Substantial progress toward the Comprehensive Plan's goal to "Promote a sound and diverse City housing stock"[88] had occurred in just a five-year period.

At 70 acres, the Farr property on Main Street has the largest undeveloped land area in the City. The Farr property's homeplace, also known as "Five Chimneys," was built in about 1880 by Richard Ratcliffe Farr[89] after Union soldiers burned the family's original home located near the intersection of Braddock Road and Route 123.[90] Its handsome brick chimneys and other historic features continue to be admired by residents and visitors.

"Community appearance has been a citywide priority at least since 1973, when a committee was established to coordinate efforts to clean up, revitalize and re-green the city."[91] That was the birth of the Community Appearance Committee (CAC) that has since shepherded the City through annual clean-ups,

Glen Shelton, Deputy Director of Public Works (left) and John Veneziano, Director of Public Works, display the Tree City USA banner at Arbor Day ceremonies at the Fairfax Museum and Visitors Center in April 1993. Courtesy of the City of Fairfax

tree plantings and appearance competitions for residential and commercial properties. So successful have the Committee's efforts been that dozens of awards for community appearance have been received by the City. Former CAC Chairman Jack Kalina commented, "We've even got gas stations competing with each other to make themselves look good."[92]

Equally successful, the Board of Architectural Review (BAR) has made sure that all new commercial construction adheres to the general appearance standards of the zoning ordinance. Even so, the City had long desired even more specific guidance for the outward appearance of new construction. On April 26, 1994, the City Council approved the Community Appearance Plan, a definitive guide for architectural and landscaping design in the downtown and along the commercial corridors for use by both the public and private sectors.[93] While serving the last month of his ten years on the City Council, Councilman Pat Rodio

praised the plan's adoption as a fulfillment of one of his long-term goals.[94]

A small business incubator, reflecting a 2020 Commission recommendation, began operating in a downtown office building on University Drive in May 1995. Initiated and financed jointly by the City of Fairfax and George Mason University, the Center offers services in business development and support and facilities and resources for very small companies and home-based businesses.[95]

Lee Highway has been an important focus of City officials since 1988 when the Comprehensive Plan envisioned the corridor as a "Business Boulevard." The Real Estate Tax Exemption program instituted in 1992 was intended to stimulate rehabilitation of properties by increasing the amount of the exemption in direct proportion to the size of the improvement. To help control seasonal flooding in specified sections of the highway, the floodplain ordinance was tightened in

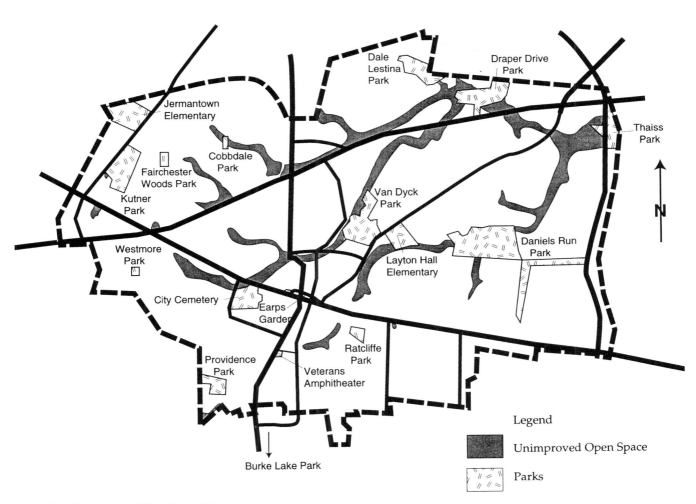

City of Fairfax Parks and Open Space Map

1993.[96] The Economic Development Authority, charged with long-term overview of the corridor, was allocated funds by the City Council in October 1996, to be used as an engineering fund for storm drainage, particularly at the intersection of Chain Bridge Road and Lee Highway.[97]

After years of study and debate, the City Council in January 1996, adopted a resolution approving a new half-mile long, two-lane road to run between the GMU entrance at Pohick Lane and University Drive at Armstrong Street.[98] Funded primarily by the State, the $2.0 million road was designed to more closely relate the activities of GMU and the City, particularly its downtown, and reduce traffic on the existing southern segment of University Drive.[99]

By June of 1996, the City's office vacancy rate had dropped to 7.5 percent, down from 20.5 percent in June 1992. Retail sales had risen from $474 million in 1990 to $560 million in 1995.[100] The City of Fairfax realized more sales tax revenue per capita than any other City in Virginia in fiscal year 1994-1995, more than doubling the amount that Williamsburg, Virginia, with its strong tourism economy, collected in the same year. In 1996, the residential real estate tax rate (99 cents per $100 of assessed value) was lower than any jurisdiction in northern Virginia except for Arlington County.[101] Despite its low tax rate, the City offers a large array of services for property owners and may have been the only jurisdiction in northern Virginia in 1996 offering backyard refuse collection.[102]

In 1996, Mayor John Mason, the only Mayor in the history of the City to be elected unopposed for three terms, on his fourth try met a challenger, Robert C. Russell. Russell was well known in the City after serving as School Superintendent from 1984 through 1995 and, earlier, as principal in local area schools for many years. John Mason became the first four-term Mayor of the City of Fairfax when reelected in May 1996.[103] Only Mayor Wood had served the community longer, having served almost five terms for the Town before the incorporation of the City. At his inauguration, Mayor Mason confirmed his goals, stating that "review and adoption of a revised comprehensive plan, built on the recommendations of the 2020 report,"[104] would be the first order of business for the newly elected City Council.[105]

The current Mayor and Council of the City of Fairfax were elected for two-year terms in 1996. They are, left to right, Gary J. Rasmussen; Jeffrey C. Greenfield; Mayor John Mason; Julia P. Lyman; R. Scott Silverthorne; J. Anthony Coughlan; and Philip Samuel Mershon. Courtesy of the City of Fairfax

The Comprehensive Plan was adopted in February 1997, the product of more than two years of drafting, mark-ups and redraftings, including 44 work sessions and two public hearings by the Planning Commission and five work sessions and two public hearings by the City Council.[106] The demographic section of the plan reported that the population had leveled off at about 20,000 in 1990, and the median age had increased from 30.8 years in 1980 to 33.5 in 1990, reflecting both national and regional trends. Over 41 percent of the City's adult population (compared with 24.5 percent in Virginia as a whole) had completed a bachelor's degree or higher. The City had one of the highest median household incomes, $50,913 in 1990, approximately 50 percent higher than the State median of $33,329. "The City's June 1993 unemployment rate of 2.2 percent was the second lowest of any jurisdiction in Virginia."[107] Figures from 1996 continued this same trend.

Government activities for the City of Fairfax over the years may be summarized best by a statement made by Mayor Mason in 1995: "The city prides itself on a sense of community. . . . In many ways, we behave like a small town. . . . And we make an extensive effort to outreach."[108]

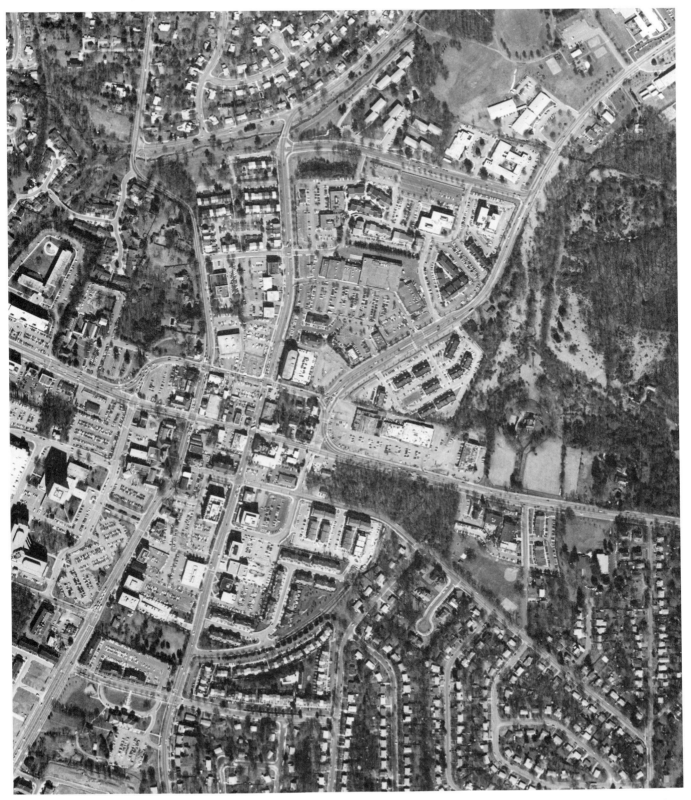

A 1996 aerial photo of part of the City of Fairfax shows the City Hall in the lower left hand corner, the historic district in left center and the post office and regional library above that on Chain Bridge Road. The Fairfax Museum and Visitors Center can be seen on the south side of Route 236 across from the Farr home place. Courtesy of Air Survey Corporation

The Legato School (built in 1876-1877) is representative of a one-room schoolhouse. In 1971 the school was moved from Lee Highway across from Legato Road to Chain Bridge Road south of Fairfax Courthouse, to mark the centennial of the Fairfax County Public School System. Courtesy of the City of Fairfax

10.

The Pursuit of Knowledge
by Mary Elizabeth Cawley DiVincenzo

Educational Issues

The newly-formed City of Fairfax had to grapple with the issue of education as never before—should the City stay with the Fairfax County Public School System or form an independent school system? The City and Fairfax County entered into a temporary contractual arrangement in which the City paid tuition to the County for City students.

By the Fall of 1964, resolution of the City-County educational arrangement became more pressing. It was estimated that the City's school population of 5,200 children would rise to 7,000 by 1970. However, the necessary school bonds could not be sold to build much-needed schoolrooms until the school system issue was resolved.[1] Indeed, an independent school system was unlikely to be up and running before the 1968-69 school year.[2] Those who favored an independent school system believed that Fairfax County might shortchange City children; in addition, they feared the loss of control over education. Those who wished to stay with the County school system pointed to Fairfax County's experience in running a school system, and questioned the cost, quality, and demographics of an independent system. Debate arose over the probable pupil/teacher ratio, cost per pupil, and teachers' salaries.[3]

In March 1965, the City-County "Peace Treaty" was endorsed by the City Council for submission to Fairfax County. The County Board of Supervisors made minor changes, approved it, and on July 1, 1965, the City-County Agreement went into effect. Many were pleased by the end of uncertainty, and happy to be joined to a school system with a proven record of success, but there were those who saw the end of hostilities as submission on the part of the City. The 1965 City-County Agreement stated that Fairfax County would administer and operate the City's schools in return for tuition payments based on the school-age population and net expenditures. The Agreement also stated that the Fairfax County School Board would endeavor to provide City pupils with an education commensurate with County pupils. In addition, it stipulated that a non-voting member of the City School Board would attend and present the City's

A young school crossing guard holding back other students. Judging by the "Get Smart" lunchbox, the photograph was probably taken in the 1960s. Courtesy of the City of Fairfax

views at County School Board meetings, and that a bond referendum "will not be held until the city's legal debt limit will permit purchase of the schools if such is the will of the citizens."[4]

Although the County was responsible for regular maintenance of the schools, capital improvements were the City's responsibility. Capital improvements, however, could not be carried out until the City actually owned the schools. The City Council had to trust that the County would make the most pressing improvements, adding the costs to the purchase price. The 1965 City-County Agreement allowed the City to buy the County schools located in the City. Part of the tuition payment that went to Fairfax County was earmarked toward the eventual purchase of these schools, valued at $5,864,955.[5]

Improvements were desperately needed. In 1955, the Town of Fairfax had a school-age population of 634 students. By 1961, the new City's school enrollment had jumped to about 3,780 students.[6] By the 1963-64 school year, the student population approached 5,000.[7] Most of the schools were crowded; Jermantown Elementary, with over 1,000 students (almost twice its 540-child capacity) was practically under a state of siege. Fairfax High used six trailers to supplement classroom space, and expected that number to double during the 1965-66 school year. The high school cafeteria lunch times ranged from 10:30 to a 2:30 "high tea"; science and art classes were meeting in unsuitable rooms[8]—and the school-age population was still rising.

These quonset huts (c. 1958) at the former Fairfax High School helped to contain the overflowing school population. Heated by kerosene stoves, the quonset huts, with concrete floors and corrugated metal interiors, must have had interesting acoustics. Courtesy of Fairfax County Public Library Photographic Archive

Proponents of an independent city school system were not pleased with the City-County Agreement, believing that the City had a sufficient tax base to warrant independence, and fearing that the County School Board had far too much power, and far too few checks, in their control of the City's schools. The City's electorate could not use their votes to show dissatisfaction with the County School Board's actions, for the Fairfax County School Board was appointed by the County Board of Supervisors; City residents can't vote for supervisors. For supporters of an independent system, this situation smacked too much of "taxation without representation."

The independent versus County school system debate was put before City residents in a July 12, 1966 referendum, which asked the electorate to decide whether the City of Fairfax should own, operate and carry out construction on its own schools, or merely carry out construction and renovation.[9] Mayor Edgar A. Prichard supported rejecting both bond issues, and staying with the County School system, emphasizing that the City could establish a separate school system in the future. Prichard further noted that "every year that portion of our tuition payment which is applied to the retirement of County bonds is deducted from the price of the County schools we have the option to buy. Every year the price goes down."[10] Voters agreed, and the third option (rejecting both bond issues) won handily, by a two and one-half to one margin.[11]

Although Fairfax County had begun the desegregation of its schools, the 1964 Civil Rights Act hastened the process; in June of 1964 the Fourth U.S. Circuit Court of Appeals ruled that Fairfax County "must completely desegregate its schools, probably meaning elimination of the all-negro character of the seven schools."[12] Before integration, the City's African-American elementary students went to Eleven Oaks School on School Street. Over a two-year period, Eleven Oaks Elementary was phased out, and its pupils were sent to surrounding schools. By the 1966-1967 school year, Eleven Oaks was used as the kindergarten annex of Green Acres Elementary.[13] Integration led to the Federal Headstart Program. The City's integrated Headstart class (and a preschool office) were housed in Eleven Oaks Elementary.[14]

Before integration, the City's African-American eighth to twelfth graders went to Luther Jackson High School. Fairfax County followed Virginia's model for integrating high schools. Formerly "colored" high schools were converted into integrated intermediate schools, and the formerly segregated high school's students were sent to nearby high schools. In this manner, Luther Jackson High School reopened in 1964 as Luther Jackson Intermediate School.[15]

Rising enrollment and years of meager educational spending had created perilously crowded schools. Nationally, Virginia had been among the low spenders for public education. In 1965, Fairfax County's cost-per-pupil was below the national average, although its residents' income was higher than average.[16] This ratio changed, seemingly overnight, as both Federal and state money buttressed local spending. (Federal funds obtained from the Impact Aid Program partially financed John C. Wood Elementary School).[17] In one year, spurred by the 1966 General Assembly, Virginia moved from thirty-eighth to twenty-fifth place in local, state, and federal spending on schools.[18] Fairfax County did its part by struggling to respond to the population boom with a prodigious construction program, building, during the 1960s, a classroom a day.[19] Nonetheless, county and city schools had to cope with the much-despised temporary trailers.

The surge in students that sparked so many school issue debates crested in 1969-1970, when the City of Fairfax had almost 6,000 students in its schools.[20] However, a steady decline in enrollment in recent decades has given rise to new concerns. The City has fewer elementary schools. Fairfax Elementary closed in 1976, and John C. Wood followed suit in 1983.

John C. Wood Elementary School, which closed in 1983, reopened in 1985 as the John C. Wood Municipal Complex, including the Police Department and the Parks and Recreation Department. Courtesy of the City of Fairfax

Eleven Oaks Elementary, phased out as a school in 1967, is now being used as a County School system administrative office.

City children do attend county schools, and the reverse is true. According to the terms of the 1978 School Services Agreement, the County should pay a fee for County children attending City schools, but the City School Board routinely waives the fee. The relatively small amount of money involved is not as important as maintaining an appropriate number of children in the schools.[21] Enrollment has been slowly rising since 1989;[22] the total 1995-96 enrollment in the six City schools was 2,366, about half of them elementary students.

By the late 1960s, Fairfax High School, built in 1935, stood in need of serious renovation or replacement. The County and City had planned to convert Sidney Lanier Intermediate into a high school facility, turning Fairfax High into the City's intermediate school.[23] This plan was seen by some City residents as County meddling, and became the focus of another fight for an independent school system. The voters, in an advisory referendum, voted for a new high school rather than go along with the County's switch and conversion plan. The result was the construction of the $8 million "new" Fairfax High School on Old Lee Highway.[24]

The issue of an independent system lay quiescent for some years, although generating enough tension that twenty-nine teachers and principals requested transfers to non-City schools, fearing that an independent system would lead to lower salaries and retirement benefits.[25] In 1978 the issue of independence versus renegotiating the County Contracts led a record number of voters (50% of the electorate) to reject the pro-independence slate; a landslide of votes went to every City Council candidate that espoused a pro-County philosophy.[26]

Since 1978 the relationship between the City schools and the Fairfax County School System has been regulated by the School Services Agreement (SSA). The SSA stipulated that the City was responsible for building (and owning) any additional elementary schools, which the County would operate and maintain. The City had previously purchased several city-located schools, and purchased the rest within several years of the SSA. The County was responsible for building and operating additional intermediate or high school buildings.[27]

Although the County is responsible for maintaining the City schools, and for minor improvements, the City must handle major capital improvements. The City's Capital Improvement Program charts schools' probable needs for the coming five years, following recommendations made by a citizens' board appointed by the School Board. In 1984, the elementary schools were 21 to 30 years old, and the twelve-year-old Fairfax High building had roof problems. Renovations added multipurpose rooms to the elementary schools (to serve as gymnasiums), repaired the high school roof, and, mercifully, granted all the schools the boon of central air conditioning.[28]

The City of Fairfax School Board oversees the School Services Agreement. The board develops its budget and the Capital Improvements Budget, and champions the needs of the City schools before the City Council and the Fairfax County School Board. The City School Board employs a City Superintendent, an administrative assistant, and a supervisor of construction projects. The School Board had been appointed by the City Council until November 1993, when citizens voted to change to an elected board of five voting members and one non-voting student member elected for a one-year term by students of Fairfax High School. The first School Board elections were held in May 1994.

The City's general education expenses have always made up a significant part of the City's budget. During the boom decades of the 1960s and 1970s, general education expenses made up 50 percent or more of the budget,[29] a result of the high numbers of school-age children in the City.[30] As the school-age population dropped, so did education's percentage of the budget. During the 1980s, education made up 40 percent of the budget; by 1996 education accounted for 35.2 percent of the budget.[31]

The tuition contract with Fairfax County takes up the lion's share of the City's total educational expenditures. Over the past ten years the tuition contract accounted for a little more than 97 percent of total educational expenditures. The remaining educational expenditures are allotted to capital improvements, debt service, and administrative costs. The tuition contract is far and away the largest of all the City's contractual services with the County. Since 1980, the tuition contract has made up about 78 percent of the City's total contractual services with the County.[32]

Public Schools

Westmore Elementary

Westmore, built in 1953, is the oldest public school still in use in the City. One of Westmore's most remarkable characteristics is the long-time nature of the faculty and staff; few leave willingly. Typically, teachers or staff leave due to retirement or a spouse's transfer. Helen Amorosa Rapson noted that she and Nancy Slusher have taught children—and their children. The biggest change in staff (and students) occurred when seasoned Westmore veterans were transferred to the newly-built Fairfax Villa School. Many Westmore students went with the staff; Westmore's enrollment of about 800 children split almost in half. Since the mid 1980s, Westmore has had about 310 to 340 students.[33]

Jean Dair taught at Westmore from 1963 to 1985; for 17 years she was a kindergarten teacher. All that time she had the same teacher's aide, Margaret Griggs. Dair remembers 49 children to a class in those pre-airconditioned days, and many trailers for classrooms. She remembered that Westmore was that modern rarity, an "all-walkers" school in the years before Mosby Woods students began to attend Westmore.[34]

In 1964, Virginia was putting all the schools through their first accreditation process, an arduous situation. Rapson, a brand-new William and Mary graduate, recalled that Principal Nellie Brown (1953-66), who had planned to retire, stayed on to guide the school through the shoals of accreditation. Brown was followed by Serena Genovese (now Watts), who was also a wonderful principal, but with a very different approach—she thought nothing of skateboarding down the hall.[35]

Westmore rejoices in good relations among employees, parents, and students. Back in the glory days of the Redskins, one custodian, a Dallas Cowboys fan, took to leaving teasing blackboard messages for the Redskin-loving teachers when a game was imminent. When the Redskins beat the Cowboys, the teachers left pitying, gloating messages for the custodian - all secure in the knowledge that the tables could be turned by the next game.[36]

Good custodial relations couldn't prevent a comical situation early in Rapson's career, when a fellow teacher and his students were stuck in their classroom. A rather mischievous student told Rapson that Mr. Williams was locked in his classroom, and signaling for help. Rapson discounted this seemingly foolish story, but the boy persisted. When Rapson investigated, she realized the lock on William's door had jammed. A group of resourceful Brownies in his class were supposed to have left early for a camping trip, and, amid tears, asked to be lowered (by ropes) from the windows to the ground. The hinges, after years of assiduous varnishing, were inexorably stuck; in the end a locksmith freed them all.[37]

In the little circle in front of the school is a dogwood tree, reputed to have been planted there when the school was opened. Once a thing of beauty, it is now known mostly for its unsettling vertical profile. Attempts to remove it and plant a new tree have been fruitless; the city arborist has stated that the tree, a state symbol, is still alive. A red maple, planted by the kindergartners to honor long-time kindergarten aide, Mrs. Griggs, is doing very well.[38] (This tree is not the only "planted" item at Westmore; a time capsule was buried on Westmore's 35th anniversary in 1988, and will be opened in the twenty-first century).

Westmore has a fine stand of trees running behind it, trees that have inspired a long-time school legend, that a naked man was seen in the woods. Rapson said that virtually every year one of the older children claims to have seen him. Invariably, the older children want to hunt for him, and the younger children are suitably spooked; no doubt the point of the legend.[39]

In 1992, Principal Ken Buterbaugh led Westmore's "World Peace Program". Thirty doves (actually, homing pigeons) were set free by children to represent world peace. Children wore simple costumes of their native countries. The World Peace Program was more than a one-day event; during the previous three months, children had run 24,901 laps on the school track, to represent circling the earth.[40]

Four years ago Mary Lou Johnson and Chris Stunkard developed a partnership between Westmore and ManTec International, a partnership now maintained by Principal Joyce Dantzler and Stunkard. ManTec, which concentrates on space experimentation and environmental issues, provides tutors and mentors to Westmore. In turn, Westmore provides ManTec with artwork, musical entertainment and programs. Westmore students who have toured ManTec's facilities noted that every room had a computer, underlining the need for computer literacy.[41]

Layton Hall Elementary

Layton Hall Elementary, built in 1956, takes its name from Joseph and Belle Willard's home, Layton Hall, although it was originally part of the Farr property.[42] Martha Wilkins, principal for sixteen years, was officially presented with the school keys by Superintendent W. T. Woodson.[43] Jim Smith, a former school board member, said Wilkins did a fine job.

Opening with 389 students and 10 classrooms,[44] Layton Hall was so crowded that children went to school for half-days for almost two years. Children who lived very close to the school nevertheless rode a bus, for at that time Old Lee Highway was very narrow, had no sidewalk, and trees came to the edge of the road.[45]

Jack Liedl, the first PTA president at Layton Hall, got into a bureaucratic tangle for his direct action, after learning someone had put a padlock on the cafeteria door; he took his wire-cutters to school and cut the padlock off. When his action was greeted with a fusillade of threats for destroying County property, Liedl offered to take his opponents around to discuss the situation with the Fire Marshal, a daunting invitation that cooled their wrath.[46]

Students in the late 1950s and early 1960s received ballroom dancing instructions and endured nerve-wracking air-raid drills. After obedient hours in class, some children enjoyed playing on the Farr property, which ran behind the school; their pleasure was spiced with the fear of being shot for trespassing. Students

Mayor John Russell speaks to a group of Layton Hall students on a tour of City Hall in the 1960s. Courtesy of the City of Fairfax

also enjoyed fording Daniels Run.[47] At times this bucolic landscape was <u>too</u> bucolic; occasionally, cows from the Farr property made a break for it, and wandered onto the playground, an exciting but maddening occurrence when recess had to be canceled. A student's father took care of the herd; the student sometimes reported on the cows' adventures.[48]

Since 1989, Layton Hall has had a "business partnership" with George Mason Bank. The partnership teaches the children banking and financial methods, using student tellers and depositors.

Layton Hall, under Principal Marian Sanders, acquired the Model Technology Program. Qualifying for this program was like trying to win a grant; the staff had to show they were willing and able to embrace technology and demonstrate that they used it in teaching. The program provided for computer training for first- to fourth-grade teachers. During the second year of the program, Sanders arranged for Green Acres Elementary Principal Gayle Andrews to receive equipment that was available, but that, due to regulations, Layton Hall could not receive. The City of Fairfax School Board worked with the City Council to provide the Model Technology Program to all the elementary schools for the 1996-97 school year, and helped Layton Hall receive the hardware, software, and teacher training for fifth and sixth grades.

Sanders noted that Layton Hall students enjoy the school's diversity. Layton Hall's parental liaison is a tremendous help. The liaison is always bi-lingual, usually in Spanish. She makes calls, helps register children, and helps with complaints. She maintains the foreign language brochures that are available at the school and has helped Sanders develop a group of "parent leaders" who can communicate in the proper language with other parents. In addition, Layton Hall is the site of the "Family Literacy" program for the City schools. ESL (English as a Second Language) classes are held for parents of school children. Children can get homework help as their parents learn English and are taught basic business skills.[49]

When John C. Wood Elementary closed in 1983, its students merged with Layton Hall. Layton Hall teacher Jan Green Dowdy, who also taught at John C. Wood, has seen many social changes over the years. She noted that children have not changed. They still come to school eager to learn, eager to succeed - and the teachers are still happy to oblige them.[50]

Jermantown Elementary

Jermantown Elementary opened its doors in 1957 to an overflow of 750 students. Until 1960, first graders to seventh graders occupied the first floor. Fairfax High eighth-graders controlled the second floor (Fairfax County had no intermediate schools until 1960).[51]

Music was taught to the eighth-graders in the library, recalled Robert C. Russell, then a high school music teacher; "We just used every inch of that building." Jermantown's elementary students overflowed into a quonset hut and several dismal trailers. Longtime school secretary, Millie Holdaway, remembered physical education being taught "in the main hall during lunch while other students used the multi-purpose room as a cafeteria".[52]

The Jermantown Parent Teacher Association (PTA) carried out a reading program called "Read-in-92—Count Me In". Parents read tales from around the world to students, and then marked the country on a world map. The Jermantown PTA received a Virginia "Count-Me-In" Grant for this successful program. In June 1992 the National PTA selected the Jermantown PTA as one of "eight PTAs in the Nation to receive an Advocates for Children Award." Such efforts led the City of Fairfax School Board to pass a resolution honoring the Jermantown PTA.[53]

Jermantown Elementary reflects modern technology and changing demographics. Student broadcasters use WJES, the school's closed-circuit television, to keep students up-to-date on local, national, and international events. Jermantown also has a business partnership with Cincinnati Bell Information Systems; the company renders material aid to the school in the form of tutors, school volunteers, and grants for teachers. Jermantown has had a Spanish-speaking parent liaison working part-time at the school to help bridge the gap between the school and non-English speaking parents.[54]

Green Acres Elementary

Green Acres opened in 1962, under the leadership of Dorothy Collier, the well-seasoned principal of 13 years at Fairfax Elementary. Collier brought with her to Green Acres the "ungraded primary" system, which had been in place for three years at Fairfax Elementary (one of two schools in the County to try this innovation). Rather than be classified into first, second or third graders, children met eight goals at their own pace.[55]

Like a queen bee going to a new hive, Collier led almost half of Fairfax Elementary's staff to the new school. They were followed by about 600 students from Fairfax Elementary and Mantua Elementary, who were shifted to Green Acres on the last two days of the 1961-62 school year. The new students had access to 1800 books, almost three times as many books as most new schools.[56]

Dance has always been an integral part of Green Acres. In the 1960s, the annual spring program highlighted themes such as "Peace through Understanding and Communication," featuring over 600 students, group dancing, and costumes. Today, Green Acres features "Dance Electric" a fourth, fifth, and sixth-grade specialty, unique to Green Acres.[57]

Students combined learning and pleasure in 1969, when they celebrated what they had learned of American history, from the Revolution to the Civil War, by reciting speeches, making costumes, dancing, and auctioning off bag lunches.[58] This program was further refined by 1971, when principal Roberta Mahoney sported an authentic 19th century outfit, and children marked "End of the Civil War Day" with games, spelling bees, and two 19th century academic tools, rote arithmetic and blab sessions.[59]

In 1981, Green Acres Students were filmed for the national "Reading is Fundamental" (RIF) program. The film was destined for 4,000 RIF programs in the country. The children sang RIF cheers, praised reading, and displayed their usual school spirit.[60]

Green Acres SACC (School Age Child Care) teachers choose a motif for learning each year, such as "human geography." Children are taught where they live in relation to their city, state and country, what states one would cross when travelling between two cities, and similar teaching games. Green Acres' SACC students have planted geraniums at City Hall, carried out a community care project at Commonwealth Nursing Home, focusing on the Alzheimers patients, and have gone on trips to many places - all within one mile of the school.[61]

Sidney Lanier Middle School

Sidney Lanier Middle School, named for the 19th century Georgia poet, was built in 1960. Middle schools, originally called intermediate, were new to Virginia. Before World War II, Virginia had a 7-4 educational system, i.e., seven years of lower school, four years of high school. Eighth grade developed after World War II as a review year for high school. In 1960, Fairfax County began building eight intermediate schools to relieve crowded high schools and elementary schools.[62] No longer would seventh graders be at the top of the elementary school heap; no longer would eighth graders be the lowest form of life at Fairfax High School.

The concept of intermediate schools was so new in Virginia that the state specifications were for "upper elementary" schools. Consequently, students had to bend way over to use the water fountains, and some had to get on their knees to use the showers.[63]

Sidney Lanier was not completely ready when classes began; lacking a completed gym, P.E. instructor Rich Wells marched students into surrounding

Named for the 19th century Georgia poet, Sidney Lanier Middle School (formerly Intermediate) was built in 1960. Lanier was one of eight intermediate schools begun by Fairfax County in 1960 to relieve overcrowded elementary schools and high schools. Lanier is the site of the Robert C. Russell Theater, named in honor of the former principal and City of Fairfax superintendent of schools. July 1997, courtesy of the photographer Randolph Lytton

neighborhoods, where, as Wells noted, "you could walk out into the field and see cows and horses across the street."[64]

The early yearbooks at Sidney Lanier underline the differences and similarities of early students with those of today. The first two yearbooks were exceedingly austere; students, faculty, even Principal Bob Russell were unnamed. There were two labeled group pictures, however; the girls were called the "Yabadabado Flintsticks," and the boys were the "Aardvarks." Over the years, girls teams sported such names as "The Exterminators," "The El Ka Bongs," "The Bloomers," and "The Lovin' Spoonfuls." A boys group was called "The Lanier Knights." Sidney Lanier had a chess club, archery club, 4-H club, and a marionette club. The bus patrols, judging by their proud expressions, took their responsibilities seriously. Music was very important; bands, glee clubs, and choruses abounded.

Some yearbooks feature candid shots with captions. Several evocative examples: 1966: a girl with another girl standing on her back says "Just because I took her surfer cross!" 1967: a laughing student exclaims, "Mr. Russell on roller skates!" 1970: a distraught teacher cries, "The Skins lost????" Featured in the 1973 Yearbook was a drawing of the moon, and the caption, "That was the Year that Was: Apollo 17 to the moon, and a landslide to Mr. Nixon."[65]

Lanier's school colors are blue and gold, and the school emblem is the American bald eagle. During the school year, Sidney Lanier houses an after-school teen center for studying or relaxing. During the summer the teen center, called the "Lanier Summer Wreck" is open during the day.[66] The Lanier Theater is the site of many performances by community groups.

Today, as one walks into the school, one is greeted on the right by the "Wall of Fame", featuring some of the school's notable students. Sidney Lanier students come from around the world; the cultural richness of the school can be visually appreciated as soon as one enters the building. The ceiling tiles are beautifully painted with many national flags; outside, the Stars and Stripes fly over all.

Fairfax High School

Dedicated on January 30, 1972, the "new" Fairfax High School replaced the 1935 Fairfax High School. In the much larger, technologically sophisticated school, educators and students had to struggle hard to foster a sense of unity. To some extent, they quickly succeeded. In 1975 the National Community Education Association selected Fairfax High School as one of the finest community schools in the Metropolitan area, due to its academic program, and use as a community center for recreation, culture, and higher education for adults.[67] Indeed, the use of the high school by the community at large figured in the conception of the new school. A citizens' group went to Flint, Michigan, to learn about its "Community School" concept. Tailoring the high school to serve the community as well as students led to the inclusion of "features from the Flint plan, such as a large fieldhouse, racquetball courts, a sauna, and a multi-use auditorium."[68] Fairfax High's classrooms, auditorium, field house and sports facilities are used by the community for sports, civic meetings, college courses and musical occasions. The completed school's versatility and availability led to Fairfax High School's receiving an award as "one of the nation's top community educational facilities. . . .Fairfax High was singled out as an excellent example of how educational facilities can be used for a wide range of community activities."[69]

More than just technology or size separated the two schools' experiences: the all-white, mostly all-American student body of the old Fairfax High (until its last years) was a vastly different student body from the new school, where, during a discussion on the Gulf War, the students were "Iraqi, Kurdish, Saudi-Arabian and Kuwaiti, as well as children of the American military." Even the math is different. Fairfax High was the first high school in the continental United States to teach Hawaiian (now called "process") geometry, in which students are encouraged to discuss, argue, and learn concepts by groups.[70]

In 1986, a furor erupted at Fairfax over the school mascot, Johnny Reb, an old sword-dragging, rebel flag-flying Confederate soldier. African-American students (and some white) objected to what they saw as a racist symbol. Principal Harry Holsinger agreed, dropped the mascot, and also ordered the drill team to change their name from the "Confederettes." A group, "Fairfax Citizens for Johnny Reb" brought a lawsuit against Holsinger, claiming the loss of the mascot was a violation of the students' freedom of speech and due process. Their lawsuit was dismissed, and the group was ordered to pay court costs of $1,800.

In April 1987, the Federal Appeals Court in Richmond ruled that the lower court had erred in dismissing the case, and that it should be heard.[71] The final

Aerial view of Fairfax High School, December 1971. Old Lee Highway crosses the upper left corner. The school itself occupies eight acres of the 48-acre property. The field house seats 5,000 people. Courtesy of the City of Fairfax

ruling came when the U.S. 4th Circuit Court of Appeals ruled "A school mascot or symbol bears the stamp of approval of the school itself. Therefore, school authorities are free to disassociate the school from such a symbol because of educational concerns."[72] For some years now the school symbol has been two crossed swords, with the word "Rebels."

The elusive notion of "school spirit," so important at the former Fairfax High School, thrives at Fairfax High. Candy Contristan, a counselor at Fairfax, and a student at the former Fairfax High, said that one had to get to the old high school an hour early to get a seat in the gym, which heightened school spirit. Now, when one can actually fit the whole school on one side of the field house, there is a natural loss of urgency. However, Fairfax has noticed increased participation in dances and school functions. The old Fairfax High

was superior in staging bonfires. In 1989, Fairfax High had a bonfire, but it was not very impressive, hedged in as it was by safety regulations.[73]

Mitch Sutterfield, who attended the former Fairfax High, and was in the new Fairfax High's first graduating class, coaches wrestling and football at Fairfax High School. He believes that sports have greatly improved over the years. Athletes used to be seasonal; now to be competitive one must do at least two seasons in a chosen sport, and many athletes play more than one sport. Fairfax competes against many more high schools in the Northern Region than was formerly the case, and a number of them are big, AAA schools.

Sutterfield noted that one of the reasons Fairfax High School was built was to improve athletics. The old Fairfax High had a small gym, no track, and poor fields. Fairfax High has a 5,000 seat field house, a 69

141

by 39 foot wrestling room, a state-of-the-art track, a 10,000 seat football stadium, and great soccer and lacrosse fields. The baseball field is so marvelously level that whenever the State baseball finals are held in the area, they are held at Fairfax High School.

A major difference over the years is the explosion in girls' sports. Fairfax has girls' gymnastics, field hockey, indoor track, soccer, lacrosse, softball, and basketball (including a freshmen team). They have had a girl on the wrestling team and football team (a field goal kicker). The girls play as intensely as the boys. Sutterfield observed that the first generation of girls' coaches were men, but that the second generation of coaches tend to be young women.

Sutterfield said that high school coaching is the last bastion of amateurism. Promising athletes must abide by the same rules as raw athletes, and all must obey the coach, a startling premise for students who have had few authority figures to deal with. The drug and alcohol policy is very strict, whether on or off school grounds. In addition, all athletes must show they are passing at least five subjects every week, or they are off the team.[74]

Fairfax High's students have excelled in many fields. In 1982 the school yearbook, the *Sampler*, won "an award of excellence" from the Fairfax County Public Schools Publication Contest; the *Sampler* took second place in the Virginia High School League Competition. In addition, the school's literary magazine, *Matrix* (1982), won Fairfax County's "Award of Excellence" scoring a first place rating in the state competition.[75]

In February 1990, Lieutenant Commander Pierre Thuot, astronaut (graduate of Fairfax High, 1973), had his first space flight on Space Shuttle *Atlantis*. The drama of this flight was shared by Fairfax High sophomore Deborah Bunker, the winner among 40 students in a competition in which students "built replicas of the rocket, space shuttle, and other space equipment accompanied by written reports to compete for a trip to Cape Canaveral." Bunker made a model of Skylab, and submitted a report on digital imaging. She was accompanied to the launch by her science teacher, Sandy Shockley, and counselor, Sue Murray.[76]

As *the* City high school, Fairfax has stronger bonds to the City Council than might otherwise be the case. In 1985 the City Public Information Advisory Committee, led by Diane Cabe, designed and implemented a three-week government program for Fairfax High seniors. Students attended a seminar, and spent the day with City employees. Those seniors who had won "election" seats were matched with their counterparts for a day.[77]

In 1983 the City Council presented cash awards to three Fairfax High students who had won the Fairfax High Award, the Faculty Award, and the Student Service Award.[78] The Dr. Thomas Hill Music Scholarship and the City of Fairfax Young Citizens Award are presented at graduation. Other awards are presented to the winners at a City Council Meeting. Certificates of appreciation are also given to a representative from each athletic and academic department.[79]

Fairfax High had its first all-night, alcohol-free party in 1988, initiated by Janice Miller. The Fairfax High School Parent Teacher Student Association sponsors the party, held after commencement.

Fairfax High's City-County demographics have greatly changed. During the school's first year, all the students were City residents. In 1972, 500 eighth-graders destined for Robinson High were brought to Fairfax to ease Robinson's overcrowding. The number of County students at Fairfax has slowly risen, and now makes up about 60 percent of the enrollment; County students are necessary to keep enrollment steady. Fairfax High's enrollment has stayed in a range of about 1400 to 1600 students for some years.[80]

Fairfax High students, like their predecessors of old, help their community through such activities as food and blood drives, and visiting nursing homes. Indeed, one can find further evidence that Fairfax High possesses some of the same small-town ambiance as the old high school; since 1992, a duck has successfully nested in an enclosed courtyard at the school.[81]

Religious Schools

Paul VI Catholic High School

Paul VI High School opened in 1983 with 225 students. In 1985, Principal Father Donald Heet said, "about 94% of its students are Catholic, and religion seems to be the main reason people send their children here."[82] Paul VI is co-educational and administered by the religious congregation of Oblates of St. Francis de Sales. The faculty contains lay and religious teachers.

Paul VI High is located in the former Fairfax High School (which was for a short time George Mason University's North Campus). When Paul VI opened, the 48-year old building was in poor shape and needed major renovations; one of the first assemblies was disturbed by a gentle rain of acoustic tiles. The auditorium has been recently renovated back to its original Fairfax High School appearance, a fitting setting for the great drama department. A classroom which had been part of George Mason's art section was covered with drawings of nudes and body parts. The faculty decided to paint over the door and window, and renovate it later! Replacement windows in the front of the school were designed to match the original windows. Paul VI had a "buy a window" campaign to raise money for new windows. One parent, Dave Ingemie, said that if his son spent as much time looking out the window as he did in high school, he deserved one of his own.

The floor in the gymnasium is soft wood; for years a group of orthopedic doctors played basketball on it. The gymnasium is still used, although it is not regulation size, and fans do not like the claustrophobic conditions. At present, there is no place large enough for the school's 1,227 students to assemble at once.

The school library, which started out with two magnificent nine-foot windows, and no books, is now both aesthetically and scholastically appealing. Librarian Ellen Dumbrowski whipped it into shape, and so impressed her personality on it that when she retired, the library was re-named in her honor.

Paul VI faculty have found interesting souvenirs of the building's earlier tenants. In the basement, teachers found barrels of crackers and other items, presumably left over from Fairfax High's role as a Civil Defense bomb shelter. A floor safe in what is now the main office has resisted a locksmith's attempts to crack it, and its contents, if any, are unknown.

Parents and students have always given generously of their time. Principal Father John Lyle encourages alumnae to visit any time. Many alumni have returned to help the excellent sports program. For two years in a row, Paul VI has won the Catholic Swimming Championship. The school's other sports, particularly boy's soccer and baseball, are also doing well.[83]

St. Leo the Great Parochial School

St. Leo's School had its beginnings in the 1950s, arising in response to the growing Catholic population. The first St. Leo's classes were held at St. Charles School, Arlington; Mrs. Rita Hurley taught St. Leo's first and second graders in one classroom. For three years the "school" shifted from St. Charles, to the nave of St. Leo's Church, and then to the "annex," a two-room building behind the church. In 1959 the school

found its final home in a ten-classroom school on Old Lee Highway. Elementary and junior high students were taught by lay teachers and Sisters of the Order of St. Benedict, from Bristow, Virginia. Sister M. Anselma, principal, and Sister M. Gertrude began teaching students in 1956.[84] The Benedictines were replaced in 1966 by the School Sisters of Notre Dame from Baltimore, Maryland. In 1968 the administration of the school was carried out by the Sisters of Notre Dame, Chardon, Ohio. The Notre Dame sisters left in 1993. Principal Diane Drews now heads an all-lay faculty and administration.[85]

The Benedictines and Notre Dame Sisters had very different teaching philosophies. Sister Rita, O.S.B., maintained control by simply looking down the hall - a crook of her finger summoned any miscreant. Her steely gaze combined with lengthy essays of the "I must not" ilk quelled rebellion. The Sisters of Notre Dame opted for a more psychological method of discipline. However, an examination of one's motives in wrong-doing resulted in the same level of obedience.[86]

St. Leo's students have always had charitable projects but the unsophisticated days of saving (and naming) "pagan babies" are long over. From 1992 until 1994 the student body sponsored a three-year project to help send three Guatemalan children to school. Students also raise money for charities, send seasonal cards to shut-ins, and completed a school beautification project along Old Lee Highway.[87] During the 1995-96 school year, St. Leo's and its across-the-road neighbor, Layton Hall Elementary, carried out a very popular bike helmet safety program, which made reduced-cost helmets available to children.[88]

St. Leo's has pre-kindergarten to eighth grade. An addition was built in 1970. In March 1991, the Parish Activities Center opened, consisting of a gymnasium, meeting room, library and four classrooms. These classrooms have been the school's junior high territory.[89]

Trinity Christian School

Founded in 1987, Trinity Christian School is an independent interdenominational school, begun with strong help from Truro Episcopal Church, where it is housed. Trinity Christian School strives "to offer a high quality academic program in the classic tradition of integrating faith and learning. . . ."[90] Trinity Christian School began with grades one to three, but presently has grades one to eight; in 1997 it will begin offering ninth grade. In 1989, Trinity Christian School leased additional classroom space at Providence Presbyterian Church; in fall 1996 its preschool leased space at Christ Lutheran Church. The School's plans for the future include a campus on Braddock Road and expansion of its educational program from kindergarten to 12th grade.[91]

In 1995, Trinity Christian School students received more individual Presidential Fitness Awards than any other Virginia school in the 100-500 student enrollment range. The students thus received the State Champion Physical Fitness Award.[92]

Bygone Schools

Greenwood School (Preschool and Kindergarten)

Ruth K. "Snip" Peter founded and ran Greenwood School from 1958 to 1965, at a time when there were few preschools. Susan Hardy Johnson attended kindergarten at Greenwood, held in the lower level of the Peter's house. Johnson recalled going upstairs to bake cookies, and feeding the Peter's horses every day. The house on Orchard Drive, surrounded by farmland, had been converted from a barn by Mr. Peter. Johnson and her husband, William Page Johnson, now live in the house.[93]

Fairfax Elementary

The first Fairfax Elementary School was built in 1873, the first brick public school in Fairfax County. In 1912 an addition was placed in front of the 1873 structure. When the "new" Fairfax Elementary was built next door in 1925, the old school house became the property of the "Cavaliers of Virginia, Inc."—a KKK chapter.

The Fairfax County School Board purchased the 1873 building in 1937, and repaired the damage done by a 1932 fire. Hereafter referred to as "the Annex," it was used for Fairfax County's first special education classes in the 1950s. In later years, it was used as a school administration building and as part of the Northern Virginia Police Academy. In 1992 the building reopened as the Fairfax Museum and Visitors Center.[94]

The "new" Fairfax Elementary school was in use until 1976. Lehman Young transferred to the "new" Fairfax Elementary from the 1873 school in 1926.

Young recalled that the new school was surrounded by mud. Every now and again, the students were impressed into service to pick up rocks, and plant flowers and grass. Young noted that it was built with very little state money. Most of the money came from local businessmen, such as F. Shield McCandlish, Fred Richardson, Walter Oliver, George Robey, his father, Lehman Young, and others.[95]

Kathryn McCord, who taught at Fairfax Elementary from 1939 to 1942, was asked by Principal J. E. Bauserman to be part of an experimental program, which she undertook with some trepidation. Rather rowdy underprivileged white children from Washington, D.C. were sent to Fairfax Elementary, where it was believed country life would have a soothing effect. McCord noted that "some of the children were good and some were ornery", and that Principal Bauserman was a good man, who worked with the children on a one-on-one basis.[96]

Dorothy Collier, principal at Fairfax Elementary from 1949 to 1962, began her career in 1929 in a one-room schoolhouse in Navy, Virginia. She was not averse to new methods; Fairfax Elementary was one of two schools chosen in Fairfax County to have the "ungraded primary" system, in which children met goals at their own pace.[97]

By the 1960s, the big event at Fairfax Elementary was the annual Spaghetti Supper. Few men were in the schools then; children who misbehaved were sent to the custodian, Benny, to have the fear of God put into them. Mary Hinson was the last principal of Fairfax Elementary, which closed in 1976.[98]

Eleven Oaks Elementary

Eleven Oaks Elementary, built in 1953, was the segregated school for African-American elementary students. African-American high school students had to travel to Manassas to go to school before Luther Jackson High School was built in 1954. The 1953 red-brick school was built behind the site of the earlier "Fairfax Colored" School, a white frame building with outhouses in the back. The 1953 school had a kitchen, but no cafeteria; parents took turns volunteering to serve the children. For years Eleven Oaks schoolbooks were hand-me-downs from Fairfax Elementary; Eleven Oaks students set time aside each year to repair the books.[99] Alta Newman, who was born in Washington, D.C., and moved to Fairfax after marrying, recalled gathering pupils around the piano to teach them songs, and reading, for the first time, the lyrics to "Carry Me Back to Old Virginia." Astonished, she asked the children, "Do I speak like this? Do you speak like this?" Nonetheless, she was required to teach the song, dialect and all.[100]

Principal Janie Howard's concern that children coming to the school had low standardized test scores led to Eleven Oaks being selected as one of Fairfax County's three pilot kindergarten schools (two African-American, one white). Some children were bussed to Eleven Oaks from as far away as Centreville. The Federal Government's Head Start Program began about the same time, and a Head Start office was installed at Eleven Oaks, headed by Newman. Children coming to the integrated Head Start Program were drawn from a much smaller geographical area. Newman, recruiting students for Head Start, had to convince leery parents that Head Start play equipment was educational. The program received good local support. Woodson High School students made the child-sized furniture and kitchen appliances from wood donated by women of Truro Episcopal Church. Under the direction of Newman, the students went to a dairy farm, fire department, circus, walking trips, made art projects, and managed to keep a pet rooster alive.[101]

In 1962, Eleven Oaks students received some very pleasant publicity at the time of Col. John Glenn's orbital flight. The *Fairfax City Times*, having received almost 50 letters and poems on the subject from the City's elementary schools, printed 15 letters - 14 of them from Eleven Oaks fourth, fifth, and sixth graders. Fifth-grader Charles Carter's poem follows:

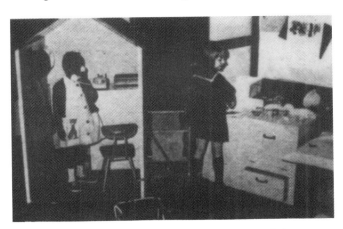

Two little girls were photographed playing in Eleven Oaks Elementary's Head Start classroom in June 1966. The play equipment and furniture were built by woodworking students at Woodson High School. Courtesy of Fairfax City Times

John Glenn was a man,
and a good man, too.
He wanted to go into space
so he had no time to waste.
It was very kind of him to go up flying.
And it was a good sight to see all the sea.
I thought he wasn't going and that made me sad.
But one morning I was made very very glad.
John Glenn went into
Orbit.[102]

As part of the integration process, Eleven Oaks School was closed, and all students attended their local elementary school. Since 1967, Eleven Oaks has been a County School system administrative office.

John C. Wood Elementary School

John C. Wood School, named after the long-time mayor, was the first city-built and city-owned elementary school; it was financed with a substantial amount of Federal funds. When the school opened, on March 1, 1965, it received students from Fairfax Elementary, Westmore, Layton Hall and Green Acres.[103] John C. Wood was an all-walking school when it opened. Students greatly enjoyed the opening of E. Calvin Van Dyck Park, with its great fields and jet plane; they used the park for their field days.[104]

This 16-room, "campus" style building had no hall. Classrooms opened directly outside, a slightly quixotic design for Virginia's climate. The school was designed this way as a result of the student enrollment boom. It was believed to be far easier to add onto the school's modular style than onto the old-fashioned "egg-crate" style of school. Children had no problems with it.[105]

Wood's first principal, Aurelia Howland, was fair and helpful. Teacher Jan Green Dowdy said that many of the schools' teachers believed that if it had not been for Howland, the founding of the new school would have been a struggle. She was a very organized woman, who ensured that her teachers had all the supplies they needed.[106]

Principal Mary Roots had a very warm style. She advocated combination classes, believing that the faculty would be less stratified, and would thus work better together. There was much use of faculty "teaming," i.e., one fifth grade teacher teaching science to all the fifth grade classes. There were always fun programs, such as International Day in the spring (all classes picked a country). The PTA initiated one tremendous project. The 12 classroom teachers were each assigned a month, and each child drew a picture of that month. The paintings were transposed onto 12 eight-by-four pieces of plywood. The teachers' names were worked into the pictures, which are now in room A at the John C. Wood Complex.[107]

In April 1984, due to declining enrollment, the former school became a municipal complex for the City Police and Magistrates Office. Remaining students were transferred to Layton Hall.

"Old" Fairfax High School

Before Paul VI—before George Mason University's North Campus—the two-story red brick building at 10675 Lee Highway was the original Fairfax High School. Fairfax High was a 17-classroom, two-laboratory building. The school had no cafeteria, gymnasium, or auditorium. Built in 1935, its first student body of 468 students was drawn from the old Oakton, Lee Jackson, Clifton and McLean High Schools.[108]

Agriculture was an accepted part of the curriculum. Indeed, the first addition to the new school was a stove-heated building (with tar-paper walls) built to make agricultural studies possible.[109] A former student, John Sherwood, noted that the school didn't provide textbooks; "the only books you had were what you bought yourself, and those you bought second-hand."[110]

The Old Coach Inn's coach being lowered from the roof of the girls' gym at the old Fairfax High School. The man facing down on the left rear side of the roof is "Bill" Sheads; the unflappable student is unidentified. Photo courtesy of Gary L. "Buddy" Matthews from the Washington Daily News

Eighth grade was introduced in Virginia after World War II, and eighth graders began attending Fairfax High School in 1947. From 1957 to 1960, Fairfax High's eighth-graders, the "Plebes," split their days; mornings at Jermantown Elementary, afternoons at the high school. The 1958 yearbook, the *Sampler*, contains this rather plaintive eighth-grade caption; "In Jermantown, one-half mile away from the high school, we had a world uniquely our own."[111]

Schools have always been fertile grounds for teenage pranksters. However, one prank at Fairfax has assumed mythic proportions. Across the road from the school stood the Old Coach Inn, whose dramatically distinguishing feature was a 500-pound, seventeenth-century gentleman's coach. In 1959 the coach appeared in all its glory—on top of the girls gymnasium at school. Principal Samuel Coffey, keenly aware of the absence of pixie dust—and the presence of some gifted physics students—thundered that the offending students, if found, would be subject to all manner of punishment. The math and physics teacher, Ray Williams, was well aware of his students' recent interest in those laws of physics that involved coach-hoisting, and noted that if he learned who did it, he was honor-bound to report the names to the principal. Thus, he ordered no more talking about it. Sue Peter Jones said her brother, Paul B. "Beau" Peter, was one of the hoisters, confessing his part in the high-jacking at a reunion years later.

The escapade had been masterminded by "Pat" Jones, son of Virgil Carrington Jones. Peter, who used the family tractor to plow gardens, had arranged his schedule of plowing to park the tractor in Mr. W. T. Woodson's shed. In the dark of night he took the tractor, a very quiet Ford Ferguson, to the school. The coach was rigged with a pulley, and pulled up to the roof by the tractor, much as one would lift a bale of hale into a hayloft. This was familiar work to the plotters, who were or had been farm boys. In the end, what the students had accomplished in one night took three days and a crane to undo.[112]

Another prank of the late 1950s involved two propane tanks behind the school, which were quite close together. Their proximity prompted one or more humorists to paint a bra on the tanks, with the legend, "I dreamed I went dancing in my Maidenform bra."[113] Shortly after the coach episode Mr. Paul Peter and his son, Beau Peter, were walking across the school parking lot, and saw that the exhaust fans that stuck out of the side of the building were draped with a sheet fashioned to look like a bra. When Mr. Coffey learned of this, he ordered the custodian to remove it immediately, whereupon it was discovered that underneath the "bra" was "a well-executed painting of what is behind a bra". The artwork was immediately covered until it could be sandblasted off.[114]

School spirit was important. For many years students selected the most spirited female and male student, who were then christened, "Peppy" and "Johnny [Reb]." The teachers deemed to be the strongest supporters of student activities were dubbed with the more stately titles "Lord and Lady Fairfax."[115]

All teachers came in for a day of hazing on role-reversing "Class Day." Teachers were reprimanded when they were discovered cutting classes in favor of Tops Restaurant, chided for hoarding passes, and reminded to move to the rear of the cafeteria line. Teachers were mimicked by foolhardy students in an assembly, and ushered out to the strains of "March of the Clowns."[116] Teachers could take the ribbing, for the balance of power was quite clear, crystallized by the announcement of Mr. Peter, a very pleasant teacher, on the first day of government class, "You will learn democracy under a dictatorship."[117]

Fairfax's enrollment kept growing, reaching 2200 students at one point. Quonset huts took up the overflow.[118] The original student body had been drawn from all parts of the County. As other high schools were built in the 1960s, however, Fairfax High School's population became primarily City students. In early 1967, the boundaries for Fairfax, Woodson, and Oakton High schools (then under construction) were redrawn. Present and prospective Fairfax High students in neighborhoods such as Fairfax Villa (about a mile from the school) would henceforth be bussed five miles to Oakton High. This plan, despite vociferous parental protests, had the combined blessings of the City and County school boards, who believed it was appropriate to have the school keep its "community of interest" by largely restricting itself to City students.[119]

During the late 1960s, the County was turning many middle schools into high schools, and vice-versa. Fairfax High and Sidney Lanier Intermediate were to be treated in this fashion, but residents' demands for a new school carried the day. In 1972 the torch of learning passed to the newly-built Fairfax High, on Old Lee Highway.

Higher Education

George Mason University

George Mason University owes its existence to the success of the Northern Virginia Center, a 1950 extension division of the University of Virginia, headed by professor J. N. G. Finley. Enrollment went from 63 in 1950 to 1,900 in 1955, leading the University of Virginia Board of Visitors to authorize the development of a two-year branch college of the University of Virginia, which opened in 1957 in the former Bailey's Crossroads Elementary School.[120] Finley directed the branch college and the extension.[121]

George Mason University owes its location on the City of Fairfax's southern edge to the inspiration of Stacy Sherwood. As Edgar A. Prichard recalled, Sherwood met with Mayor Wood and Prichard and presented an attractive solution to the deadlock facing the University of Virginia Board of Visitors over the permanent location of the UVA branch college. The Board of Visitors could not decide between two proposed locations: the 68-acre Ravensworth site near Annandale (which was rather expensive) or 450 free acres, offered by the Bowman brothers, at Route 7 (in what would become Reston). Several members of the Board of Visitors opted for the free acres, but Judge Albert V. Bryan believed it was too far away from the population centers the future college would serve. Sherwood proposed buying the Willard property and offering it to the Board of Visitors, with the aim of making Fairfax into a college town like Charlottesville. A bond issue was passed to buy the land, but the Willard property proved too expensive, as did the Mathy property. Wilson Farr agreed to sell 150 acres of land at Braddock and Chain Bridge Road, receiving $750 an acre for his half interest, and Viola Orr, $1,500 an acre for her half interest. The Board of Visitors liked the property, but made two stipulations: that the Town of Fairfax provide sewer and water link-ups, and that the Board have clear title to the land. There was a squatter on the land, Andy Smith, who had long lived on the property with his dog. He acknowledged he had no right to the land, and was given a new trailer near Fairfax Circle.[122]

Beginning as the northern Virginia branch of the University of Virginia, George Mason University's first classes were held in 1957 in the old Bailey's Crossroads Elementary School. The Town of Fairfax enthusiastically purchased 150 acres of land adjacent to the town in 1958 and donated it to the university. Construction of the first four buildings was completed in 1964 and classes were held on the campus next to the new City of Fairfax. With the university's several subsequent acquisitions, the total acreage of the main campus is now 583. Courtesy of George Mason University

George Mason College, named by the Board of Visitors for the author of the Virginia Declaration of Rights, "on which the Bill of Rights of the U.S. Constitution is based," opened in 1964.[123] Two years later, George Mason College was "elevated to a four-year, degree-granting institution by the Virginia General Assembly . . . and given a long-range mandate to expand into a major university."[124] In 1970, George Mason College began graduate programs and received 422 acres of land through the George Mason College Board of Control in Northern Virginia.[125] In 1972, the City of Fairfax sold the former Fairfax High School to George Mason College. On March 1, 1972 the Virginia General Assembly declared the former branch college to be an independent institution, George Mason University. The governor signed the legislation on April 7, 1972.[126]

After weathering several rejections by the Virginia General Assembly, George Mason University succeeded in forming a School of Law in 1979, merging with the financially-troubled International School of Law. In March 1980, the George Mason University School of Law celebrated its first graduation and its accreditation by the American Bar Association.[127]

Led by former Dean Henry G. Manne, the School of Law quickly carved out its own preserve in the forest of legal academia by focusing on a cross-disciplinary approach to law and economics. Students can choose between traditional legal study and a concentration in one of five "specialty track programs (corporate and securities law, litigation, international business, regulatory law, or intellectual property)."[128] The Law and Economics Center (LEC), founded in 1974, sponsors "conferences, teaching institutes, and cutting-edge research in the field of law and economics. By educating over 400 Federal judges and over 600 law professors, the LEC's Economic Institutes have achieved a superlative national reputation."[129]

George Johnson, who became president in 1978, garnered a great deal of business support for the rapidly growing university. This growth led to stress between the university and the City. In 1976, the university, with about 6,100 students, had no on-campus quarters; almost 900 students lived in the City.[130] By 1987 enrollment had jumped to 17,412.[131]

Naturally, a fair number of student residents had a more relaxed definition of "noisy," "disruptive," and "late night" (particularly concerning fraternity or sorority parties) than did established residents. Traffic, with almost all students driving to school, became a

George W. Johnson was appointed president of George Mason University in 1978, taking over a six-year-old institution of 9,600 students that offered 56 undergraduate and master's-level degrees. During his tenure, the university achieved doctoral status, acquired a law school, and earned a national reputation for academic quality and innovation. He retired in 1996. Courtesy of George Mason University

perennial headache, escalating to migraine levels during the first week of a new semester. Students, unwilling to buy a parking decal (or unable to find a parking space) parked in residential areas. Some students believed that the City police targeted them unfairly and that City residents were hostile to the university's presence.

Relations eased somewhat as campus housing increased, and the City clearly marked parking restrictions on residential streets. In 1979 the City/University/Business Committee (CUB) was formed to reduce town and gown tensions. As better communication and greater maturity helped to ameliorate problems between the City and university, CUB has stressed the positive strength of the ties between the City, the university, and the business community. CUB highlights activities and projects of interest to the three entities, such as the City of Fairfax Golf Outing or the Central Fairfax Chamber of Commerce Trade Fest. In 1996, CUB began the Old Town Hall Lecture Series, featuring notable GMU professors and faculty, such as Dr. James Buchanan, Virginia's Nobel Laureate. CUB issues the "Community Involvement Guide," listing civic, university and business functions.[132]

Other programs and efforts have fostered amicable relations. In April 1985 the efforts of the City's Office of Community Affairs and GMU's Theater Company resulted in "Fairfax City Night" in which City residents were able to purchase cut-rate tickets to a GMU play.[133] In 1986 the George Mason University Interfraternity Council adopted Providence Park, thus becoming a member of the City's "Gifts for Parks" Program.[134] In 1988 the Northern Virginia Small Business Development Center (NV SBDC), a state program, began at GMU, designed to help one start up a business or refine business techniques.[135] For years, students have carried out the "Witch Watch" program on Halloween Night, ensuring safety on City streets for trick or treaters. In addition, student teachers from the University have both eased teachers' loads and received on-the-job training in City schools.

George Mason University is able to take advantage of the metropolitan area's resources in high technology, the humanities, and public affairs. The educational centers affiliated with George Mason carry out research and "contribute, both directly and indirectly, to the intellectual growth of the George Mason student."[136] Examples are the Institute for Conflict Analysis and Resolution, the Center for Public Choice, and the Northern Virginia Writing Project.

In 1984, thanks to a bequest from Clarence J. Robinson, the University began to offer its students the opportunity to study with the Robinson Professors, "eminent scholars dedicated to interdisciplinary and undergraduate education."[137] Robinson Professors have included Pulitzer Prize winner Roger Wilkins, Guggenheim Fellowship winner, Anthropologist Mary Catherine Bateson and scholar and playwright Paul D'Andrea.

In 1996, Alan Merten, who had headed Cornell University's Graduate School of Management, succeeded George Johnson as University President. Merten heads a university that has grown with extraordinary speed from four buildings and 356 students in 1964[138] to over 24,000 students and a sprawling campus featuring notable local attractions such as the

Dr. Alan G. Merten was Dean of the Graduate School of Management at Cornell University when he succeeded George W. Johnson as the fifth president of George Mason University on July 1, 1996. He earned his undergraduate degree in mathematics at the University of Wisconsin in 1963, his master's degree in computer science at Stanford University in 1964, and his doctorate in computer science at Stanford University in 1970. Courtesy of George Mason University

Center for the Arts, the Johnson Center and the Patriot Center. The direction in which George Mason University is developing is prototypical, a model for universities in the coming century.[139]

Northern Virginia Community College

Less than two miles from the City of Fairfax's eastern border is the Annandale Campus of Northern Virginia Community College (NVCC), a two-year state-supported college offering associate degrees, occupational-technical programs, general education, and developmental studies courses. NVCC encompasses five campuses and an Extended Learning Institute (ELI) that offers home study and telecourses. NVCC is the largest community college in Virginia, and the second largest in the nation.[140]

Upon learning that Virginia had the second-lowest "percentage of college-age population" in the nation, the Virginia General Assembly passed an act in 1964 that established the Department of Technical Education and a State Board for Technical Education. One result of the act was the speedy establishment of the Northern Virginia Technical College, first located in Bailey's Crossroads; "in just over 100 days, its president, Robert L. McKee, had interviewed and hired qualified faculty and staff, established a curriculum, scheduled classes, obtained books, notified prospective students, and enrolled them in scheduled classes."[141] The college opened in 1965, with 761 students; by Fall 1966 the enrollment had leaped to 2,226 students.[142] In 1966, the General Assembly changed what had been a technical college system to the Virginia Community College System, and Northern Virginia Technical College, the first in the state-wide system of community colleges, was renamed Northern Virginia Community College. At that time NVCC added college transfer curricula to the occupational/technical curricula.[143] In

Dr. James M. Buchanan was lured away from Virginia Tech in 1983 to teach at George Mason University, three years before he became a Nobel Laureate in 1986. The Holbert L. Harris Professor and the Advisory General Director of the Center for Study of Public Choice at George Mason University, he earned his doctorate at the University of Chicago. Courtesy of George Mason University

1967, President McKee noted that over 80 percent of enrollment was in the technical program, and about 11 percent in the college-transfer program.[144]

Annandale Campus (which houses the offices for college-wide services) was the first of five NVCC campuses to be developed; the College Board bought 78 acres in Annandale in 1966. The first permanent NVCC building constructed at the Annandale Campus opened in 1967.[145] The following year, Dr. Richard J. Ernst became NVCC's second president.[146] Annandale Campus houses the Ernst Community Cultural Center, a large complex containing, for community use, a theatre, sports activities, art gallery, and seminar rooms.[147]

In 1970, the Northern Virginia Education Television Association occupied the specially-equipped fifth building on the Annandale Campus. The Association beamed programs to Northern Virginia high schools, ran the new public television station (Channel 53), and made possible a broadcast engineering technology program for the burgeoning school.[148]

A view of the Northern Virginia Community College looking south from Route 236. It opened initially in 1965 at Bailey's Crossroads as a technical college. NVCC is a two-year state-supported college offering associate degrees and other programs on its five campuses. It is the largest community college in Virginia and the second largest in the nation. Photo by Carolou Marquet, courtesy of the Northern Virginia Community College

Dr. Richard J. Ernst became Northern Virginia Community College's second president in 1968. Under his administration, the college has grown dramatically. Its courses are aimed at meeting "the requirement for trained manpower in Northern Virginia by cooperating with local industry, business, professions and government." Photo by Carolou Marquet, courtesy of the Northern Virginia Community College

NVCC is accredited by the Commission on Colleges of the Southern Association of Colleges and Schools. The American Medical Association, the American Dental Association, the National League for Nursing and the American Physical Therapy Association accredit health technologies programs. The American Bar Association accredits the Legal Assistance Program and the American Veterinary Medical Association accredits the Veterinary Technology Program.[149] NVCC courses are aimed at meeting "the requirement for trained manpower in Northern Virginia by cooperating with local industry, business, professions, and government."[150]

President Ernst has stated:

Since becoming a community college in 1966, the college has grown dramatically. During the 1995-96 Fiscal Year, the college served 60,005 students in credit courses, 21,167 in non-credit continuing education unit courses, and 251,423 persons in a variety of community service programs. The Annandale Campus continues to be the largest of the five campuses with an enrollment of 21,860.

Further, the demographic profile of the college has changed dramatically. In terms of racial composition, 13.5 percent of the student body is African-American, 12.8 percent Asian, 7.9 percent Hispanic, and 0.9 percent Native American. Reflecting the population of the community, the college served 10,728 who were on visa and not U.S. citizens. Of that number, only 734 were on a student visa, thereby indicating their intention to return to their home country.[151]

Preparing for the future, Northern Virginia Community College's mission "is to respond to the educational needs of a changing community and its institutions, ensuring that all individuals in the northern Virginia area have an opportunity to develop and enhance their values, skills, and knowledge."[152]

Libraries in the City of Fairfax

Huddleson Memorial Library

The first Fairfax Town Library began in 1933. Housed in a corner of the County Clerk's office, it contained several hundred books formerly kept by the "Old Chamber of Commerce."[153] The Fairfax County Library was just beginning to take shape, and the distinction between the two libraries was not clear; books were loaned from one to another. When the Clerk's building was razed, Town Library books were moved to the mildew-friendly Police building, leading the school board to offer the library space in Fairfax Elementary School's second floor.[154] The Town Library had no librarian until 1937. By 1940, however, with the help of Fairfax County and Works Progress Administration (WPA) workers, the Town Library took on the trappings of a "real" library, with cataloguing, files, and indexes.[155]

In 1940, the Town Library had its first appointed Board of Trustees, and moved from Fairfax Elementary to Fairfax Town Hall[156] at the intersection of "Main and Mechanic." In 1946, the Library received a $10,000 bequest from Elizabeth Chilcott, vice-president of the Library Board, and a staunch volunteer, in memory of her parents, Dr. and Mrs. F.W. Huddleson. The Town Library operated on a shoestring budget. Volunteers ran the Library, and money was raised for it through annual teas.[157] In May 1962 the Fairfax Town Library was re-named the Huddleson Memorial Library.[158]

For years Huddleson Library was run by a succession of volunteers devoted to its preservation. Roberdeau Walker and Delores Owens were among those who put in many hours. In 1983 Carol Cover, one of the Board members, became librarian and is still serving. Cover noted that arrangements at Huddleson are "very informal!"[159] She can recommend particular books for long-time patrons, or help new patrons with selections.[160]

The Library has changed little since the 1960s. It is still old-fashioned, with a card catalog and a checkout system maintained in a small wooden box. Books are not weeded out, so old favorites remain for decades. The Library contains many local histories, Civil War histories, and mysteries. Huddleson Library receives $600 a year from the City of Fairfax, and about $1,000 a year from the fund set up by Elizabeth Chilcott.[161]

The Fairfax City Regional Library

Fairfax City Regional Library, a part of the Fairfax County Public Library System, began about the same time as the Huddleson Memorial Library. In 1939, the Fairfax County Board of Supervisors voted in favor of a free library system, and a Board of Trustees for the Fairfax County Public Library was formed. The Trustees received $250 from the Board of Supervisors, and sought matching funds from the State Library Board and the WPA. Thanks to the WPA's statewide library project, the Fairfax Library received "funds for the librarian's salary, a bookmobile, and driver, books, and personnel."[162] The Board of Supervisors authorized a 24-foot-square cinderblock building for books (located behind the Courthouse, on what is now the County parking lot) and a WPA-required garage for the bookmobile.

The first professional librarian was John Mehler, who persuaded the Board of Supervisors to "provide service to black residents."[163] Population increases in the County led the Board of Supervisors to authorize getting a larger bookmobile, and expanding the cinderblock library to three times its original size, an

A southern view from Huddleson Memorial Library, 1988. Lori Crockett photo; courtesy of the City of Fairfax

This view of the east side of the Fairfax City Regional Library shows a rare sight—an empty parking lot. Photo in 1988 by Brian Conley, courtesy of the Fairfax County Public Library Photographic Archive

expansion completed in 1950.[164] The Library and its four employees took up temporary quarters in the Duncan Chapel Methodist Church basement at the corner of South Payne (Chain Bridge Road) and Court House Drive.[165] The expansion was all too small for the County's population boom. The lack of branch libraries, poor quality collection, and inadequacies of the bookmobile led citizens' groups to petition for change. In 1953 the Board of Supervisors appointed Mary Katherine McCulloch as library director, charged with leading the overhaul of the library system.[166] In November 1959, following years of effort by Friends of the Public Library organizations, Fairfax County voted to spend $2 million to build a headquarters library and six branch libraries.[167]

In early 1961, the design for the proposed headquarters library, to be located in the Town of Fairfax, was displayed. Some objected to what they perceived as a clash between its style and Fairfax Courthouse's colonial style. Architect Russell Bailey stated that he had incorporated "colonial elements in his design, and the stone and red-brick materials planned were traditional."[168]

The Town of Fairfax became a city on July 1, 1961, and was thus "ineligible for County tax-supported services after June 30, 1961." The Board of Supervisors considered selling the headquarters library, which was under construction, but was persuaded by the Library Trustees to finish the building, deferring until later whether to use it as a warehouse and administrative center, or as a library. Fairfax County and the City of Fairfax worked out a temporary contract ensuring that City residents could use the Library's services. The 1965 City-County Agreement stipulated that the City would contract for some services, including the libraries, and be entitled to have a resident sit on the County Library Board of Trustees.[169]

The Fairfax County Headquarters Library opened on July 8, 1962; it was birch-paneled, air-conditioned, could hold 150,000 volumes, and was projected to meet Headquarters' needs for 15 to 20 years. It included the Virginiana Room, a public meeting room, and a "dock" for the Bookmobile.[170] Headquarters Library began to form a Music Collection from donations, a collection which quickly expanded. The Library offered film programs, inter-library loans, a "special Business and Technical section, active participation in the Suburban Washington Library Film Service, and a Professional Library (for use of staff and library science students)."[171] The Library also had

a Civil Defense Bomb Shelter, and had food and water stored in case of an attack.[172]

Less than a year after it opened, the library was embroiled in controversy over a film program that celebrated National Library Week by showing films that promoted international good will and brotherhood. The films were denounced as subversive and, in one case, "preaching evolution."[173] The library was also denounced for carrying such "obscene" books as *Catcher in the Rye*. The Board of Trustees and the Executive Committee of the Fairfax County Federation of Citizens Associations supported Library Director Mary McCulloch, her assistant, Joseph Runey, and the Library for sticking to their guns and allowing all the public to judge the merits of artistic works. In May 1963, a lawsuit over obscenity in four library books was dismissed by Judge Albert V. Bryan "on the grounds that Virginia's obscenity statute expressly exempts public libraries from its application."[174]

Headquarters Library flourished; 1964's circulation of over 319,000 items was a "78% increase in circulation."[175] By 1970 the library was again pressed for space. To make room for the collection, many functions, including administration and cataloging, moved to the Ravensworth Industrial Complex.[176]

The revamped library was now called the Central Library. Central Library's "Library Outreach" program brought books to the elderly, the housebound, and people in jail or Work Camp 30. In 1974, the library received a Steinway grand piano, courtesy of the Library's Music Friends. These were high points of the 1970s, otherwise dogged by recession and fuel shortages. The Central Library had to cut hours, and closed completely from January 31 to February 9, 1976, due to the frigid weather and gas shortage.[177]

In 1980, the approval of a $10.43 million bond issue meant the Library could be renovated. The Library's 200,000-plus collection of books moved into the South Wing of Fairfax Courthouse, and some library staff services and collections were sent to other branches. The Library's name was changed again, first to the Central Regional Library, and then to the Fairfax City Regional Library.[178]

Perhaps disoriented by their move to the Courthouse, some of the library staff took a slight departure from their appointed rounds, and proudly presented the well-rehearsed Fairfax City Regional Library Precision Book Cart Drill Team, trophy winners at the 1983 Independence Day Parade and the 1984 2nd Annual Gross National Parade.[179]

The Fairfax City Regional Library Precision Book Cart Drill Team, performing in the 1990 Independence Day Parade.   Photo by William Haegele, courtesy of the City of Fairfax

The library's renovations were completed in 1984, and sixty staff members returned to a library with a new entrance on Whitehead Street and entirely new configurations inside. The first floor housed "circulation services; a media center; a meeting room; video cassettes; records; the children's collection; adult fiction; a storytelling program area; and a 'Magic Mountain' for children to just enjoy." The second floor contained information services; business and technical material; inter-library loans; periodicals; nonfiction; the music collection; staff facilities; and a conference room.[180]

On February 28, 1988, a Sunday morning, a piece of the Library's stone cornice broke off and fell into the parking lot. Examination proved that more of the cornice was dangerous, so the Library was closed until April 1988. Repairs were completed in early 1989.[181]

The reference librarians deal impartially with their daily allotment of questions, whether academic, bet-solving, or earnestly goofy. One patron, stymied by a copy of "Macbeth," wanted to know if there was an English version. Another patron wanted a photograph of Adam and Eve and was astonished that the Library could not provide it.[182]

Since the 1984 renovation, the Virginia Room has occupied the entire third floor. Originally called the Virginiana Room, it began as a state and local history collection, but has since expanded its focus, and holds strong genealogical and government information collections. The Virginia Room also keeps a commanding photographic archive, manuscripts, and videos of the City of Fairfax Council and School Board meetings. Increasingly, the Virginia Room uses modern technology, such as the Legislative Information Service (LIS), and the Family Search System.[183] The Family Search System, which allows one to carry out genealogical research using information contained in social security records, military service, and the like, is a CD-ROM system, and the hardware and software could not have been covered by the library's budget. The Friends of the Fairfax City Regional Library raised the money to purchase it and many other items, such as computer terminals for book information, home computer dialup to access the catalog system, and other special equipment purchases. The Friends are volunteers who handle all the logistics involved in the library's book sales (most books are donations, and the rest culled from the library's collection).[184]

The Fairfax Museum and Visitors Center opened with a ribbon-cutting ceremony on July 4, 1992. Present were, left to right, John Gano, president of Historic Fairfax City, Inc.; former Mayor George Hamill; Mayor John Mason; State Senator Jane Woods; Jim Moyer and Charlene Hurt, Head of Libraries, George Mason University. Courtesy of the City of Fairfax

Suzanne Rehder, Regional Branch Manager of the Fairfax City Regional Library, noted that the Friends of the Fairfax City Regional Library are an invaluable support in a time of lean budgets and increased services. Rehder stated that in fiscal year 1996 the library handled almost 586,000 check-outs; the first nine months of fiscal year 1997 showed a 13% increase. The 1996 door count was 350,000 people; almost 22,000 people received new library cards.

Rehder said that electronic services are the trend of the future and drive many expenditures. The Internet, in particular, is a very popular and helpful service.[185]

The public library has come a long way from the little cinderblock building. Yet, the increase in size and complexity has not quenched the original core of community spirit— Fairfax City Regional Library consistently outstrips all other Fairfax County libraries in number of volunteer hours.[186]

Fairfax Museum and Visitors Center

The Fairfax Museum and Visitors Center (FMVC), opened in 1992 in the historic Old Fairfax Elementary School. FMVC offers exhibits of northern Virginia's history, a 90-minute guided walking tour of the City's historic district, and the Futuristic Peek into the Past (FPP Project), a collaborative Fairfax High School/ Fairfax Museum and Visitors Center research project. Fairfax High School students research the City's past, putting their completed research on the HyperCard Program, and plan to create a multimedia computer presentation, available to FMVC visitors and Fairfax High school staff and students.[187] FMVC's latest project, for the City's fourth-graders, is an historical interest newspaper. Woodson High School graphics department students will set up the layout and graphics, and fourth-graders will submit letters and stories.

About 36 percent of the FMVC's business is devoted to its role as a visitors center. FMVC is on the Virginia and Fairfax County websites, and distributes City, County, and State brochures. In 1993, the FMVC had 72 requests for mailed information; such requests were up to 3,000 in 1996. Daryl Ann Humrichouser, the Museum's director and curator, noted that the complete renovation of Old Fairfax Elementary School took less than five years through funding provided by a city referendum. Humrichouser thinks the FMVC has flourished due to strong community support and especially to its dedicated volunteers.[188]

John Gano, President, Historic Fairfax City, Inc., conducts Nicholas, Lord Fairfax, through the Fairfax Museum and Visitors Center, June 11, 1992. Photo by Chris Fow, courtesy of the City of Fairfax

A determined player in the Fire Safety Olympics, 1989. Photo by Craig Bogan, courtesy of the City of Fairfax

11.

The Resources of a Giving Community:
Civic, Safety, and Sports Organizations
by Mary Elizabeth Cawley DiVincenzo

The City of Fairfax is served by a loyal network of service clubs and fraternal and civic organizations, the majority founded after World War II. With so many groups devoting themselves to community improvement, the need for oversight is crucial so that one cause does not overshadow other equally needy causes. In 1977, Charles W. Mowerey, a member of the Fairfax Host Lions Club, formed the Inter-Service Club Council of the City of Fairfax, to coordinate the efforts of these groups. The Inter-Service Club Council seeks to improve the community by fostering good relations among its organizations and providing a forum for discussing community problems. Representatives from George Mason

University, the City government, the Chamber of Commerce, and the Fairfax City Regional Library attend meetings in order to disseminate pertinent information to the Council's organizations.[1]

Following are short histories of many of the organizations that have supported the City.

American Legion Post 177

American Legion Post 177, founded in 1945, has a long tradition of service to veterans, families and the community; their motto is "For God and Country." In 1946, Amos Chilcott, a World War I veteran, donated 10 acres of land to American Legion Post 177. The American Legion held an open house in October 1951 to display the foundations of the Legion Hall. The cornerstone was a piece of Fairfax County Aquia Creek sandstone that had been part of the White House until renovations in 1950. The American Legion made Chilcott a Life Member, and later named the Legion Hall and adjoining stadium in his honor. Chilcott Hall was used for many social events. The Woman's Club of Fairfax held their first antique show there in 1957.[2]

In 1996, the Legion's 900 members supported the Independence Day Celebrations (as they have every year), held a Christmas party and Easter Egg Hunt for children, served luncheons to senior veterans in area nursing homes, and held a dinner and bingo night at the Post each week. In 1995, American Legion Post 177 donated funds to the community, schools, youth activities, veterans' organizations, the Volunteer Fire Department, Crimesolvers and Heroes, Inc.[3]

At several highway entrance points to the City of Fairfax, service club boards display names of some of the many community organizations active in the City. This particular one is located on Route 50 as it enters Fairfax Circle going west. Courtesy of the photographer, Scott Boatright

159

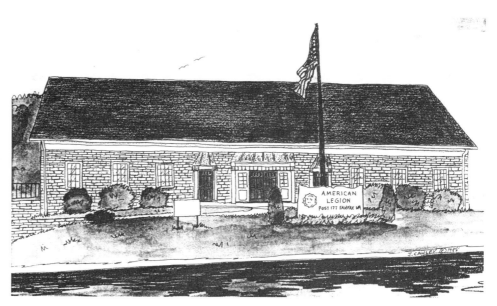

American Legion Post 177 was founded in 1945. The Legion Hall, built on land donated by First World War veteran Amos Chilcott, opened in 1951. Its cornerstone, a piece of Aquia Creek sandstone, had been part of the White House until renovations in 1950. The Hall has been the site for Legion dinners, bingo, and a host of community events. Courtesy of the artist, Jackie Cawley

American Legion Auxiliary (Unit 177)

Fairfax Unit #177 of the American Legion Auxiliary, chartered in January 1949, has twice won the Kate Waller Barrett Trophy, awarded to Virginia's outstanding American Legion Auxiliary Unit. In conjunction with American Legion Post 177, the Auxiliary members devote their attention to veterans, children and community issues. Unit 177 visits the Veterans Affairs Medical Center in Washington, D.C., where Unit 177 holds monthly parties and distributes comfort items. The unit sends comfort and gift shop items to the three Virginia veterans' hospitals so veterans can shop free of charge for their families. In addition, the Auxiliary sponsors local high-school juniors as delegates to Girls State. In 1995, Unit 177 sent 21 girls to Longwood College, Farmville, Virginia, for this "week-long crash course in government."[4]

The Auxiliary raises money selling poppies, the American Legion memorial flower, around Memorial Day.[5] The members also raise money for charity by running a Valentine's Sweetheart Dance and handling the bingo night concession stand, yard sales and breakfasts at the Legion Post.

Veterans of Foreign Wars Blue and Gray Post 8469

VFW Post 8469 began in October 1946. Despite the Post's location at Fairfax Station, they feel great ties to the City; the members originally met on Old Town Hall's second floor.[6] VFW Post 8469 has no bar or bingo at their post but holds a well-attended monthly dinner.

VFW Post 8469 focuses on veterans, firefighters, police and students. Members visit patients and run bingo games at the Veterans Affairs Medical Center in Washington, D.C. They hold Veterans Day ceremonies at the Courthouse and Fairfax Cemetery, and the Post banded together with American Legion 177 to get a flagpole for the Fairfax Museum and Visitors Center. VFW Post 8469 honored City firefighters for their response to the December 1995 fire at Old Town Hall and honored City Police for their help with the Independence Day Parade, fireworks and other events. In addition, VFW Post 8469 oversees the "Voice of Democracy," a VFW national speech contest for high school students.[7]

The Rotary Club of Fairfax

The Rotary Club of Fairfax, chartered in April 1931 by local businessmen, was the pre-eminent Town club, and was very popular with townspeople.[8] It now has 85 to 90 members. The Rotarians have the "Donate Eight" program, in which volunteers are asked to perform eight hours of community service a year. This program encourages people to volunteer without fear of getting in over their heads. Last year the Rotarians worked with "Christmas in April" to rehabilitate a home and gave money to George Mason University. They worked with the Salvation Army at Christmas time, assisted community support groups delivering

For quite a few years, the Veterans of Foreign Wars (VFW) held their meetings in the Old Town Hall. Shown in this 1948 photo are members, left to right, front row: Edward Blumenfeld, Frederic Kielsgard, far right, unknown; middle row, Everett Long, Elmo Owens, Howard Stull and Morris Katz; top row, Calvin Long, George Dalby and James McAllister. Calvin Long, Ed Blumenfeld and Howard Stull were the first three police officers for the Town of Fairfax, in 1950. Courtesy of Howard Stull

food, helped cook at a transitional house, and assisted in national immunization days at Children's Hospital. They provided the FPYC sign-up boards that dot the City. In 1996, they sponsored a spring golf tournament and a November auction extravaganza to raise money.[9]

Kiwanis Club of Fairfax

The men and women of the Kiwanis Club of Fairfax (founded 1956) have committed their efforts to aiding the community, youth, and children. The Kiwanians have long sponsored Key and Keyette Clubs at local high schools and sponsor a Circle K Club at George Mason University. They also carry out community service projects for the Northern Virginia Training Center, the Fall Festival, Fairfax County Senior Adult Picnic, Thanksgiving meals, a Christmas Party for Senior Adults and a drug awareness program.[10]

The Kiwanis Club of Fairfax helped Children's Hospital and supported the effort to eradicate Iodine Deficiency Disorder (IDD). They also support the Young Astronaut Program, the Little League, shopping trips for foster children and the Hugh O'Brian Youth Foundation.[11] In 1972, children were the beneficiaries of an unusual Kiwanis program. Led by President James F. Brooke III, the Kiwanis Club (which had been on a two-year waiting list) arranged for the installation of a T-33A jet in E. Calvin Van Dyck Park.[12]

E. Calvin Van Dyck Park, featured the Air Force T-33A jet installed in 1972, thanks to the efforts of the Kiwanis Club of Fairfax. The Park was named in honor of E. Calvin Van Dyck, who died at age 51. Van Dyck, who had been the City Attorney, was a notable athlete, and was the highly-respected jurist of the 16th Judicial Circuit Court. Courtesy of the City of Fairfax

Fairfax Host Lions Club

The men and women of the Fairfax Host Lions Club, dedicated in 1951, concentrate their efforts on sight and hearing needs. The Fairfax Host Lions hold an eye clinic at Fairfax Hospital with another Lions Club, carry out a Diabetes Awareness Program, and buy leader dogs for sight-impaired people. Any blind person in the City of Fairfax area can come to the Lions for help; if one club runs short on needed funds for projects, another Lions (or Lioness) club will help out.

The Fairfax Host Lions run clinics for hearing exams, give people hearing aids, and provide hearing dogs for hearing-impaired people. In addition, they provide scholarships for disabled students, give food baskets to needy families, and support the Police D.A.R.E. Program. They support Little League and the Babe Ruth Baseball League.

The Fairfax Host Lions' major fund-raisers are the three citrus fruit sales held each year. They volunteer at the Independence Day Parade and the Fall Festival, sell hot dogs, and collect contributions outside stores for the visually handicapped and hearing impaired.[13]

The Fairfax AM Lions Club

The Fairfax AM Lions Club was chartered in August 1975, sponsored by the Fairfax Host Lions Club. A Mid-Day Lions Club, chartered in 1967, had folded. This smaller club focuses, as do all the Lions Clubs, on eye and hearing problems. Mr. Ronald G. Hoopes of the Fairfax AM Lions noted that Helen Keller called the Lions Clubs the "White Knights of the Blind." The Fairfax AM Lions work at the Fall Festival, sell hot dogs, soft drinks and candy at the Bailey Crossroads Lions Club Bingo and turn their attentions to drug awareness, youth activities, and helping individuals as needed.[14]

The Clifton-Fairfax Lioness Club

The Clifton-Fairfax Lioness Club, formed in 1978, concentrates on sight and hearing problems, and diabetes awareness, particularly juvenile diabetes. The Clifton-Fairfax Lionesses hold fund-raisers, raising money at the Fall Festival, Christmas Craft Show, and Clifton Days. They collect used eyeglasses and hearing aids, and also help out during "White Cane" days. They help with the Lions' sight and hearing van that goes to schools, and they make up holiday food baskets for the needy.

They donate clothing and presents to the Northern Virginia Training Center, money for children to get closed-captioned televisions, hearing aids and glasses, and support high school alcohol-free parties. The Lionesses give money for the leader-dog program, in which clubs sponsor a blind person to go to Michigan to train for several months with a leader dog. They also give money to the Lions youth camp near Winchester, Virginia.[15]

Noonday Optimist Club of Fairfax

Founded in 1973, the main mission of the Noonday Optimist Club of Fairfax is to support the youth of the Fairfax City community. The Noonday Optimists, with about 85 members, conduct oratorical and essay contests for City school students, and sponsor Youth Appreciation Week (when the Optimist Club honors outstanding students from Fairfax High School, Paul VI High School, Lanier Middle School and seventh and eighth-graders from St. Leo's).

The Noonday Optimists lend their support to such youth activities as Little League, Cub Scouts, Boy Scouts and the D.A.R.E. Program. They also carry out Respect for Law Week, to honor law enforcement agents from the City of Fairfax, the Sheriff's Department and George Mason University.[16]

Many people have vowed to "clean up City Hall"—but the Brownies and the Scouts did it. Courtesy of the City of Fairfax

The Optimist Club of Central Fairfax

The Optimist Club of Central Fairfax, founded in June 1986, evolved from the Noonday Optimist Club. They focus on recognizing and assisting young people; indeed, the Optimist Club motto is "Friend of Youth." The Central Fairfax Optimists have programs at three area schools: Robinson High School, Oak View and Laurel Ridge Elementary Schools. They established two youth clubs at Robinson High, and hold an oratorical contest, a communication contest for hearing-impaired children, and bestow awards on academically successful immigrant students who have overcome such obstacles as having to learn a new language. They also hold a Teen Leadership Workshop at Robinson High School.

Both Optimists Clubs support ChildHelp, a national program that sets up treatment facilities for severely abused children. The local facility is outside Culpeper, Virginia. The Optimists raise money for the children and buy them Christmas gifts. They also help families in need at Christmas.[17]

The Civitan Club of Fairfax

Founded in 1962, the Civitan Club of Fairfax concentrates on helping mentally and physically disabled persons. The Civitans hold two parties a year at the Northern Virginia Training Center and adopted a group home, "Wellspring," for mildly retarded women. Civitans of Fairfax supported the development of the School for Contemporary Education. The Club helped this special education school get off the ground by writing proposals and winning grants, demonstrating to the business world that the school had grass-roots support, thus winning business support for the school.

The Civitans raise money by participating in the Fairfax Fair, the Fall Festival and Independence Day activities by running pony rides and cooking hot dogs. Money raised through guest speakers goes to such causes as the Virginia Head Injury Foundation and Alzheimers.[18]

Friends of Fairfax

Formed in 1982 by City Council members Rob Lederer, Ron Escherich and Gene Moore, the not-for-profit Friends of Fairfax have helped many groups, often supplying "nice-to-have" items that are not covered by an organization's budget. They have bought furniture for the Police Department waiting room, equipment for the Northern Virginia Training Center, donated money for jackets for Wildflour Bakery employees, given money to the Washington Ear,[19] helped the Fairfax City Regional Library's Virginia Room and bought a portable piano for City Hall.[20] In 1983 the Friends of Fairfax organized the Fairfax City Gala, a dinner-dance designed to bring together business owners and members of neighborhood civic organizations, such as Fairfax Mews, Ardmore and Great Oaks.[21] The Friends of Fairfax also arranged the Festival of Lights and Carols and are involved in the Chocolate Lovers Festival.[22]

Henry Lodge No. 57 (AF&AM)

Henry Masonic Lodge No. 57, chartered in 1869,[23] met in various places, including Fairfax Courthouse, until 1900. The trust that conveyed the newly-built Fairfax Town Hall to the Trustees of Fairfax Town Hall stipulated that Henry Lodge No. 57 be permitted to hold regular meetings on the second floor, and that the Lodge ". . . have exclusive use of the small northeast room on the second floor of said Hall."[24] The Lodge met in Fairfax Town Hall until 1971, when they moved into their new temple on Oak Place. Money raised by Henry Lodge goes to the Grand Lodge in Virginia, and charities are then given money. The

The first Henry Masonic Lodge at Fairfax Court House was chartered in December 1849 and was in existence until December 1855. A new Henry Mason Lodge, No. 57, was chartered by the Grand Lodge of Virginia in December 1869. The Lodge met in rented quarters until member Joseph E. Willard and his wife Belle conveyed the newly-built Town Hall in part to the Masons for a meeting hall. In 1971, a new Lodge Hall was completed at 10503 Oak Place in Fairfax Acres. After more than a century of continuous existence, more and more brethren have "discovered how pleasant it is to dwell together in unity." Courtesy of Henry Lodge No. 57, A.F.&A.M.

163

Lodge has a scholarship program for a high school graduate. Henry Lodge sponsors three Masonic youth groups, the only lodge in Virginia to sponsor all three. They are the International Order of Job's Daughters, the International Order of DeMolay, and the International Order of Rainbow for Girls. These youth groups confine themselves to general leadership programs.[25]

Fair Oaks Hospital Auxiliary

Fair Oaks Hospital Auxiliary began in 1978 as Commonwealth Hospital Auxiliary, devoted to raising money to purchase hospital equipment. The Auxiliary's by-laws forbid using funds raised for anything but their Hospital, but the community benefits in the end. In 1987, Commonwealth Hospital's staff and equipment changed sites, moving to Fair Oaks Hospital, and the Auxiliary was renamed Fair Oaks Hospital Auxiliary.[26]

Fairfax Nursing Center

Fairfax Nursing Center is a privately owned 200 bed skilled facility providing specialized care by dedicated professionals. Robert and Charmaine Bainum began Fairfax Nursing Center in 1964 and continue to guide its progress. The Center remains family owned and operated. The Fairfax Nursing Center places great importance on professional nursing care for the residents of the Center. Over 50% of the nursing staff are RNs and LPNs, the highest ratio to residents at any facility in the northern Virginia area. Approximately 25 percent of Fairfax Nursing Center is devoted to the care of residents with Alzheimer's and other related diseases. The Center has regular activities for its residents. It has added animals, birds and plants to the Center to enrich the lives of the residents, their families and the employees of the Center. Each year the entire Fairfax community enjoys the elaborate holiday decorations in front of the Center -- a different display for each season of the year.

The Central Fairfax Chamber of Commerce

The Central Fairfax Chamber of Commerce (motto: "Better Business is our Business") began in 1956 as the "Court House Square Businessmen's Association." In 1958 members elected George Hamill as their first president, and Kathryn Everhart their first secretary. Among other actions, the Association monitored and responded to legislative action that affected business. In 1963 the newly dubbed City of Fairfax Chamber of Commerce, hitherto an all-volunteer organization, hired its first executive director, Arthur D. Stamler.[27] During the 1960s, the Chamber supported the formation of Northern Virginia Community College, established

Hubert Dulaney was the longtime owner of Fairfax Hardware Store, which opened in January 1953. He was the Grand Marshal of the 1992 Independence Day Parade. In 1995 the Woman's Club of Fairfax sold a Christmas ornament of Fairfax Hardware, the first time a business had been so honored, as a tribute to Dulaney's community spirit, particularly his neighborly morning coffee club at the store. Courtesy of the City of Fairfax

Cub Scout Pack 1513, led by Cub Master Lieutenant Colonel William G. Arnold, held a "Pine Wood Derby" on May 5, 1969, racing models designed and built by the Pack, and rated for speed and beauty by five judges, four of whom are kneeling at the end of the race track. From left to right they are Warren Carmichael of WEEL radio, Wayne Orme of the National Bank of Fairfax, Fairfax County Police Officer Joe Higgs, and William Garber of the National Bank of Fairfax. Courtesy of the City of Fairfax

relations with George Mason College, and focused on resolving traffic problems. In 1974, the Chamber began the practice of meeting with the City Council and City staff, in order to alert them to business issues.[28] The Chamber sponsors events such as the TradeFest, now included in the Fall Family Festival Business Expo, Fairfax Quality Day, and participates in the Chocolate Lovers Festival. In 1994, the Chamber and George Mason University and other organizations became partners in the creation of the Enterprise Center[29]; in 1996, the Chamber's Business Showcase exhibited over 100 local businesses' products and services.[30]

The Chamber honors achievers all year long: Business Leader of the Year, Public Safety Awards, Small Business Awards, Community Appearance Awards, scholarships and the Athena Award. The Athena Award, given to women who facilitate the rise of other women in business, is a national award from Oldsmobile. The Central Fairfax Chamber of Commerce works with Farrish Oldsmobile to bestow this award.[31]

Fairfax Junior Chamber of Commerce

The Fairfax Junior Chamber of Commerce (Jaycees), founded 1994, welcomes men and women between 21 and 39 years of age. Jaycee members acquire management, communication and leadership skills as they develop community service projects. The Jaycees volunteer at the Fall Festival and the Fairfax Easter Egg Hunt, manage canned food drives, sell donuts to raise money for Cystic Fibrosis, and hold a "Dating Game" fund-raiser for "Camp Virginia," the Jaycee camp for disabled children. They visit nursing homes and hold international dinners, dollar movie nights and bar-of-the-month outings.[32]

Downtown Fairfax Coalition

The Downtown Fairfax Coalition seeks to protect and revitalize Old Town Fairfax. The coalition is a public/private partnership of residents, merchants, business and property owners and City officials. Leadership is provided by an 18-member board of directors that includes elected officers, a city-appointed official, a State Senator and State Delegate and a full-time salaried executive director.

The coalition was formed in 1990 in response to an economic blow to the City: the relocation of Fairfax County's government from the Massey Building to the Fairfax County Government Center. To replace the loss of the connected business infrastructure, coalition programs have sought to create, in Old Town Fairfax, an eclectic mix of retail on the first floors of buildings, with business and legal offices on upper floors.

Since 1994, coalition programs and activities have greatly expanded. They include the Chocolate Challenge, Spring Clean-up Day, an Arts and Services Auction, the Saturday Morning Community Market, the annual City of Fairfax Championship Golf Tournament and the Expo Room at the Holiday Craft Show. The coalition publishes a quarterly newsletter, the "Main Street News," and a restaurant, merchant and service guide, which are distributed to residents, tourists and George Mason University students. The Downtown Fairfax Coalition relies on George Mason University interns and area volunteers to assist with the multitude of programs and events they sponsor throughout the year.[33]

Historic Fairfax City, Inc.

Historic Fairfax City, Inc.(HFCI), founded in 1983 as a non-profit organization, acts as advocate for the City's historic heritage. HFCI generates interest in, and support for, the City's historic properties, public and private, including Old Town Hall and the Ratcliffe-Allison House. In 1987, the City's Office of Planning, at the behest of the City Council, succeeded in having the City's "old and historic district" placed on the National Historic Register, a measure that carries a federal tax break for owners of historic buildings, and as Planning Chief David Hudson noted "validated the idea that Fairfax is historic." In 1990, a zoning review committee changed the name of the "Old and Historic District" to the "Old Town Fairfax Historic District."[34]

In March 1971 the Garden Club of Fairfax presented $500 to Mayor John Russell for Old Town Hall landscaping renewal, a donation in honor of Kitty Pozer and her efforts to preserve Old Town Hall. Club president Kathryn McCord, Mrs. Walter Oliver and Mrs. John Elliot presented the check. Courtesy of the City of Fairfax

HFCI, under President John Gano (1989-1996), oversaw the procurement, fund-raising, and renovation necessary to turn Old Fairfax Elementary School into the Fairfax Museum and Visitors Center. HFCI oversaw the transformation from school to museum by gathering a collection of artifacts and by training docents.[35] HFCI also highlights the need for tax-deductible contributions to buttress City spending for historic renovation. Jeanne Johnson Rust gave the rights to the reprinting of her 1960 book, *A History of the Town of Fairfax* , to HFCI.[36]

The Garden Club of Fairfax

Organized in 1926, the Garden Club of Fairfax is affiliated with the Garden Club of Virginia. Kitty Pozer, who restored the Ratcliffe-Allison House and turned it over to the City, was a member. During the last week of April, the Garden Club of Fairfax participates in Historic Garden Week; proceeds go to the Garden Club of Virginia.

They carry out community projects on a regular basis. They had a landscape artist draw up a plan to redo a courtyard at Woodburn Center for Community Mental Health, which they then carried out. The Garden Club of Fairfax planted a memorial garden around the little house by the pond in front of George Mason University's Center for the Arts and dedicated it to Mrs. Ebie Stull. Some years ago they carried out a project for the Northern Virginia Training Center, winning the Commonwealth Award, given yearly by the Garden Club of Virginia.[37]

Ladies Auxiliary of the Fairfax Volunteer Fire Department

The Ladies Auxiliary, a perennial presence at City gatherings, was founded in 1928. All money raised by the Auxiliary is used for the benefit of the Fairfax Volunteer Fire Department. The Auxiliary raises money for the Fairfax Volunteer Fire Department through Friday night bingo at Station #3. They run the kitchen at Station #3 and do catering. They have a bakestand at the Fourth of July Parade and the Fall Festival, sell craft items at the Chocolate Lovers Festival and hold flea markets. When Fairfax was a small town, the Ladies Auxiliary used to run social dances for high school clubs.[38]

The Tuesday Afternoon Club

The Tuesday Afternoon Club began in 1947, inviting women from throughout Fairfax County.

Members of the Tuesday Afternoon Club honored their founder at a special tea given in the summer of 1957 observing their tenth anniversary. Left to right are "Dickie" Kitchen, Dorcas Henderson, Marion Macomber, Kitty Smith, Virginia Curran, "Ebie" Stull and "Snip" Peter. Courtesy of the Fairfax County Public Library Photographic Archive

They have always had a civic interests committee, and have arranged speakers on topical subjects, such as political change or welfare reform. Many speakers have presented information on Fairfax County subjects. The Tuesday Afternoon Club awarded scholarships at a time when such scholarships were unusual, selecting from Fairfax County high schools. Originally, the scholarship was always given to a woman (selected by her school), for women rarely received scholarships. Now, the scholarship is just as likely to be awarded to a man as a woman.[39]

The Woman's Club of Fairfax

Organized in May 1956, the Woman's Club of Fairfax devotes its attention to charities, fund-raising, and social activities. The members have raised money through fashion and antique shows, card parties, and the sale of cookbooks, baked goods and Christmas ornaments designed by local artists. Funds raised have gone to many groups, including the Northern Virginia Training Center, the Fairfax Museum and Visitors Center, Northern Virginia Community College, George Mason University, scholarships, and specific medical or social cases, such as medical supplies for a wheelchair bound child. The Woman's Club organized the first senior citizens' club in the area and also helped to organize Meals on Wheels.[40]

Celebrating their 40th anniversary, in October 1996, were the following members of the Woman's Club of Fairfax: left to right, Betty Dittman, Outstanding Citizen for 1996; Eldrey Appler, charter member; Dolores Testerman, Second Vice President, and Patricia Pflugshaupt, President. Courtesy of the Woman's Club of Fairfax

Fairfax Ferns Garden Club

The Fairfax Ferns Garden Club, formed in 1960, carries out beautification projects. The members have, for the past ten years, decorated Old Town Hall for

Christmas. After Old Town Hall's December 1995 fire, they took down their decorations, waited for speedy renovations, then put them back up (not leaving until 1:00 in the morning) to have Old Town Hall ready for a wedding the next day. For the last eight years, they have maintained the garden in the front of the Ratcliffe-Allison House. For several years, they have been planting flowers in the boxes in Old Town; in Spring 1996, they planted 800 flowers in the boxes, and filled the boxes with flowers in time for the Fall Festival. The Fairfax Ferns' efforts turned the former smoking atrium at Fairfax High School into a pretty garden. In 1995, the ladies planted a garden around two benches at Rust Curve. They dedicated the garden to the memory of Paul I. Barthol, the spouse of a Fairfax Ferns member.[41]

American Association of University Women

The Fairfax City Chapter of the American Association of University Women (AAUW) was chartered in July 1973. By 1996, the Fairfax Chapter had 70 women in the City of Fairfax area. The AAUW members aid the community by serving on PTAs, library boards, watchdog committees and school committees. For years they helped coordinate the City of Fairfax Halloween Party. For the past six years they have run the GEMS (Girls Excelling in Math and Science) Conference. The AAUW raise money to fund a graduate-level scholarship at George Mason University for a City of Fairfax woman.[42]

The Zonta Club of Fairfax County

The Zonta Club of Fairfax County, founded in 1957, is part of Zonta International, a world-wide network of professional women dedicated to raising the status of women. The Zonta Club of Fairfax carries out service projects that focus on education. Zonta scholarships at Northern Virginia Community College encourage young women to prepare for non-traditional fields. Zonta funds the Edith Clark Nalls graduate-level scholarship at George Mason University. The Zonta Club and Northern Virginia Community College's Division of Business sponsor the annual "Women in the Workplace" seminar. The Club supports "Project Opportunity," a Fairfax County program that inspires and assists pregnant teenagers to finish high school, and lends a hand to battered women, the aged, pregnant teens and foster children.[43]

Soroptimist International of Fairfax County

Soroptimist International is a service organization of professional women, open to any woman who is a president, officer or owner of a business. Soroptimist International of Fairfax County gave women nursing scholarships when no one else did, sending women to Richmond for their education. When nursing scholarships became more common, the Soroptimists turned their attention to other projects, such as their Youth Citizen and women's Opportunities Scholarships, Hospice of Northern Virginia, Aids, breast cancer research and battered women. For fundraising purposes, they have sold food and ornaments including White House Christmas ornaments at the Fall Festival. However, their biggest moneymaker has been the annual antiques show held at George Mason University.[44]

Civic Associations

The City's civic associations, formed to define or maintain a subdivision or neighborhood's interests, also serve as a link between a neighborhood and City Hall. Civic associations have "adopted" neighborhood parks, donating time, money and equipment to maintain them. Many of the City's civic associations publish newsletters.

These and other organizations, such as the Widowed Persons Service, the American Red Cross, Welcome Wagon of Fairfax-Burke and the Salvation Army Auxiliary, are part of an altruistic network, whose efforts have strengthened the community. Asking for donations on a freezing day, battling bees while running a cotton-candy booth, or cooking steaming hot dogs on a steaming day may be typical, seemingly thankless, club activities. But allied with this labor is a tremendous sense of camaraderie, accomplishment, and as Elden Wright of the Fairfax Host Lions noted; "We have fun; if we didn't have fun, we wouldn't do it!"[45]

Country Clubs

Fairfax Army Navy Country Club

The Army Navy Country Club of Fairfax began when the Arlington Army Navy Country Club (ANCC) sought to expand to allow more golfing opportunities. The ANCC focused on property which had originally been the site of the Swayze farm on Old Lee Highway. John Connolly, a former ANCC greenskeeper, from 1940 to 1949, purchased and developed this property into the Fairfax Country Club. He eventually sold the club to developers, who sold the club to the Arlington ANCC. The newly-christened Fairfax Army Navy Country Club opened in 1958. The Fairfax ANCC, with its "topiary letters" of ANCC visible from Old Lee Highway, has golf, swimming and tennis courts, including two all-weather courts.[46]

The Country Club of Fairfax

In 1947, John Alexander and John H. Rust, Sr. led a group of twenty men interested in starting another country club. On September 17, 1947, they bought the Haight dairy farm south of Fairfax, between Fairfax Station and Fairfax Courthouse. They built the Court House Country Club on the farm property, selling shares to the community to buy the land. On June 26, 1948, the Court House Country Club officially opened, with a four-hole golf course known as "the Famous Four." The original farmhouse served as the first clubhouse. During the club's first year, wheat was raised on part of the property to help fund the development of the golf course. The twenty original founders devoted their time and physical labor to develop the club. Senator John W. Rust was the club's first president, continuing as such for almost a decade. On July 31, 1949, the original nine-hole golf course opened; a tennis court was also available to members.

In 1955, the current clubhouse opened. The same year the swimming pool, more tennis courts and a second nine holes of golf opened. During the 1970s, more tennis courts were added, and a bubble for winter tennis playing was leased. In 1986, the club name was officially changed to the Country Club of Fairfax. Several years later the clubhouse was completely renovated, reopening on August 8, 1992. The thriving Country Club of Fairfax has over 800 members with over 500 full golfing members.[47]

Police, Fire and Rescue Community Activities

The City of Fairfax's Fire and Rescue and Police Departments increasingly augment their regular missions of emergency responses and crime prevention with many community improvement and prevention programs. These programs educate the community (especially children) on fire safety, drug issues and health maintenance. All help make the City a nicer and safer place to live.

Fairfax Police Youth Club Marching Band in the Independence Day Parade, c. 1971. Courtesy of the City of Fairfax

D.A.R.E. (Drug Abuse Resistance Education), first taught at St. Leo's in 1992, is now taught by City Police to all City fifth graders. D.A.R.E., an alternative to regular drug enforcement efforts, seeks to educate children before they are confronted by drugs. A uniformed police officer covers such topics as peer pressure, self-esteem, violence and risk-taking, and assigns homework and a final essay. D.A.R.E. wraps up with an assembly, at which the winning essays are read aloud, and the winners are presented with a Darren the D.A.R.E. Bear Mascot.[48]

D.A.R.E. hosts summer events for parents and children. A popular event is the D.A.R.E. Air Show at Manassas Airport, run by the D.A.R.E. Officers Association; the underlying theme of the show is that a person with a drug-clouded mind can't fly, skydive or do anything that requires skill. Fortunately, D.A.R.E. has cost the City very little money to support it. Money has come from state grants and community groups, such as the Lions, the Downtown Fairfax Coalition and the Chiropractors Association.[49]

The Community Bike Patrol began as a method to give the police a stronger community presence, as they patrol parks, schools and pools. The Patrol has also proven surprisingly effective at stopping crime. Indeed, one officer made six "driving under the influence" and several drug arrests; officers have caught larcenies in progress.

As in all Fairfax County high schools, a police officer is assigned to Fairfax High School. Officer Tim Haines splits his time between Fairfax High and Lanier Middle School. He maintains order, speaks in government classes on such issues as search and seizure, attends sporting events, and acts as a mentor. He has solved several cases by his presence at the school.[50]

Officer Haines and Officer Dave Sharp are taking part in the City's "Officer Residency Program." They moved into apartments along Jermantown Road where, as residents in an area "in transition," they take part in community meetings, meet with residents, and drive home marked police cruisers. The officers must learn Spanish, and act as officer liaisons at Jermantown Elementary School and Lanier Middle School. The officers live rent-free, thanks to owner, A. J. Dwoskin. This program, which City Police Chief John J. Skinner refers to as part of a "community policing" trend, has been very successful.[51]

The City of Fairfax Police raise money for good causes. In February 1996, the City Police were part of the "Polar Plunge" fund-raiser for the Special Olym-

pics; participants jumped into the Atlantic Ocean. In June 1996 the City Police, sponsored by American Legion Post 177, raised a team to participate in a "plane pull" at Dulles Airport, to raise money for the Special Olympics.[52]

There are, of course, many other programs: the all-volunteer Fairfax Police Youth Club has, since 1964, acted as sponsor for children's sports activities. The community unit performs various functions, such as taking the ever-popular radar board (which displays the speed of approaching vehicles) out into the streets. At times the community unit has set up a law enforcement Explorer Unit for the Boy Scouts. Perennial programs, such as fingerprinting children or free engraving of serial numbers on valuables are aimed at the same goal — improving the security and quality of life in the City.

Fire and Rescue Community Activities

Smoke detectors and sprinkler systems have greatly reduced the loss of life due to fires; not content with this reduction, the City of Fairfax's Fire and Rescue

Mayor George Hamill, accompanied by Lt. Freeland Young of the Fairfax County Fire Marshal's Office, giving Junior Fire Marshals Joseph Wolfe, Dean Fortney, and Mike Jackson a proclamation declaring October 8, 1969 "Junior Fire Marshal Day" in the City. Courtesy of the City of Fairfax

Department seeks to further reduce death and injury in the community with an aggressive risk management program. Four programs in particular seek to achieve this goal:

> H.E.L.P. (Health Education and Lifesafety
>   Program) in the Schools
> H.E.L.P. in the Community
> Aluminum Cans for Burned Children
>   (ACBC)
> COACH (Cardiac Outreach and Cardiac
>   Health)

H.E.L.P. in the Schools seeks to alert students to preventable dangers to their health and safety. One engine or station company is assigned to one parochial elementary, five public elementary schools and the middle school. Two rank-level officers are assigned to each school to develop a safety program. Three activities are required parts of each school's program: semi-yearly safety assemblies, Fire Safety Olympics and a Safety Message Board.[53] The Fire and Rescue Drug Program is handled differently than the Police D.A.R.E. program; the health side of drug, tobacco and alcohol use is discussed by medics.[54] In 1996, firefighters planted trees in front of Jermantown and Layton Hall Elementary schools, on which students hang safety messages, using what they have learned from the firefighters.[55] The Fire and Rescue Department also teamed up with George Mason University's Pi Kappa Alpha Fraternity to hold a fire essay contest for City-area fifth and sixth graders.[56]

H.E.L.P. in the community offers safety classes to citizens, safety inspections for businesses and civic groups and free home inspections. Fire and Rescue will install, at no cost, smoke detectors donated by Circuit City.[57] The COACH program sends blood pressure testing machines to such places as stores and libraries. Under the COACH program, citizen CPR classes are offered each month. In the ACBC Program, the proceeds from recycled aluminum cans are placed into a program account. Proceeds finance a summer camp and medical treatment for young burn victims and purchase special equipment, such as hands-free telephones.

City of Fairfax Sports

There are many facets of sports life in the City of Fairfax. Three private pools (Mosby Woods, Fairfax, and Country Club Hills) accept memberships from the community. Starlit Pool, which trained many swim-

Girl Scout "Daisies" helping with the Aluminum Cans for the Burned Children program, 1989. Courtesy of the City of Fairfax

mers, closed in the early 1980s. There are many sports-related businesses in the city, such as the Fairfax Ice Arena, Bowl America Bowling Alley, Fast Eddie's Billiards Cafe, Gold's Gym and the Fairfax Racquet Club.[58] Within the City, youth and adults can participate in a variety of organized sports activities.

Fairfax Little League

In May 1955, Hugh Tankersley successfully spearheaded the move to create a Fairfax Little League; 250 boys played that first season. Fairfax Little League, incorporated in March 1956, began their 1955-56 season with four Major teams, four Minor teams and two Farm teams. The League worked hard to develop fields and stadiums. The Little League leased Chilcott Stadium from the American Legion for five years. With the Babe Ruth League, the Little League oversaw the construction of three Minor and Major League fields on Pickett Road. After these fields had been expanded, they dedicated the Pickett Road site to Fred Thaiss, a tireless volunteer and former Little League president.

During the 1964-65 season 650 boys played in "eight Major, eight Minor AAA teams, eight Minor AA teams and eight Minor A teams in each League."[59] By the 1967-68 season, 1,183 boys were in Fairfax Little League, which expanded to three Leagues for the 1968-69 season: American, Dominion and National Leagues. During the 1971-72 season, Fairfax Little League had over 1,350 boys playing on 96 teams. By the 1974-75 season, however, there were 900 players on 74 teams. The 900 players included girls for the first time.

Fairfax Little League teams have repeatedly won the District 10 Championship and sent a team to the

State Championship. In the 1972-73 season, the Fairfax Dominion Team won the Virginia State Championship and traveled to the Southern Regional Playoffs in Florida, where they lost. In 1993-94, Fairfax Little League hosted the 15-team state tournament at Chilcott Stadium.

Starting in 1978, the number of Fairfax Little League players began to rise again. By the 1995-96 season, there were 1,368 players on twenty-four Major teams, 62 Minor teams, 24 T-Ball teams and four Challenger teams. The Challenger Division teams, for disabled children, was formed in 1989-90; 1995-96 was the first year for two Junior Division teams.[60]

Fairfax Babe Ruth League

Fairfax Babe Ruth Baseball began in 1957, for 13- to 16-year-old boys. By 1966, there were 313 boys playing on 12 Major League Teams, three Senior League Teams and four "Taxi Squads." Elizabeth Wells recalled the many hours her family devoted to the game. Her husband, Grafton Wells (a former semi-pro baseball player), coached a team. Mrs. Wells raised funds "selling many a hot dog and a coke for a quarter." She and her sons maintained the field, mowing grass and weeding. Babe Ruth's sponsors were very supportive. Wilton Crouch shares Mrs. Wells' pleasant memories of Babe Ruth, with one galling addition. In 1962, his son was on the only undefeated Babe Ruth team, sponsored by Arlington-Fairfax Savings and Loan. Eight of the nine boys on the team qualified for the All Stars Team, and the team batting average was .333. Unfortunately, the commissioner failed to submit the team roster on time - - and they were disqualified from going on to the State Championship.[61]

Billy Fairfax played Babe Ruth baseball, and remembered the team camaraderie. Many players went to Fairfax High School. When the City was smaller, most of the teams and players knew each other. He recalled a mother, who, frustrated by an umpire's calls, yelled until the umpire threatened her with eviction from the field. Rather than resort to legal threats or escalating anger, she calmed down, and shook hands with her friend the umpire — after the game.[62]

Fairfax Babe Ruth has always had good teams, and in the last several years, the Senior Babe Ruth team (16-18-year-olds) has won the State Tournament.

The Fairfax Police Youth Club

The Fairfax Police Youth Club (FPYC), which sponsors children's sports activities, was incorporated in 1963 as the Boys Club of America. City of Fairfax Police Chief Murray Kutner and Fairfax County Police Chief William Durrer were instrumental in combining the Boys Club and a small Girls Club into the Fairfax Police Youth Club in 1967. The FPYC has a permanent position for both a City and County police officer on their Board.[63] The FPYC clubhouse in Providence Park opened in 1995 after seven years of planning and labor by volunteers, civic groups, City of Fairfax Parks and Recreation and local businesses.

FPYC has a tremendous number of participants. In 1996-97, there were about 5,000 children ages 5 to 18 in FPYC sports, supported by almost 1,000 volunteers (parents and others). The high number of athletes is a tribute to the FPYC's reputation and efforts, for "the

Fairfax City Police Chief Murray Kutner, who was instrumental in the formation of the Fairfax Police Youth Club, awaits FPYC director Neil Neilson's signal to begin the Dollar-a-Minute Marathon to raise funds for the FPYC. This marathon lasted 25 hours. Courtesy of the City of Fairfax

In 1971, the Washington Redskins gave pointers on the art of football to the Fairfax Police Youth Club "Hornets." The adults in the back row, from left to right, are FPYC coach Joe Shepherd, Redskins players Bob Brunet, Jeff Jordan, Diron Talbert, Sonny Jurgensen, Fairfax City Police Officer Gilbert Barrington, Redskins Ron McDole, Len Hauss, Billy Kilmer, and FPYC Coach John Meehan. Courtesy of the City of Fairfax

jurisdiction in which FPYC operates is not in a high population growth area."[64] FPYC affords athletes the opportunity to play more than one season a year in a particular sport or learn a new one.

FPYC soccer's popularity allows the league to hold two massive tournaments, "the largest in Virginia and among the largest on the East Coast."[65] In 1996, they had their 13th Annual Fathers Day Tournament (with almost 5,000 players), and 17th Annual Labor Day Tournament (with over 6,500 travel team players using 50 local fields). In 1995, FPYC Football had seven teams (152 boys and one girl) grouped according to weight, from the "Blue Devils" to the "Anklebiters." FPYC cheerleaders cheer for the FPYC football teams. Softball (which includes T-Ball) is divided into intermediate, junior and select teams. The Running Club, for boys and girls age nine to 13, train, participate in a formal run, and shorter "fun runs." FPYC wrestling offers training to wrestlers from seven to 14 years of age. In 1995-96, they had a ratio of one coach to four players. Basketball had almost 700 players in 1995-96. Lacrosse trains from fourth grade to high school; in the fall season, players can hone their skills with a series of games.

FPYC's Youth Challenged League (YCL) offers coaching and games to children who are mentally or physically challenged. YCL sports are basketball, soccer and softball. Players are taught in controlled scrimmages and play in regular games and tournaments such as the Special Olympics. YCL basketball, open to five- to 18-year-olds, provides players with weekly practices and several tournaments. YCL soccer, open to five- to 16-year-olds, includes practices, games and tournaments. YCL softball has played against a YCL League from Woodbridge.[66]

"Fairfax Furnitures" Team - Industrial League Baseball

Many sports have industrial leagues, allowing athletes to play into adulthood. The "Fairfax Furnitures," a sandlot baseball team, was created in the 1970s by Woody Harris and Wilton Crouch to allow their sons to play baseball after college. Fields were at a premium, and the team could not get into the Virginia Industrial League, so they joined the Maryland Industrial League. When they won the Maryland State Championship, they were presented with a small Maryland flag. Crouch asked if they could get a larger flag if they won the next year. Official Louis Goldstein said, "Listen, if you win next year I will get you a flag that has flown over the Statehouse!" They won the next year, but Mr. Goldstein could not be at the banquet, and they did not get the flag. It may be presumed there was little joy in Mudville, or Maryland, that night.[67]

People derive pleasure from sports by playing, volunteering or just watching the action. As one dedicated sandlot baseball player said, "There's never a true athlete who has his heart in the game who can just give it up."[68]

Spotlight on the Arts poster. Courtesy of the City of Fairfax

12.

City Lights: Artistic Endeavors and Seasonal Events
by Mary Elizabeth Cawley DiVincenzo

T he City of Fairfax has played a significant part in the formation of northern Virginia's artistic world. Since the 1950s, the hard work and dedication of artistically-inspired City residents resulted in symphonies, bands, theaters and galleries springing up, seemingly overnight. Following are histories of these artistic institutions, beginning with the oldest, the Fairfax Symphony Orchestra.

Fairfax Symphony Orchestra

The Fairfax Symphony Orchestra (FSO) began in 1957, fostered by the efforts of Dorothy Farnham Feuer, a recent arrival to the Town of Fairfax from Connecticut. Finding no group with which to play her violin, Feuer and members of the Woman's Club of Fairfax canvassed for possible members of an orchestra. Feuer was aided by Penelope and John Farris; John, band leader of Annandale High School, and Penelope (who would develop the Northern Virginia Youth Symphony) became long-time orchestra members. They were joined by Frederick Wygal, who would later start the Fairfax Choral Society. In 1961, Thomas Hill, future director of the City of Fairfax Band, became orchestra president. Other officers were Lois Wygal, Doris Dakin, Byron Woodside and Richard Sherman.[1]

The FSO's first rehearsal was April 12, 1957. Phil Fuller and guest conductors held rehearsals with them until the first conductor, Harvey Krasney, was hired. The 52-member orchestra held its first concert in November 1957 at the former Fairfax High School for an audience of about 200. Krasney conducted the FSO until his retirement.

The FSO had always had some professional musicians, particularly those who played with military bands, yet wanted orchestral experience. Nonetheless, Penelope Farris said that the Fairfax Symphony Orchestra was a good, but not yet great orchestra. Indeed, a 1968 study carried out by the American Symphony Orchestras League recommended merging the FSO with another group. Instead, the FSO dug in its heels, hired William Hudson as resident conductor - - both the Board and Orchestra had voted for him - - and steeled themselves to accept the rigors inherent in developing a first-class orchestra.[2] Hudson, on the faculty of the University of Maryland, has been credited with much of the FSO's subsequent success, insisting on the highest possible standards. Hired as conductor in 1970, Hudson continues as music director in 1997.[3]

The FSO has long encouraged children's musical education. Orchestra members carry out educational and elementary school programs, such as "Overtures to Orchestra" and "Simply Symphonic" to acquaint children with symphonic orchestras.[4] Indeed, in the early 1960s, Feuer strove to convince Fairfax County Schools to provide stringed instrument instruction as they did for band instruments. When Feuer died in 1963, at the age of 35, the FSO created the Dorothy Farnham Feuer Memorial String Scholarship. Many winners of the scholarship have performed as soloists at the FSO's Young People Concerts.[5]

Years of hard work transformed a small orchestra of dedicated volunteers into a near 100-person orchestra, performing six concerts a season in George Mason University's Center for the Arts, and serving as orchestra in residence at the Shenandoah Valley Music Festival. The Fairfax Symphony Orchestra, called by the *New York Times* "one of the finest regional orchestras in the country,"[6] won the Governor's Award for the Arts in Virginia, and has received numerous accolades from world-class performers.

Northern Virginia Youth Symphony Association

In 1964, the Fairfax Symphony Orchestra appointed Penelope Farris to develop a youth symphony to make up for the lack of strings training in Fairfax County schools. Auditions pointed up the need for two groups, based on proficiency levels. Novices made up the Strings Training Sessions, where they gained all-important ensemble experience. More highly skilled musicians made up the Northern Virginia Youth Symphony. Rehearsals were directed by Gerald Brobst, a former National Symphony Orchestra player turned teacher at T.C. Williams High School. The Northern Virginia Youth Symphony's first concert was held in May 1965.

The FSO, with the help of parent volunteers, administered the Youth Symphony for several years. Players were charged a small fee; expenses were low, for they could rehearse in public schools. In the mid-1970s, the Youth Symphony became independent of the FSO. The Northern Virginia Youth Symphony Association (NVYSA) was incorporated in 1972.

The NVYSA grew rapidly, for schools began to add strings programs, and good private string teachers became available. The NVYSA sponsors four orchestras: the American Youth Philharmonic, the Virginia Youth Symphony, String Orchestra and String Ensemble. The American Youth Philharmonic has its own concert series and has performed at the Kennedy Center and the Youth Symphony Festival in Scotland.

NVYSA students profit from rich ensemble experience and excellent training. Most NVYSA coaches are from the National Symphony Orchestra, the Fairfax Symphony Orchestra, or Fairfax County Public Schools. Students are afforded the opportunity to perform with such virtuosos as Daniel Heifetz and Leonard Slatkin.[7]

Fairfax Choral Society

The Fairfax Choral Society, the oldest singing group in northern Virginia, was begun by members of the Fairfax Music Guild. In October 1962, Louise Vore and Geraldine Sherwood (former head of Fairfax High School's choral department), asked an Arlington chorus director, Frederick Wygal, to start and direct a chorus. He agreed, asking only that they put an ad in the paper requesting that persons interested in singing in a performance of Handel's "Messiah" in December show up at Fairfax High School. To his astonishment, 101 people came. The newly-formed chorus was a little short on tenors, so Wygal persuaded his friends to fill the gap.

The first performance of the "Fairfax County Choral Society," at Fairfax United Methodist Church, was very well received, as was their performance of Brahms' *Requiem* in Spring 1963. They soon changed their name to reflect the all-inclusive nature of the group. The Fairfax Choral Society has presented both traditional and modern works. The members were proud to present the Virginia premier of Carl Orff's *Carmina Burana*, an unpublished *Magnificat* by Felix Mendelssohn and works by local composers.[8] They have performed with the Fairfax Symphony Orchestra and the City of Fairfax Band, the Arlington and Alexandria Symphony Orchestras, and the American Youth Philharmonic, and have appeared on all of the major stages in the Washington area. Two of the Fairfax Choral Society's three performing groups were part of the 1997 City of Fairfax Spotlight on the Arts. The Society has had only three directors since 1962: Frederick Wygal (now director of the Reston Chorale), Robert McCord, and Douglas Mears. In 1996, the Society had almost 120 members in the adult chorus and the adult chorale, and 83 children in the junior and senior divisions of the Children's Chorus. It has sponsored young vocal artists competitions and workshops for singers and choral directors. All three ensembles rehearse at locations in the City of Fairfax.[9]

The City of Fairfax Band

The City of Fairfax Band, mainstay of so many City celebrations, has changed greatly over its history. The City Band, an ensemble principally composed of high school students at its beginning in 1969, has evolved into a polished symphonic band of nearly 100 members, composed of amateur and a few professional musicians.[10]

During its early years, the City of Fairfax Band was principally composed of high school students. Photo from the early 1970s. Courtesy of Tom and Ruth Hill

The City Band was co-founded by Phillip Fuller, supervisor of music for Fairfax County Public Schools and first band director at the former Fairfax High School, and Matthias (Matt) Hynes, Fairfax High School's band director. Although the original idea was Fuller's, it was Hynes who organized and administered the band for its first few years. In 1971, Dr. Thomas Hill became the City Band's conductor, and his wife, Ruth Hill, became band librarian. John Mauro became associate director in 1977, a position he maintains in 1997. The Hills held their positions until they retired in 1993 (when Hill, due to his years of unflagging service, received the first Fairfax Award given by the City Council). Upon Hill's retirement, the City Band elected as director Robert Pouliot, a former conductor and executive officer of the United States Air Force Band.

The City Band's first concert was held on the City Hall steps, July 30, 1969. In 1971, the City Band held its first Children's March, in which a drum major led the children in the audience, and began its tradition of marching in the Independence Day Parade. For some years it was the only band in the parade.[11] In 1972, the band added a pre-fireworks concert at the newly

Thomas Hill, Grand Marshal of the 1994 Independence Day Parade, and Ruth Hill. The Hills retired in 1993 after 23 years respectively as band conductor and band librarian. Courtesy of Tom and Ruth Hill

built Fairfax High School, which has served as home for the band ever since.

The Independence Day Parade and pre-fireworks concerts typify the City Band's "home town" performances. The Band also carries out seasonal concerts at Veterans Amphitheater, and plays for civic ceremonies, festivals, dedications and George Mason University commencements. However, the Band's polished style has drawn it into a wider musical orbit. In 27 years, the band played almost 350 concerts in Virginia, Maryland, Delaware, Washington, D.C. and New Orleans. The City Band has performed at Wolf Trap Farm Park, Baltimore's Inner Harbor, Christmas Eve Concerts at the Kennedy Center, summer concerts at Bethany Beach and Rehoboth and national conferences.

The band has had many memorable performances. In 1985, the City band was invited to perform at the Association of Concert Bands Conference. In June 1996, the City band, led by music director Robert Pouliot, accepted an invitation to play at the National Band Association Convention. The National Band Association, the world's largest and most prestigious band association, selects one community band to perform for their convention each year.[12]

Perhaps the most notable event in the band's history was the invitation by the Virginia Independence Bicentennial Commission to "represent the state of Virginia at the opening ceremonies of the Yorktown Bicentennial," October 16, 1981.[13] Representatives from France, Great Britain and the Federated Republic of Germany were also present.[14] The City of Fairfax Band shared the stage with a choral group from Williamsburg. The entire day was a success: crystalline weather, the French Marine Marching Band, flags flying, people in costumes and, as the City Band played the National Anthem, a contingent of jets roared overhead.[15]

Small ensembles have developed within the Band. The oldest is *Alte Kameraden* (The Old Comrades), formed in 1977, and directed by Samuel Laudenslager, Jr. Other ensembles are the Swing Band, directed by Richard Parrell; Potomac Brass, managed by Sharyl Abell; and the Fairfax Saxophone Quartet, led by James Francis. Ken Stegeman and Ken Murphy lead a Dixieland Band, and Bill Warnell leads the Just Jazz Septet. Ensembles have performed in City schools, and offered musical clinics to high school students.[16]

The City Band, incorporated as a non-profit organization in 1982, has been blessed by energetic and devoted volunteers. David Ray Abell, president of the City of Fairfax Band Board of Directors, and his wife, Sharyl, have worked to ensure smooth sailing for the Band's myriad activities. Stanley Shelton has had the magician's task of making the Band's intricate financial affairs read as smoothly as music. Dr. Hill credited Samuel Laudenslager, Jr., with arranging "many of the concerts presented outside the City, as well as exercising his considerable public relations skills in furthering the band's mission."[17]

The City Band has also prospered through the concern and efforts of several music-loving Mayors. Mayor George Snyder gave the Band more than moral support. At the opening of Fair City Mall, Robert Haft of Crown Books learned from Snyder that the Band was his "favorite charity." Soon afterwards, Snyder presented the band with a check from Haft. Snyder, remembered by Dr. Hill as "a real Boston Irishman, with a wonderful sense of humor" was declared an honorary conductor in 1992 by Ray Abell. Mayor John Mason has also strongly supported the City Band through his dedication to the arts in Fairfax. Hill noted that Mason has "built up the arts and done a lot of good."[18]

The City Band offers small musical scholarships to George Mason University-bound students. In 1995, the First Annual Young Artists Competition began; the winner received an award for college and an appearance as a soloist with the Band. After Hill retired, the

Mayor John Mason cordially greets the City's guests at the City of Fairfax Band concert and reception in honor of Nicholas, Lord Fairfax and Annabel, Lady Fairfax, June 11, 1992. Courtesy of the City of Fairfax

City Council set up a musical scholarship at Fairfax High School in his honor.[19]

Guest artists and groups have performed with the City Band. Some, like radio personality John Lyon, have become regulars. The band has performed with Agathe von Trapp; William Warfield; Harden and Weaver; the Mormon Choir of Washington, D.C.; "David and Dorothy;" Barbara DeMaio; and Harvey Phillips. The City Band has hosted the *Dorfmusikappel Unterbrun* from Munich and the *Akkordeon Orchestra* JMK Rhineland, Cologne.

The Band has often had to deal with the wonders of weather. Hill vividly recalled the 1988 Spotlight on the Arts, when he led the Band on a windy, 50-degree day. Miss Virginia, Heidi Lammi, gamely performed her dance routine in a knee-length tunic, controlling chattering teeth. This chilly day was a vast improvement over the Band's demoralizing experiences during Virginia Day, 1979, at Wolf Trap Farm Park. Logistical difficulties forced the City Band out of the big building and into a tent, on a day when the skies opened. Water accumulated on the tent, which began

Former Mayor George T. Snyder, Jr. seen here with Ray Abell in 1992, was dubbed honorary conductor of the City Band. Courtesy of Tom and Ruth Hill

World-famous blues singer and guitarist John Jackson, performing with his son James, c. 1987. Jackson, who lives in Fairfax Station, has a repertoire of southern blues that goes back to colonial times. A master of the "Mississippi Delta Blues" jazz form, Jackson has performed across America, and toured other countries in cultural exchanges sponsored by the State Department. Photo by Theresa Newton, courtesy of John Jackson

ominously to sag, as the band played a memorial piece written by Glenn Smith for one of the deceased members of the band, a rather sad piece of music. Then, the conductor of the next band had a heart attack while conducting. As Dr. Hill recalled:

> They had the rescue squad coming in the rain, and the tent was sagging. We were supposed to be in the covered area and we weren't, and Glenn's piece was not a very jolly piece anyway, and oh, talk about memorable days, that was one of them. If that tent had ever let go. . . tons of water![20]

Old Town Hall Performance Series

The Old Town Hall Performance Series began in 1990 as an offshoot of the Spotlight on the Arts. Councilman (later Mayor) John Mason, who had arranged the Spotlight on the Arts, asked Commission on the Arts member Bonita Lestina to recommend a musical offering. Lestina arranged for a flute quartet to perform. It was such a hit that the commission decided to have artistic selections, one each month, from January to April, the April performance occurring during the Spotlight on the Arts. The following season they offered selections twice a month from October to April. Lestina has been in charge of the selections, which she dubbed the Old Town Hall Performance Series for she wanted to attract and offer more than music. Lestina strives for varied programs, such as poetry reading, chamber music and theater. However, the biggest audiences have turned out for musical selections, perhaps because Old Town Hall's intimate setting best suits music. The Performance Series, free to the public, is sponsored by the Commission on the Arts and supported by the Friends of the Old Town Hall Performance Series.[21]

FairStage Productions

FairStage Productions, managed by Glenn White, started in 1988, sponsored by the Commission on the Arts. FairStage's first play, *1776*, financed by a wealthy benefactor who liked colonial life, was staged at George Mason University's Harris Theater. It was very well received. There was no benefactor for the following year's production of *Godspell*, so it was held in the large room at John C. Wood Complex; members of FairStage built stages and put in lights. White thought that their production was good, but blighted by

a very hot day, a tremendously aggravating situation for both players and audience. *1776* and *Godspell* formed a part of 1989 and 1990's Spotlight on the Arts.

FairStage Productions went into hiatus when White went to Germany for two years. On his return he produced *The Andersonville Trial* in Fairfax Courthouse's renovated Courtroom, a very appropriate setting for a courtroom drama based on the most famous military trial of the Civil War. The actors attempted to draw the audience into the play as courtroom spectators, and White felt they succeeded very well. Fairfax Courthouse was used the following year when FairStage put on *Gilbert and Sullivan are Alive and Well and Laughing in Fairfax*. Words to Gilbert and Sullivan songs were changed to fit topical issues; e.g., "Titwillow" became "Whitewater."

In 1995 FairStage produced the courtroom drama, *Twelve Angry Men*. In the Lanier Middle School Theater, FairStage members built a very narrow set, around which the jury members sat, walked, or shouted. Around the stage they built risers so audiences could be close to the action. Some members of the audience sat only a few feet from the actors.

Although this setting made for a riveting production, it was very expensive. White figured that expenses at a City facility would be low, but unforeseen costs, including liability insurance, raised the costs of mounting a production. In 1996, White went back to the Commission, and learned that, due to budget cuts, he could only get a small portion of the amount needed to stage a production. The combination of low funds and White's plans to retire away from the City led him to fold FairStage's tent. The pleasure audiences took in FairStage's performances convinced White that theater will rise again in Fairfax![22]

Children's Theater

Children's Theater, sponsored by the City of Fairfax Parks and Recreation and the Commission on the Arts, has been in production since 1992. Performances for children had been at Fairfax High School, but are now held in the Lanier Theater. Productions are put on in the wintertime. Programs have included the Bob Brown Marionettes and Theatre IV (a Richmond touring performance group, which gets a grant from the Virginia Commission on the Arts, thus reducing the costs to the City of Fairfax). In 1996, the Children's Theater put on performances of *Tom Thumb* and *Cinderella*.[23]

Fairfax Art League

The Fairfax Art League (FAL) was formed in 1986 by six artists: Kathryn Higgins, Donya Bauer, Jackie Cawley, Art Cole, Deron Decesare and Deb Smith. Their works were first exhibited at the John C. Wood Complex in space arranged through the Friends of Fairfax. In 1987, these artists chose the name "Fairfax Art League" to emphasize their "covenant to promote art in the community"; indeed, FAL's motto is "original art at affordable prices."[24] Incorporated as a non-profit group in 1989, FAL now has over 100 artist members. Each month FAL holds league activities for its members at the John C. Wood Complex. FAL board business is discussed, and guest artists demonstrate their talents and techniques.

Kathryn Higgins said that before FAL acquired its permanent gallery at Old Town Hall, she displayed artists' works during the Spotlight on the Arts by hanging paintings in historic buildings, such as the Ratcliffe-Allison House and Draper House. After trying to get Fairfax Elementary School for a gallery, Higgins inspected Old Town Hall's second floor, a dusty, paint chip-strewn mess. Higgins noted that City officials rejected her request to use it as a gallery, stating the City didn't have the money to fix it up. Higgins declared that FAL members could knock it into shape, whereupon City officials, in some haste, stated that professional repair people would be called in to do the job.[25]

Volunteer members staff the FAL Gallery. A setback for FAL occurred in December 1995, when a fire at Old Town Hall damaged the newly-renovated gallery; however, the Gallery was re-opened in time for the April 1996 Spotlight on the Arts. Monthly receptions are held there, at which the public can vote for their favorite piece of art, which then receives a "People's Choice Award."

During the Spotlight on the Arts, FAL holds a reception for its exhibition at Old Town Hall Gallery. FAL maintains exhibits in unorthodox places, bringing art to those who have no time for regular gallery visiting. FAL displays artistic works at the Fairfax County Government Center, the Central Fairfax Chamber of Commerce and City Hall. FAL also has a yearly Christmas Exhibit. In October 1996, FAL held its First Annual Juried Art Show at Northern Virginia Community College, Ernst Gallery, Annandale Campus.

Topkapi Middle Eastern Folkloric Dancers

Linda Caldwell, inspired by the dancing she had seen in Turkey, began this dance troupe in 1978, named for the Topkapi Imperial Palace in Istanbul. The Topkapi Dancers, a non-profit organization, try to be as authentic as possible. They have been practicing their routines for years at the Fairfax City Regional Library Meeting Room. The Topkapi Dancers, whose numbers have ranged from about six to 12, perform the folk dancing of Turkey, Persia, Morocco, Egypt, Tunisia, Sinai and Greece. They also perform cabaret dancing and folk dancing with instruments such as finger cymbals, Turkish spoons, tar (a hand-held Turkish drum) and karkabs, a northern African steel drum. Each dance is preceded by a short history of its source and significance. The Topkapi Dancers have performed at the National Theater, the Old Post Office Pavilion, Wolftrap Farm Park Children's Festival, nursing homes and other places. Colette Ashley, a Topkapi dancer who doubles as seamstress for the Washington Opera, sews their costumes.

Dancing in authentic costumes can be exciting - and risky. Dorothy Jackson and another dancer were performing at the Falls Church Community Stage, doing a dance with canes. Her cane hit a fluorescent light, that promptly exploded on part of the stage. Jackson said that the audience was riveted, but the other dancer never missed a beat. She just moved over on the stage to allow Jackson room, and the dancers glided on, ignoring the litter of glass near their bare feet.[26]

Good Vibration Dancers

The Good Vibration Dancers, who perform upbeat jazz and tap "Broadway" routines, developed from Fairfax County's recreation program, but have been associated with the City of Fairfax's Parks and Recreation since 1993. At present there are about 20 dancers, ranging in age from 20 to 76. They have performed in many places: Spotlight on the Arts, Spotlight on the Season, the Post Office Pavilion, community fairs - even the Central Intelligence Agency. Each performance includes one audience participation routine. They have even developed a spin-off group of male dancers, the City Slicks.[27]

Commission on the Arts

In 1979, the Fairfax City Council, mindful of the manifest economic and cultural benefits that result from a strong artistic community, created the Commission on the Arts. The Council charged the commission "to encourage, to promote, and to provide opportunities for artistic expression within our City" by supporting existing artistic endeavors and encouraging new ones. The Commission supports the arts in the city schools, and uses City-owned buildings in ways that encourage the arts.[28]

The Commission provides funds for the Spotlight on the Arts, Fairfax Art League, Community Children's Theater and the City of Fairfax Band (including grants for guest artists). The Old Town Hall Performance Series is supported by the commission. The commission, which has supported visual arts, music and theater, is also prepared to support other group artistic activities, such as dance or creative writing. In fact, in March 1985 the commission launched a song contest for a march to be called "The City of Fairfax." (The winning composer was Virginia Wayland).[29]

Katherine B. Jones, age 15 months, exchanges handshakes with stars of the puppet show "Cinderella," which was performed on the west lawn of Fairfax City Hall in July 1972. Other weekly entertainments offered to area residents that summer included a magic act, a rock group and performances by military bands. Courtesy of the City of Fairfax

Artistic Sites

The City's buildings lend themselves to a variety of artistic activities. Veterans Amphitheater at City Hall has been the site of numerous performances since 1981. Old Town Hall houses the Old Town Hall Performance Series and the Fairfax Art League. Old Town Hall has room for about 150 people on both floors, and is equipped with an elevator for easier second-floor access. Lanier Middle School and Fairfax High School offer larger performing venues. The Lanier Theater, named after Robert C. Russell by the City School Board in 1996, seats 300, contains a well-lighted and equipped stage, and has an elevator. The superior acoustics and lighting of Fairfax High's 1,310 seat auditorium has led to its popularity among performers.[30] The newly renovated Heet Auditorium at Paul VI High School seats 750, and has been rented for orchestra ensembles, the Swan Ballet, one-act plays and Irish music.[31]

George Mason University's Center for the Arts contains a cornucopia of settings. The 2,000-seat Concert Hall, which opened in October 1990, is the heart of the Center for the Arts Complex. The Holbert L. Harris Theater, in Robinson Hall, has 530 seats for music, theater and dance performances. The Performing Arts Building contains the Dance Performance Studio and TheaterSpace which is the home of the Theater of the First Amendment, featuring contemporary writing for the stage. Cinema offerings are presented in the Johnson Center.

The visual arts have acquired new locations for exhibition. Fairfax High School artists are able to display their works at John C. Wood Complex. Fairfax High photographers have their work displayed at an annual photography show at Us Too Studio.

Seasonal Events

The City of Fairfax has sponsored events that define the City's image and seek to draw the larger community to the City. By the 1990s, the City had established a series of crowd-pleasing seasonal events designed to stimulate one's patriotism, artistic bent, intellect, nostalgia—and palate.

Spotlight on the Arts

Spotlight on the Arts, developed in 1986 by Mayor John Mason (then a City Council member), is an arts festival designed to showcase local performers, artists

The Desert Storm Support Group at the City Hall Amphitheater, February 1991. This picture was sent to city residents who participated in Operation Desert Storm. Courtesy of the City of Fairfax

and cultural opportunities. Spotlight on the Arts was begun by the Friends of Fairfax, the Central Fairfax Chamber of Commerce, the City of Fairfax, the Fairfax City Commission on the Arts, Historic Fairfax City, Inc. and George Mason University. Spotlight on the Arts is now sponsored by the City of Fairfax in cooperation with George Mason University. Spotlight on the Arts encompasses a kaleidoscope of artistic endeavors produced by participating organizations. Mason said that Spotlight on the Arts evolved "to enhance the general public's awareness of the existing cultural opportunities, and to encourage and help grow organizations that would be essentially community oriented."[32]

The 1986 Spotlight on the Arts lasted three days, and offered music, a play, art, dance, film, photography and readings. One highlight was the Fairfax Pyramid of Schools Arts Festival, wherein City students presented their artistic endeavors. An important feature of Spotlight on the Arts is that City students have their artistic efforts recognized. The 1990 Spotlight on the Arts included "Spotlight Outreach in the Schools," a program in which performers and artists went to City schools to demonstrate their crafts

and offer professional instruction to students. Principals tailored the program to best fit their own students' talents.

Spotlight on the Arts is now almost two weeks long. Spotlights have featured art walks, historic open houses, street festivals, living history reenactments, library open houses, "Artistry on Ice" (featuring Michael Weiss), the Arts and Services Auction, photography shows and the Northern Virginia Folk Festival. Luminaries such as William Warfield, Richard Bausch and Norman Mailer have been a part of this springtime art festival.[33]

Community/Farmers Market

Sponsored by the Downtown Fairfax Coalition, the Community/Farmers Market is held Saturdays from mid-May to mid-November, across University Drive from Firehouse #3 in the City. The vendors sell fresh produce and fish, honey, herbs, plants, baked goods, crafts, antiques and flowers. The Market is also the site for periodic voter registration and Fire and Rescue Department Blood Drives.

The City/County sponsored Farmers Market, May 1988. Photo by Lori Crockett, courtesy of the City of Fairfax

City-sponsored Farmers Market

Since 1981, the City of Fairfax and Fairfax County have sponsored a weekly Farmers Market from early May to early November. The Market has roamed from parking lots at the Massey Building, Draper Drive Park, and Fairfax High. It is presently located in the City-owned lot next to Truro Episcopal Church. All products sold (fruit, vegetables, jams, honey and baked goods) must be home-grown and certified as such by Fairfax County's Agricultural Department.[34]

Independence Day Celebrations

The City's Independence Day Parade and Fireworks began in 1967. Organized by the Delta Alpha Chapter of Beta Sigma Phi Sorority, the parade has developed into the largest in northern Virginia. The parade has all the requisite ingredients for the 4th of July: marching bands, civic floats, Shriners' little cars and big motorcycles, old fire engines, horses, clowns, gymnasts and scorching sun. The parade has featured

The flags of the United States, the Commonwealth of Virginia, and the City lead the procession in the Independence Day Parade, 1992. Photo by William Haegele, courtesy of the City of Fairfax

flyovers by the Flying Circus Aerodrome, and, in 1996, a hot air balloon race, sponsored by radio station WXTR-104 FM. The parade is sometimes followed by an old-fashioned Fireman's Day, in which area fire companies compete. Finally, evening brings a concert by the City of Fairfax Band, ushering in the long-awaited fireworks.

In the early, small-parade days, the Independence Day festivities could be handled by volunteers, assisted by the City's Public Information Office and supported by such stalwart sponsors as American Legion Post 177 and VFW Blue and Gray Post 8469. During the 1980s, the City's Parks and Recreation Department began overseeing the festivities. However, the parade's entrants, sponsors, and community groups became increasingly numerous, rendering the all-volunteer nature of the parade unfeasible. Thus, in 1990 the Independence Day Committee incorporated as a not-for-profit

Two Oak View gymnasts in the 1977 Independence Day Parade, accompanied by coach Jim Moyer. Courtesy of the City of Fairfax

Indian Guides and Princesses (fathers and daughters) marching in the 1992 Independence Day Parade. Photo by William Haegele, courtesy of the City of Fairfax

Kena Temple's little cars and canny drivers at the Massey Building in the 1992 Parade. Photo by William Haegele, courtesy of the City of Fairfax

The 4th of July Parade in 1997 featured the Fairfax Rotary Club float, which highlighted the forthcoming publication of Fairfax, Virginia: A City Traveling Through Time. *Seated on the float were Bonnie Fairbanks and Pat Sowers, members of the Living History Group. They were portraying Louisiana (Locian) Ratcliffe, Richard Ratcliffe's wife and Elizabeth Hannah, their friend. Courtesy of the photographer, Douglas Schauss,* Fairfax City Observer

organization. It now receives City funding and staffing assistance from Parks and Recreation.[35]

Each year, the Independence Day Parade has a theme and a grand marshal. Children in City schools have submitted themes for many of the Independence Day celebrations. The parade's grand marshals have been a diverse group, such as retired Colonel Lloyd L. "Scooter" Burke (Korean War Medal of Honor Winner), television meteorologist Bob Ryan, James and Sarah Brady, and a cluster of former Mayors and involved citizens.[36]

Fall Festival

The Fall Festival, in Old Town Fairfax, is held on the second Saturday in October. Begun in 1977 as a craft show, it has greatly expanded. Although there are still plenty of crafts (500 crafters in 1996), the Fall Festival also offers children's activities: pony, amusement and hay rides; Octoberfest beer gardens; a new car show; the Central Fairfax Chamber of Commerce TradeFest; and good food. In 1996, Country Music radio station WMZQ sponsored the Main Stage for music; there was also a children's stage. The Fall Festival is always a blaze of red, white and blue, as political aspirants and supporters distribute balloons, banners and stickers in preparation for coming elections.[37]

Old Town Hall Lecture Series

Seeking to emphasize the positive side of having George Mason University on the City's doorstep, City Council Member Jeffrey C. Greenfield and the City/University/Business Committee (CUB) devised the Old Town Hall Lecture Series, beginning October 1996. A survey of City residents showed that topics of interest for a lecture series were "health, history, anthropology, the arts and social issues."[38] The free lectures have provided GMU faculty, beginning with President Alan Merten, with a forum for pertinent issues.[39]

Festival of Lights and Carols

Winter's approach can be heralded by Fairfax Nursing Home's elaborate holiday display or Weber Tire's rooftop tree of lights. However, the season is properly ushered in with the Festival of Lights and Carols, begun by the Friends of Fairfax in 1982, and now sponsored by the Central Fairfax Chamber of Commerce and the City of Fairfax. The Festival offers sleigh/hay rides, Yule log fires, cider, music, children's shows, caroling and the Christmas tree lighting. Decorations for the Christmas tree have been made by such groups as the Lamb Center (a non-profit group that assists homeless people), and residents of the Fairfax Nursing Center.[40] Local merchants offer samples, prizes and promotional events.

The festivities vary somewhat each year. In 1995, children could share a free pizza lunch with Santa Claus at Picco's Restaurant (courtesy of Picco's and the Downtown Fairfax Coalition) or pose with Santa at two dramatically different locations: Old Town Hall or the Dharma Coffee House. Visitors could sing along with the Jubil-Aires, or listen to the Fairfax High School and Lanier Middle School choruses and bands.[41]

The very-well attended Fall Festival is held the second Saturday in October. Courtesy of the City of Fairfax

The Commonwealth Doctors Hospital was built to serve the City of Fairfax and its environs in 1968. Its status changed when INOVA Fair Oaks Hospital (formerly Fair Oaks Hospital) was built nearby in 1987. Commonwealth became a nursing home and an emergency care facility (INOVA Emergency Care Center, formerly ACCESS) under the INOVA system, a northern Virginia multi-hospital corporation. The nursing home, now known as INOVA Commonwealth Care Center, is a 137-bed facility. In November 1996 a 70-bed assisted-living facility opened in an adjoining building. Courtesy of the INOVA system.

Fairfax Nursing Center, 10701 Main Street, was built by Robert and Charmaine Bainum in 1964 and continues to be family-owned and operated today. It is home to 200 long term care residents who enjoy a home-like atmosphere which includes live-in pets and plants. Courtesy of the Fairfax Nursing Center

The Chocolate Lovers Festival

Beginning in 1993, the Chocolate Lovers Festival, brightening dreary February, is a weekend designed to enhance one's appreciation for this confection in a festival sponsored by the Central Fairfax Chamber of Commerce, the Downtown Fairfax Coalition, the Friends of Fairfax, Combined Properties, George Mason University and the City.[42] The sybaritic pleasures include tasting chocolate treats at Old Town Hall, viewing chocolate sculptures at the Old Court-house and playing children's games in Fair City Mall. In 1996, Fair City Mall featured America's largest brownie, baked by the staff at Wildflour Bakery, and an interview with Washington Redskin Gus Frerotte by sportscaster, Rene Knott. The Living History Foundation presented performances about chocolate and 18th century life at Fairfax City Regional Library. At the Wood Complex, the Ladies Auxiliary of the Fairfax Volunteer Fire Department presented a craft show. Shuttle buses transported starry-eyed chocolate lovers from site to site.[43]

Notable Events from the City's First Decade

John Mosby Days

John Mosby Days (May 15-21, 1966), a week-long event sponsored by the City of Fairfax Chamber of Commerce, was meant to entertain, to teach citizens the historical significance of Fairfax, and to make them aware of a threat facing the oldest buildings in the City. The proposed widening of Main Street would bring the road quite close to the Courthouse, and necessitate removing the porch on the Ratcliffe-Allison House ("Earp's Ordinary"). The City and Chamber of Commerce wanted citizens aware of what could be lost.[44]

Mosby Days included tours of old houses, lectures on the Civil War by writer, Virgil Carrington Jones, costumed dancers performing the minuet in the lobby of the National Bank of Fairfax (now NationsBank) and a band concert by the First United States Army Band. In addition, members of the 9th Virginia Cavalry formed a picket line on Main Street, the 17th Virginia Infantry bivouacked behind the County printing office, and all enjoyed the Woodson High School Musket team volleys.

The highlight of Mosby Days was the lantern light tour of Old Town Fairfax. The Washington Gas Light Company installed butane gas lamps, Virginia Power turned off the street lights, and traffic was halted, so Main Street between Chain Bridge Road and Old Lee Highway would be lit only by gas lamps or interior candles. Main Street was festooned with Old Glory and Confederate flags. The center line on Main Street was diplomatically painted blue on one side, and gray on the other.[45]

"Old Virginia City", a frontier town on Route 29-211 (Lee Highway) west of the City, operated during the 1960s. It featured cowboys, Indians, can-can girls, a real steam train, historical exhibits, and an operating printing press.
    In March 1963 the Fairfax City Times *reported that owner Robert Sprinkle's attempts to expand this rootin', tootin' western town were successfully opposed by "effete easterners", who objected to the steam train's whistle and the "noisy and disturbing gun battles." From the postcard collection of Tony Chaves*

In March 1955 the Town of Fairfax held an observance of Mosby Week, commemorating the 92nd anniversary of Col. John S. Mosby's capture of Union General Edwin Stoughton. Virgil Carrington Jones delivered an address on the subject of Mosby. Mayor John C. Wood laid wreaths on Mosby's grave in Warrenton and Antonia Ford's grave in Oak Hill Cemetery, Georgetown. Courtesy of the Cawley family

Heritage Week

Heritage Week (May 21-27, 1967), sponsored by the Fairfax City Chamber of Commerce and the City, began with the tolling of church bells from nine City churches. Heritage Week marked the rededication, by the Fairfax County Bar Association, of the restored Fairfax County Courthouse Courtroom. Municipal buildings had open houses; the Fairfax City Regional Library displayed historical memorabilia; City businesses sold products at "century-old prices;" and the City again enjoyed a lantern light tour of Old Town.

The United States Army performed its Torchlight Tattoo for the first time outside Washington, D.C. Other participants in the Tattoo were the United States Army Band and Chorus, Third Infantry Regiment, U.S. Army Fife and Drum Corps and the Army Drill Team. The "Massing of the Battle Colors" was performed by the Marine Corps Silent Drill Team and Drum and Bugle Corps.[46]

Old Town Hall Fairs

A summer event, starting in 1965, and continuing into the 1970s was the Old Town Hall Fair. In 1964, Mrs. Charles "Kitty" Pozer and Mrs. Walter Oliver formed a group, the Friends of the Old Town Hall, to raise money to repair the 64-year old building, which had fallen into disrepair. They designated July 30, 1965 "Old Town Hall Day" and held their first fair, displaying paintings, selling food, and holding a white elephant sale. The fair was supported by the Friends of Old Town Hall, the Fairfax Woman's Club, and church organizations in the City.[47]

The City of Fairfax has given rise to many stimulating events and organizations. Some have flourished for years, while others have bloomed a short while, then vanished. All, however, have brought pleasure to the community and are a tribute to those citizens who performed these labors of love for the benefit of their community.

Nine children enjoying a jungle gym at Providence Park in 1971. Courtesy of the City of Fairfax

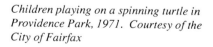

Children playing on a spinning turtle in Providence Park, 1971. Courtesy of the City of Fairfax

A hearty hail and farewell from the children at Van Dyck Park. Courtesy of the City of Fairfax

A contemplative moment on a City footbridge. Courtesy of the City of Fairfax

OK TIL, I'LL TAKE THE CITY OF FAIRFAX AND YOU CAN HAVE THE REST OF THE COUNTY!

Eighteenth and early nineteenth century entrepreneur, Richard Ratcliffe, visits Fairfax in this modern-day cartoon about ownership of valuable local land. Carrying a copy of the 1997 City of Fairfax history book, he proposes dividing the City and County land with John "Til" Hazel, modern entrepreneur. Courtesy of The Connection *newspapers*

Legends, Local Lore and Laughter
By Nan Netherton

I n an old community like Fairfax, which has seen almost 200 years of recorded history, stories have been told and retold and even passed on down as oral tradition to younger generations so many times that it is sometimes difficult to separate truth from fiction. But it is all interesting and many of the accounts are amusing. A few examples follow.

* * * * *

Andrew M. D. Wolf tells an interesting story in his study, "Black Settlements in Fairfax County, Virginia During Reconstruction." After the Civil War, there was a good-sized population of freedmen in the Town of Fairfax. Of the 380 population registered in the 1880 census, 125 were black, or almost one-third of the the Town. Without a doubt the most distinguished black entrepreneur of this community was James Ferguson, known by most as Jim Fogg. It seems that Fogg began his business career at the age of 38, when he purchased the "Allison Stable Lot," and began a livery stable. The lot was acquired at a public auction, probably because the previous owner had failed to keep up with his taxes. Fogg could always count on his best business every third Monday, according to William West of Vienna, when officials came from various parts of the County to attend meetings at the courthouse. Apparently, Fogg did not reside in his own home until 1874, when he purchased a lot through another auction "in front of the door of the Courthouse"

for $160, the highest bid. However, he had been renting the lot for some time. Perhaps encouraged by his success as a livery stable owner, Fogg opened up a restaurant at some point between 1870 and 1880. The census of the former year lists him as owning a livery stable; the 1880 census records both the livery stable and "eating house." His wife served as the chief and only cook. Not listed in the land records was the hotel he also ran, probably consisting of three or four rooms above the little restaurant. Men who wanted to sacrifice the comfort of the town's main hotel to save money would always stay with Ferguson. William West remembers that this thrifty black earned an excellent reputation. "If you want something good to eat," they used to say, "go on down to Jim Fogg's!"

* * * * *

The bell at the courthouse called 300-400 people to business, to law and to religion for many years. But its use was not always authorized. Unidentified pranksters in the Town were disturbing the peace in 1882 to the extent that the County court clerk wrote in the official court minute book: "Some person or persons have entered the Court House Building in the night, without authority and have damaged Said building and have greatly annoyed the citizens living nearby by violently ringing the bell. It is therefore ordered by the Court, that such trespass . . . will be punished to the full extent of the law."[1]

* * * * *

In addition to being a well-known practicing physician in the area and in the Town of Fairfax, Dr. F. M. Brooks was also a farmer, merchant, and banker. The remedies Dr. Brooks suggested for his patients' problems were sometimes a bit unusual. Dr. Brooks always mixed his own medicines which he bought wholesale in large quantities from Philadelphia. Apparently, he often put in a dab or pinch of a number of medicines into a single medication on the theory that if one did not work, perhaps another might. They must have tasted terrible as several patients vividly remember them to this day. Dr. Brooks once treated Wilson Farr's severe aches and pains by winding bandages tightly around most of his body. When the patient mentioned that the bandages would make it difficult to bathe, Dr. Brooks commented: "Well, if you bathe in the winter, no wonder you are sick!"[2]

* * * * *

Energetic boys who resided in the Town of Fairfax in the 1920s and 1930s had a variety of activities to utilize the vast amount of pent-up energy that grade-school age boys world-wide seem to have. Frederic Kielsgard recollects some of his experiences in that period when he attended the old Fairfax Elementary School, now the Fairfax Museum and Visitors Center. Homespun fun included mainly baseball and basket-ball played outside on a dirt court. Local boys usually got their first pocketknife when eight to nine years old, which was neat for playing "mumblety-peg"—a knife-tossing game which is a test of skill. The knives had a very useful purpose also. They could be used to prepare snares to catch rabbits and put meat on the family table when money was a scarce commodity.

All was not play for the older boys. There was a long, rectangular stove in the school which operated on firewood. When trees were cut to clear space for the new brick "colonial style" school next to Fairfax Elementary about 1925, large stumps were left standing. The school supplied the axes, and the boys cut the wood from the stumps.

Almost all boys, in Town and outside, received their own rifles by the age of nine or ten. They were used for target practice and the shooting of small game. Sometimes pranksters in Town waited until the jailer had left his residence in the jail to tend to his farm located near Fairfax Circle on Old Lee Highway. Then

This portrait of Dr. F. M. Brooks was taken sometime in the 1920s. He was the epitome of a country doctor of his time and a successful businessman in the Town of Fairfax. Courtesy of Lee Hubbard

they did a little target practice on the numerous starlings which habitually sat on the cresting ornament atop the jail roof. The good marksmen were able to reduce the number of the noisy fowl for that day, giving temporary relief to human ears in downtown Fairfax.[3]

* * * * *

During the period from 1929 to 1939, when the Reverend Herbert A. "Mike" Donovan served as rector of Truro Episcopal Church in Fairfax, a memorable Sunday School pageant was presented one Christmas season. Sheild McCandlish, George Robey and Dr. Ramsay Taylor played the parts of the three kings bringing gold, frankincense and myrrh. They were garbed in flowing robes and beards which to strangers probably looked authentic enough. But to those who knew them, they presented an extremely funny sight as they came down the church aisle singing "We Three Kings." George Robey had on a red beard which didn't quite fit, and he looked like Henry the Eighth. He was wearing overshoes and they were plainly visible. Sheild McCandlish had on a pointed beard which made him look like Shylock in *The Merchant of Venice*. He was wearing glasses. Eleanor Rust and Mary Walton McCandlish were dressed as angels and standing behind the manger. They could not help laughing, and Mrs. Anne Rust, who was playing the organ, had to put her hand over her mouth and put her head down on the organ to keep from laughing out loud. Mike Donovan was having just as much trouble keeping from laughing and soon the whole congregation was laughing, which detracted considerably from the solemnity of the occasion.[4]

* * * * *

In 1933, a quilt was made by the volunteer class of the Fairfax Methodist Church in honor of Mamie C. Wiley, who was their Sunday school teacher. It is composed of 28 blocks of signatures of families, friends, Pastor Royal A. Rice, (who was the pastor of the church at that time), and many prominent persons of that era.

In the spring of 1995, in Greensboro, N.C., Robert Hutchinson discovered this quilt in the attic of the house he inherited from his mother Mary Sue Wiley Hutchinson. He found out that the quilt was made by his grandmother, Betty Jones Wiley, and some of her friends and family in their adult Sunday School class in 1933. He sent the quilt to the Fairfax United Methodist Church.

Miss Wiley was known as "Aunt Mame" to those who knew and loved her. She was teacher of the volunteer class of the Fairfax Methodist Church from about 1925 to 1940. It is believed that this class consisted of ladies between the ages of about 25-40. "Aunt Mame" was a Charter Member of the United Daughters of the Confederacy, Fairfax Chapter, organized in 1912. She was the aunt of Mary Sue Wiley Hutchinson.

This quilt was sent to the Fairfax United Methodist Church in 1995 for its historic value. It was given for permanent display to honor 1930s member Mamie C. Wiley, other church members in her time, and her present descendants. Holding the quilt for the photo are, left to right, Mavis Cobb, Diane Swart, church historian, and Norma Darcey. Courtesy of the Fairfax United Methodist Church

In the 1940s, there were still actively cultivated farms within the Town limits. Some of them had cattle. Students from Fairfax High borrowed a cow and left her in the school's Senior Courtyard. This caused a great deal of merriment for years as the story was passed on down to new students. The story was retold again recently after the City had become thoroughly urbanized. The listener, a relative newcomer, said in astonishment, "A cow? Where did they find a cow in Fairfax?"[5]

* * * * *

The National Gallery of Art opened on Constitution Avenue in Washington, D. C., in 1941. A convoy of school buses carried students from the Town of Fairfax to see this new treasure house of fine art. In the first exhibits, the students quickly separated into groups of boys and girls, giggling over the numerous depictions of nudes of both sexes. The teachers, most of them young women, realized that deportment would soon be uncontrollable. They calmly and quickly loaded everyone back into the school buses and took their young charges down the street to the Smithsonian's Natural History Museum where the giant stuffed elephant greeted visitors in the central rotunda and the exhibits in the building were less titillating.[6]

* * * * *

In 1941, the United States became directly involved in World War II. Life was profoundly changed, especially among the Fairfax High School boys. The Virginia National Guard disappeared as young men went into military service. To replace them, the state instituted the Virginia State Guard in the more populous areas. Farming communities such as Fairfax were provided with a less trained emergency force known as the Virginia Reserve Militia (VRM).

Such a VRM trained every Thursday evening at Fairfax High. The few officers were World War I veterans, including Master Sergeant W. T. Woodson, Superintendent of Schools. The men in ranks were Fairfax High School boys, ages 15 to 17. They were trained in mob control, response to a riot, and how the unit was to respond to a search for a dangerous criminal.

One weekend, a drill was held at Paul Kincheloe's farm near Clifton. The last exercise for training was

Wilbert T. Woodson served as Fairfax County's superintendent of schools from 1929 to 1961. He took over a mixture of one- and two-room wooden schoolhouses with potbellied stoves, outhouses and water buckets and modernized the school system with the strong support of Town and County voters. His task was to meet the spectacular growth in population and educational demands of his time. Courtesy of the Fairfax County School Board

the location and capture of a vicious, armed and dangerous criminal. The unit's sergeant decided that W. T. Woodson was perfect for the part. So he took off through the woods with two pistols (unloaded), smoke pots and tear gas grenades, followed by the foot soldiers. A blustery, cold March wind was blowing the smoke pots and the troops came unexpectedly upon Mr. Woodson, who pulled a tear gas grenade from his bag and pulled out the pin. "Gas," yelled one of the leaders, and each soldier threw himself on the ground as he struggled to pull on his gas mask. Blaine Friedlander broke out one of the eyeglasses in his mask, and the grenade rolled to his head, giving him a full dose of tear gas, an unexpected accident. Two officers pulled him away from danger. Blaine's throat was raw and painful. His eyes hurt from the gas. He became the first casualty wounded while protecting Fairfax against a vicious criminal, the beloved School Superintendent. When the "gassed" soldier and the "criminal" met again twenty years later at Fairfax Hospital, they took the opportunity, like two old "war buddies," to relive the mock battle. And like all old soldiers who recount their experiences, every word spoken was, of course, true and no fact was embellished or manufactured.[7]

* * * * *

During World War II, Edgar A. Prichard and his wife, Nancy, both worked in the Office of Strategic Services (OSS), the forerunner of the Central Intelligence Agency. Nancy McCandlish took a bus to

Washington, D. C., every day, then caught the OSS bus back to the Town of Fairfax, where the OSS had located its top-secret "Assessment Building" in the old Willard house—across Chain Bridge Road from her house. She had to take great care no one saw her or realized what line of work she was involved in.[8]

* * * * *

Future Fairfax Mayor Nat Young was in the Army Air Force during World War II. When he was learning to fly, he buzzed the town in a trainer. He was not a UFO—the townspeople knew the only local boy learning to fly was Nat Young.[9] John Rust recalls, however, that Lehman Young also knew how to fly and had his own plane.

* * * * *

For a rural school, Fairfax Elementary offered a rich cultural experience. Students watched World War II from their *Current Events* reports and discussions. They studied Shakespeare and in the fifth grade produced *The Merchant of Venice.* They were exposed to French, Spanish and Italian and to the world of music. To prepare for future citizenship, students were taught to follow *Robert's Rules of Order* and learned debating and public speaking.[10]

* * * * *

On Christmas Day 1947, Edward and Elizabeth Cawley, residents of Westmore, were most pleasantly surprised by the appearance of their mailman, Stacy Swart, carrying a very large package. Mr. Swart had accurately identified this late-arriving package as a "grandparents'" box, full of presents for little ones, and went out of his way to bring pleasure to the family's three little children on the holiday.[11]

* * * * *

When Fairfax was still a Town in the 1950s, several pranks were successfully executed. Two of them had to do with the old courthouse. Every Halloween, unknown "spirits" rolled large cannonballs down Main Street until they disappeared in the culverts at University Drive. Examination of photographs from the early 1900s to the 1960s shows gradual depletion of the two pyramids of cannonballs which once stood near the Marr Monument, now no longer to be seen. Another prank had to do with one of the cannons. Students borrowed it from the courthouse lawn, pushed it to the Kamp Washington intersection (Routes 236, 50, 29 and 211), and left it there in the dark of night.[12]

* * * * *

The *Herald* published the following unusually formal announcement in the August 3, 1951, edition: "Smoky, a handsome male Dalmatian, or as the breed is more commonly known, coach dog, has recently been appointed to the post of official mascot of the Fairfax Fire Department and has entered upon the discharge of his duties at the firehouse. The gift of a friend of the firemen in Vienna, Smoky is now ready to receive visitors who may wish to pay their respects to the new mascot. Coach dogs are the traditional mascots of all fire departments and in the old days of the horse drawn engines, could often be seen racing alongside the teams to fires."[13]

* * * * *

"The Fairfax Fire Department is rejoicing over the return of Jeannie, the Dalmatian firehouse dog who has been missing for about 18 months. No one knows where Jeannie has been and she has maintained a discreet silence on the subject. All that is known is that on Sunday morning she scratched on the firehouse door, asking admittance. She is well-nourished and in good condition, from which it is evident that she has succeeded in getting good meals while she was away from home." (February 1960)[14]

* * * * *

Aspen Grove, at 4300 Roberts Road, is approximately 250 years old, built on a corner of the Fitzhugh estate, "Ravensworth." There have been many mysterious occurrences at Aspen Grove in recent years. In fact, an NBC show on haunted houses included Aspen Grove as one of the major haunted houses in the U. S., according to Ted Heflin, a former owner.

Anna Sue Day, a long-time owner and resident of the house in the 1960s, is very skeptical about ghosts, but she states there were occurrences at Aspen Grove that were just too incredible to be coincidental.

She first suspected the ghost's presence in 1964, just three days after moving in. One of her first nights

Two classic participants in the Old-Fashioned Firemen's Day activities following the Independence Day Parade in 1992 were this Dalmatian coach dog and his flame-haired owner. Photo by William Haegele, courtesy of the City of Fairfax

* * * * *

"Cats" played City Hall Tuesday night, March 24, 1987, to a "standing-room-only crowd."[16] Unlike the popular Broadway musical, however, there was no music or dancing. Featured instead were 26 fervent monologues directed pro and con at a proposed "cat trespass law."[17] As described by a critic in one of many reviews after the lively performance, "the fur flew when the pet owners and neighbors finally bared their claws."[18] As finally reported by the *Washington Post*, "The Meows Have It As Fairfax Votes Down Cat Trespassing Bill."[19]

The proposed ordinance originated when Maria Bocchino complained to City Hall that "Pretty, a long-haired, gray fluffy cat, repeatedly . . . [defecated] in the . . . children's sandbox—and then . . . spread her

All that remains of the old "High Offley" estate on which the County's Massey Building now stands is a small tombstone. It marks the resting place of the family's favorite cat, Clem. Courtesy of the photographer, Randolph Lytton

at Aspen Grove, she was in bed when she heard footsteps on the staircase. It was especially frightening because her husband was away on a trip at the time. The footsteps would stop each time she checked. It happened night after night. She never told her husband about her experience, but he soon heard steps and told her of them.

After some research, Day learned that the house was supposedly haunted by the ghost of a Union soldier killed while occupying Aspen Grove. Legend has it that the soldier rushed outside with bare feet after hearing a noise in the yard. He was shot to death by the enemy and still returns to Aspen Grove, racing noisily up and down the main stairs in search of his army boots.

Aspen Grove changed hands many times during the war. The house served both armies as a shelter and a hospital. Initials and bloodstains can still be seen on the pine floors in the dining and living room. The house has sheltered a lot of anxiety, emotion and pain.[15]

droppings throughout the family's backyard. . . . The smell was so bad we couldn't even sit in our backyard any more,"[20] said Bocchino. Thus, the ordinance came to City Hall for an airing.

New language in the City Code "made it a class four misdemeanor for an owner to allow an animal or fowl, including domestic cats, to go on the premises of another after having been requested by the owner of said premises not to permit this." Nineteen cat lovers opposed to the new law, in the midst of audience applause, argued that "a cat's natural inclination is to roam";that the "proposed ordinance will punish the many for the crimes of the few;" and pointed out the difficulty of establishing "which cat was the perpetrator as many cats looked similar." A supporter of the proposal stated that "cats were very smart animals that could be trained not to go out a door . . . if the owner took the responsibility." Another speaker urged a "yes" vote, stating that "cats rarely defecate in their own yards but instead went in other people's yards, gardens and sandboxes."[21]

In the end, however, City Council members appeared to be swayed by the majority opposition and the law's unenforceability as they unanimously voted down the ordinance. Mayor George Snyder remarked that he "would like to see greater participation on the more *substantial* issues that face Fairfax City." Prior to the debate on the trespass law, the Council had held a public hearing on the proposed $41.2 million budget and it attracted only three or four speakers, contrasted with the full house that spoke that night on the "cat trespass law."[22]

* * * * *

It was Monday, December 4, 1995, at about 10:45 p.m. when the Fairfax Ferns Garden Club had just completed the holiday decorating at Old Town Hall for the tenth consecutive year. Just before the door was closed the members looked back at their work and complimented themselves on a job well done. Decorating the Hall is the club's Christmas gift to the citizens of the City of Fairfax and great pride is taken in this endeavor.

A few minutes before 9:00 a.m. on Wednesday, December 6, 1995, fire sirens could be heard for miles around. The phones started ringing. The bad news was that Old Town Hall was on fire! The fire was touched off by a contractor's heat gun while removing old paint. The fire raged through the second floor and

ceiling of the building, causing an estimated $250,000 in damage. There was also considerable water damage to the first floor.

It was most fortunate that there was no more damage than there was. An unknown person was astute enough to realize that the holiday decorations would be completely ruined if left in place, and removed as many of them as possible, placing them in the front office. At this point the biggest damage to the decorations was smoke and water. The Ferns received a call early Thursday morning saying that they might come in and salvage what decorations they could. Also, would they please redecorate by Friday, December 8? There was to be a wedding reception at the Hall on Saturday, and we couldn't disappoint the bride and groom.

On Thursday, Fern members Pat Beck and Hildie Carney removed and salvaged most of the holiday decorations. The entire day was spent in dusting off the many wreaths and silk greenery with paint brushes to remove the ashes; fluffing the bows; and finding new fresh greens to replace those that had been damaged by the heat from the fire. The big pine cone garland (on the front stair railing that extended from the first floor to the second floor) was washed in dishwashing detergent in a bathtub to remove the smoke odor. Pine cones close up tightly when wet. Of course, this was not acceptable—so up went the thermostat on the furnace and out came the hair dryers. The cones opened. New electric candles for the windows were replaced. We were back in business!

On Friday, December 8 about 9:30 p.m., when the clean-up crew was still working, the members of the Fairfax Ferns met again at Old Town Hall. Object: To redecorate. City employees, clean-up crews, contractors for the building and the Ferns members were all there waiting to pitch in to help wherever help was needed. There was a sense of magic in the air—a sense of strong community spirit and pride. There was a job to be done, and those there knew what it was. One of the electricians helped the Ferns to hang the kissing balls. One of the Ferns pointed out the missed spots on the floor that was being waxed. City employee Joe Kirby was trying to hang the window swags. Jane Stange, a Fern member and an interior designer, was not pleased with his efforts. So she said, "Let me do this. This is what I do for a living. You go and help put the tablecloths on the tables and make sure they are on straight!" And up the 14-foot ladder Jane went. Everyone there helped where help was needed.

While removing old paint from the exterior of the Old Town Hall on Wednesday, December 6, 1995, a contractor's heat gun set fire to the second floor. The fire department for the City of Fairfax quickly responded to the alarm and saved the damaged building. The Fairfax Ferns Garden Club redecorated the inside of the building in time for a scheduled wedding reception on Saturday. Courtesy of the City of Fairfax

The redecorating was completed by midnight. Saturday's wedding reception took place as planned. That was a major community effort. "We really don't live in a small town, but with that type of all-out project you get the small town atmosphere," said Pat Beck, president of the Fairfax Ferns. "It just makes you feel good. It's what Christmas is all about— giving. It shows that when people get together for a worthwhile purpose, wonders can happen."[23]

* * * * *

Jana Klopp, did not realize that when she married her husband Ben in 1989, she also married the City of Fairfax. He lived in Fairfax, enjoyed it and did not want to move. Jana soon found out why it is so attractive: it is convenient to major highways and transportation, yet it has a small city's charm and local taxes are low. Many destinations are within walking distance of their home. She can walk to City Hall to pay her water bill and have lunch or dinner in historic Old Town Fairfax. The local post office, the Fairfax City Regional Library and George Mason University

are also within walking distance. Seasonal events such as the annual Fourth of July parade, the community market, the Fall Festival, the Holiday Craft Show, the Festival of Lights and Carols, the Chocolate Lovers' Festival, and the Spotlight on the Arts give residents and visitors a sense of community, pride of place, and a comfortable, small-town atmosphere.[24]

CHOCOLATE LOVERS FESTIVAL

CITY OF FAIRFAX
February 12 – 14, 1993

Endnotes

Chapter 1. Prehistory to 1800
Indians, Rangers and English Settlers

1. Walter Biscoe Norris, Jr., ed., *Westmoreland County, Virginia* (Montross Virginia, Westmoreland County Board of Supervisors, 1983), pp. 5-9. William Waller Hening, *Statutes of Virginia*, I (New York, 1823), pp. 274, 337-8, 352-353, 362.
2. The Northern Virginia Chapter, Archaeological Society of Virginia, *Prehistoric Fairfax County: Surveys and Excavations 1988* (Falls Church, Virginia, Fairfax County Office of Comprehensive Planning, 1989).
3. Thomas G. Lilly, Jr. and Daniel F. Cassey, *Archeological Assessment, Predictive Model, & Management Plan for the City of Fairfax, Virginia* (Raleigh, North Carolina: Garrow & Associates, Inc., 1994), p. 1, pp. 33-37.
4. Fairfax Harrison, *Landmarks of Old Prince William* (Baltimore: The Prince William County Historical Commission, 2nd reprint, 1987), pp. 79-85, 342.
5. Beth Mitchell, *Beginning at a White Oak . . . Patents and Northern Neck Grants of Fairfax County, Virginia* (Fairfax, Virginia, Fairfax County Office of Comprehensive Planning, 1977), pp. 19, 931, 168-173.
6. Stuart E. Brown, Jr., *Virginia Baron: The Story of Thomas 6th Lord Fairfax* (Berryville, Virginia: Chesapeake Book Company, 1965).
7. Pohick Church, *Minutes of the Vestry, Truro Parish, Virginia 1732-1785* (Lorton, Virginia, 1974).
8. Nan Netherton, et al., *Fairfax County, Virginia: A History* (Fairfax, Virginia, Fairfax County Board of Supervisors, 1978), pp. 722-723; *Minutes of the Vestry*, pp. 157-159.
9. Fairfax Harrison, *Landmarks*, pp. 405-408.
10. Nan Netherton, et al., *Fairfax County*, p. 723; Pohick Church, *Minutes*, pp. 158-9.
11. Ross D. Netherton and Ruby Waldeck, *The Fairfax County Courthouse* (Fairfax County Board of Supervisors, History Commission, and Office of Comprehensive Planning, July 1977), pp. 7-9.
12. Netherton, et al, *Fairfax County*, pp. 83-117.
13. H. R. McIlwaine, ed., *Official Letters of the Governors of the State of Virginia* (Virginia State Library, 1926), Vol. I, p. 182; Vol. II, p. 418.
14. C. Eugene Hamilton, ed., *Minutes of the Vestry, Truro Parish, Virginia 1732-1785* (Lorton, Virginia: Gateway Press, Inc., reprint, 1995), p. 159.
15. Nan Netherton, et al., *Fairfax County*, p. 39.
16. For a full discussion of the work of John Ariss in Virginia, see Thomas Tileson Waterman, *The Mansions of Virginia, 1709-1776* (New York: Bonanza Books, 1945), pp. 243-337.
17. Hamilton, *Minutes*, pp. 96-97.
18. Constance K. Ring, "Richard Ratcliffe: The Man, His Courthouse, and His Town," *Yearbook*, The Historical Society of Fairfax County, Vol. 25, 1995-96, pp. 97-98, 99-101; Fairfax County Court Orders 1772-3, p. 275.
19. Laurence Mitchell, "Official Records of the Colonial Period in Fairfax County," Historical Society of Fairfax County, *Yearbook*, Vol 11, 1971, pp. 20-23.
20. Harrison, *Landmarks*, p. 324.
21. William Walter Hening, *Statutes at Large* (New York, 1823), 3 January 1798.

22. Netherton and Waldeck, *Courthouse*, p. 74.
23. Peter Henriques, *Northern Virginia Heritage*, Vol. V, No. 3, pp. 11-14.
24. Ruth P. Rose, "Dr. David Stuart," *Northern Virginia Heritage*, Vol. X, No. 1, pp. 9-14.
25. John C. Fitzpatrick, ed., *The Writings of Washington*, Vol. 31, pp. 344-345.
26. Gertrude B. Richards, ed., "Dr. David Stuart's Report to President Washington on Agricultural Conditions in Northern Virginia," *Virginia Magazine of History and Biography*, Vol. 31 (1953), pp. 286-294.
27. Ibid., p. 292.
28. Ox Road was the old Copper Mine Road constructed around 1729 by the Frying Pan Company, organized by Robert "King" Carter in partnership with his sons, Robin and Charles, and his son-in-law, Mann Page of Rosewell, to establish a copper mine on Frying Pan Run. The road led from the copper mine near present-day Herndon to the Occoquan River, where the port of Colchester would be established in 1753.
    Around 1729, another road began to appear on maps and documents of the area, Walter Griffin's Rolling Road, which joined the Copper Mine Road where Braddock Road now runs westward from the junction of the two. It was later extended to the Bull Run Mountains, where it joined the old Indian hunting path. Rolling roads were used to roll ox-drawn hogsheads of tobacco to ports for shipping abroad. Walter Griffin, Jr. and Benjamin Griffin patented 350 acres of land on Pope's Head Run in 1719. The rolling road that bore Walter's name was known as the Mountain Road in 1800, at the time of the building of the new courthouse. Harrison, *Landmarks*, pp. 422-425, 476.
29. Ring, "Ratcliffe," p. 85.
30. Robert S. Gamble, *Sully: The Biography of a House* (Chantilly, Va.: Sully Foundation, Ltd., 1973), pp. 15-54.
31. Fairfax Deed Book Z, p. 477.
32. Virginia Historical Society Manuscripts Division, Mss1 F5785 b12.
33. Thomas Jefferson Papers, Library of Congress, Microfilm Series I, March 27, 1804.
34. Charles Carter Lee, Unpublished autobiography, C. C. Lee Papers, microfilm, Library of Virginia.
35. Ring, "Richard Ratcliffe," pp. 89-95.
36. *Ibid.*, pp. 95-96.
37. *Ibid.*, pp. 96-97.
38. *Ibid.*, p. 104.
39. *Ibid.*, p. 97.
40. *Ibid.*
41. *The Columbian Mirror and Alexandria Gazette*, June 20, 1795; August 1, 1795.
42. Ring, p. 99.
43. Fairfax County Minute Book 1800-1801, n.p.
44. Netherton and Waldeck, *Courthouse*, p. 3.
45. Fairfax County Minute Book 1800-1801, p. 29.
46. *Ibid.*, p. 33.
47. John W. Wayland, *The Washingtons and their Homes* (Berryville, Virginia, facsimile reprint, 1973), p. 318.
48. *The Columbian Mirror and Alexandria Gazette*, April 24, 1800.
49. John O. and Margaret T. Peters, *Virginia's Historic Courthouses* (Charlottesville and London, University Press of Virginia, 1995), pp. 35-36.

Chapter 2. 1800 to 1860
The Town of Providence at the New Courthouse

1. Netherton and Waldeck. *Courthouse*, pp. 14, 18, 24.
2. Ring, "Ratcliffe," pp. 96-99, 102; an obituary for Richard Ratcliffe appeared in the *Alexandria Gazette*, September 27, 1825; post office names, years of establishment, and names of postmasters in Fairfax County were published by Robert Lisbeth in *Way Markings*, February 1977, pp. 4-50.
3. Samuel Shepherd. *Statutes at Large of Virginia, 1792-1806*, Vol. iii, pp. 48, 177. (Richmond, Va., reprint).
4. Albert C. Rose. *Historic American Highways*. (Washington, D. C.: American Association of State Highway Officials, 1953), pp. 37-38; Netherton, et al., *Fairfax County*, pp. 192-193, 198.
5. Netherton and Waldeck, *Courthouse*, pp. 59-60, 65.
6. Harrison. *Landmarks*, pp. 441-445, 466-467, 476.
7. Artemel in Netherton, et al., *Fairfax County* (1978), pp. 190-191.
8. Netherton, et al. *Fairfax County* (1978), pp. 163-167.
9. John W. Bell. *Memoirs of Gov. William Smith of Virginia: His Political, Military and Personal History*. (Published by Moss, 1891), pp. 3, 6, 7, 21.
10. Joseph Martin. *A New and Comprehensive Gazetteer of Virginia and the District of Columbia*. (Charlottesville: Moseby & Tompkins, Printers, 1835), p. 168.
11. Virginia State Archives; Virginia Board of Public Works, Loose Papers, Library of Virginia, Richmond. Box 249, #198, 1846-1854.
12. Cordeila G. Sansone. "Coombe Cottage, first girls' academy in Fairfax County, Virginia." *Yearbook*, The Historical Society of Fairfax County, Va., Inc. Vol. 16, pp. 25-51.
13. *Ibid.*; Jeanne Johnson Rust. *A History of the Town of Fairfax*. (Washington, D. C.: Moore & Moore, Inc., 1960), p. 36.
14. Netherton, et al. *Fairfax County* (1978), pp. 266-267.
15. Virginia State Archives, Board of Public Works, O&A RR, Loose Papers, Library of Virginia, Richmond.
16. Nan Netherton and Ruth Preston Rose. *Memories of Beautiful Burke, Virginia*. (Burke: Burke Historical Society, 1988), p. 12.
17. Netherton, et al. *Fairfax County* (1978), pp. 596-597.
18. R. & B. Freson, eds. *St. Mary's: Fairfax Station, Virginia, 1858-1983*. (Fairfax Station, Va.: St. Mary's, 1983), pp. 7-8.

Chapter 3. 1861-1870
Caught in the Crossfire: War and Its Aftermath

1. *Population of the United States in 1860; Compiled from the Original Returns of the Eighth Census, Under the Direction of the Secretary of the Interior, By Joseph C. G. Kennedy, Superintendent of Census.*
2. D'Anne A. Evans, *The Story of Oakton, Virginia: 1758-1990*, Second Edition (Oakton: The Optimist Club of Oakton, 1991). See Chapter II for a discussion of the changing nature of farming in Fairfax County during the first half of the 19th century.
3. Patricia Hickin in Netherton, *et al., Fairfax County, Virginia: A History* (Fairfax: Fairfax County Board of Supervisors, 1978), pp. 315-316.
4. *Ibid.*
5. Nan Netherton and Whitney Von Lake Wyckoff, *Fairfax Station: All Aboard* (Fairfax Station: Friends of the Fairfax Station, 1995), p. 27; also Hickin in Netherton, *et al., Fairfax County* (1978), p. 318.
6. Hickin in Netherton, *et al., Fairfax County* (1978), p. 318.
7. *Ibid.*, p. 320. See also, Thomas Chapman, Jr., "The Secession Election in Fairfax County, May 23, 1861," *Yearbook of the Historical Society of Fairfax County*, Vol. 4 (1955).
8. Jeanne Johnson Rust, *A History of the Town of Fairfax* (1960), p. 42.
9. Netherton and Wyckoff, *Fairfax Station* (1995), p. 27.
10. Hickin in Netherton, *et al., Fairfax County* (1978), p. 319.
11. D'Anne A. Evans, *The Story of Oakton* (1991), p. 31.
12. Hickin in Netherton, *et al., Fairfax County* (1978), p. 321; "Ellsworth, The First to Fall," Fort Ward Museum, (September 1991); and "The Life of James W. Jackson, the Alexandria hero, the slayer of Ellsworth, the first martyr in the cause of southern independence; containing a full account of the circumstances of his heroic death, and the many remarkable

incidents in his eventful life, constituting a true history, more like romance than reality, Pub. for the benefit of his family." (Richmond: West & Johnston [Macfarlane & Fergusson, printers], 1862).
13. *Ibid.*, Life of Jackson.
14. D'Anne A. Evans, *The Story of Oakton* (1991), p. 31-32.
15. *Ibid.* pp. 33-35.
16. Rev. Joseph Hodge Alves and Harold Spelman, *Near the Falls, Two Hundred Years of the Falls Church* (Falls Church: The Falls Church, 1969), pp. 32-33.
17. *Ibid.*, p. 33. See also, *Diary of a Southern Refugee During the War*, by a Lady of Virginia [Judith B. McGuire] (New York: 1868).
18. Alice Maude Ewell, *A Virginia Scene* (Lynchburg: J. P. Bell Co., 1931), pp. 56-57.
19. Governor William Smith, "The Skirmish at Fairfax Court House," in *Fairfax County and the War Between the States* (Fairfax County Civil War Centennial Commission, 1961), pp. 1-8. See also, Rust, *A History of the Town of Fairfax*, pp. 43-45; Joseph A. Jeffries, "The Night Attack at Fairfax Court House," in *The Southern Magazine*, September 1899 (Vol. 1, No. 4) (Manassas: The Southern Publishing Company), pp. 250-254; and letter from J. P. Machen to his brother, Arthur W. Machen, dated June 11, 1861, in *The Letters of Arthur W. Machen, With Biographical Sketch*, compiled by Arthur W. Machen, Jr. (Baltimore: Privately Printed, 1917), pp. 291-293.
20. *Ibid.*
21. Charles D. Walker, *Memorial, Virginia Military Institute Biographical Sketches of the Graduates and Eleves of the Virginia Military Institute Who Fell During the War Between the States* (Philadelphia: J. B. Lippincott & Co., 1875), pp. 359-363.
22. For a photograph of the dedication of the Marr monument, see Netherton, *et al., Fairfax County* (1978), p. 470; for a poem read at the dedication of the Marr monument, see "The Night Attack, A Ballad of Fairfax," in *Songs of Love and War*, by Henry Mazyck Clarkson (Manassas: Manassas Journal Publishing Company, 1910), pp. 107-110.
23. Geoffrey C. Ward, *The Civil War, An Illustrated History* (New York: Alfred A. Knopf, Inc., 1990), pp. 62-69.
24. *Ibid.*
25. Hickin in Netherton, *et al., Fairfax County* (1978), p. 326; see also, Benjamin Franklin Cooling, *Symbol, Sword, and Shield: Defending Washington During the Civil War* (Hamden, CT: Archon Books, 1975), especially pp. 73-80.
26. Ross D. Netherton and Ruby Waldeck, *The Fairfax County Courthouse* (Fairfax County Office of Comprehensive Planning, 1977), p. 34; see also Rust, p. 48; and Stephen Woodworth, *Davis and Lee at War* (Lawrence, Kansas: University Press of Kansas, 1995), pp. 62-69.
27. For a good discussion of raids and skirmishes between Federal and Confederate forces in Fairfax County during the winter of 1861-62, see Netherton and Wyckoff, *Fairfax Station* (1995), p. 29; see also Cooling, *Symbol, Sword, and Shield* (1975), Chapter 4, "Watchfires of a Hundred Circling Camps," pp. 81-101.
28. Cooling, *Ibid.*, p. 112.
29. Unpublished letter from William Maris Clark to his brother, Edward R. Clark, and his sister, S. Emma Clark, dated April 27, 1862, provided by Chris Mullen, Fairfax, Virginia.
30. Hickin in Netherton, *et al., Fairfax County* (1978), p. 333.
31. For a discussion of the Wheeling conventions, see Charles H. Ambler, *Francis H. Pierpont* (Chapel Hill: University of North Carolina Press, 1937), especially pp. 84-90.
32. Hickin in Netherton, *et al., Fairfax County* (1978), p. 332.
33. *Ibid.*, p. 336.
34. For a scholarly and readable account of the Shenandoah Valley campaign during the Summer of 1862, see John Hennessy, *Return to Bull Run, The Campaign and Battle of Second Manassas* (New York: Simon & Schuster, 1993).
35. *Ibid.*
36. Robert Ross Smith, "Ox Hill, The Most Neglected Battle of the Civil War, 1 September 1862," in *Fairfax County and the War Between the States* (Fairfax County Civil War Centennial Commission, 1961), pp. 19-64.

37. Hennessy, *Return to Bull Run* (1993).
38. There are a number of good biographies of Clara Barton, including the most recent by Stephen B. Oates, *Clara Barton* (1992).
39. Netherton and Wyckoff, *Fairfax Station: All Aboard* (1995), p. 31.
40. These troop movements are memorialized on a roadsidehistorical marker on westbound U.S. Route 50 at its intersection with Jermantown Road.
41. Unpublished letter from William Elbridge Knight to his wife, Jane Rhoda Martin Knight, dated December 12, 1862, provided by Judith M. E. Fugate, St. Cloud, Florida. For an additional description of Fairfax C.H. in October, 1862, see "Civil War Letter of Col. David Thomson," *Historical Society of Fairfax County, Virginia, Inc. Yearbook*, Volume 20 (1984-1985), pp. 86-88.
42. Unpublished letter from William Elbridge Knight to his wife, Jane Rhoda Martin Knight, dated December 14, 1862, provided by Judith M. E. Fugate, St. Cloud, Florida.
43. Unpublished letter from William Elbridge Knight to his wife, Jane Rhoda Martin Knight, dated December 25, 1862, from "near Fairfax Court House, Va.," provided by Judith M. E. Fugate, St. Cloud, Florida.
44. Unpublished letter from William Elbridge Knight to his wife, Jane Rhoda Martin Knight, dated December 27, 1862, provided by Judith M. E. Fugate, St. Cloud, Florida.
45. Netherton and Wyckoff, *Fairfax Station: All Aboard* (1995), pp. 32-33.
46. The text of the telegram is taken from Burke Davis, *Jeb Stuart, The Last Cavalier* (New York: Holt, Reinhart & Winston, 1957), p. 262. Davis notes that he was unable to locate the exact text of the telegraph message from a primary source; several slight variations are included in various secondary sources.
47. *Ibid.*
48. Unpublished letter from William Elbridge Knight to his wife, Jane Rhoda Martin Knight, dated January 9, 1863, provided by Judith M. E. Fugate, St. Cloud, Florida.
49. Unpublished letter from William Elbridge Knight to his wife, Jane Rhoda Martin Knight, dated January 22, 1863, provided by Judith M. E. Fugate, St. Cloud, Florida.
50. Ross D. Netherton and Ruby Waldeck, *The Fairfax County Courthouse* (Fairfax County Office of Comprehensive Planning, 1977), p. 36.
51. *Ibid.*, pp. 37-38. See also, Eugene E. Prussing, *The Estate of George Washington, Deceased* (Boston: Little, Brown and Co.,1927), pp. 39-40; and "Martha Washington's Will and the Story of its Loss and Recovery by Fairfax County," *Yearbook of the Historical Society of Fairfax County, Virginia*, II (1952-53), pp. 40-62.
52. Emory M. Thomas, *Bold Dragoon, The Life of J.E.B. Stuart* (New York: Harper & Row, 1986), pp. 83, 86, 90, 110-11; Hickin in Netherton, *et al.*, *Fairfax County* (1978), pp. 354-55; for more detailed treatment of Mosby, see Virgil Carrington Jones, *Ranger Mosby* (Chapel Hill: University of North Carolina Press, 1944); and V.C. Jones, *Gray Ghosts and Rebel Raiders* (New York: Henry Holt and Company, 1956).
53. Hickin in Netherton, *et al.*, *Fairfax County* (1978), p. 355.
54. *Ibid.* See also, "An Account of Mosby's Raid, By One of Stoughton's Men," as told to Herbert A. Donovan, *The Historical Society of Fairfax County, Virginia Yearbook*, Volume 4 (1955), p. 72. This short article tells of a visit to the Rectory of the then Zion Church (formerly the Gunnell House) in 1940 by a former New York soldier who had been part of Stoughton's guard detail and who himself had been captured by Mosby.
55. Linda J. Simmons, "The Antonia Ford Myst," *Northern Virginia Heritage*, October 1985, p. 4.
56. Jeanne Johnson Rust, *A History of the Town of Fairfax* (1960), pp. 53-54; Hickin in Netherton, *et al.*, *Fairfax County* (1978), p. 355.
57. Garnett Laidlaw Eskew, *Willard's of Washington* (New York: Coward-McCann, Inc., 1954), pp. 17-18.
58. *Ibid.*, pp. 61-79.
59. Hickin in Netherton, *et al.*, *Fairfax County* (1978), pp. 351.
60. Hickin in Netherton, *et al.*, *Fairfax County* (1978), p. 362. For background on Pierpont's views on slavery, see Charles H. Ambler, *Francis H. Pierpont* (Chapel Hill: University of North Carolina Press, 1937); and *Proceedings in Statuary Hall and the Senate and the House of Representatives Upon the Unveiling, Reception, and Acceptance from the State of West Virginia of the Statue of Governor Francis Harrison Pierpont*

61. (Washington, DC: Government Printing Office, 1910), especially pp. 5, 13-17.
62. Ralph LeRoy Milliken, "Then We Came to California: A Biography of Sarah Summers Clarke," *Yearbook of the Historical Society of Fairfax County, Virginia*, Volume 8 (1962-63), pp. 30.
63. Hickin in Netherton, *et al.*, *Fairfax County* (1978), p. 366-367. See also the *Journal of the Convention which Convened at Alexandria on the 13th Day of February, 1864.* (Alexandria, Va.: D. Turner, Printer to the State, 1864.)
63. *Ibid.*, p. 369.
64. Milliken, *Historical Society of Fairfax County Yearbook*, Vol. 8 (1962-63), p. 39.
65. Eric Foner, *Reconstruction, America's Unfinished Revolution, 1863-1877* (New York: Harper & Row, 1988), p. 78.
66. Hamilton James Eckenrode, *The Political History of Virginia During the Reconstruction* (Baltimore: Johns Hopkins University Press, 1904), pp. 40-41.
67. *Ibid.*, p. 58.
68. Hickin in Netherton, *et al.*, *Fairfax County* (1978), p. 381-382.
69. Eric Foner, *Reconstruction, America's Unfinished Revolution, 1863-1877* (New York: Harper & Row, 1988), p. 271.
70. Hickin in Netherton, *et al.*, *Fairfax County* (1978), p. 379.
71. Eckenrode, op cite, p. 88-89.
72. *Ibid.*, pp. 87-103.

Chapter 4. 1871-1899
School Days, a War Memorial, and a Masonic Hall

1. Patrick Reed in Netherton, et al., *Fairfax County* (1978), p. 392.
2. *Fairfax News*, September 5, 1873.
3. *Ibid.*
4. *Fairfax News*, January 17, 1873. The *Fairfax News* was published by J. Simpson from 1872 to 1875.
5. *Fairfax News*, May 23, 1873.
6. *Fairfax News*, February 21, 1873.
7. *Fairfax News*, November 7, 1873.
8. *Fairfax News*, December 25, 1874.
9. Virginia Acts of Assembly, 1874, 1891-92, 1908.
10. *Fairfax News*, March 28, 1873.
11. *Ibid.*
12. *Fairfax News*, June 13, 1873.
13. Reed in Netherton, et al., *Fairfax County* (1978), pp. 445-446.
14. *Ibid.*
15. *Ibid.*, p. 418.
16. R. Walton Moore. "R. Walton Moore: Reflections in His 80th Year." Dictated to Helene Mitchell, November 1939. Unpublished. Copyright: S. William Livingston, Jr. Alexandria, Va., p. 24.
17. Richard W. Stephenson. *Cartography of Northern Virginia.* (Fairfax, Va.: Office of Comprehensive Planning, 1981), p. 92.
18. Chataigne's *Virginia Gazetteer*. Richmond, 1884.
19. *Richmond State*, January 31 and February 2, 1882.
20. Reed in Netherton et al., *Fairfax County*, p. 403.
21. Richard L. Thompson. "Captain John Newton Ballard: A Dyed-in-the-Wool Confederate." *Yearbook*: Historical Society of Fairfax County, Va., Vol. 21, pp. 95-105.
22. *Ibid.*
23. *Ibid.*
24. Chataigne's *Virginia Gazetteer*, cited in *Fairfax County In Virginia: Selections from Some Rare Sources.* (Fairfax, Va.: Office of Comprehensive Planning), 1974, p. 88.
25. Rust, *Fairfax*, p. 64.
26. Petitions re: liquor licenses, 1888, Fairfax County Circuit Court Archives, Judicial Center.
27. Netherton and Wyckoff, *Fairfax Station*, p. 49.
28. Albert C. Rose. *Historic American Highways.* (Washington, D. C.: American Association of State Highway Officials, 1953.)

29. Noel Garraux Harrison *City of Canvas: Camp Russell A. Alger and the Spanish-American War.* (Falls Church, Va.: Falls Church Historical Commission and Fairfax County History Commission, 1988), pp. 1-2, 72.

30. Sadie C. Detwiler, Fannie Johnson, Hollie Nickel, and Katharine Harrison. *Fairfax County Geography Supplement.* (Charlottesville: University of Virginia, Fairfax County School Board, 1925), p. 7.

31. Ring, "Richard Ratcliffe", *Yearbook*, Vol. 25, p. 136.

Chapter 5. 1900-1930
Rails, Roads, Fairs and a Fire

1. *Fairfax Herald*, August 31, 1900.
2. Netherton, et al., *Fairfax County* (1978), pp. 460-461.
3. *Fairfax Herald*, 1900-1910, numerous weekly advertisements.
4. Netherton and Wyckoff, *Fairfax Station*, p. 59.
5. Reed, in Netherton, et al., *Fairfax County* (1978), pp. 473-75.
6. *Ibid.*
7. *Ibid.*
8. City of Fairfax Public Information Office, *City of Fairfax Historic Sites*, (Fairfax, Va.: City of Fairfax, 1988), p. 30.
9. Netherton and Wyckoff, *Fairfax Station*, p. 52.
10. Reed, in Netherton, et al., *Fairfax County* (1978), p. 468.
11. *Fairfax Herald*, August 24, 1900; April 19, 1901; October 13, 1905; November 10, 1905.
12. Susan Hunter Walker, "Confederate Monument at Fairfax, Va.," *Confederate Veteran*, v. 12 (1904); Emily J. Salmon, ed., *A Hornbook of Virginia History.* (Richmond: Virginia State Library, 1983), p. 80.
13. Fairfax, *Historical Sites*, p. 31; Lee Hubbard on bank opening.
14. *Fairfax Herald*, July 29, 1904; August 26, 1904.
15. Fairfax County Board of Supervisors, *Historic, Industrial Fairfax County*, (Fairfax, Va.: 1907).
16. *Fairfax Herald*, November 17, 1905.
17. *Ibid.*, November 17, 1905; May 29, 1908; August 13, 1909; June 19, 1928.
18. *Ibid.*, August 26, 1904; July 5, 1906; April 24, 1908; September 9, 1932.
19. *Ibid.*, May 18, 1917; January 4, 1918.
20. *Ibid.*, July 5, 1906.
21. *Ibid.*, August 31, 1906.
22. *Ibid.*, July 5, 1906.
23. *Ibid.*, December 21, 1906; January 4, 1907.
24. *Ibid.*, September 20, 1935.
25. *Ibid.*, July 14. 1922, p. 3; February 23, 1923, p. 5; March 13, 1925, p. 3.
26. *Ibid.*, August 16, 1907, p. 2; May 27, 1921, p. 3; March 13, 1931, p. 1; May 3, 1935, p. 1; May 29, 1936, p. 1.
27. *Ibid.*, October 7, 1921; November 11, 1921; March 18, 1927.
28. "Martha Washington's Will and the Story of its Loss and Recovery by Fairfax County," *Yearbook of the Historical Society of Fairfax County, Va.:* Vol. 2 (1952-1953), pp. 40-62; Letter to J. P. Morgan from Mary Grimsley Barbour, November 10, 1913; Virginia v. John Pierpont Morgan, Supreme Court of the U. S., Term, October 1914, Commonwealth of Virginia, complainant, J. P. Morgan, defendant. Returned in October 1915.
29. *Fairfax Herald*, October 13, 1914.
30. *Ibid.*, October 23, 1914.
31. *Ibid.*
32. Fairfax City Regional Library, Virginia Room, (Rare), *1920 Program for the Fairfax County Colored Fair.*
33. *Ibid.*
34. *Fairfax Herald*, 1916-1918.
35. Virginius Dabney, *Virginia: The New Dominion.* (Garden City, New York: Doubleday & Co., Inc., 1971), p. 464-65.
36. Arthur Kyle Davis, *Virginia Communities in Wartime*, (Richmond, Va.: The Executive Committee), 1927.
37. Reed, in Netherton, et al., *Fairfax County*, pp. 591-92.
38. Dabney, *Virginia*, p. 475.
39. *Ibid.*, pp. 461-62.
40. *Ibid.*, pp. 462-63.
41. Dabney, *Virginia*, p. 477.
42. *Fairfax Herald*, August 31, 1920.
43. *Ibid.*, June 15, 1923.
44. Town Council Minutes, November, 1936; September 6, 1939.
45. *Ibid.*, January 7, 1921; February 11, 1921.
46. Fairfax County Agriculture Extension Agent, Annual Report, 1923. Virginia Room, Fairfax City Regional Library, Fairfax.
47. From *The Historic Fairfax Elementary School*, a fact sheet published by the Fairfax Museum. No date.
48. Reed, in Netherton, et al., *Fairfax County*, p. 534.
49. *Fairfax Herald*, April 10, 1925; May 29, 1925.
50. *Ibid*, November 19, 1926, p. 5.
51. *Ibid.*, March 18, 1927.
52. *Ibid.*, April 22, 1927.
53. *Ibid.*, September 20, 1935.
54. *Ibid.*, January 2, 1925.
55. Indictment was announced in the *Herald*, May 21, 1926, p. 3; May 28, 1926.
56. Excerpt from a letter of recollections sent to John Rust, Jr. by his father, John Rust, Sr., March 17, 1996; letter of recollections to John Rust, Jr. from E. A. Prichard, March 14, 1996.
57. Interview with Patsy and Scotty Allensworth, Vienna, February 7, 1997; Rust to Rust letter, March 17, 1996; *Fairfax Herald*, December 8, 1922, p. 3; July 14, 1922, p. 3; February 23, 1923, p. 5; March 13, 1925, p. 3; *Fairfax Herald*, December 8, 1922, p. 3; July 14, 1922, p. 3; February 23, 1923, p. 5; March 13, 1925, p. 3.
58. *Fairfax Herald*, September 7, 1928.
59. *Ibid.*, November 23, 1928; a copy of the 1924 film, *The Road to Happiness*, may be seen in the Virginia Room of the Fairfax City Regional Library.
60. *Ibid.*, December 24, 1909; Fairfax VFD history notes from Bill Sheads, November 1996.
61. *Fairfax Herald*, March 14, 1930.
62. *Industrial Directory of Virginia, 1929*, Town of Fairfax, Virginia.
63. Rust to Rust letter, March 17, 1996.
64. Town *Council Minutes* March 7, 1928.
65. *Ibid.*, October 9, 1928; *Fairfax Herald*, October 26, 1928, p. 1.
66. *Ibid.*, March 7, 1929.
67. *Ibid.*, February 4, 1929.
68. Special Town Council Meeting, June 25, 1929; Recollection of John Rust, Sr.
69. *Fairfax Herald*, January 4, 1929.
70. "Klan Day at Fairfax County Fair Draws Immense Throngs," *Fairfax Independent*, September 19, 1929.
71. *Fairfax Herald*, September 20, 1929.
72. Town Council Minutes, December 2, 1929.
73. "Flint Hill" report, Historic American Building Survey Inventory, Fairfax County Office of Comprehensive Planning, #67, November 24, 1970.

Chapter 6. 1931-1960
Cows, Corn and Commuters

1. Netherton, et al., *Fairfax County* (1978), p. 553 quoting Derr, *Reports*, 1930, 1931, 1932. See also Fairfax County white corn, pp. 517 and 549.
2. Derr, *Reports*, 1930.
3. *Ibid.*, 1931.
4. *Ibid.*, 1932.
5. Town Council Minutes, November 11, 1930; November 21, 1930; November 29, 1930; December 1, 1930.
6. *Fairfax Herald*, November 24, 1931.
7. Town Council Minutes, July 20, 1933.
8. *Ibid.*; 1933 Acts of the Assembly, Chapter 51.
9. *Ibid.*, June 4, 1934.
10. Dabney, *Virginia*, pp. 461-462.
11. Town Council Minutes, November 6, 1933.
12. *Ibid.*, August 31, 1934.
13. *Fairfax Herald*, December 8, 1933.
14. *Ibid.*, December 15, 1933.

15. *Ibid.*, December 29, 1933.
16. *Ibid.*, January 29, 1932.
17. *Ibid.*, December 6, 1935.
18. Town Council Minutes, April 10, 1935.
19. *Ibid.*, June 3, 1935; July 1, 1935.
20. *Ibid.*, November 23, 1935.
21. *Ibid.*, July 6, 1936.
22. *Fairfax Herald*, December 27, 1935; March 27, 1936.
23. Town Council Minutes, April 4, 1938.
24. *Ibid.*, November 2, 1936.
25. Netherton, et al., *Fairfax County* (1978), p. 553.
26. Blaine Friedlander memorandum to the author, November 24, 1996.
27. Public Law No. 74-641, 49 Stat. at 774, August 24, 1935.
28. Friedlander memorandum, November 24, 1996.
29. Public Law No. 396, 79th Congress, 60 Stat. 230.
30. Interview with Vaughan MacDonald, historian, Country Club of Fairfax, on April 15, 1997, by Nan Netherton.
31. Memoirs of R. Walton Moore, 1939, unpublished.
32. *Fairfax Herald*, December 8, 1939.
33. Netherton, et al., *Fairfax County* (1978), p. 617.
34. Fairfax Council Minutes, February 7, 1940.
35. *Ibid.*, April 3, 1940.
36. Letters to John Rust, Jr., from E. A. Prichard, March 14, 1996, and John Rust, Sr., March 17, 1996.
37. *Fairfax Herald*, August 31, 1934.
38. *Historic, Progressive Fairfax County*, Fairfax Chamber of Commerce, 1928, p. 32.
39. *Ibid.*, p. 38.
40. *Fairfax Herald*, May 23, 1941.
41. *Ibid.*, December 3, 1941.
42. Letter, Rust to Rust, March 17, 1996. There are unfortunate gaps in the Town Council of Fairfax Minute books. The City of Fairfax clerk's office's earliest minutes begin in June 1927. Books are missing that would have included December 1941 to April 1946, and the first 141 pages in the October 1951 to March 1953 minute books are missing. The books that covered almost exactly the period of World War II would have been enlightening had we had them.
43. Fairfax Council Minutes, February 5, 1941; March 5, 1941.
44. *Ibid.*, August 6, 1941.
45. 1943 *Fare Fac Sampler*, Fairfax High School Annual, p. 5.
46. *Ibid.*, p. 89.
47. *Ibid.*, p. 91.
48. 1944 *Fare Fac Sampler*, p. 105.
49. The OSS Assessment Staff. *Assessment of Men: Selection of Personnel for the Office of Strategic Services.* (New York: Rinehart & Company, Inc.), 1948, pp. v, 3-5.
50. 1945 *Fare Fac Sampler*, p. 10.
51. *Fairfax Herald*, July 17, 1891, p. 3.
52. *Ibid.*, May 12, 1939.
53. *Ibid.*, September 7, 1945.
54. *Ibid.*, September 9, 1960.
55. *Ibid.*, December 5, 1947.
56. *Ibid.*, March 13, 1925.
57. Town Council Minutes, February 4, 1948; April 7, 1948.
58. *Ibid.*, March 5, 1941.
59. *Ibid.*, May 15, 1946.
60. *Ibid.*
61. *Ibid.*, July 7, 1948.
62. *Ibid.*, October 6, 1948; January 17, 1949; April 6, 1949.
63. *Ibid.*, June 1, 1949.
64. *Ibid.*, September 7, 1949.
65. *Ibid.*, January 8, 1947.
66. Letter from R. M. Loughborough to Fairfax Town Council, February 5, 1947.
67. Fairfax Council Minutes, December 3, 1947.
68. *Ibid.*, September 7, 1949.
69. *Ibid.*, December 7, 1949.
70. *Ibid.*, September 7, 1949.

71. *Ibid.*, October 5, 1949.
72. *Ibid.*, July 2, 1941; May 7, 1947.
73. Fairfax Council Minutes, December 7, 1949.
74. *Ibid.*, Books from 1927 to 1961.
75. *Ibid.*, December 5, 1951.
76. *Ibid.*, February 8, 1950; January 16, 1952.
77. *Ibid.*, September , 1954.
78. *Ibid.*, February 16, 1953; March 12, 1953; May 19, 1953.
79. *Ibid.*, June 30, 1953.
80. *Ibid.*, April 7, 1954.
81. *Ibid.*
82. *Ibid.*, May 5, 1954.
83. *Ibid.*
84. *Ibid.*, May 14, 1952; August 6, 1952.
85. *Ibid.*, May 14, 1952; June 4, 1952.
86. *Ibid.*, November 10, 1954; December 17, 1954.
87. *Ibid.*, January 5, 1955.
88. *Ibid.*, April 27, 1954; May 5, 1954.
89. *Ibid.*, November 16, 1954.
90. *Ibid.*, August 8, 1956.
91. *Ibid.*, September 12, 1956.
92. *Ibid.*
93. *Ibid.*, May 5, 1952.
94. *Ibid.*, March 9, 1955.
95. *Ibid.*, February 3, 1960.
96. *Ibid.*, May 4, 1960.
97. Netherton et al., *Fairfax County* (1978), p. 581.
98. 1953 *Fare Fac Sampler*, p. 89.
99. 1954 *Fare Fac Sampler*.
100. *40th Anniversary Program*, Fairfax Symphony, 1996; Ross and Nan Netherton, *Fairfax County in Virginia: A Pictorial History*, Norfolk, Va.: The Donning Company, Publishers, 1986, p. 140.
101. Netherton, et al., *Fairfax County* (1978), pp. 578-581.
102. *Ibid.*, p. 582.
103. Fairfax Council Minutes, October 19, 1954.
104. *Ibid.*, October 7, 1959.
105. *Ibid.*, June 18, 1952; September 10, 1952.
106. *Ibid.*, July 8, 1953.
107. *Ibid.*, September 19, 1952.
108. *Ibid.*, December 17, 1954; January 5, 1955.
109. *Ibid.*, February 9, 1955.
110. *Ibid.*, June 8, 1955.
111. *Ibid.*, March 15, 1956.
112. *Ibid.*, September 23, 1959.
113. *Ibid.*, December 2, 1959.
114. *Ibid.*, February 29, 1960; March 3, 1960.
115. *Ibid.*, April 5, 1961.
116. *Ibid.*, August 6, 1952.
117. *Ibid.*, July 23, 1954; November 7, 1956.
118. *Ibid.*, March 6, 1957.
119. Interview with Fairfax City Manager Robert Sisson by Nan Netherton, January 31, 1997.
120. Fairfax Council Minutes, January 7, 1953; February 4, 1953.
121. *Fairfax Herald*, January 10, 1958, pp. 3 and 6, map.
122. *Ibid.*, July 4, 1958.
123. *Ibid.*, December 4, 1959.
124. *Ibid.*, May 20, 1960, p. 1.
125. Fairfax Council Minutes, May 3, 1961.
126. *Ibid.*, July 5, 1961.

Chapter 7. 1961-1968
From Sleepy Town to Vibrant Small City

1. *City of Fairfax Annual Report, 1961.*
2. Interview with E. A. Prichard, May 28, 1996.
3. *Fairfax City Times*, October 3, 1963.
4. Interview with John H. Rust, Jr., March 26, 1997.
5. *Fairfax City Times*, October 3, 1963.

6. *Ibid.*
7. *Ibid.*
8. Town of Fairfax Council Minutes, May 3, 1961.
9. City of Fairfax Council Minutes, June 21, 1961.
10. *Free Press Publications,* June 4, 1964.
11. *Northern Virginia Sun,* May 11, 1961.
12. *City of Fairfax Annual Report,* 1958.
13. Community Inforum Summary, April 18, 1995.
14. *Code of Virginia.*
15. City of Fairfax Council Minutes, October 4, 1961.
16. *Ibid.,* September 13, 1961; January 17, 1962; June 6, 1962; June 20, 1962.
17. *Fairfax City Times,* November 21, 1963.
18. *Ibid.*
19. *Northern Virginia Sun,* June 25, 1963.
20. *Ibid.,* June 26, 1963.
21. City of Fairfax Council Minutes, February 6, 1963.
22. *Ibid.,* April 15, 1964.
23. *Ibid.,* March 6, 1963; *Fairfax County Sun Echo,* October 17, 1963.
24. City of Fairfax Council Minutes, April 3, 1963.
25. *Fairfax City Times,* May 8, 1964.
26. City of Fairfax Council Minutes, August 19, 1964.
27. *Ibid.,* May 1, 1963; July 13, 1963; October 20, 1963; December 18, 1963; January 15, 1964; March 4, 1964; March 18, 1964; July 1, 1964.
28. Interview with E.A. Prichard, May 28, 1996.
29. *Northern Virginia Sun,* June 10, 1964; *Washington Post,* June 10, 1964; *Fairfax City Times,* August 28, 1964.
30. *Northern Virginia Sun,* December 14, 1965.
31. *The City of Fairfax Annual Report,* 1965.
32. City of Fairfax Council Minutes, June 18, 1968.
33. *Fairfax City Times,* May 15, 1964.
34. *Northern Virginia Sun,* December 22, 1965.
35. *Fairfax City Times,* June 11, 1965.
36. *Northern Virginia Sun,* June 19, 1968; *Fairfax Globe,* August 22, 1968; *Alexandria Gazette,* September 4, 1968; Files, Parks and Recreation Department, City of Fairfax.
37. *City of Fairfax Annual Report,* 1966-67.
38. *Fairfax Sentinel,* July 1, 1971.
39. *Northern Virginia Sun,* March 5, 1965; March 10; 1965; March 16, 1965.
40. *Fairfax City Times,* September 11, 1964.
41. *Ibid.,* March 5, 1965.
42. *Alexandria Gazette,* July 14, 1967.
43. *Northern Virginia Sun,* April 8, 1966.
44. *Fairfax City Times,* August 17, 1967.
45. *Northern Virginia Sun,* August 16, 1967; *Fairfax City Times,* August 17, 1967.
46. *Fairfax City Times,* April 9, 1965.
47. *Loudoun Times Mirror,* May 27, 1965; *Northern Virginia Sun,* June 25, 1965.
48. *Community Inforum Summary,* April 18, 1995.
49. *Fairfax City Times,* November 10, 1966.
50. *Ibid.,* June 8, 1967; *Fairfax Globe,* November 2, 1967.
51. *Northern Virginia Sun,* January 7, 1966.
52. *Ibid.*
53. *City of Fairfax Annual Reports,* 1964 and 1968.
54. *Northern Virginia Sun,* February 8, 1968.
55. *Fairfax Globe,* March 14, 1968.
56. *Fairfax City Times,* September 10, 1965.
57. City of Fairfax Council Minutes, June 18, 1968.
58. *Northern Virginia Sun,* June 3, 1968.

Chapter 8. 1968-1978
The Changing Face of the City

1. *Virginia Sentinel,* May 21, 1970.
2. *Ibid.,* June 23, 1970.
3. *Ibid.*
4. *Ibid,* February 17, 1972.

5. *Ibid.,* March 13, 1972; April 27, 1972; *The Fairfax Globe,* May 11, 1972; May 25, 1972.
6. *Northern Virginia Sun,* December 6, 1972; *Fairfax Journal,* December 7, 1972; *Fairfax City Zoning Ordinance, 1968 (As Amended), Section 15, Erosion and Sedimentation Control,* October 10, 1972.
7. *Northern Virginia Sun,* December 8, 1972.
8. *Virginia Sentinel,* August 18, 1974; August 25, 1974.
9. *Fairfax Journal,* November 9, 1974.
10. *The News,* March 21, 1974.
11. *Virginia Sentinel,* May 16, 1974; *Fairfax County Sun Echo,* October 17, 1973; *Northern Virginia Sun,* May 8, 1973.
12. *Virginia Sentinel,* June 27, 1974.
13. *Northern Virginia Sun,* May 14, 1976.
14. *Fairfax Journal,* June 12, 1975; Interview with John H. Rust, Jr., March 26, 1997.
15. *Northern Virginia Sun,* August 25, 1975.
16. *The Fairfax Globe,* January 2, 1976.
17. *Fairfax Journal,* June 22, 1976.
18. *Washington Post,* December 14, 1976.
19. *Ibid.*
20. *Northern Virginia Sun,* February 26, 1977.
21. *The Gazette,* March 4, 1977.
22. *Northern Virginia Sun,* May 28, 1977.
23. *Washington Post,* November 9, 1977; interview with John H. Rust, Jr., March 26, 1997.
24. *Fairfax Journal,* February 3, 1978.
25. *Northern Virginia Sun,* May 5, 1976; April 6, 1977.
26. *Ibid.*
27. *The Fairfax Globe,* June 9, 1977.
28. *Ibid.,* June 16, 1977.
29. Fairfax City Council Minutes, September 6, 1977.
30. *Washington Star,* November 1, 1977.
31. *Ibid.,* December 13, 1977.
32. *Ibid.*
33. *The Fairfax Globe,* December 22, 1977.
34. Fairfax City Council Minutes, January 3, 1978.
35. *Ibid.*
36. *Ibid.,* January 17, 1978.
37. *Ibid.*
38. *Fairfax Journal,* January 20, 1978.
39. *Northern Virginia Sun,* January 11, 1978.
40. *Washington Star,* January 2, 1979; *Washington Post,* February 6, 1978.
41. *Ibid.*
42. *Ibid.*
43. *Northern Virginia Sun,* July 15, 1977.
44. Interview with Ellen Wigren, November 15, 1996.
45. *Washington Post,* October 3, 1978; *Northern Virginia Sun,* October 23, 1978.

Chapter 9. 1978-1996
Two Decades of Progress and Change

1. *Fairfax Journal,* July 13, 1983.
2. *Ibid.,* July 19, 1983.
3. *Ibid,* July 13, 1983.
4. Fairfax City Council Minutes, February 12, 1985.
5. *Fairfax Journal,* November 4, 1981.
6. *Northern Virginia Sun,* November 4, 1981.
7. *Ibid.,* November 3, 1982.
8. Files, Community Relations Office, City of Fairfax, Virginia.
9. *Northern Virginia Sun,* February 27, 1984.
10. *Fairfax Journal,* May 2, 1984.
11. *Fairfax Connection,* June 28, 1990.
12. *City of Fairfax Annual Report,* 1985-1986.
13. *Fairfax Connection,* September 17, 1992.
14. *Ibid.,* December 12, 1991; Files, Department of Community Development and Planning, City of Fairfax.

15. *Burke Times,* November 24, 1993; Files, Department of Community Development and Planning, City of Fairfax.
16. *Northern Virginia Sun,* January 24, 1979.
17. *Fairfax Journal,* November 18, 1982.
18. *Northern Virginia Sun,* September 13, 1983.
19. Fairfax City Council Minutes, December 17, 1985 and February 25, 1986.
20. *Washington Post,* September 1, 1982.
21. *Northern Virginia Sun,* August 18, 1983.
22. *Fairfax Connection,* May 21, 1992, and *Washington Post,* July 9, 1992.
23. Interview with John Gano, January 1997.
24. *Fairfax Connection,* July 16, 1992.
25. Daryl Humrichouser, Director, Fairfax Museum and Visitors Center.
26. Historic District Survey Forms, Department of Community Development and Planning, City of Fairfax, August 27, 1987.
27. *Washington Times,* February 19, 1992.
28. Certified Local Government files, Department of Community Development and Planning, City of Fairfax, 1991-1993.
29. *Washington Post,* October 16, 1986.
30. *Northern Virginia Sun,* November 12, 1980.
31. *City of Fairfax Annual Report, 1986-1987.*
32. *Northern Virginia Sun,* April 3, 1990; *Washington Post,* April 5, 1990.
33. Community Inforum Summary, City of Fairfax, April 18, 1995.
34. *City of Fairfax Highlights, 1983-1984.*
35. *Washington Post,* February 7, 1980.
36. Interview with James Shull, Former Director of Public Works, City of Fairfax, July 23, 1996.
37. *Fairfax Journal,* January 1, 1988; *Washington Post,* November 5, 1987; *Fairfax Journal,* November 4, 1987.
38. *City of Fairfax Annual Report, 1986-1987.*
39. *City of Fairfax Landscaping Study,* Rhodeside and Harwell (no published date).
40. *City of Fairfax Annual Reports, 1986-1987 and 1987-1988.*
41. Interview with John H. Rust, Jr., March 26, 1997.
42. City Inforum Summary, City of Fairfax, April 18, 1995.
43. Files, Department of Community Development and Planning, City of Fairfax 1985-1988.
44. *The City of Fairfax Zoning Ordinance, Article XVI.1, Highway Corridor Overlay District,* November 8, 1988.
45. Rezoning Activity in the City of Fairfax, 1980-1985, Department of Planning, 1985; Computer Base and Rezoning Files, Department of Community Development and Planning, 1996.
46. *Fairfax Journal,* March 9, 1989.
47. Summary of Rezoning Activity, January, 1975-July, 1980, Office of Planning, 1981; Rezoning Activity in the City of Fairfax, 1980-1985, Department of Planning, 1985; Computer Base and Rezoning Files, Department of Community Development and Planning, 1996.
48. Interview, Edward J. Cawley, Director of Finance, City of Fairfax, November 13, 1996.
49. *City of Fairfax Annual Report, 1986-1987.*
50. *Ibid.*
51. *City of Fairfax Annual Report, 1985-1986.*
52. *City of Fairfax Annual Report, 1986-1987.*
53. *The Comprehensive Plan of the City of Fairfax,* November 29, 1988.
54. *Washington Post,* November 30, 1989.
55. *Fairfax Connection,* January 4, 1990.
56. *Fairfax Connection,* January 11, 1990.
57. *Fairfax Journal,* May 2, 1990.
58. *Fairfax Connection,* March 1, 1990.
59. *Fairfax Journal,* January 10, 1991; *Fairfax Connection,* January 10, 1991; *Washington Post,* January 21, 1991; *Fairfax Connection,* April 4, 1991.
60. *Fairfax Journal,* November 5, 1990.
61. *Washington Post,* April 30, 1992.
62. Interview, Barry Baker, Assistant Chief, Fire and Rescue Services, January 3, 1997.
63. *Fairfax Connection,* January 23, 1992.
64. Files, Community Development and Planning Department, City of Fairfax, 1992.
65. *Fairfax Connection,* August 6, 1992.
66. *Fairfax Connection,* August 20, 1992.
67. *Washington Post,* May 7, 1987; *Fairfax Journal,* May 19, 1988; City of Fairfax Planning Commission Minutes, June 10, 1991; *Fairfax Journal,* December 4, 1992; *Washington Post,* October 19, 1989; *Washington Post,* January 1, 1989; *Fairfax Journal,* October 19, 1989; *Economic Development Facts, City of Fairfax,* 1996.
68. *Fairfax Connection,* August 13, 1992.
69. *The City of Fairfax Zoning Ordinance, Sections 26-45 (d) Business openings and sales events signs, and 26-39.3 Off-street parking in Old Town Fairfax,* March 24, 1992, and April 28, 1992.
70. *Fairfax Connection,* January 28, 1993.
71. *Fairfax Journal,* January 11, 1993.
72. *Fairfax Connection,* September 17, 1992.
73. *Ibid.*
74. *Tradition with Vision, 2020 Commission,* March, 1994.
75. Files, Community Development and Planning Department, City of Fairfax, March, 1994.
76. Offices of Economic Development and Community Relations, City of Fairfax, 1996; *Cityscene,* June, 1996; City of Fairfax Council Minutes, October 11, 1994.
77. Interview, Adrian Schagrin, City Engineer, January 13, 1996.
78. *Ibid.*
79. *Historic District Survey Forms, Department of Community Development and Planning, City of Fairfax,* 1990.
80. *City of Fairfax Budget, 1996-1997.*
81. *Ibid.*
82. *City of Fairfax Comprehensive Plan,* November 1988.
83. *Fairfax Journal,* October 8, 1992.
84. *Home Pride Update, Department of Community Development and Planning, City of Fairfax,* 1996.
85. Interview, Earl Berner, Economic Development Coordinator, City of Fairfax, December 2, 1996.
86. *Fairfax Journal,* August 14, 1995.
87. *Ibid.*
88. *City of Fairfax Comprehensive Plan,* November 1988.
89. Historic District Survey Forms, Department of Community Development and Planning, City of Fairfax, 1990.
90. *Fairfax Connection,* May 23-29, 1996.
91. *Washington Post,* June 2, 1989; *Community Appearance Plan,* April 26, 1994.
92. *Ibid.*
93. *Community Appearance Plan,* April 26, 1994.
94. *Fairfax Journal,* May 2, 1994.
95. *Fairfax Journal,* April 26, 1995; *Fairfax Times,* April 20, 1995.
96. *Community Inforum Summary,* April 18, 1995.
97. Interview, Earl Berner, Economic Development Coordinator, City of Fairfax, January 13, 1997.
98. City of Fairfax Council Minutes, January 23, 1996.
99. *Fairfax City Observer,* February 22, 1996; *Fairfax Times,* January 26, 1996.
100. Office of Economic Development, City of Fairfax, 1996.
101. Interview, Edward A. Cawley, Director of Finance, City of Fairfax, November 25, 1996.
102. *Washington Post,* May 1, 1996.
103. *Fairfax Journal,* May 8, 1996.
104. *Fairfax Connection,* July 3-10, 1996.
105. *Fairfax Journal,* May 1, 1996.
106. Files, Department of Community Development and Planning, City of Fairfax; *Fairfax City Observer,* September 5, 1996.
107. *Comprehensive Plan of the City of Fairfax,* February 1977.
108. *Fairfax Connection,* March 23, 1995.

Chapter 10. 1961-1996
The Pursuit of Knowledge

1. "School Factors studied for Speedy Resolution," *Fairfax City Times*, September 11, 1964, page 1.
2. "School Board Gives Nod to Contract Plan," *Fairfax City Times*, March 19, 1965, page 1.
3. "A City School System: Cost, Quality at a Glance," *Fairfax City Times*, January 31, 1964, page 6.
4. "Council—County Agree on Formula for Reciprocal Tuition Charges," *Fairfax City Times*, July 30, 1965, p. 1.
5. "School Board Gives Nod to Contract Plan," *Fairfax City Times*, March 19, 1965, page 1. The schools were Fairfax High, Sidney Lanier Intermediate, and Westmore, Green Acres, Layton Hall, and Eleven Oaks elementary schools. Fairfax Elementary was turned over to the City without cost.
6. *Comprehensive Plan of the City of Fairfax*; Planning Commission and Office of Planning, 1975, p. 5.
7. City Children will study in County Schools Again," *Fairfax City Times*, April 11, 1963, p. 1.
8. "Educational Equality guaranteed in County Agreement with City," Fairfax *City Times*, May 7, 1965, pages 1 and 16.
9. "Referendum splits Council; No. 2 takes Beating," *Fairfax City Times*, July 1, 1966, p. 1.
10. *Fairfax City Times*, July 8, 1966, p. 23.
11. "Voters Reject Separate Schools", *Fairfax City Times*, July 15, 1966, page 1.
12. "Quiet Desegregation Expected on all Fronts," *Fairfax City Times*, July 10, 1964, p. 1. (The 2500-member Fairfax Education Association, after studying the issue, voted to integrate with the 100-member Fairfax Teachers Association, composed of African-American teachers. "FEA Open to all Races Now.", *Fairfax City Times*, February 21, 1963, p. 2).
13. "Desegregation Complete in County Schools", *Fairfax City Times*, February 5, 1965, p. 1.
14. "Headstart Program Grows in Fairfax County," *Fairfax City Times*, June 10, 1966, p. 14.
15. "A County First," *Fairfax City Times*, June 18, 1965, page 3.
16. "Proposed Budget Set for Schools," *Fairfax City Times*, January 15, 1965, p. 18.
17. "Quiet Desegregation Expected on All Fronts," *Fairfax City Times*, July 10, 1964, p. 1.
18. *Fairfax City Times*, January 12, 1967, p. 7.
19. Interview with George Stepp, Fairfax City Superintendent of Schools, May 31, 1996.
20. *Comprehensive Plan of the City of Fairfax*; Planning Commission and Office of Planning, 1975, p. 7.
21. George Stepp, May 31, 1996.
22. "City Schools" [chart], *Community Inforum*, 18 April, 1995.
23. *Comprehensive Development Plan*, Planning Commission and Office of Planning, 1968, p. 20.
24. *Comprehensive Plan of the City of Fairfax*, Planning Commission and Office of Planning, 1975, p. 9.
25. "Educator Exodus in Fairfax City", *Fairfax Journal*, May 16, 1974, p. 1.
26. "Fairfax Says 'No' to Independent Schools," *Fairfax Globe*, May 4, 1978, p. 1.
27 *School Services Agreement*, August 10, 1978, pp. 2, 3.
28. "So What's With the Fairfax City Schools," undated brochure.
29. *City of Fairfax Annual Financial Reports, for the Fiscal Years ending 30 June, 1962 - 1979.*
30. Interview with Edward J. Cawley, Jr., Director of Finance, City of Fairfax, Virginia, June 17, 1996. (That the City Budget for education was over 50% of the total budget reflects an operating ratio for budget planning: for every one percent of a certain population, one can expect to spend three percent of the budget).
31. *City of Fairfax Annual Financial Reports, for the Fiscal Years ending 1980- 1996.*
32. *Ibid.* Some state and federal funds go right to the County and are then reflected as credit towards the City's tuition payment.
33. Interviews with Mary Lou Johnson, May 24, 1996; Nancy Slusher, June 19, 1996; Jean Dair, June 19, 1996; and Helen Amorosa Rapson, July 2, 1996.
34. Interview with Jean Dair, June 19, 1996.
35. Interview with Helen Amorosa Rapson, July 2, 1996.
36. Rapson Interview, July 2, 1996.
37. Rapson Interview, July 2, 1996.
38. Rapson Interview, July 2, 1996.
39. Rapson Interview, July 2, 1996.
40 "Hope on the Wing — Pupils let fly with Doves of Peace," *Fairfax Journal*, December 23, 1992, p. A1.
41. Chris Stunkard Interview, April 3, 1997.
42. Edgar A. Prichard Interview, April 3, 1997.
43. Mary Fox Interview, June 17, 1996.
44. *Ibid*.
45. Interview with Candy Contristan, October 15, 1996.
46. Interview with Jackie Cawley, January 20, 1997.
47. *Ibid*.
48. Interview with Jan Green Dowdy, January 22, 1997.
49. Interview with Layton Hall Principal Marian Sanders, January 23, 1997.
50. Dowdy Interview, January 22, 1997.
51. Interview with Bob Russell, June 19, 1996.
52. "Jermantown School Hits 50," *Fairfax Connection*, October 15, 1987, p. 7.
53. "Jermantown PTA named Most Outstanding by National PTA", Press Release, The National PTA, June 1992; City of Fairfax School Board Resolution, October 1992.
54. "Safety, Social Work Keeps Pupils Busy," *Fairfax Journal*, November 7, 1994, page A8.
55. "Introducing Principal, Mrs. Dorothy Collier," *Fairfax County Sun-Echo*, February 8, 1962, p. 4B.
56. "Parents Visit Green Acres, Like School," *Fairfax County Sun-Echo*, May 24, 1962, p. 6.
57. Interview with Robin Bahn, June 11, 1996.
58. *Fairfax Globe*, May 20, 1969, p. 3
59. "Rebel Yells Resound Across Green Acres," *Virginia Sentinel*, April 8, 1971.
60. "Students are 'Stars for a Day' for National Reading Program," *Alexandria Gazette*, October 31, 1981, p. A1.
61. Robin Bahn Interview, June 11, 1996.
62. Bob Russell Interview, June 19, 1996.
63. Bob Russell Interview, April 4, 1997.
64. "30 Years and 6,000 students", *Fairfax Connection*, 1990, p. 5.
65. *The Chattahoochee*, Sidney Lanier Yearbook, Fairfax City, Virginia, 1960 - 1974, passim. (Bob Russell noted that the early yearbooks were actually "memory books", and were intentionally spartan to keep the price low; they sold for $1.00).
66. *Fairfax Cityscene*, May 1996, page 8, "Teen Center opens at Lanier, FHS." The "Lanier Summer Wreck" is not the first such teen center in the city. From 1965 to 1966, a teen center, "The Crow's Nest" was located at various spots in the city, including Vincent's Octagon (now Fuddruckers Restaurant) on Chain Bridge Road.
67. "National Education Unit Honors Fairfax School," *Fairfax Journal*, September 18, 1975, A10.
68. "Community Activities Office Report," Community Activities Office, Fairfax High School, Fairfax, Virginia, 1987.
69. *Fairfax Cityscene - A Report to the Citizens of the City of Fairfax*, Office of the Mayor, Fairfax, Virginia, February 1983, volume 13, no. 2, p. 2.
70. "Fairfax High's 60 Years of Tradition," *Fairfax Journal*, October 31, 1994, C5.; George Derner Interview, March 31, 1997.
71. *Fairfax Journal*, April 23, 1987, p.1
72. "Johnny Reb Ban in Fairfax Upheld on Appeal," *Washington Post*, August 6, 1988, p. B1.

73. Interview with Candy Contristan, October 15, 1996.
74. Interview with Mitch Sutterfield, January 23, 1997.
75. *Fairfax Cityscene*, January 1983, Vol. 13, No. 1, p. 1.
76. "Fairfax High Teachers, Pupil, to Watch Graduate's Blastoff," *Fairfax Journal*, February 21, 1990, p. A3.
77. *Fairfax Cityscene*, May 1985, vol., 15, No. 5, p. 5; Diane Cabe interview, January 14, 1997 (Cabe, of the City's Community Relations Office noted that this program continued for a number of years, but came to an end one year when too many snow days had to be made up).
78. *Fairfax Cityscene*, July 1983, Vol. 13, No. 7, p. 1.
79. Diane Cabe Interview, April 4, 1997.
80. "Fairfax High: 60 Years of Tradition", *Fairfax Journal*, October 31, 1994, p. C-5.
81. Interview with Pat King, June 19, 1996.
82. "Private Schools Match Public School Growth," *Fairfax Journal*, August 16, 1985, p. S5.
83. Interview with Barbara Rannazzisi, January 20, 1997.
84. "Dedication [of St. Leo's Church]," June 18, 1966, St. Leo's Catholic Church, Fairfax, Virginia.
85. *Ibid.*
86. Personal recollection, Mary Elizabeth DiVincenzo.
87. "St. Leo the Great Summary Report," (unpublished), St. Leo's Catholic School, Fairfax, Virginia, June 17, 1996.
88. Interview with Diane Drews, Principal, St. Leo's Catholic School, June 19, 1996.
89. Drews Interview, June 19, 1996.
90. "Trinity Christian School: Building Solid Foundations," Trinity Christian School brochure, Fairfax, Virginia, undated.
91. Interview with James L. Beavers, Trinity Christian School, January 30, 1997.
92. Trinity Christian School brochure.
93. Interview with Susan Johnson, February 18, 1997.
94. "The Historic Fairfax Elementary School" Information, undated.
95. Interview with Lehman Young, January 23, 1997.
96. Interview with Kathryn McCord, April 3, 1997. (In 1940, Principal Bauserman requested $200 from the Community Chest in order to purchase shoes for County children, who would otherwise miss school in cold weather.)
97. "Introducing Principal, Mrs. Dorothy Collier," *Fairfax County Sun-Echo*, February 8, 1962, p. 4B.
98. Interview with Janice Miller, January 14, 1997.
99. Interview with Alta Newman, September 24, 1996.
100. Newman Interview, September 24, 1996.
101. Newman Interview, September 24, 1996; "Headstart Program Grows in Fairfax County," *Fairfax City Times*, June 10, 1966, p. 14.
102. "Letters to the Editor", *Fairfax City Times*, March 1, 1962, p. 2.
103. *Fairfax City Times*, March 5, 1965, p. 24.
104. Interview with Jan Green Dowdy, January 22, 1997.
105. Interview with Janice Miller, January 14, 1997.
106. Interview with Jan Green Dowdy, January 22, 1997.
107. Interview with Janice Miller, January 14, 1997.
108. "Past Principals Recall Fairfax High of 1935," *Fair Facts* [Fairfax High School Newspaper], December 10, 1971, Vol. XXXVII, No. 6, p. 3.
109. *Ibid.*
110. "Fairfax HS Celebrates 50 Years," *Fairfax Journal*, October 7, 1985, P. A3.
111. *1958 Sampler of Fairfax High School*, 22nd ed., Anne Connery, Ed., p. 81.
112. Interview with Pat King, June 19, 1996; Interviews with Sue Peter Jones, June 19, 1996 and February 2, 1997.
113. Interview with Pat King, June 19, 1996.
114. Interviews with Sue Peter Jones, June 19, 1996 and February 2, 1997. (Lee Hubbard answered the vexing question of just where the exhaust fans were located.)
115. *Fairfax City Times*, September 23, 1966, p. 2.
116. "Teen News", *Northern Virginia Sun*, May 26, 1959, p. 18.
117. Interview with Edward J. Cawley, Jr., September 27, 1996.
118. "Past Principals Recall Fairfax High of 1935," *Fair Facts* [Fairfax High School Newspaper], December 10, 1971, Vol. XXXVII, No. 6, p. 3.
119. "Boundary Disputes Split City, County,"; "Parents Protest School Boundaries," *Fairfax City Times*, February 2, 1967, pp. 18-19.
120. Netherton, *Fairfax County*, p. 587.
121. *Ibid.*, p. 588.
122. Interview with Edgar A. Prichard, April 4, 1997.
123. George Mason University School of Law: Law School Information.
124. Netherton, *Fairfax County*, p. 588.
125. *Ibid.*
126. *Ibid.*
127. "Reasons to Celebrate". *Fairfax Journal and Globe*, March 22, 1980, p. A2.
128. George Mason University School of Law Information.
129. George Mason University School of Law Information; Interview with Steve Davis, Director, Public Relations, George Mason University School of Law, Arlington, Virginia, January 20, 1997.
130. *1976 Comprehensive Plan of the City of Fairfax*, Department of Community Development and Planning, Fairfax, Virginia, 1976, p. 28.
131. *1988 Comprehensive Plan of the City of Fairfax*. Department of Community Development and Planning, Fairfax, Virginia, adapted 29 November 1988, pp. 5-6.
132. Interview with Jeffrey C. Greenfield, January 7, 1997; "Lecture Series Sprout from Window of Opportunity", *Fairfax City Observer*, October 21, 1996, p. 5; Community Involvement Guide, prepared by the City of Fairfax and George Mason University City/University/Business Committee (CUB), Fairfax, Virginia.
133. *Fairfax Cityscene - A Report to the Citizens of the City of Fairfax*. Office of the Mayor, Fairfax, Virginia, April 1985, Volume 15, No. 4, p. 3).
134. *Fairfax Cityscene*, May 1986, Volume 16, No. 5, p. 3.
135. Northern Virginia Small Business Development Center (NV SBDC) Brochure.
136. George Mason University Graduate Catalog, 1990-1991, p. 6.
137. *Ibid.*, p. 7.
138. Twenty-fourth Annual Spring Commencement, George Mason University, 1991, no page number.
139. Interview with Helen Ackerman, Vice-President for University Relations, George Mason University, January 7, 1997.
140. Interview with Wallace Hutcheon, Northern Virginia Community College, August 1, 1996. (In 1995-96, 2.3 percent of NVCC students were City of Fairfax residents (1,398 students). The average age of NVCC students in 1996 was 29.26 years old; the average age of City of Fairfax NVCC students was 28.3 years old.)
141. Netherton, *Fairfax County*, pp. 588-589.
142. Northern Virginia Community College Catalog, 1996-1997, p. 13.
143. *Ibid.*
144. "Technical Skills", *Fairfax City Times*, October 25, 1966, p. 3.
145. Northern Virginia Community College Catalog, p. 13.
146. *Ibid.*
147. Statement by Wallace Hutcheon, February 24, 1997.
148. Netherton, *Fairfax County*, p. 589.
149. Northern Virginia Community College Catalog, p. 13.
150. *Ibid.*
151. Statement by President Richard Ernst, February 24, 1997.
152. Northern Virginia Community College Catalog, p. 14.
153. "The F. W. Huddleston [sic] Memorial Library", *The McLean-Providence Journal*, September 11, 1964, p. 2)
154. *Ibid.*
155. *Ibid.*
156. Nan Netherton, *Books and Beyond: Fairfax County Public Library's First Fifty Years* (Fairfax, Virginia: Fairfax County Public Library, 1989), p. 1.
157. "Fairfax Town Library Annual Tea June 20", *Fairfax County Sun Echo*, June 25, 1959, p. 1.
158. *Fairfax City Times*, May 10, 1962, p. 1.
159. Interview with Carol Cover, Librarian, Huddleson Memorial Library,

Fairfax City, Virginia, 28 January 1997.

160. "No Microfiche Here", *Fairfax Journal*, November 7, 1994, p. A8.

161. *Ibid.*

162. Netherton, *Books and Beyond*, p. 1.

163. *Ibid.*, p. 1.

164. *Ibid.*, p. 4.

165. *Ibid.*, p. 24.

166. *Ibid.*, p. 7.

167. *bid.*, p. 9.

168. *Ibid.*, p. 10.

169. *Ibid.*, p. 10.

170. *Ibid.*, p. 26.

171. *Ibid.*, p. 26.

172. "Fairfax City Regional Library", three page summary, no author, undated.

173. "National Library Week Brings Film Furor to Fairfax County", *Library Journal*, June 1, 1963, pp. 2216-2217.

174. Netherton, *Books and Beyond*, pp. 10-11.

175. *Ibid.*, p. 26.

176. *Ibid.*, pp. 26-27. Library functions moved to Ravensworth Industrial Complex included administration, cataloging, computer input, acquisitions, mail room, printshop, book selection, central registration and overdues (CRO) and the children's and reference coordinator.

177. *Ibid.*, p. 27.

178. *Ibid.*, p. 27.

179. *Ibid.*, p. 26; "Fairfax City Regional Library," p. 2.

180. *Ibid.*, p. 27.

181. "Fairfax City Regional Library", p. 3.

182. "Questions Quest just a Phone Call Away", *Fairfax Journal*, April 24, 1990, p. A3.

183. Interview with Suzanne Levy, Librarian, Virginia Room, Fairfax City Regional Library, January 29, 1997.

184. "Friends of the Fairfax City Regional Library" Newsletter, November 1996. (All Friends of the Fairfax Library groups are non-profit, non-stock 501(c)(3) tax-exempt corporations.)

185. Interview with Suzanne Rehder, Regional Branch Manager, Fairfax City Regional Library, January 26, 1997.

186. Rehder Interview, January 26, 1997.

187. "Futuristic Peek into the Past (FPP Project)", (unpublished summation).

188. Interview with Daryl Ann Humrichouser, Director, Fairfax Museum and Visitors Center, Fairfax, Virginia, November 22, 1996.

Chapter 11.
Resources of a Giving Community

1. Interview with Patricia Beck, President, Inter-Service Club Council of the City of Fairfax, November 6, 1996; "History of the Inter-Service Club Council of the City of Fairfax, Virginia", *Fairfax City Observer*, June 6, 1996, p. 7. (In 1996 the Inter-Service Club Council revived an earlier custom: an annual volunteer recognition night, lauding volunteers nominated by their organizations. "Inter-Service Club Council presents Awards to city volunteers," *Fairfax City Observer*, August 29, 1996, p. 4.)

2. "Fairfax Legion Post News", *Fairfax Herald*, January 18, 1946, p. 1; "New Legion Home Opened", *Fairfax Herald*, October 31, 1952, p. 1; "Legion names Bowman to assist McKenna on Home," *Fairfax Herald*, March 20, 1953, p. 1; Interview with Dolores Testerman, March 15, 1997.

3. Interview with Jim Donovan, Second Vice-Commander, American Legion Post 177, October 31, 1996.

4. Interview with Lorene Heriot, American Legion Auxiliary 177, October 31, 1996; American Legion Auxiliary 177 Information, unpublished.

5. "By law, every penny collected by this means must go for the benefit of veterans and their dependents."; American Legion Auxiliary 177 Information, unpublished.

6. Interview with Howard Stull, November 21, 1996.

7. Interview with Commander Robert VanHouten, November 19, 1996.

8. Interview with Edgar A. Prichard, April 4, 1997.

9. Interview with Marshall Groom, Rotary Club of Fairfax, November 6, 1996.

10. "Kiwanis Club of Fairfax", 1995-96 Brochure.

11. *Ibid.*

12. *Fairfax Cityscene: A Report to the Citizens of the City of Fairfax*, Office of the Mayor, Fairfax, Virginia, February 1972, Vol. 1, No. 2, p. 1. (Unfortunately, in 1977, "Due to vandalism, resulting in exposed sharp edges, the aircraft in Van Dyck Park and Providence Park will be removed starting April 1." ; "City to Remove Planes", *Fairfax Cityscene*, March 1977, Vol. 7, No. 3, p. 2.)

13. Interview with Elden Wright, Fairfax Host Lions Club, November 20, 1996. The Lions name their clubs for the time of day at which they meet. The Fairfax Host Lions Club meets in the evening.

14. Interview with Ronald G. Hoopes, Fairfax AM Lions Club, November 11, 1996. Mr. Hoopes noted that the Lions ask for used eyeglasses; by law, they cannot be given to others in the United States, but are sent overseas to help people.

15. Interview with Terry Smith, Clifton Fairfax Lioness Club, January 10, 1997. (Women do not have to be married to Lions members to become Lionesses.)

16. Interview with Edward J. Cawley, Jr., Noonday Optimists Club of Fairfax, November 15, 1996.

17. Interview with Anthony DiGregorio, the Optimists Club of Central Fairfax, November 16, 1996.

18. Interview with Mary Beth Jacobs, President, Civitans of Fairfax, January 12, 1997. All Civitan clubs send money to the Civitan International Research Center, in Birmingham, Alabama.

19. The Washington Ear is a free reading and radio service for the blind and visually impaired; the radio reading service includes books, newspapers, and important publications.

20. Interview with Gene Moore, February 4, 1997; Interview with Phylis Salak, Friends of Fairfax City, December 2, 1996.

21. Interview with Jackie Cawley, January 31, 1996.

22. Salak Interview, December 2, 1996.

23. *Henry Lodge No. 57, AF&AM: 125th Anniversary Celebration*, October 8, 1994, Fairfax, Virginia, p. 6. (Henry Lodge No. 40 existed in Fairfax from 1849 to 1855).

24. *Ibid.*, page 12.

25. Interview with Leonard "Nick" Carter, Henry Lodge No. 57, AF&AM, Fairfax, Virginia, November 18, 1996.

26. Interview with Kathy Newcombe, Fair Oaks Hospital Auxiliary, January 13, 1997.

27. "History of the Central Fairfax Chamber of Commerce" (unpublished), by Max Bassett, with assistance from Claire Luke, Executive Vice President, Central Fairfax Chamber of Commerce, 1995, p. 3.

28. *Ibid.*, p. 4.

29. *Ibid.*, p. 6.

30. "Business Showcase Comes to Patriot Center", *Main Street News*, Vol. II, No. II, Spring 1996, p. 6.

31. Interview with Claire Luke, Executive Vice-President, Central Fairfax Chamber of Commerce, November 1, 1996.

32. "The Fairfax Jaycees: A Message from the President"; *Main Street News*, Spring 1996, Vol. II, No. II, p. 5; "The Fairfax Jaycees: Now Serving the City of Fairfax"; *Main Street News*, Winter 1996, Vol.. II, No.1, p. 8.

33. Interview with Gary Powers, Executive Director, Downtown Fairfax Coalition, 21 November 1996; Fax Message from Downtown Fairfax Coalition, Fairfax, Virginia, January 14, 1997.

34. "City put on Historic Register", *Fairfax Connection*, October 1987, p. 4 ; Interview with Sue Otto, City of Fairfax Office of Planning, March 27, 1997.

35. "John Gano is King for a Day in the City of Fairfax"; *Fairfax Museum and Visitors Center Volunteer Newsletter*, August 1992, p. 1.

36. Historic Fairfax City, Inc., publicity information, October 26, 1990, pp. 1-2.

37. Interview with Jackie Anderson, Garden Club of Fairfax, January 20, 1997.

38. Interview with Karen Snitzer, Ladies Auxiliary of the Fairfax Volunteer Fire Department, November 27, 1996; Interview with Evelyn Boehm, Ladies Auxiliary of the Fairfax Volunteer Fire Department, December 2, 1996.

39. Interview with Vivian Sprigg, Tuesday Afternoon Club, January 22, 1997.

40. Interview with Dolores Testerman, Woman's Club of Fairfax, November 5, 1996, and March 15, 1997; "History of the Woman's Club of Fairfax" (unpublished) by Betty Dittman, undated.

41. Interview with Patricia Beck, President of the Fairfax Ferns Garden Club, Fairfax, Virginia, November 6, 1996.

42. Interview with Carol McNeil, President, American Association of University Women, November 7, 1996. The GEMS Conference provides workshops for young girls, led by female experts, in fields that require mathematics and science backgrounds, such as electrical engineering or medicine.

43. "Zonta: Opportunity for Action . . . Avenue for Change" Brochure; Interview with Marion H. Earle, charter member, Zonta of Fairfax, November 16, 1996. The Zonta motto is "Successful Executives Serving the World."

44. Interview with Ruth Watson, Soroptimist International of Fairfax County, November 18, 1996. A few years ago, they were the largest classified organization for women. Watson stated that the Soroptimists are a classified organization to avoid getting too many women from one occupation, such as teachers, and thus becoming a de facto teachers organization. Soroptimists' rules stipulate that only one woman from a profession can belong until there are 20 members; then, two women per profession can belong until there are 40 members. There must be 18 members to start a chapter.

45. Interview with Elden Wright, Fairfax Host Lions Club, November 20, 1996.

46. *Army Navy Country Club: 1924-1989 Historical Review.* Army Navy Country Club, Arlington, Virginia 1989, pp. 47-109 passim.

47. Information on the Country Club of Fairfax from John H. Rust, Jr., to Randolph Lytton, May 1997; "A Brief History of the Country Club of Fairfax", unpublished.

48. Interview with Sgt. Scott Dulaney, Fairfax City Police Department, and Officer William L. Thomas, Jr., Fairfax City Police Department; June 11, 1996. All children in the D.A.R.E. program receive a D.A.R.E. T-shirt.

49. Dulaney and Thomas Interview, June 11, 1996.

50. *Ibid.*

51. "At-Risk Communities get Neighbors in Blue", *Fairfax Journal*, January 9, 1995, p. 4.

52. "FCPD Pulls for Special Olympic Athletes", *Fairfax City Observer*, June 6, 1996, p. 5.

53. Interview with Battalion Chief Kenneth R. Hahn, City of Fairfax Fire and Rescue Department, June 11, 1996; H.E.L.P. in the Schools: Health Education Lifesafety Program Manual (unpublished), City of Fairfax Fire and Rescue, 1995.

54. Hahn Interview, June 11, 1996.

55. *Fairfax Cityscene*, April 1996, Vol. 16, No. 4, p. 3.

56. *Fire and Rescue Journal: An Informational Newsletter for the Citizens of the City of Fairfax*, November/December 1996, Vol. 1, No. IV, p. 1.

57. Hahn Interview, June 11, 1996.

58. Nan Netherton Interview with City of Fairfax Manager Robert Sisson, February 3, 1997.

59. "Our 42nd Year: Fairfax Little League, 1996 Season" (Fairfax City, Virginia: Fairfax Little League, 1996), p. 11. (The first scheduled Little League games were the Aces versus the Raiders and the Little Bucs versus the Green Hornets.)

60. "Fairfax Little League", p. 2, pp. 10-15 passim; Interview with Patrick Rodio (Fairfax Little League President, 1962-63 Season), January 6, 1997.

61. "Babe Ruth League in Fairfax is Ten Years Old", *Fairfax City Times*, July 1, 1966, p. 38; Interview with Elizabeth Wells, February 18, 1997; Interview with Wilton Crouch, February 21, 1997; "Three Area Babe Ruth League Champs set for State Tourney Wednesday", *Northern Virginia Sun*, July 23, 1962, p. 11.

62. Interview with Billy Fairfax, March 1, 1997.

63. Interview with John A. C. Keith, legal advisor, FPYC, January 20, 1997.

64. "Scoreboard: Fairfax Police Youth Club", Vol. 19, No. 1, Winter 1996, p. 1.

65. "Scoreboard: Fairfax Police Youth Club", Vol. 19, No. 3, Fall 1996, p. 3.

66. "Scoreboard", Vol. 19, No. 1, Winter 1996, pp. 1-4 passim; "Scoreboard", Vol.19, No. 3, pp.1-4 passim. Interview with Bill Mundy, Director, YCL, FPYC, February 4, 1997.

67. Thomas Boswell, *How Life Imitates the World Series, including the Newest Statistic, Total Average*. (Garden City, New Jersey: Doubleday and Company, Inc., 1982), pp. 158-161; Interview with Wilton Crouch, February 21, 1997.

68. Boswell, *How Life Imitates the World Series*, p. 159.

Chapter 12.

City Lights: Artistic Endeavors and Seasonal Events

1. "Fairfax Symphony Tuning its Strings for Fall Season", *Fairfax City Times*, September 31, 1961, p. 10.

2. "Rags to Riches: FSO Company Boasts of Musical Success Story," *Fairfax Tribune*, July 25, 1980, p. 8.

3. "Life Begins at 40": Fairfax Symphony Program, September 28, 1996, p. 18.

4. *Fairfax Tribune*, March 19, 1987, p. 11.

5. "Symphony Announced D. F. Feuer Memorial Scholarship Fund", *The Journal-Standard*, September 19, 1963, p. 3; "Life Begins at 40": Fairfax Symphony Program, September 28, 1996, p. 23.

6. "Life Begins at 40": Fairfax Symphony Brochure, 1996-1997 Season.

7. Interviews with Penelope Farris, October 22, 1996 and November 4, 1996; Interview with Rhonda Endicott of the NVYSA, 17 October 1996.

8. Interview with Frederick Wygal, October 17, 1996; "Fairfax Civic Chorus", *Fairfax Herald*, October 5, 1962, p. 1.

9. Interview with Carol Dunlap, Managing Director, Fairfax Choral Society, September 27, 1996.

10. "The City of Fairfax Band: A Thumbnail History", (unpublished) by Thomas and Ruth Hill, 1996.

11. Interview with Dr. Thomas Hill and Mrs. Ruth Hill, Fairfax City, March 11, 1996.

12. *Fairfax Cityscene - A Report to the Citizens of the City of Fairfax*, Office of the Mayor, Fairfax, Virginia, August 1996, Vol. 26, No. 9, p. 3.

13. "Fairfax Band History", 1996.

14. *Fairfax Cityscene*, September 1981, Vol. 11, No. 9, p. 2.

15. Hill Interview, March 11, 1996.

16. "Fairfax Band History", 1996.

17. Hill Interview, 11 March 1996.

18. "Fairfax Band History", 1996.

19. *Fairfax Cityscene*, November 1994, Vol. 24, No. 11.

20. Hill Interview, March 11, 1996.

21. Interview with Bonita Lestina, September 27, 1996.

22. Interview with Glenn White, September 9, 1996.

23. Interview with Michael Cadwallader, City of Fairfax Parks and Recreation Department, October 1, 1996.

24. "Introductory Guide to the Fairfax Art League", December 11, 1993.

25. Interview with Kathryn Higgins, Fairfax Art League, September 24, 1996.

26. Interview with Colette Ashley, September 11, 1996; Interview with Dorothy Jackson, September 17, 1996.

27. Interview with Teri Westbrook, November 1, 1996.

28. "Commission on the Arts", *Fairfax City Artscene*, January - August 1996, Vol. 1, No.1, p. 2.

29. *Fairfax Cityscene*, Vol. 15, No. 3, March 1985, p. 1

30. *Fairfax City Artscene*, September - December 1996, Vol. 1, No. 2, p. 2.

31. Interview with Kate Wozniak, Paul VI High School, October 16, 1996.

32. *Fairfax Cityscene*, Vol. 16, No. 4, p. 1, "Spotlight on the Arts, 25-27 April"; Interview with Mayor John Mason, City of Fairfax, January 6, 1997.

33. *Fairfax Cityscene*, 1986-1996, passim.
34. Interview with Earl Berner, Director, Economic Development, City of Fairfax, November 25, 1996; Interview with Jack Baggett, March 31, 1997.
35. "Community Profile: Ellie Schmidt, 20 Years of Community Service", *Main Street News*, Spring 1996, Vol. II, Issue II, p. 7.; Interview with Betsy Beckman, October 31, 1996.
36. *Fairfax Cityscene*, 1971 - 1997, passim. Jackie Garris of Jermantown Elementary submitted the winning Independence Day Theme for 1997, "Symbols of America".
37. *Fairfax Cityscene*, 1977 to 1996; "Fairfax Fall Festival", *Fairfax City Observer*, October 8, 1996, pp. 9 - 11; "Fairfax Fall Festival", *Fairfax City Observer*, October 21, 1996, p. 6. The Fall Festival was an attempt to revive Heritage Week; this was noted in the September 1977 *Cityscene*.
38. "Old Town Hall Lecture Series Begins October 16 with GMU President Merten", *Fairfax Cityscene*, October 1996, p. 2.
39. "Lecture Series Sprout from Window of Opportunity", *Fairfax City Observer*, October 21, 1996.
40. "Decking the Hall at Old Town Hall", *Fairfax Cityscene*, December 1993, p.1.
41. Publicity Handouts for Festival of Lights and Carols, 1989 - 1996.
42. "Indulge in Chocolate February 10 - 11 at the Festival", *Fairfax Cityscene*, February 1996, p. 2.
43. *Fairfax Cityscene*, February 1993-1996, passim.
44. "The Rough Beginnings of City's 'Mosby Days'", *Fairfax Globe*, May 1, 1969, p. B3.
45. "The Rough Beginnings of City's 'Mosby Days'", *Fairfax Globe*, May 1, 1969, p. B3; "Mosby Rides Again May 15-21", *Fairfax Herald*, May 13, 1966, p. 1.; "Lantern our Feature Mosby Days Program", *Northern Virginia Sun*, May 17, 1966, pp. 1, 3.
46. "Heritage Week Highlights City's Historical Places", *Fairfax City Times*, 11 May 1967, p. 2.; "Heritage Week Highlights Fairfax City's History - Businessmen Stage Weekend Sales Finale", *Fairfax City Times*, 25 May 1967, p. 23; "Fairfax Heritage Week Begins Sunday, Restored Court Open", *Fairfax Herald*, 19 May 1967, p. 1.
47. *Fairfax City Times*, July 22, 1965, p. 1; "Old Town Hall Fair is 'Most Successful Yet'", *Fairfax Globe*, July 31, 1969, p. 3.

Chapter 13.

Legends, Local Lore and Laughter

1. Fairfax County Court Minute Book, 1882-1885, p. 34. The bell presently hanging in the cupola was cast by TW & RC Smith of Alexandria, D. C. in 1844. See Fairfax Courthouse brochure.
2. Peter R. Henriques, *Fairfax County Medical Society, 1884-1934. Early Years and Early Leaders*. (Falls Church, Va.: Fairfax County Medical Society, 1984), pp. 40-41.
3. Frederic Kielsgard memorandum to the author, January 1997.
4. From an address given by F. Sheild McCandlish, Senior Warden, to a parish meeting in 1958. From the archives of Truro Episcopal Church, Fairfax.
5. Karen Ann Moore memorandum to the author, November 14, 1996.
6. Blaine Friedlander memorandum to the author, November 24, 1996.
7. *Ibid.*
8. *Ibid.*
9. Moore memorandum.
10. Friedlander memorandum.
11. Memorandum to Nan Netherton from MECD, April 1997.
12. Moore memorandum.
13. *Fairfax Herald*, August 3, 1951, p. 1.
14. *Fairfax Herald*, February 26, 1960, p. 1.
15. "Aspen Grove," from Paula Grundset's talk on the ghosts of Fairfax; Bob Garfield, "The Haunting of Aspen Grove," *The Washington Post Magazine*, May 7, 1996, pp. 21-30.
16. *Northern Virginia Sun*, March 26, 1987.
17. Minutes, City Council Meeting, March 24, 1987.
18. *Northern Virginia Sun*, March 27, 1987.
19. *Washington Post*, April 2, 1987.
20. *Fairfax Journal*, March 24, 1987.
21. Minutes.
22. *Fairfax Journal*, March 27, 1987.
23. Letter from Patricia Beck to the author, January 28, 1997.
24. Molly Klocksin, "City of Fairfax cherishes history and charm," *The Connection*, May 30-June 5, 1996.

Appendix A
Mayors, Town of Fairfax

(A partial list)
C. L. Zoll - 1924
Thomas P. Chapman - 1927-1933
William Lindsay Carne - 1934-1936
O. B. Campbell - 1936
R. R. Farr - 1936
John Rust, Sr. - 1941
Robert D. Graham - 1946-1948
S. Gail Landon, Jr. 1950 (Acting)
Robert B. Walker - 1951
Dr. F. W. Everly - 1953 (Acting)
John C. Wood - 1953-1961

Mayors, City of Fairfax

John C. Wood - 1961-1964
Edgar A. Prichard - 1964-1968
George A. Hamill - 1968-1970
John W. Russell - 1970-1974
Nathaniel F. Young - 1974-1978
Frederick W. Silverthorne - 1978-1982
John W. Russell - 1982-1984
George T. Snyder, Jr. - 1984-1990
John Mason - 1990-present

Treasurers, City of Fairfax

Frances L. Cox - 1961
Ray Birch - 1981
Stephen L. Moloney - 1982 -

Commissioners of Revenue, City of Fairfax

Frank M. Carter - 1961
A. Howell Thomas - 1965
Juanita Dickerson - 1981 -

Appendix B
City of Fairfax School Superintendents

Robert Walker - 1961-1971
George Tankard - 1971-1977
Wayne White - 1977-1984
Robert C. Russell - 1984-1995
George E. Stepp - 1996-present

Appendix C
City of Fairfax Chiefs of Police

Frank Young - 1962-1965
Murray Kutner - 1965-1975

Leonard P. Kline - 1975-1977
Larry F. Wines - 1977-1980
Loyd W. Smith - 1980-1993
John J. Skinner - 1993-present

Appendix D
City of Fairfax Fire Chiefs

Joseph Gebauer - Oct. 1977-Dec. 1979
Harold Dailey - Jan.1980-May 1980
Gary Mesaris - Jan. 1990-present

Appendix E
Fairfax Court House Postmasters

John Ratcliffe - 7 Apr. 1802
Robert Ratcliffe - 1 Apr. 1803
Thomas Moore - 1 Oct. 1803
John Ratcliffe - 1 Jan. 180?
Hugh Violette - 1 July 1805
Christopher Neale - 1 Apr. 1806
Hugh W. Minor - 31 Dec. 180?
John Ratcliffe - 1 Jan. 1810
William P. Richardson - 17 Jan. 1817
Hiram Carver - 23 June 1824
Joel L. Harper - 3 Aug. 1825
Gordon Allison - 19 Sept. 1827
James G. Allison - 30 June 1837
Robert Allison - 1 Jan. 1841
William R. Chapman - 17 June 1857
Henry T. Brooks - 11 Apr. 1862
Walter B. Hoag - 17 June 1862
Job Hawxhurst - 1 Aug. 1865
J. W. Whitehead - 22 May 1885
Job Hawxhurst - 4 Apr. 1889

Changed to Fairfax - 8 June 1893
Postmasters — Town of Fairfax

Alfred H. Moncure - 8 June 1893
Job Hawxhurst - 8 June 1897
Richard R. Farr - 22 August 1903
Claude I. Wiley - 10 July 1913
Stephen R. Donohoe - 12 Aug. 1918
E. Mack Wiley - 18 Aug. 1918
Charles F. Cummins - 9 Oct. 1918
Miss Ludema Sayre - 3 Nov. 1923
Lewis M. Coyner - 30 June 1933
Edgar McCarthy Wiley - 29 Dec. 1937
Stacey C. Swart - 16 Jan.1944
Robert W. Miller - 27 Jan. 1956
Charles W. Harris, Jr. - 28 Mar. 1957
Charles W. Harris, Jr. - 22 July 1960

Appendix F
City of Fairfax Civic Associations

Ardmore Civic Association
Aspen Grove Civic Association
Assembly Civic Association
Breckinridge Homeowners Association
Cambridge Station Association
Comstock Homeowners Association
Council of Civic Associations
Country Club Hills Civic Association
Courthouse Square Homeowners Association
Crestmont Civic Association
Fairchester Woods Civic Association
Fairfax Mews Civic Association
Fairfax Oaks Homeowners Association
Fairfax Triangle Civic Association
Fairview Civic Association
Foxcroft Civic Association
Great Oaks Homeowners Association
Limewood Mews Homeowners Association
Little River Hills Civic Association
Lyndhurst Condominium Association
Mosby Woods Community Association
Mosby Woods Condominium Association
Old Lee Hills Civic Association
Railroad Square Civic Association
Ridgecrest Homeowners Association
Rustfield Homeowners Association
Southeast Fairfax Citizens Association
The Crossing at Fairfax
Warren Woods-Joyce Heights Association
Westmore Citizens Association

Appendix G
Properties Entered in the National Register of Historic Places

After years of studies, research, applications and hearings, the City of Fairfax Historic District was officially named to the National Register of Historic Places in October of 1987. The Register is maintained by the National Park Service. The list of historic structures and their years of construction follows:

Barbour House - 1910
Fairfax Courthouse - 1800
Oliver House - 1830
Marr Monument - 1904
Ford Building - 1835
Moore House - 1840
Donohoe House - 1880
Confederate Memorial - 1890
Truro Rectory - 1833

Old Fairfax Jail - 1885
Hav-a-Bite - 1895
T. T. Reynolds - 1895
Fairfax Hay and Grain - 1900
Fairfax Herald - 1900
Ratcliffe-Allison House - 1812
Draper House - 1810
Old Fairfax Elementary - 1873
Old Town Hall - 1900
Tastee 29 Diner - 1940

Appendix H
Boards and Commissions

No history of the City of Fairfax government would be complete without paying tribute to the nearly 200 men and women who dedicate their time and skills to the City by serving on permanent boards and commissions. Most board and commission members are City residents, but in certain instances specialized experts from surrounding areas are appointed. City staff individuals also serve as volunteers on several committees acting as liaisons and/or full or ex officio members.

These permanent committees assist City Council by reviewing, planning and, in certain cases, acting on applications, appeals and other matters. They often influence City policy as in the case, for example, of the School Board's recommended capital improvement expenditures and the Planning Commission's recommended Comprehensive Plan, the City's principal blueprint for the future. A part-time Human Services coordinator to manage City resident referral services was hired in 1987 as a result of a recommendation from the Commission for Women.[1]

Recognition also should be given to the numerous individuals who have served throughout the years on ad hoc committees, including the 112 members of the 2020 Commission appointed in 1992. At the recommendation of the 2020 Commission, the newest permanent committee, Human Services, was established by City Council in 1996.

The list below provides the authority, with dates, under which the individual boards and commissions were established and lists the appointment body for those not appointed by City Council.[2] For those mandated by *The Code of Virginia*, or with other special authority, a summary description of responsibilities is provided. For additional information, please contact the Community Relations Office, City Hall.

Board of Architectural Review

Authorized by State Code; *City Charter*, 1976; City Ordinance, 1973; Virginia Certified Local Government review authority. Conducting two regular meetings per month and special meetings as required, the BAR reviews and acts on Historic District construction, reconstruction and demolition applications and reviews site plans for the area surrounding the Historic District. The Board also reviews and acts on applications for construction and reconstruction of all visible exterior architectural and landscape features throughout the City, excluding single family homes and sign applications as provided by the Zoning Ordinance.[3]

Electoral Board

Mandated by State Code; *City Charter*, 1966; appointed by Circuit Court. Meeting several times a year and biweekly during registration and election seasons, the Electoral Board is responsible for the appointment of the Registrar and the administration of elections, including polling sites, voting machines and absentee ballots.[4]

Board of Equalization of Real Estate Assessments

Mandated by State Code; *City Charter*, 1966; appointed by Circuit Court. This quasi-judicial Board, meeting as often as necessary between May 1 and December 31, is required to hear and decide on all appeals of real estate assessments. The Board acts on individual appeals concerning equity and market value, has the authority to summon witnesses or documentation and may raise, lower, or maintain the current assessment of a property.[5]

Planning Commission

Mandated by State Code; City Ordinance, 1966. Conducting two regular meetings per month as well as numerous special meetings, the Commission reviews and acts on subdivision applications and certain site plans and prepares and recommends the Comprehensive Plan, the five-year Capital Improvement Plan and other plans as required by City Council.[6]

School Board

Mandated by State Code; *City Charter*, 1977; *City Charter* amendment, 1993, to authorize election of members. The Board's principal responsibility is oversight of the contractual agreement with Fairfax County for operation of the City Schools. Conducting one regular meeting per month and special meetings as required, the School Board determines and oversees the school budget, which constitutes approximately 37 percent of the overall City budget; administers City-owned school properties, including improvements, and recommends school policy initiatives to the Fairfax County School Board.[7]

Board of Zoning Appeals

Mandated by State Code; Town Ordinance, 1960; appointed by Circuit Court. Conducting two regular meetings per month and special meetings as required, the quasi-judicial BZA reviews and acts on appeals, Zoning Ordinance variances and interpretations and certain Special Use Permit and Special Exemption applications.[8]

Other Boards and Commissions

Commission on the Arts: City Resolution, 1979
Board of Building Code Appeals, Housing Hygiene Division: City Ordinance, 1980
City/George Mason University/Business Community Committee: Resolution, 1979
Community Appearance Committee: City Ordinance, 1973
Economic Development Authority: City Resolution, 1994
Board of Electrical Examiners: City Ordinance, 1973
Fire Service Advisory Committee: City Ordinance, 1985
Historic Fairfax City, Inc.: City Resolution, 1970
Human Services Committee: Resolution, 1996
Industrial Development Authority: City Ordinance, 1977
Parking Authority: City Resolution, 1991
Parks and Recreation Advisory Board: City Ordinance, 1969
Personnel Advisory Board: City Ordinance: 1974
Board of Plumbing Examiners: City Ordinance, 1974
Board of Refrigeration, Heating & Air Conditioning Examiners: City Ordinance, 1975
The Retirement Plan Administrative Committee: City Ordinance, 1988
Transportation Safety Commission: City Resolution, 1967; City Ordinance, 1981
Commission for Women: City Resolution, 1984

Board and Commissions Notes

1. Interview, Louise Armitage, Human Services Coordinator, February 7, 1997.
2. Interview, Jackie Henderson, City Clerk, February 6, 1997.
3. *Chapter 26, City Code of Fairfax, Virginia*
4. Interview, Kevin Dunn, Registrar of Voters, February 7, 1997.
5. Interview, Dorothy Bennett, Real Estate Assessor, February 7, 1997.
6. *Chapters 2, 21 and 26, Code of City of Fairfax, Virginia*
7. Interview, George Stepp, Superintendent of Schools, February 7, 1997.
8. *Chapter 26, Code of City of Fairfax, Virginia*

Appendix I
Portraits in the Old Courthouse

James Roberdeau Allison (1864-1927) - Sheriff of Fairfax County
Paul E. Brown (1904-1968) - Fairfax County Commonwealth's Attorney and Senior Court Judge
Bryan Fairfax (1737-1802) - Justice of Fairfax County Court, Episcopal Minister, Eighth Lord Fairfax, 1800-1802
C. Vernon Ford (1871-1922) - Fairfax County Commonwealth's Attorney
William Edwin Graham (1850-1916) - Clerk of the Circuit Court

George Johnston (1700-1766) - Member of House of Burgesses, attorney

Walter Jones (1776-1861) - Attorney, practiced law in Fairfax and Loudoun Counties

William Henry Fitzhugh Lee (1837-1891) - Confederate Major-General of Cavalry, State Senator and Congressman

George Mason (1725-1792) - Fairfax County Court Justice. In 1774 principal author of the Fairfax Resolves; 1776, principal writer of the Virginia Constitution and Declaration of Rights

Robert Walton Moore (1859-1944) - State Senator, Congressman, counselor of Department of State, attorney, member Board of Visitors, University of Virginia and College of William and Mary

Ferdinand Danson Richardson (1808-1880) - Clerk of the Fairfax County Court,

Frederick Wilmer Richardson (1853-1936) - Clerk of Fairfax County Courts

Henry Wirt Thomas (1812-1890) - Fairfax County Commonwealth's Attorney, state legislator, judge and lieutenant governor

John Webb Tyler (1795-1862) - Fairfax County Circuit Court judge

George Washington (1732-1799) - Surveyor, burgess, justice, general, first President of the United States, 1789 & 1793

Joseph Edward Willard (1865-1924) - Attorney, lieutenant governor, minister and ambassador to Spain under Woodrow Wilson

Appendix J
City of Fairfax Housing by Neighborhoods

Alfred Mickelson - 1957-60
Ardmore - 1955
Aspen Grove - 1988-89
The Assembly - 1969-70
Autumn Woods - 1986
Barrister's Keepe - 1996-97
The Boltons - 1996-97
Bruin Heights - 1950-68
Cambridge Station - 1967
Chancery Square - 1995-97
Cobbdale - 1950-60
Comstock - 1974-76
Country Club Hills - 1954-56-61
Courthouse Square - 1968/1980-89
Courthouse Square III (Breckinridge) - 1988-93
Crestmont - 1995-97
The Crossing - 1995-96
East Fairfax Park - 1957
El Hogan - 1952

Fairchester - 1953-54-59
Fair Oaks - 1950-62-70
Fairfax Acres - 1947-60
Fairfax Country Club Estates - 1950-69-76
Fairfax Heights - 1941-54
Fairfax Oaks - 1987
Fairfax Town Estates - 1959-61
Fairfax West - 1964
Fairfax Woods - 1951-60
Fairmont Estates - 1957-66
Fairview - 1951-52-54
Foxcroft Colony - 1963
Great Oaks - 1974-85
Green Acres - 1954-56
Greenway Hills - 1955-57
Halemhurst - 1942-75
Heritage Manor 1963
Hill Street Estates - 1990-91
Holly Park *(see also Ridgecrest, Sharon Ct. & Kirkwood)* - 1928-41-59-88
Jermantown Village - 1930-60
Joyce Heights - 1954
Kirkwood - 1996-97
Layton Court - 1968-70
Layton Hall - 1957-64
Limewood Mews - 1987
Little River Hills - 1953-60
Lord Fairfax Estates - 1955-56
Lyndhurst - 1964
Maple Hills - 1952-61
Maple Terrace - 1952-85
Moore & Oliver - 1939-54
Mosby Glenn - 1967
Mosby Woods - 1961-67
Mosby Woods Condos - 1963
Netherdale - 1961-62
Old Post Estates - 1964-76
Orchard Knolls - 1976
Providence - 1972
Pumpkin Place - 1979
Railroad Square - 1985
Ridgecrest - 1994-96
Rust - 1948
Rustfield - 1980-85
Sharon Court - 1988
Singing Pines *(see Wren's Courtyard)* - 1948-66
Town & Country Forest - 1960
Trammel Commons - 1993-94
Tusico Villa - 1956
Warren Woods - 1953-55
Westmore - 1929-67
Wren's Courtyard - 1993-94

Source: City of Fairfax CD & P, 1997

INDEX